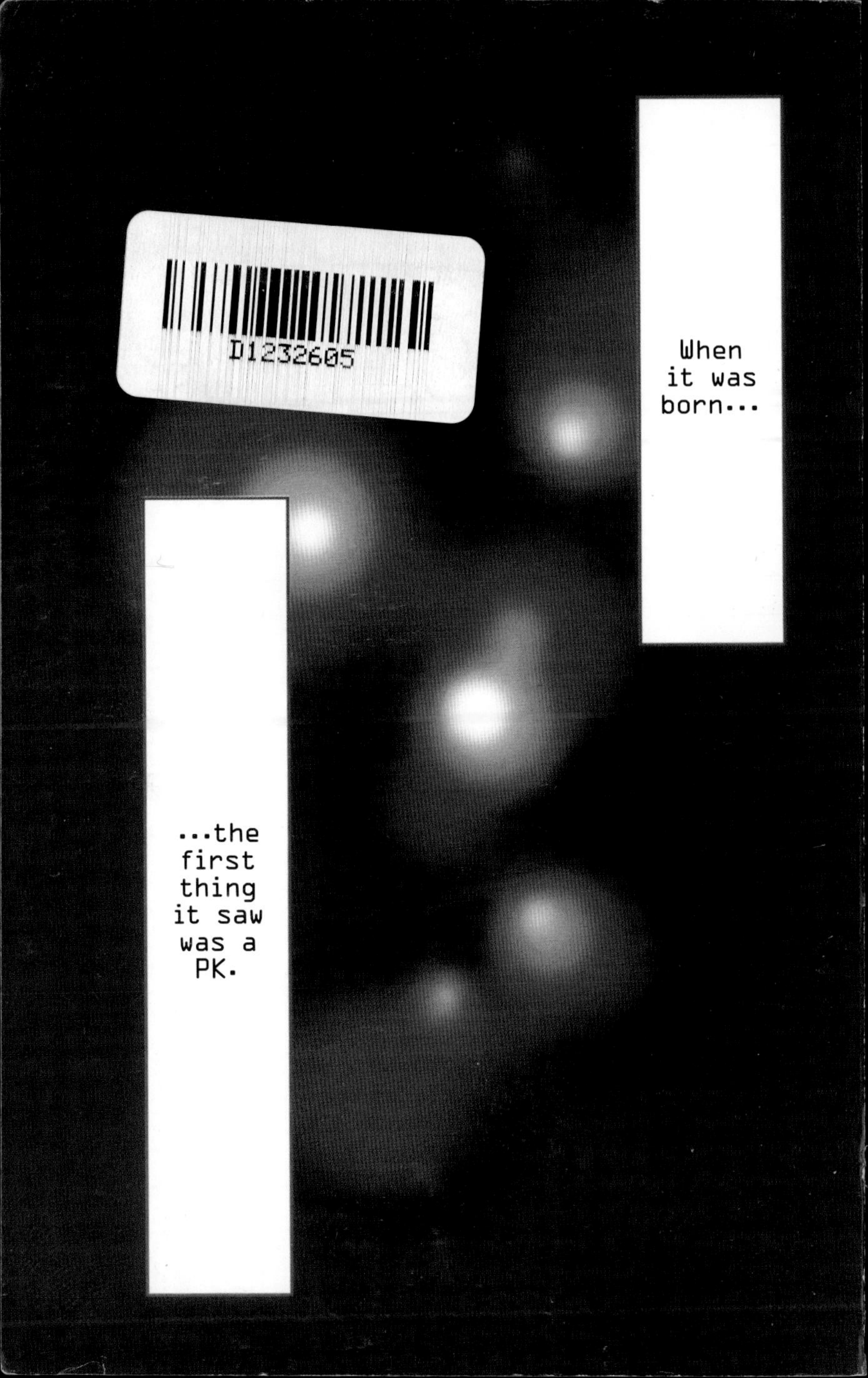
When it was born...
...the first thing it saw was a PK.

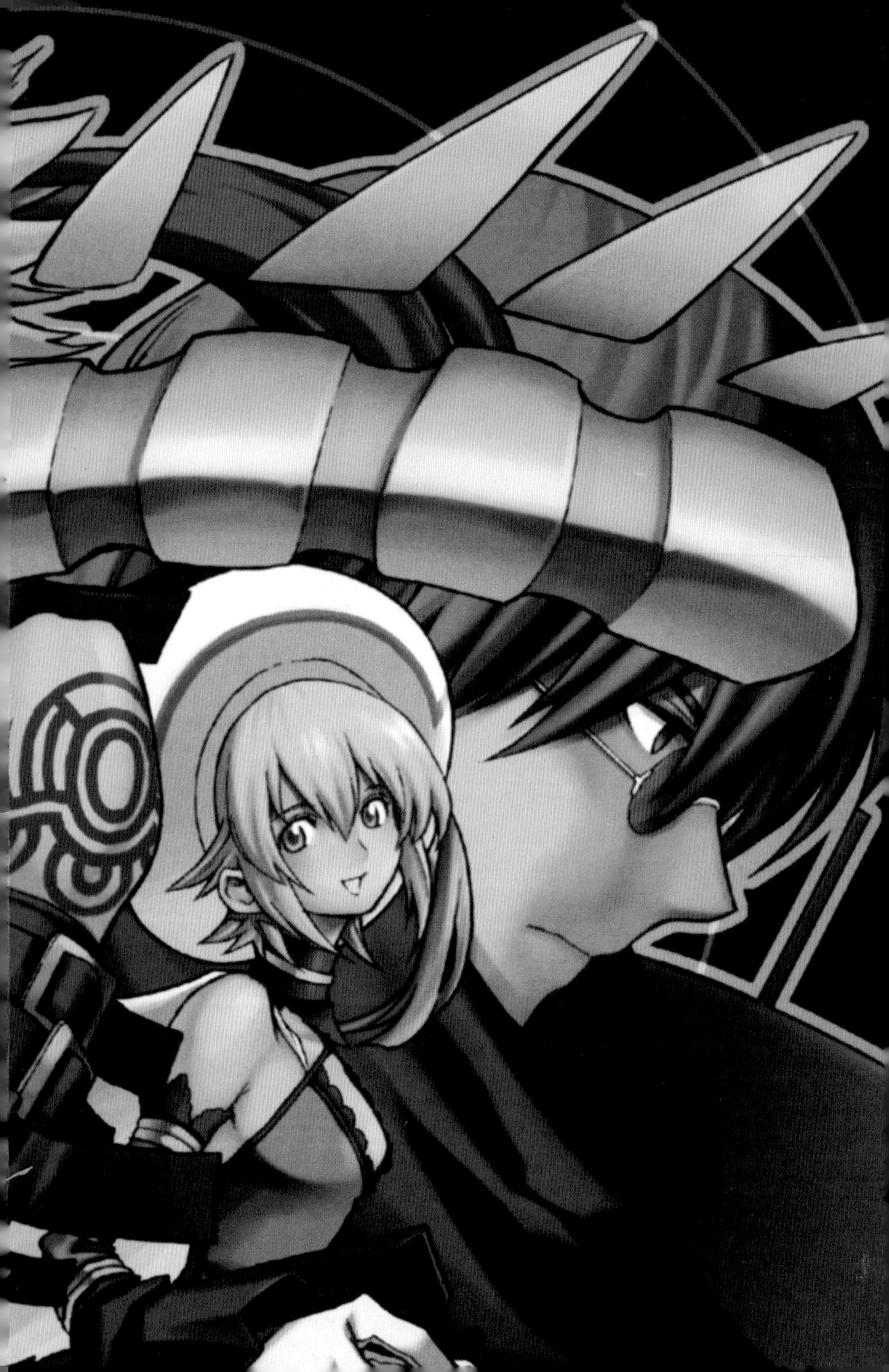

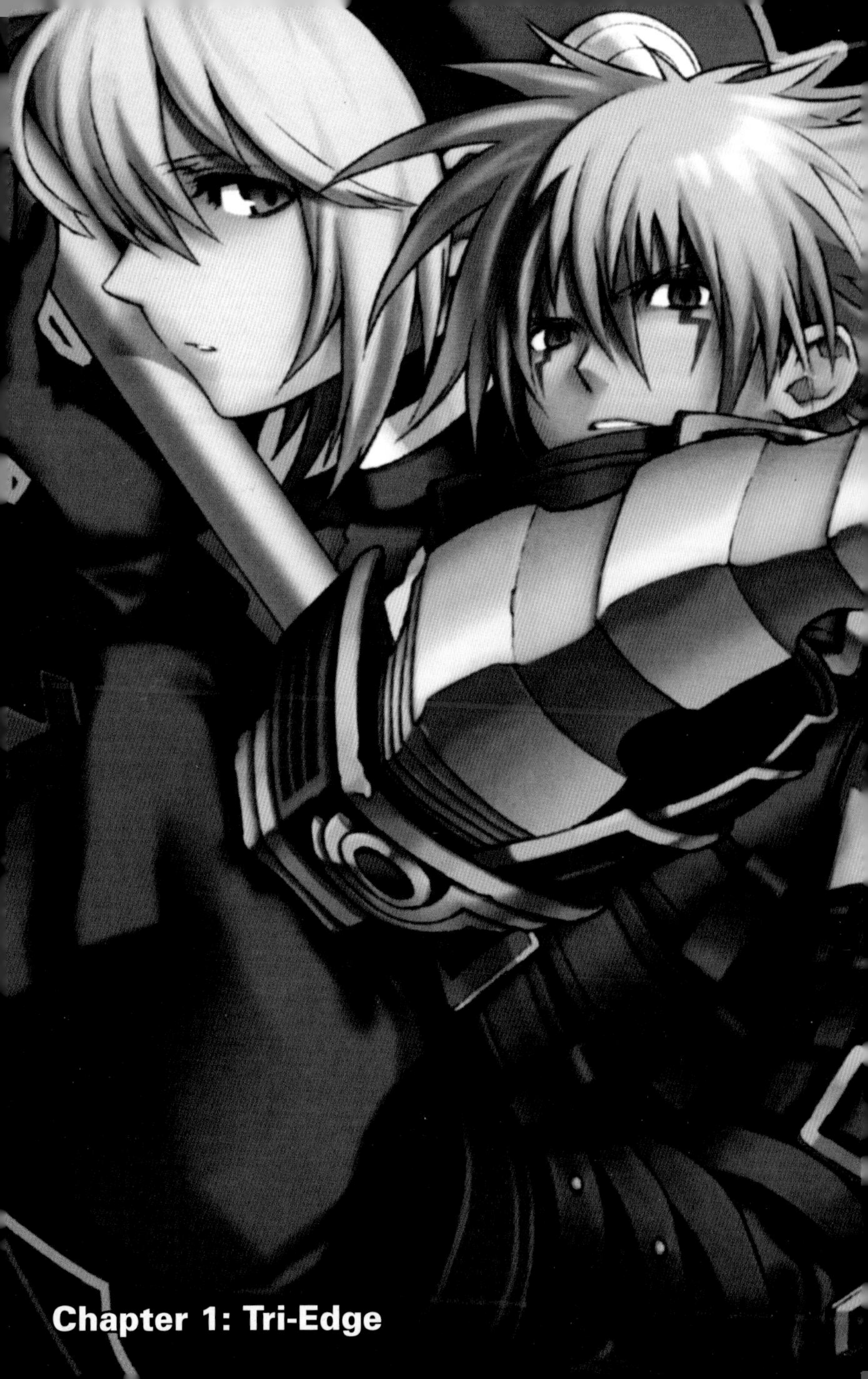

Chapter 1: Tri-Edge

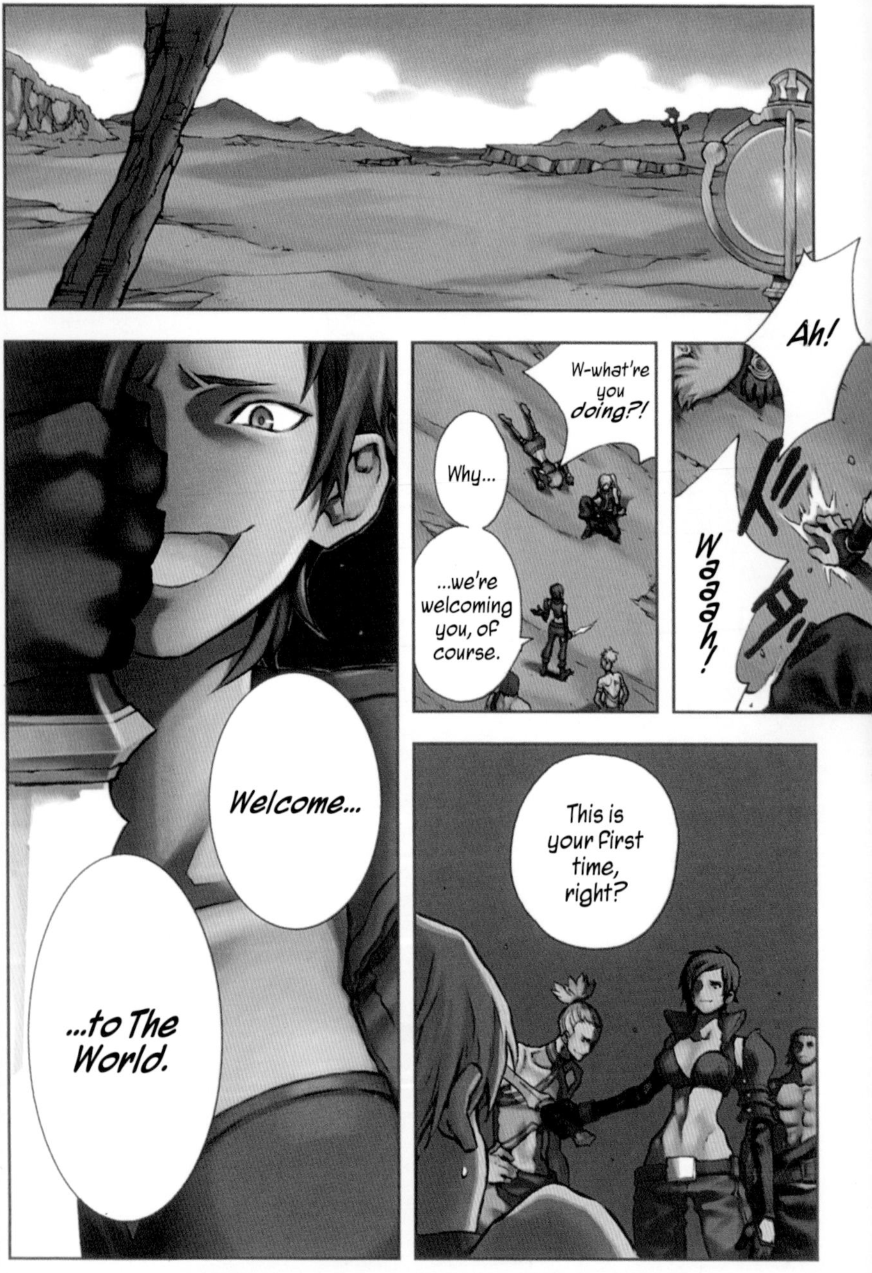

Ah!
Waaaah!
W-what're you doing?!
Why...
...we're welcoming you, of course.
This is your first time, right?
Welcome...
...to The World.

.hack//G.U.+

Volume 1

Story by Tatsuya Hamazaki
Art by Yuzuka Morita

HAMBURG // LONDON // LOS ANGELES // TOKYO

.hack//G.U.+ Volume 1
Story By Tatsuya Hamazaki
Art By Yuzuka Morita

Translation - Ryan Peterson
English Adaptation - Marc Lunden
Fan Consultant - Christopher Wagner
Retouch and Lettering - Star Print Brokers
Production Artist - Courtney Geter
Graphic Designer - Tina Corrales

Editor - Peter Ahlstrom
Digital Imaging Manager - Chris Buford
Pre-Production Supervisor - Erika Terriquez
Production Manager - Elisabeth Brizzi
Managing Editor - Vy Nguyen
Creative Director - Anne Marie Horne
Editor-in-Chief - Rob Tokar
Publisher - Mike Kiley
President and C.O.O. - John Parker
C.E.O. and Chief Creative Officer - Stuart Levy

A  Manga

TOKYOPOP Inc.
5900 Wilshire Blvd. Suite 2000
Los Angeles, CA 90036

E-mail: info@TOKYOPOP.com
Come visit us online at www.TOKYOPOP.com

.hack // G.U. + vol.1 © 2006 .hack Conglomerate © 2006 NBGI First published in Japan in 2006 by KADOKAWA SHOTEN PUBLISHING CO., LTD., Tokyo. English translation rights arranged with KADOKAWA SHOTEN PUBLISHING CO., LTD., Tokyo through TUTTLE–MORI AGENCY, INC., Tokyo. English text copyright © 2008 TOKYOPOP Inc.

ISBN: 978-1-4278-0635-2

First TOKYOPOP printing: February 2008
10 9 8 7 6 5 4 3 2 1
Printed in the USA

CONTENTS

History of [The World]

2004.8
Emma Weilant dies, her epic poem Epitaph of Twilight unfinished.

2005.12.24
Pluto's Kiss incident: The Internet is shut down by a virus.

2006.1
Harald Hoerwick sells his game Fragment to CyberConnect Corp.

2007.12.24
Fragment, now renamed The World, is released to instant success.

2009
.hack//AI buster: Albireo meets Lycoris.

2010
.hack//SIGN: Tsukasa is trapped in The World. Aura awakens.
.hack//INFECTION, MUTATION, OUTBREAK, QUARANTINE /
.hack//Another Birth: Kite and BlackRose seek to help coma
victims. Aura is reborn. Alternately told in .hack//XXXX.

2014
.hack//Legend of the Twilight: Shugo and Rena help Zefie find Aura.

2014.12.24
The World crashes temporarily. Aura disappears.

2015.12.24
The World R:2 is released.

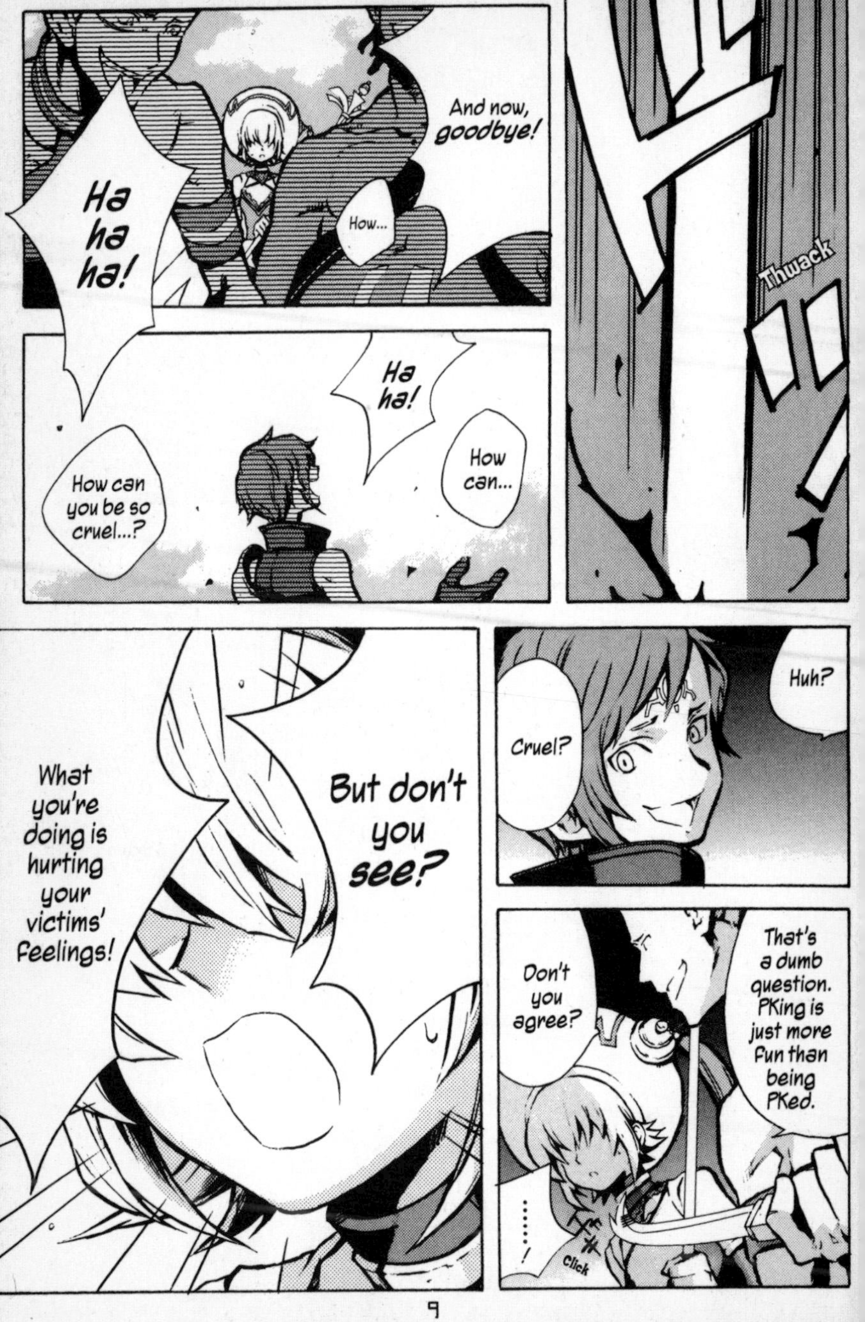
Thwack
And now, goodbye!
How...
Ha ha ha!
Ha ha!
How can...
How can you be so cruel...?
Huh?
Cruel?
That's a dumb question. PKing is just more fun than being PKed.
Don't you agree?
......!
Click
But don't you see?
What you're doing is hurting your victims' feelings!

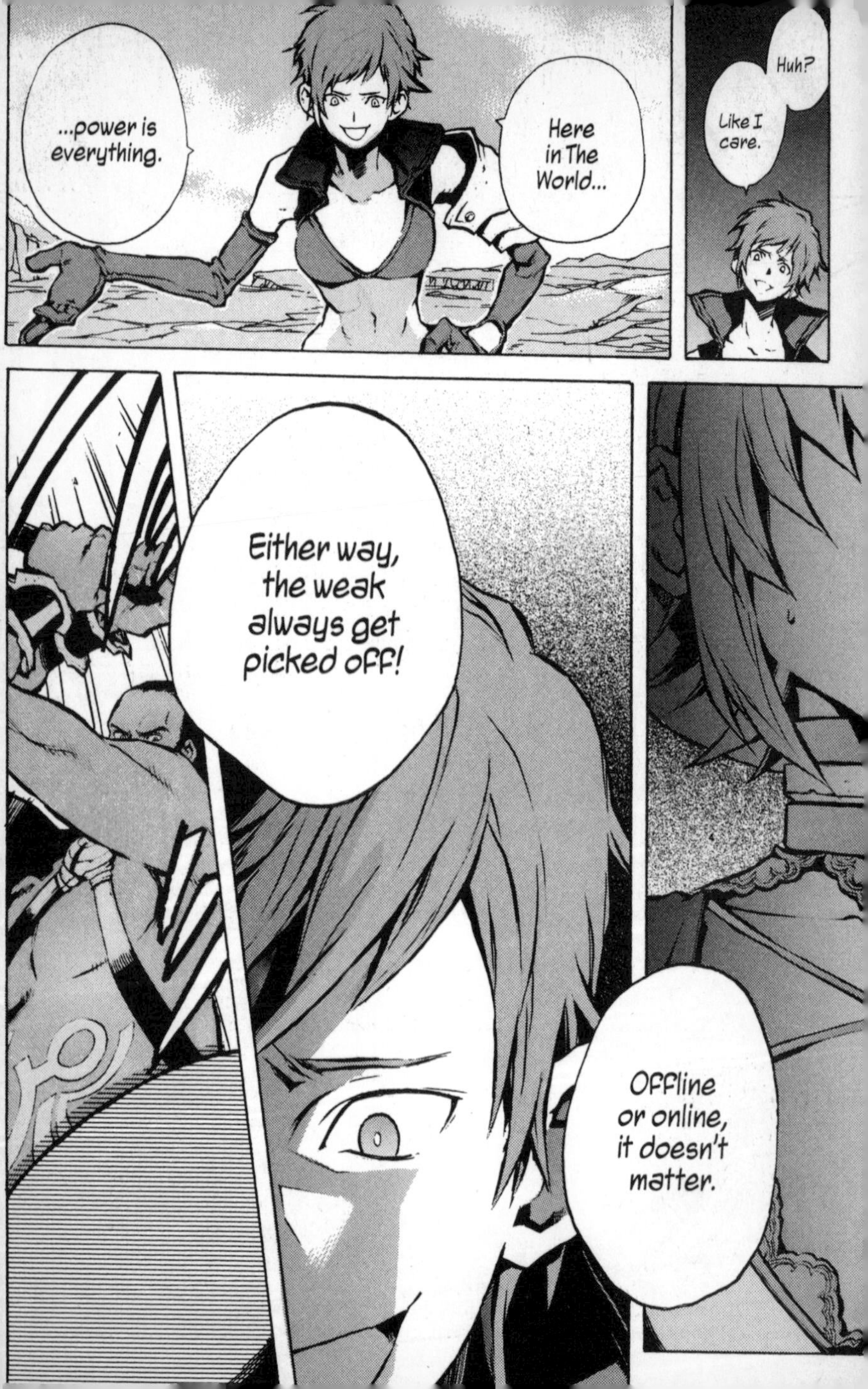
Huh?
Like I care.
Here in The World...
...power is everything.
Offline or online, it doesn't matter.
Either way, the weak always get picked off!

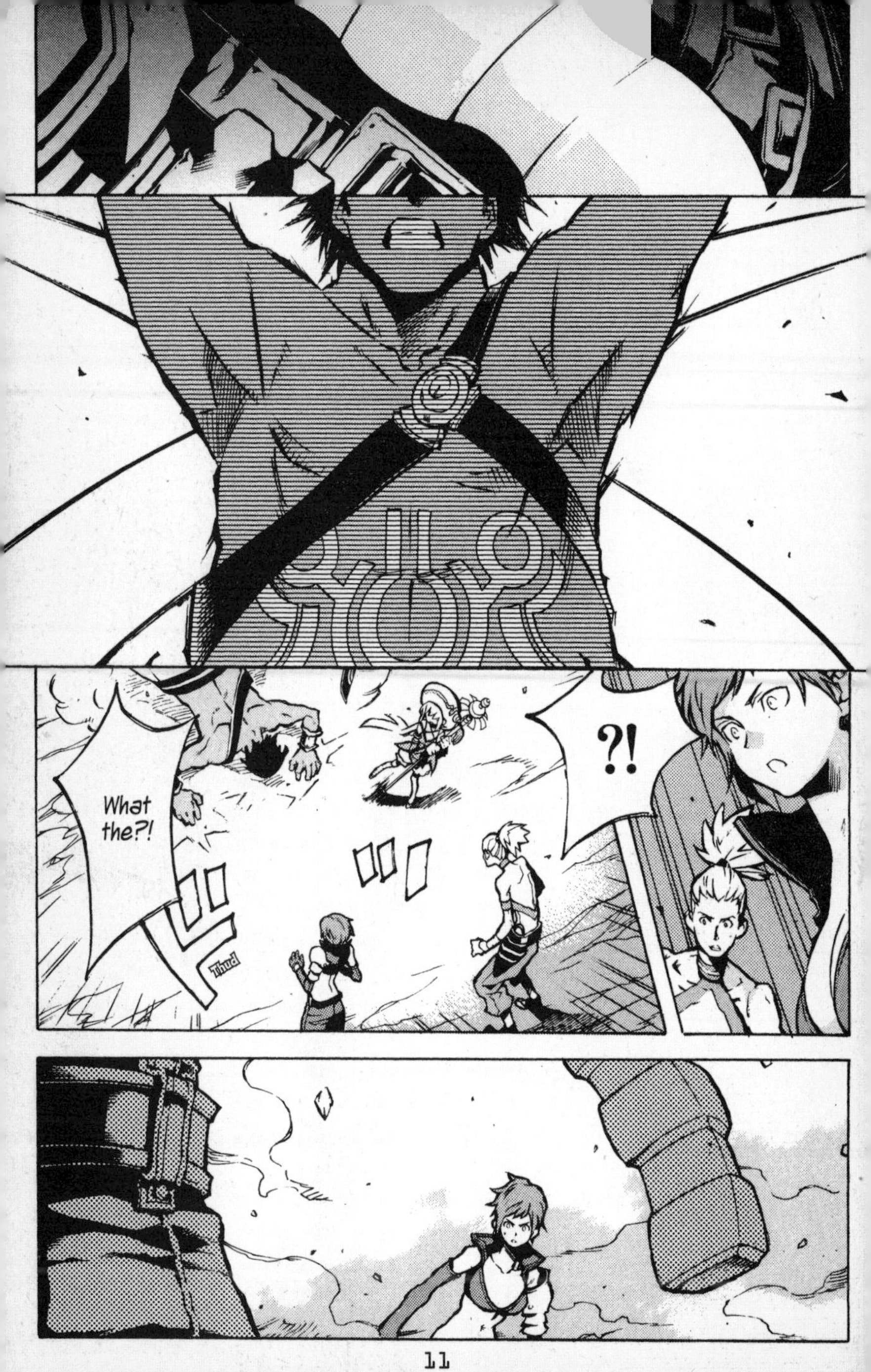
?!
What the?!
Thud

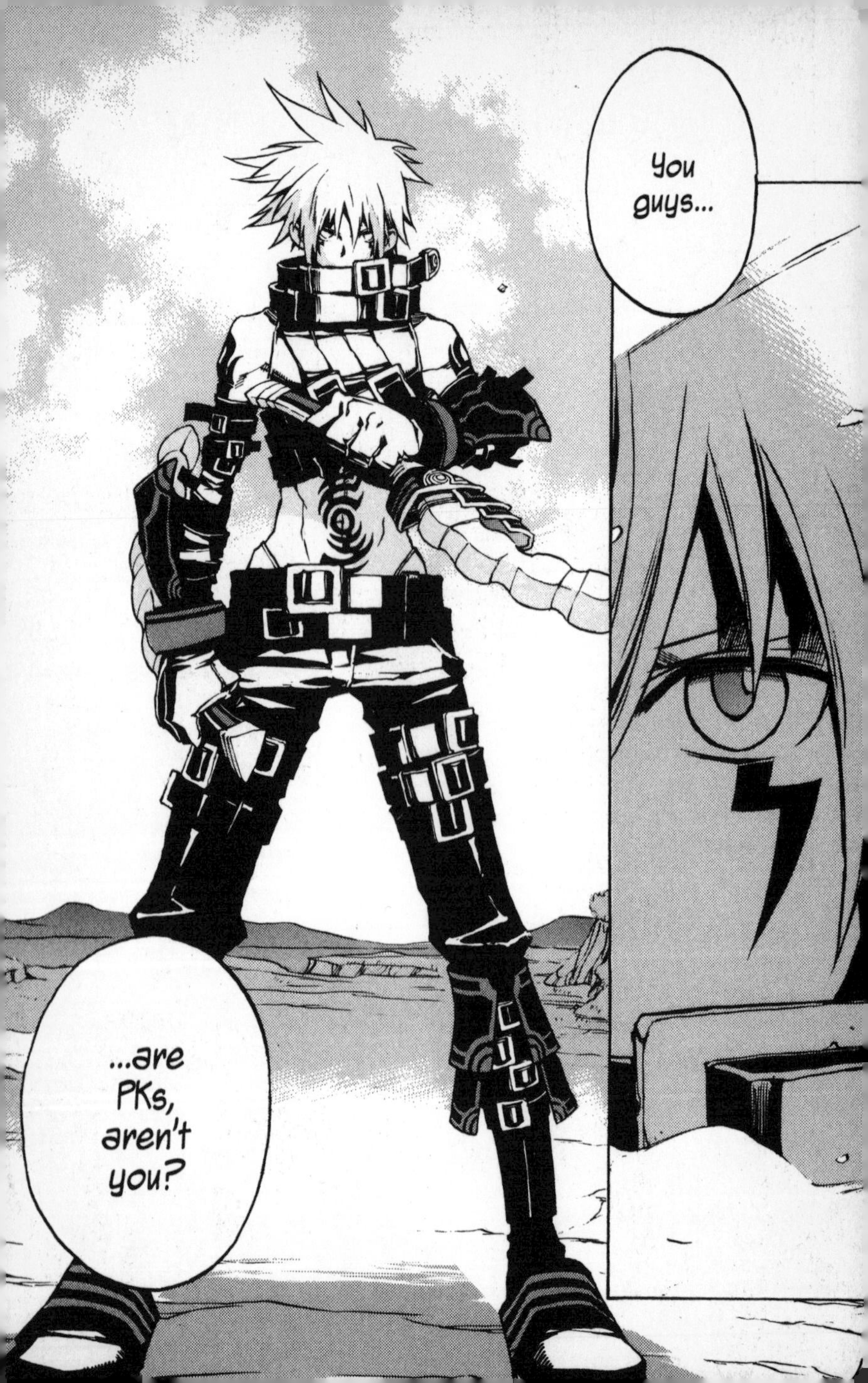
You guys...
...are PKs, aren't you?

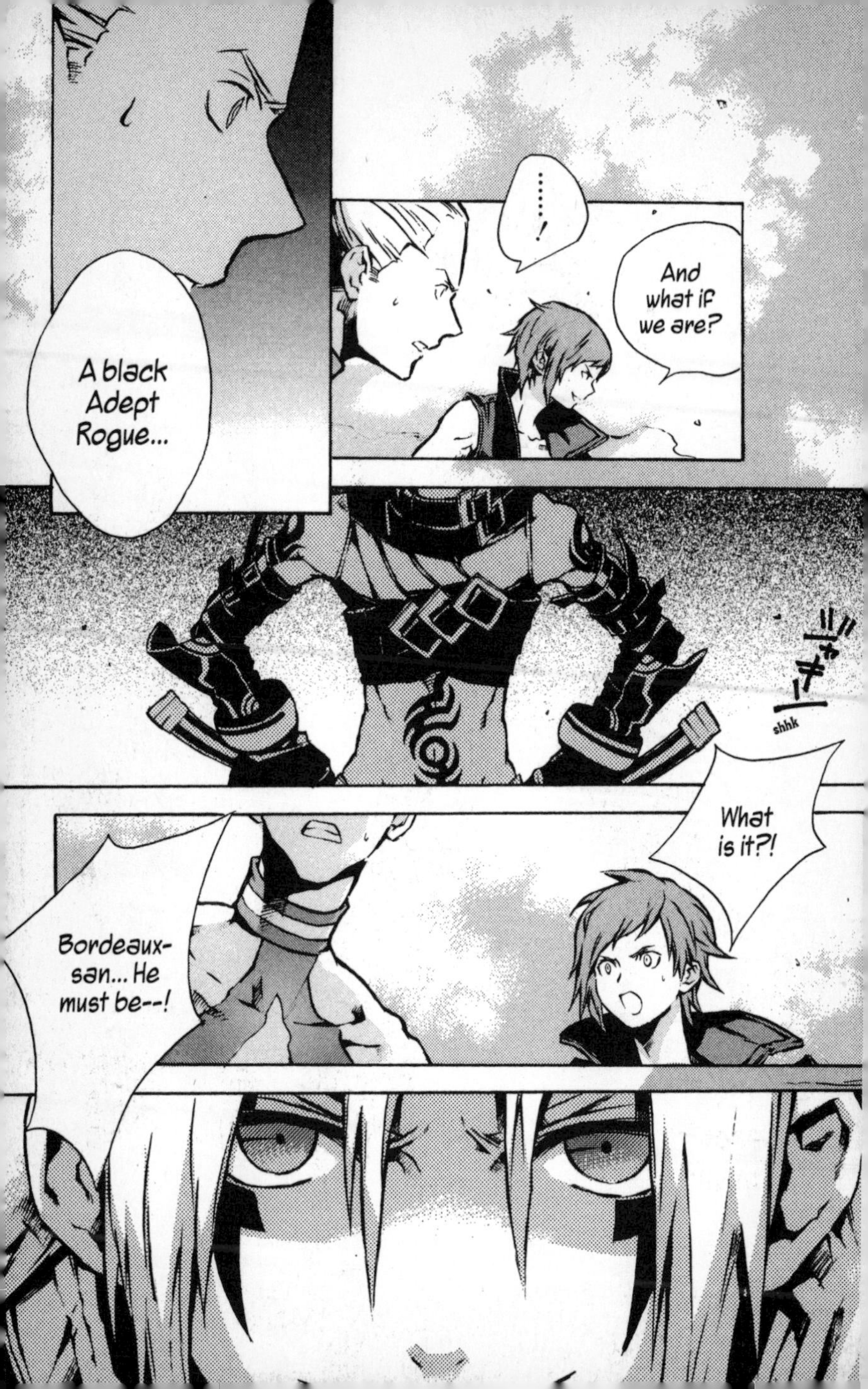
And what if we are?
......!
A black Adept Rogue...
shhk
What is it?!
Bordeaux-san... He must be--!

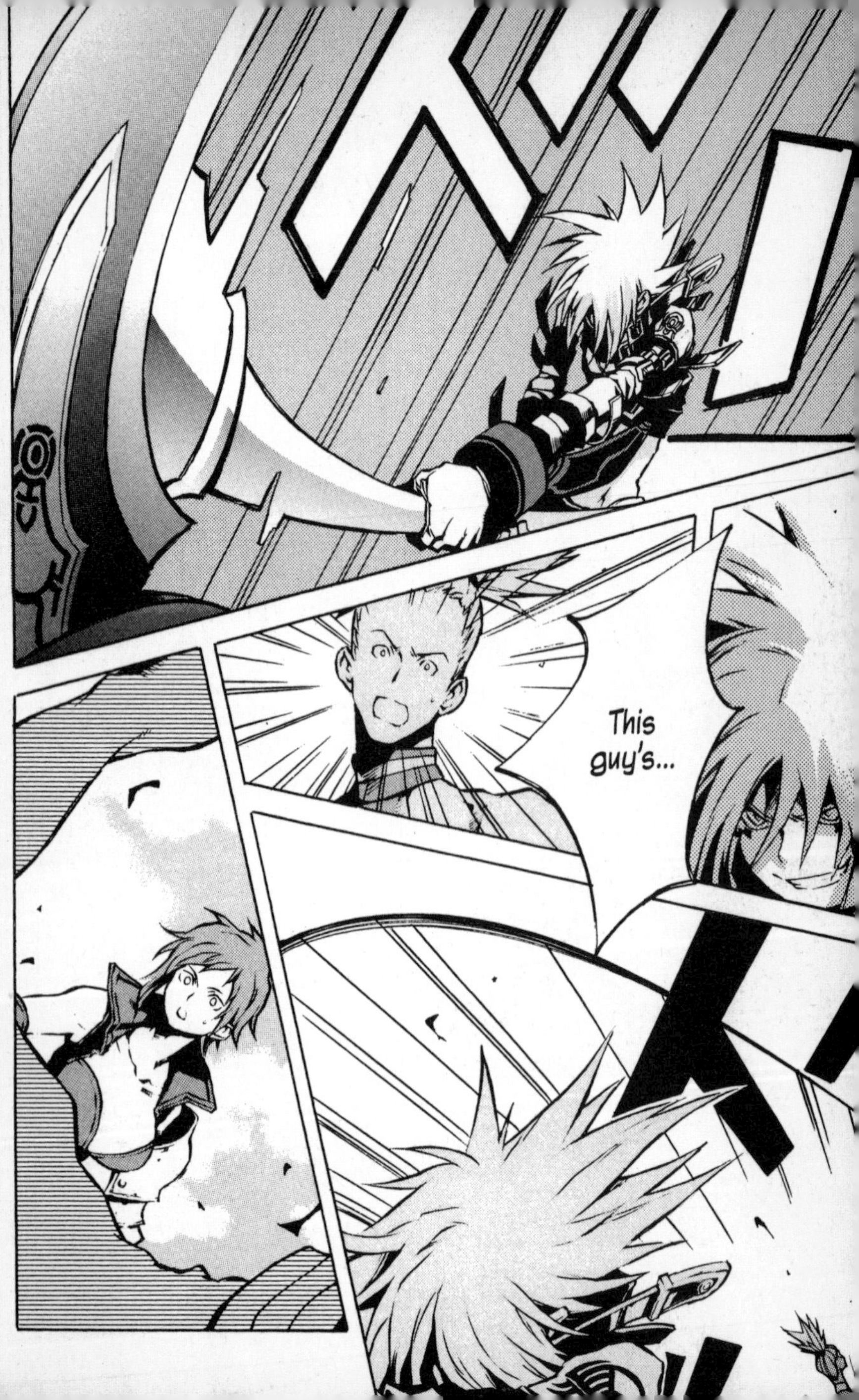
This guy's...

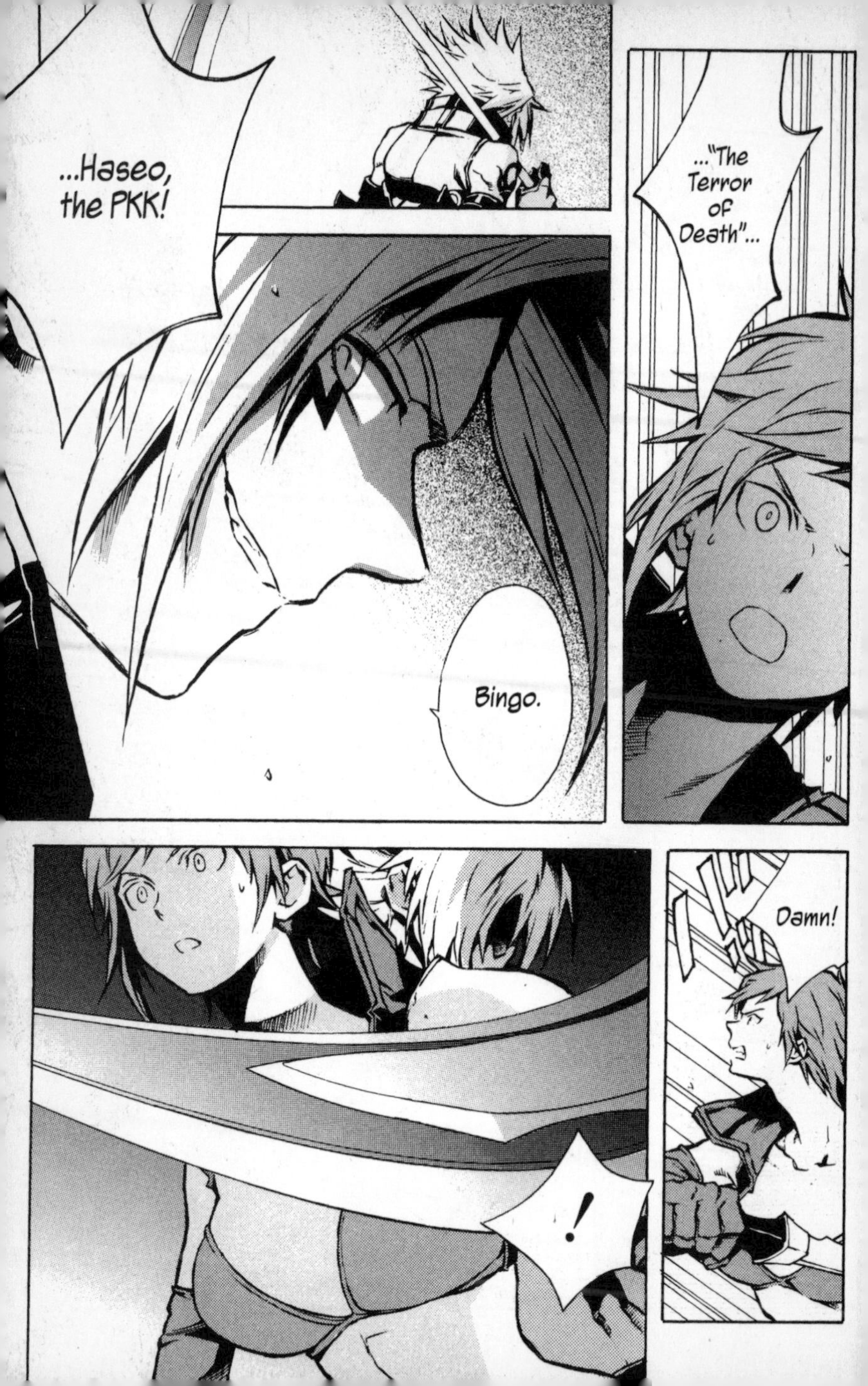
..."The Terror of Death"...
...Haseo, the PKK!
Bingo.
Damn!
!

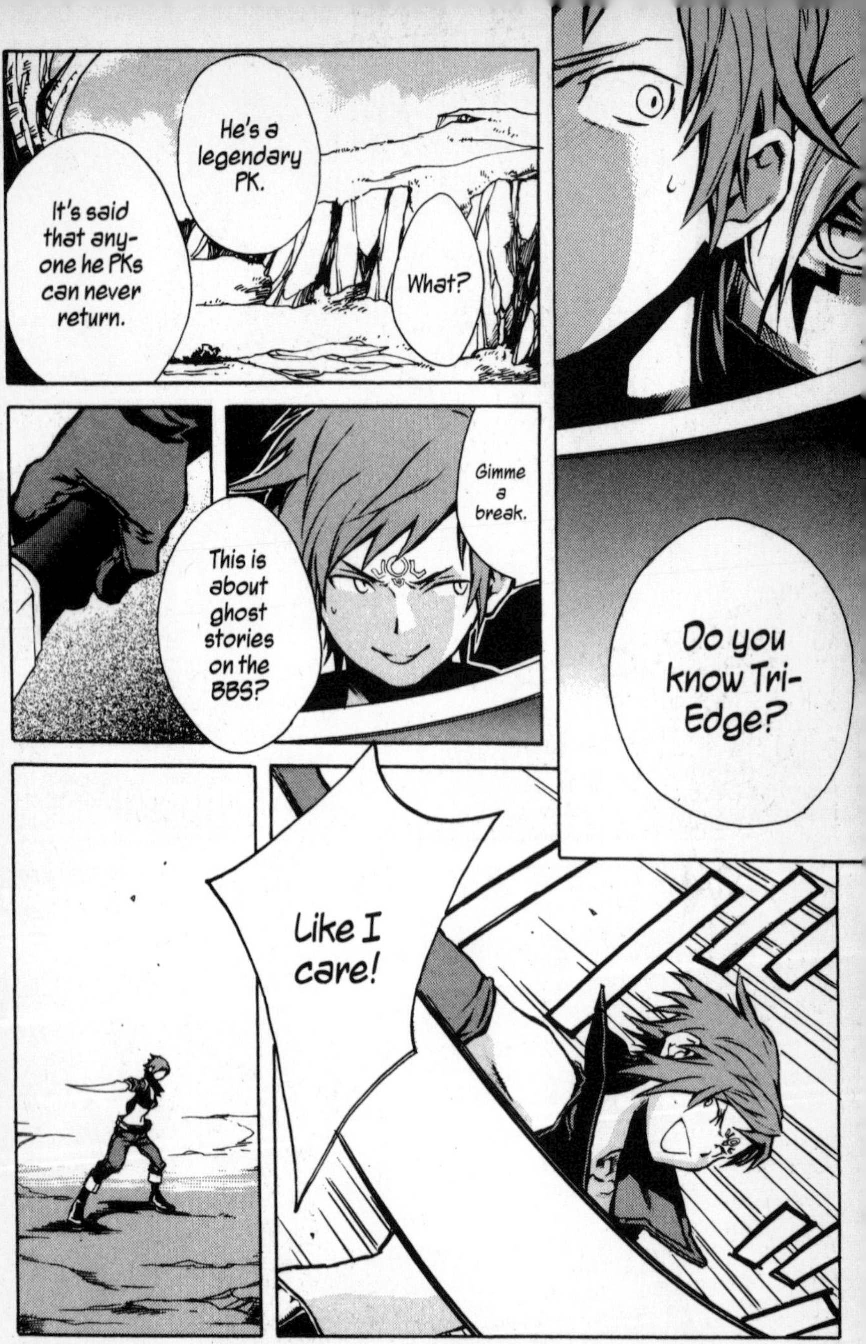
Do you know Tri-Edge?
What?
He's a legendary PK.
It's said that any-one he PKs can never return.
Gimme a break.
This is about ghost stories on the BBS?
Like I care!

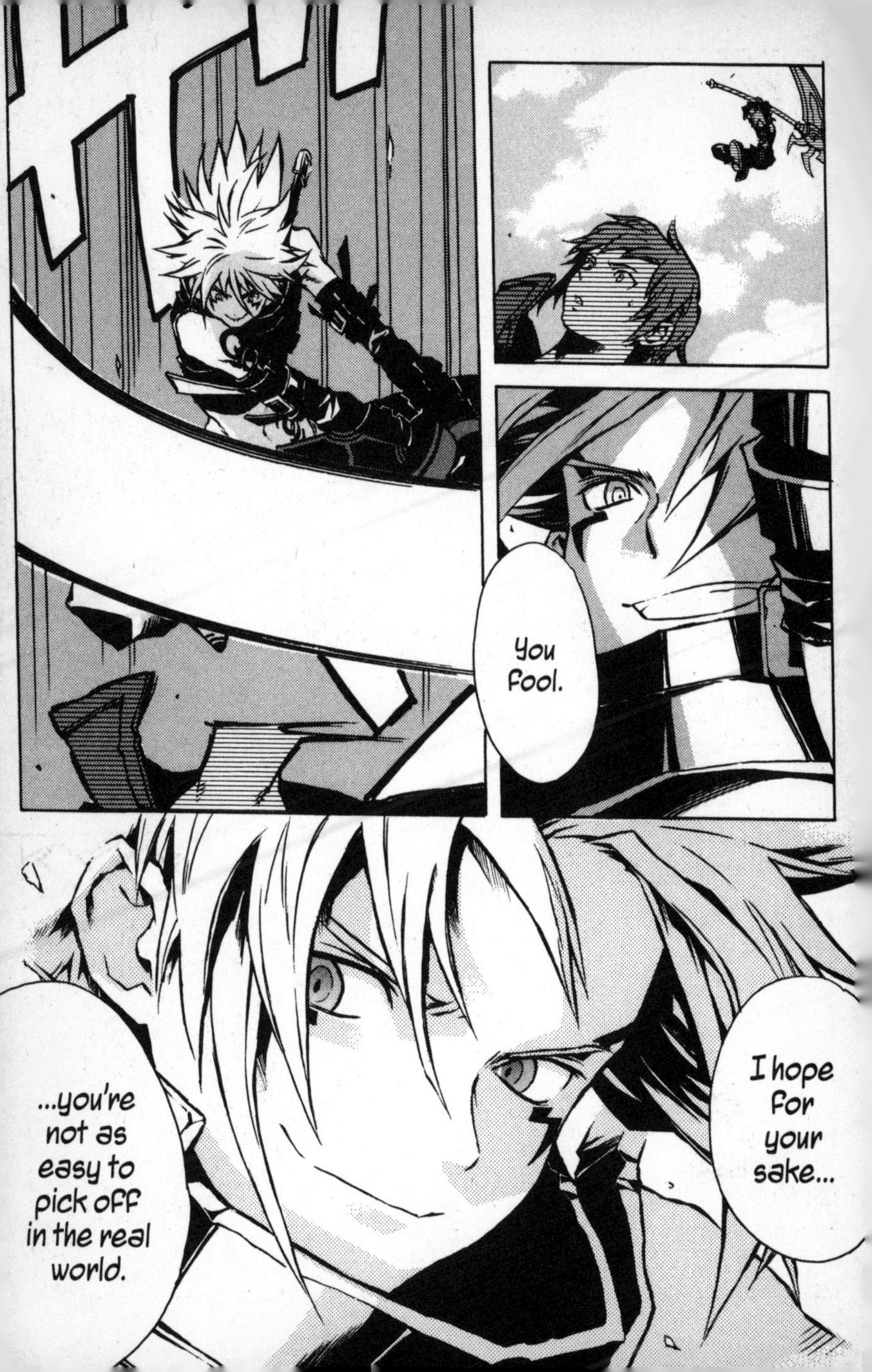
You fool.
I hope for your sake...
...you're not as easy to pick off in the real world.

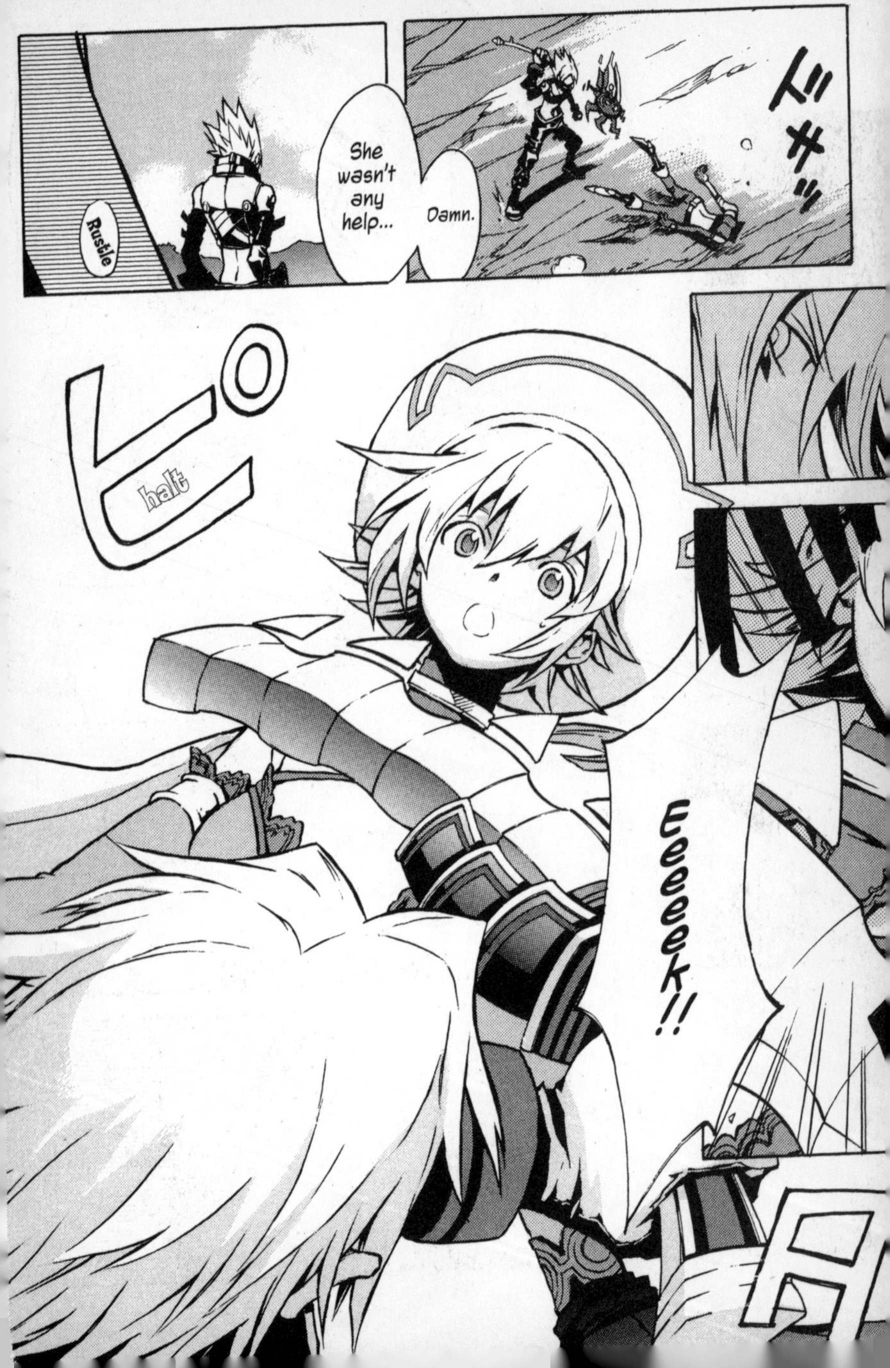

ドギッ
Damn.
She wasn't any help...
Rustle
ピ
halt
Eeeeek!!

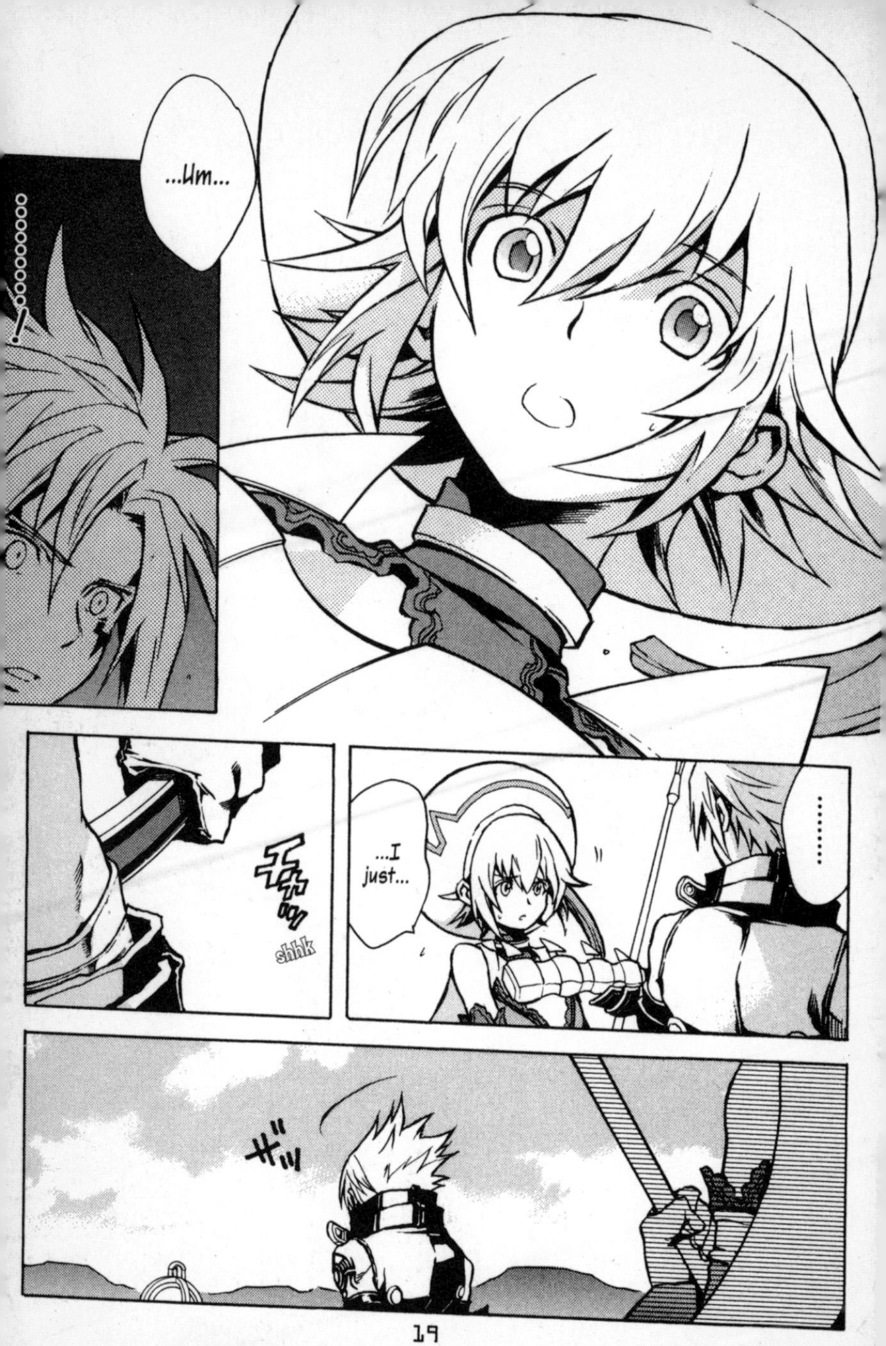
...Um...
ooooooooo!
......
...I just...
shhk

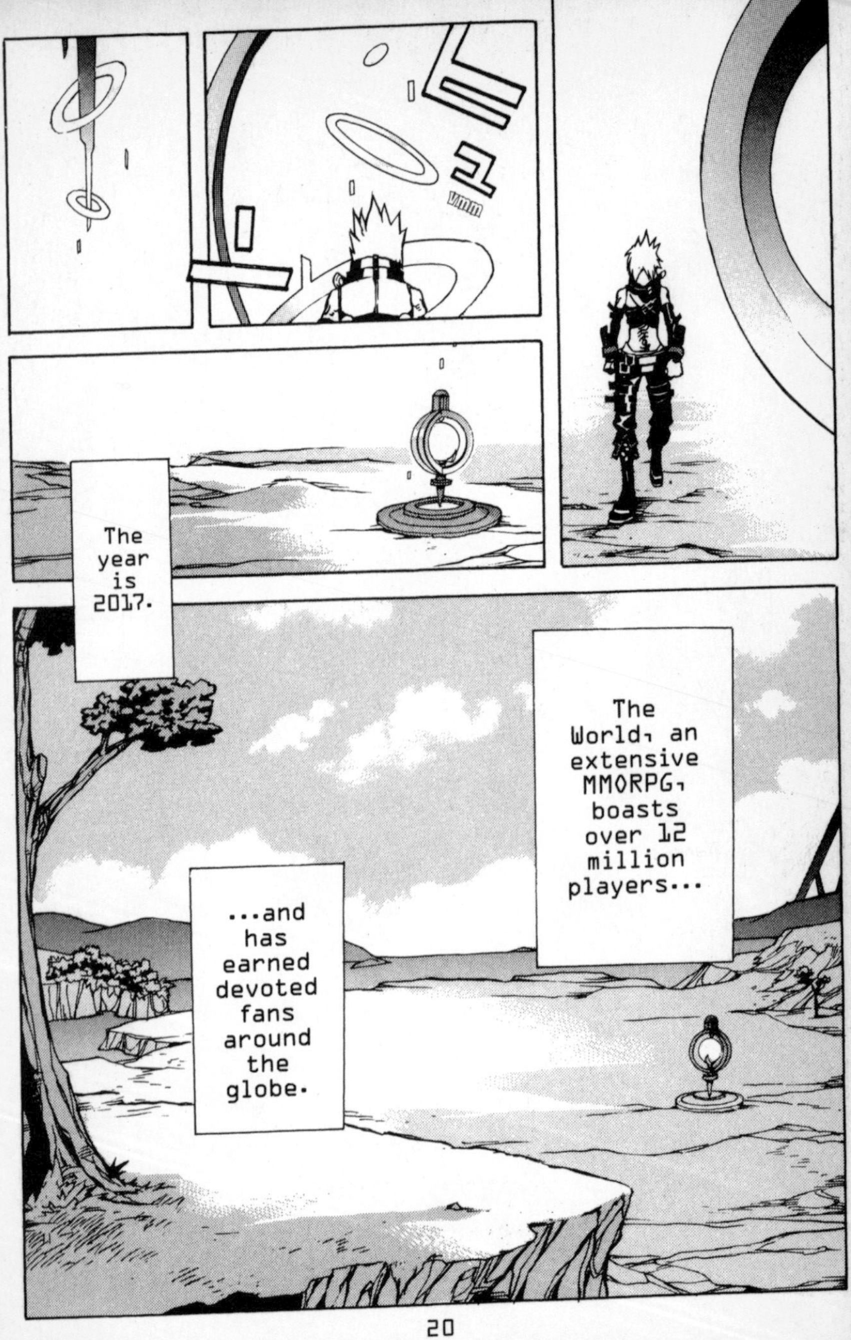
vmm
The year is 2017.
The World, an extensive MMORPG, boasts over 12 million players...
...and has earned devoted fans around the globe.

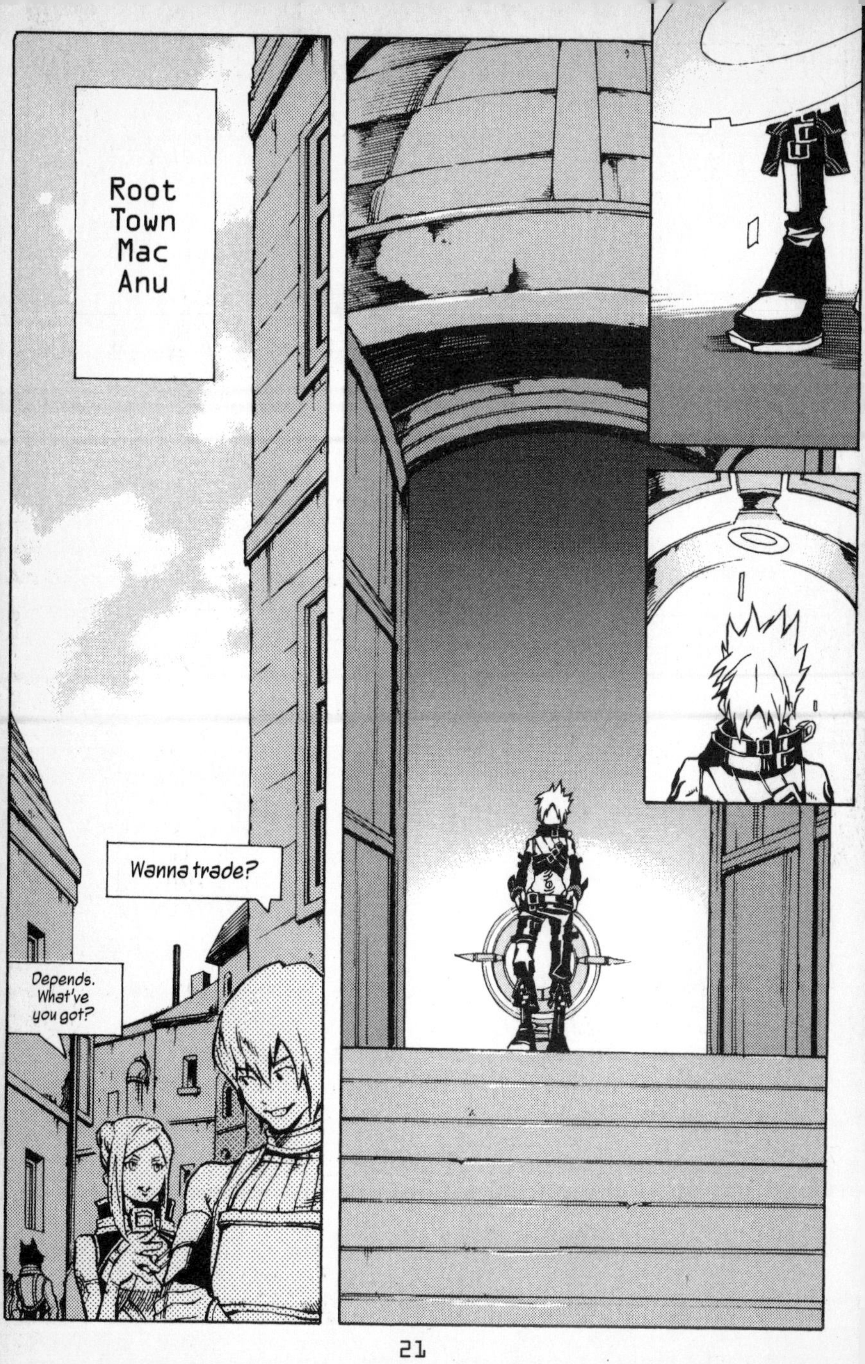
Root Town Mac Anu
Wanna trade?
Depends. What've you got?

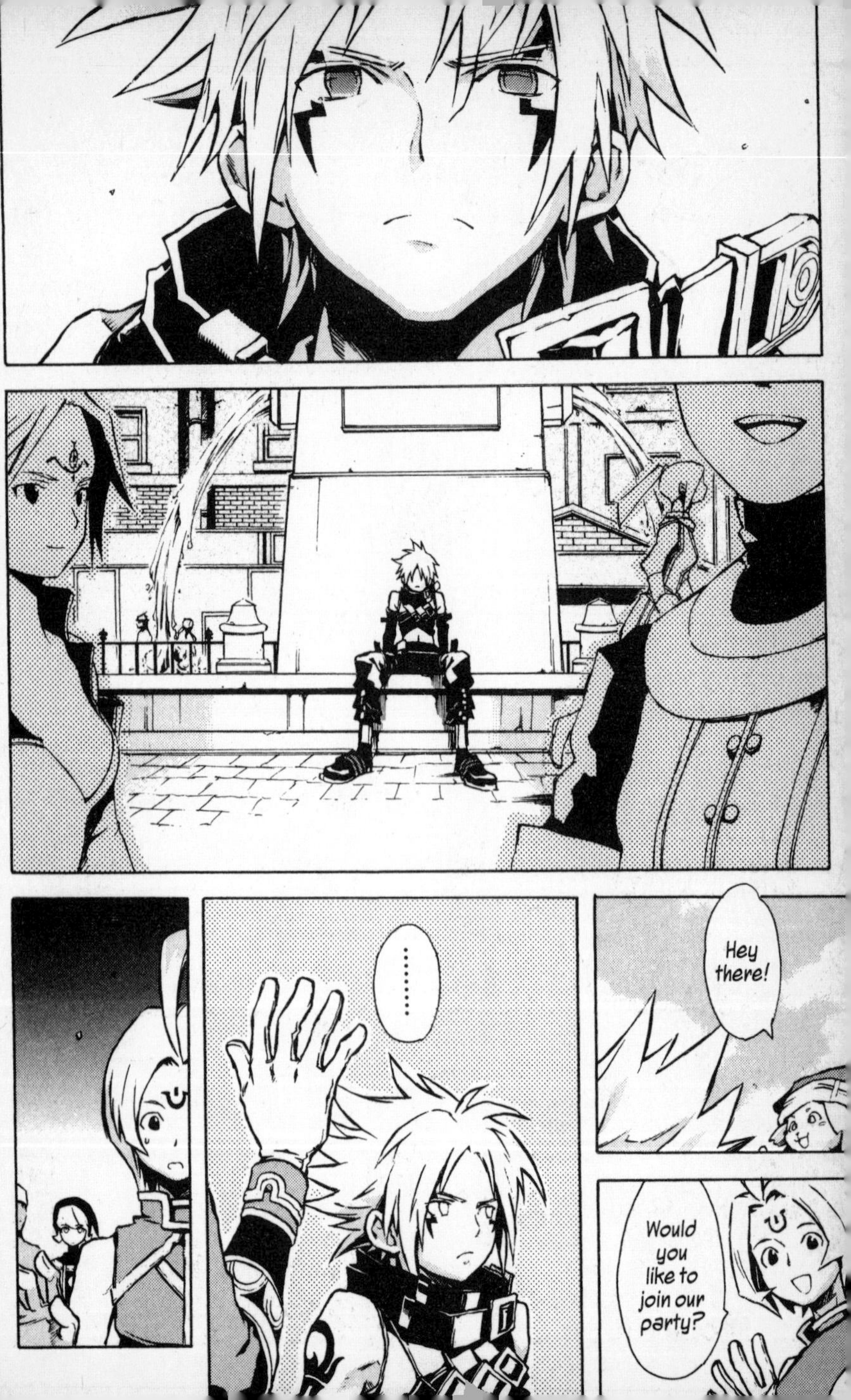
Hey there!
Would you like to join our party?
......

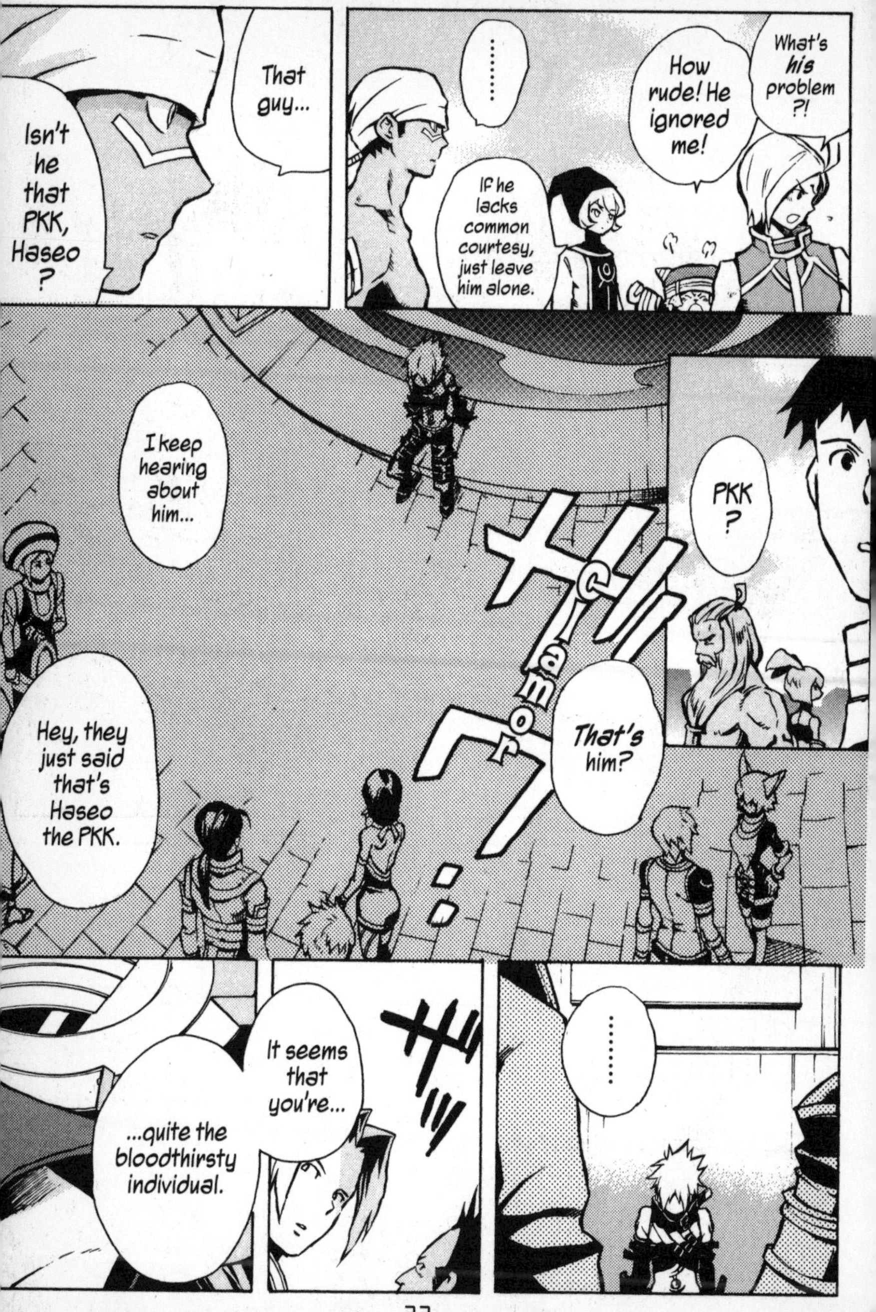
What's his problem ?!
How rude! He ignored me!
......
If he lacks common courtesy, just leave him alone.
That guy...
Isn't he that PKK, Haseo ?
PKK ?
That's him?
Clamor
I keep hearing about him...
Hey, they just said that's Haseo the PKK.
......
It seems that you're...
...quite the bloodthirsty individual.

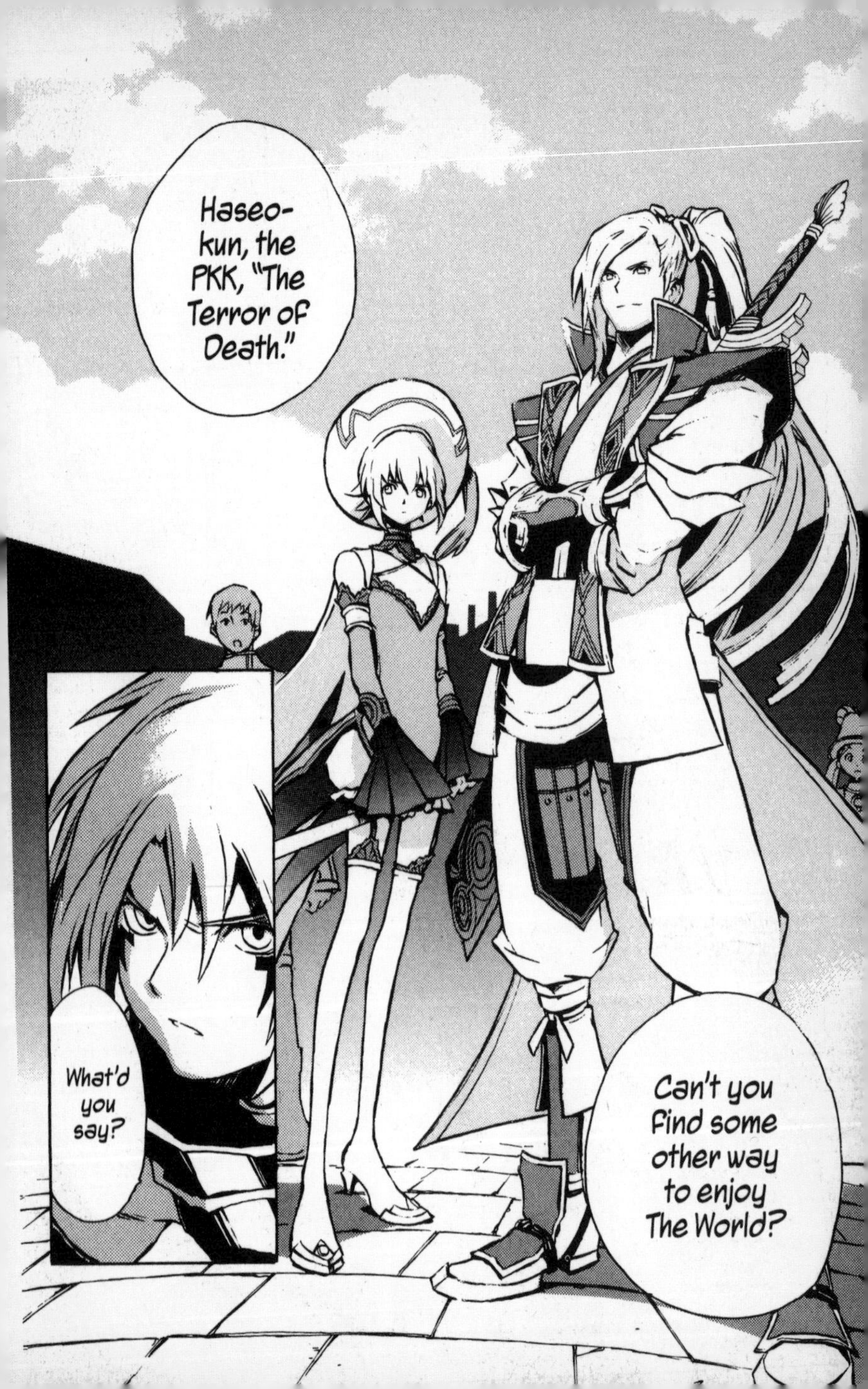
Haseo-kun, the PKK, "The Terror of Death."
Can't you find some other way to enjoy The World?
What'd you say?

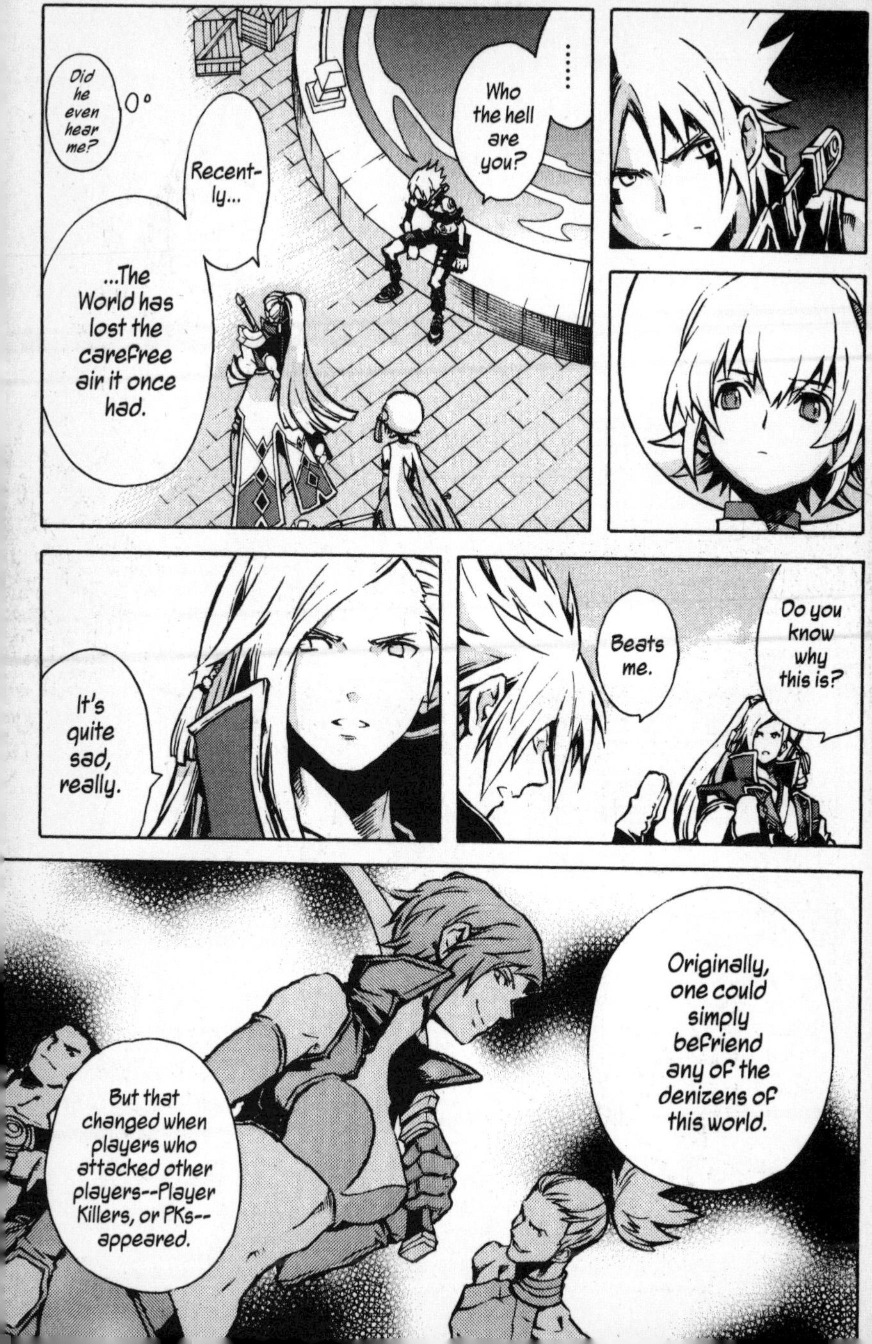
......
Who the hell are you?
Recent-ly...
Did he even hear me?
...The World has lost the carefree air it once had.
Do you know why this is?
Beats me.
It's quite sad, really.
Originally, one could simply befriend any of the denizens of this world.
But that changed when players who attacked other players--Player Killers, or PKs--appeared.

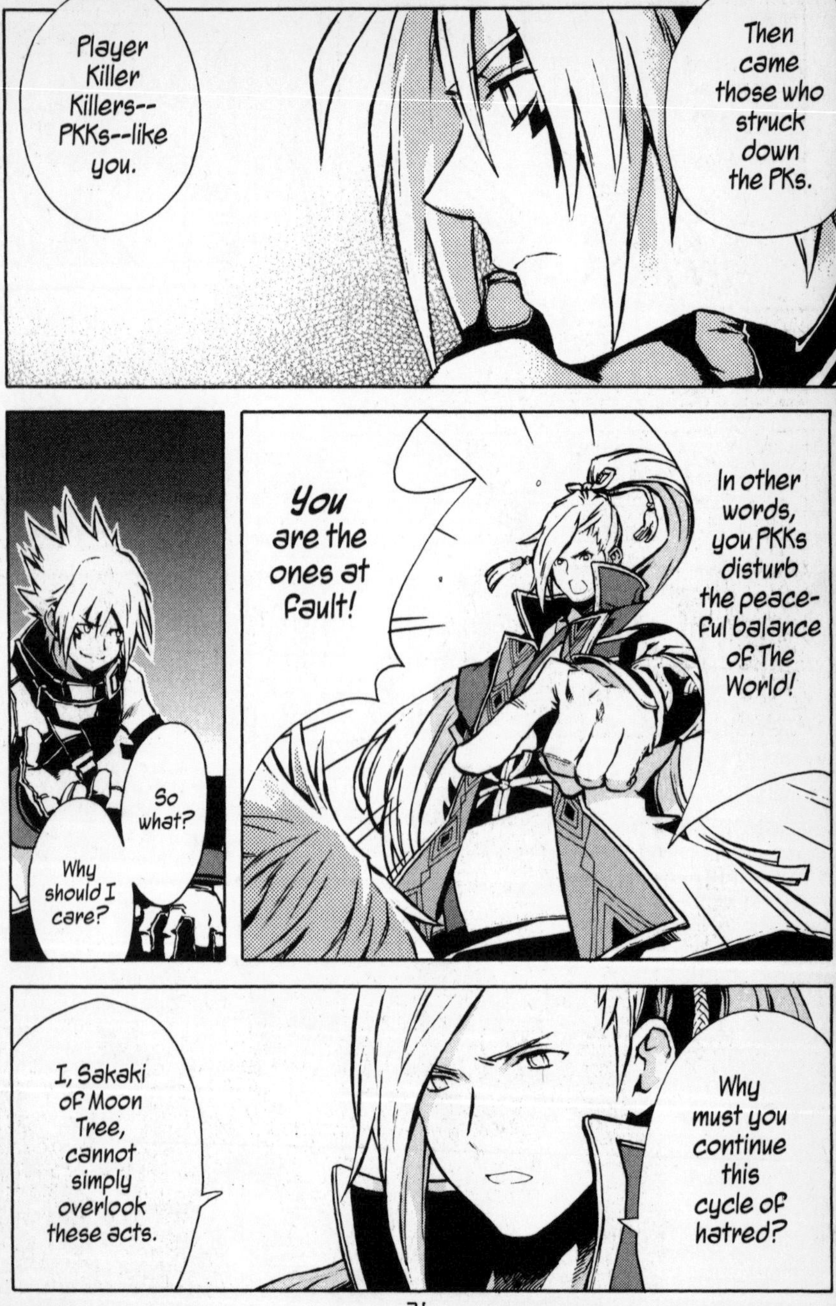
Then came those who struck down the PKs.
Player Killer Killers--PKKs--like you.
In other words, you PKKs disturb the peace-ful balance of The World!
You are the ones at fault!
So what?
Why should I care?
Why must you continue this cycle of hatred?
I, Sakaki of Moon Tree, cannot simply overlook these acts.

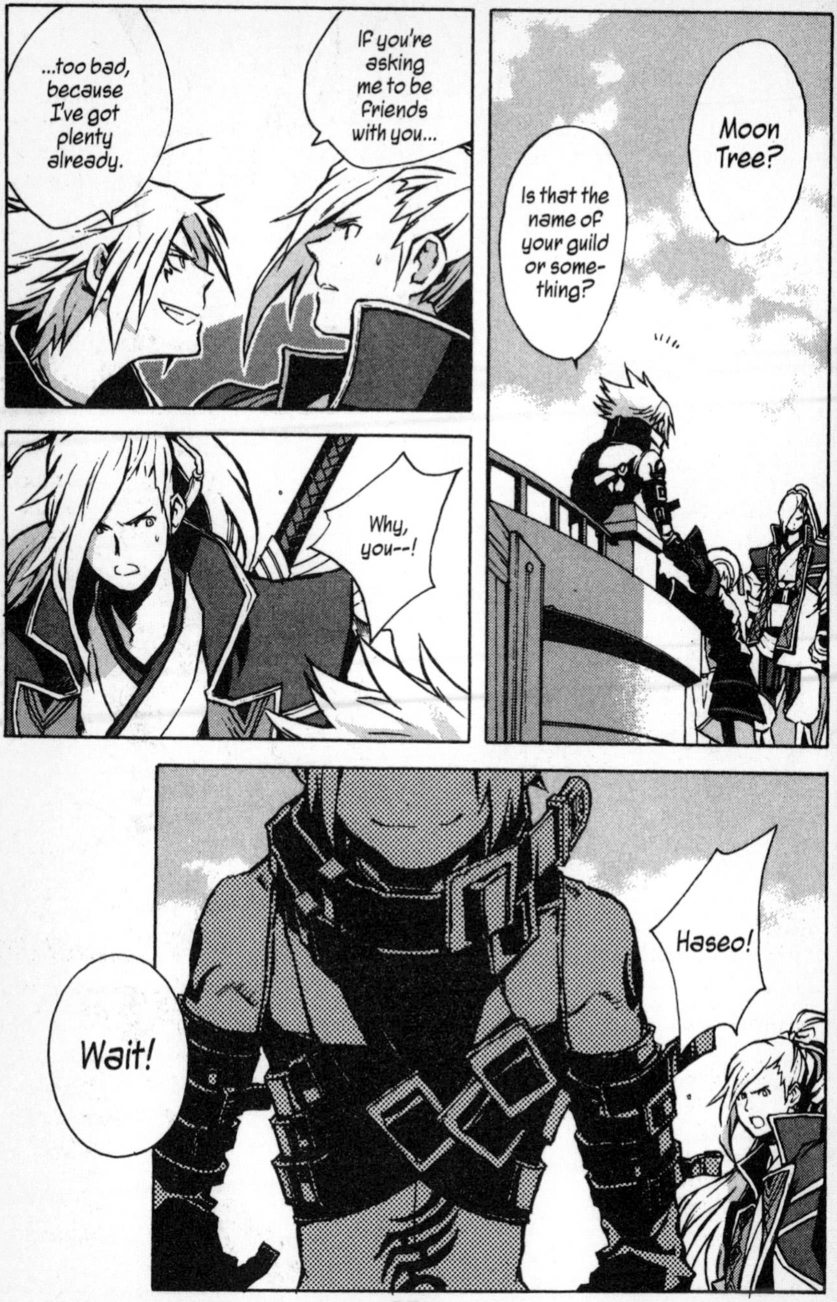
Moon Tree?
Is that the name of your guild or some-thing?
If you're asking me to be friends with you...
...too bad, because I've got plenty already.
Why, you--!
Haseo!
Wait!

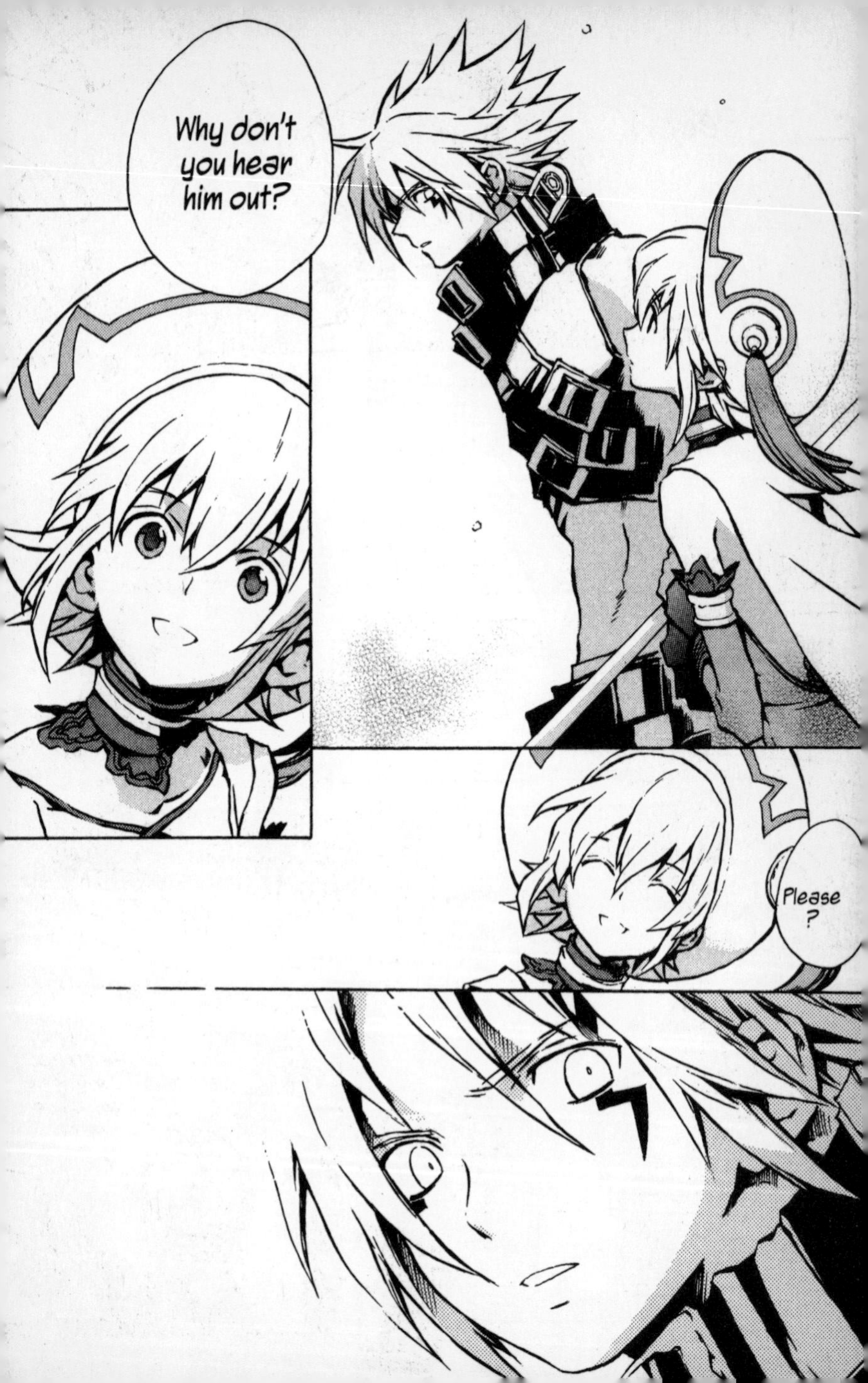
Why don't you hear him out?
Please ?

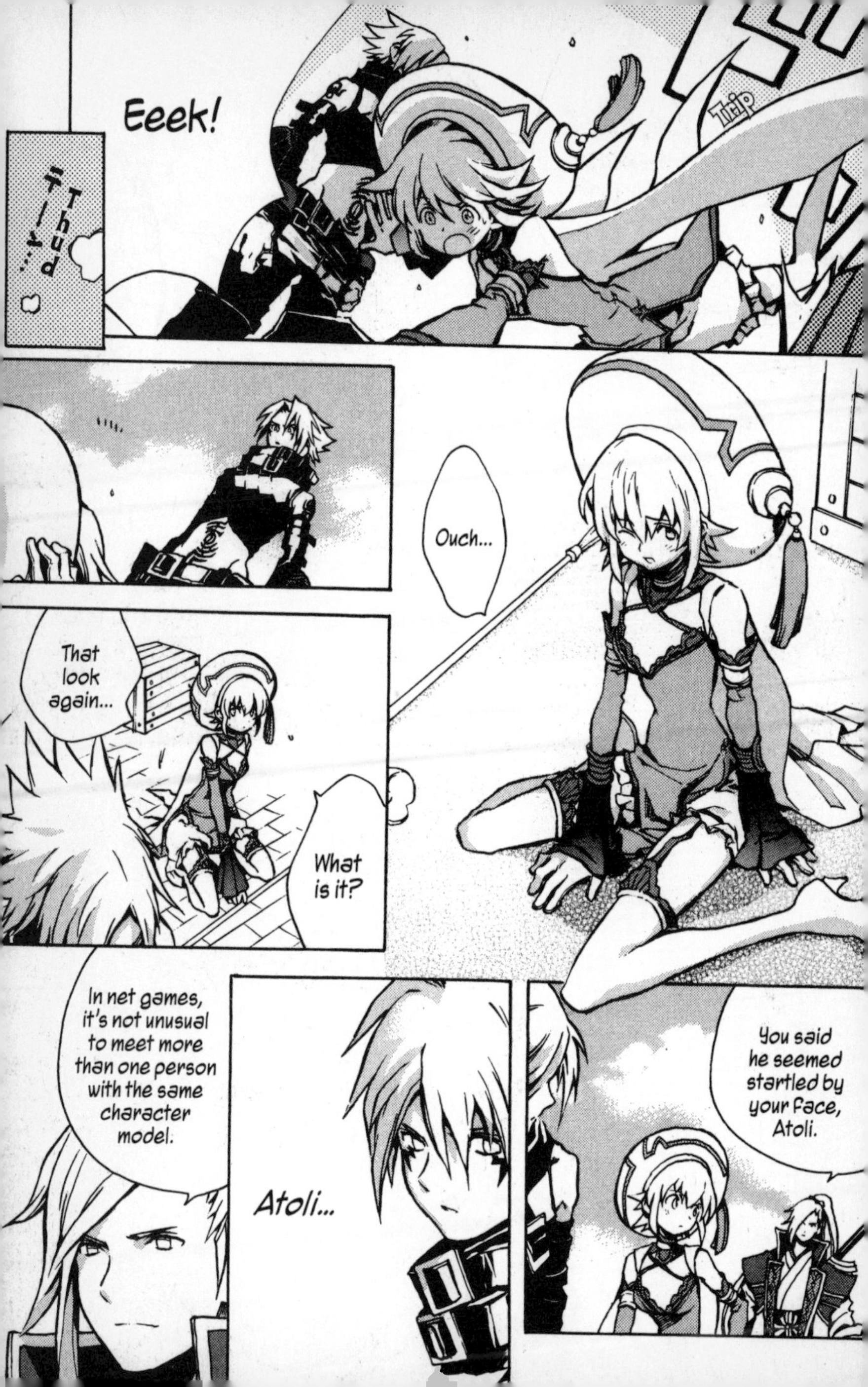
Trip
Eeek!
Thud...
Ouch...
That look again...
What is it?
You said he seemed startled by your face, Atoli.
Atoli...
In net games, it's not unusual to meet more than one person with the same character model.

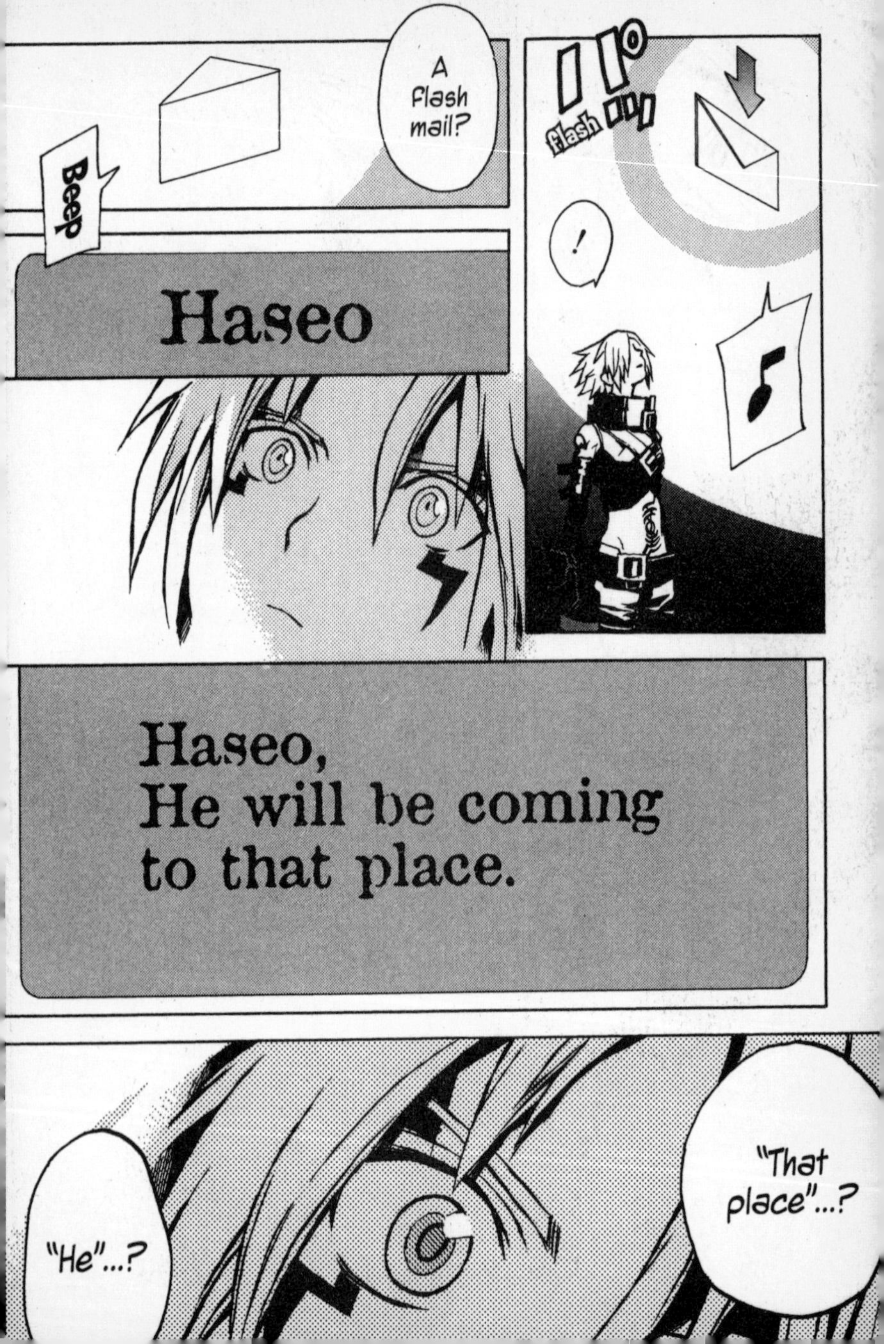
flash
!
A flash mail?
Beep
Haseo
Haseo,
He will be coming
to that place.
"That place"...?
"He"...?

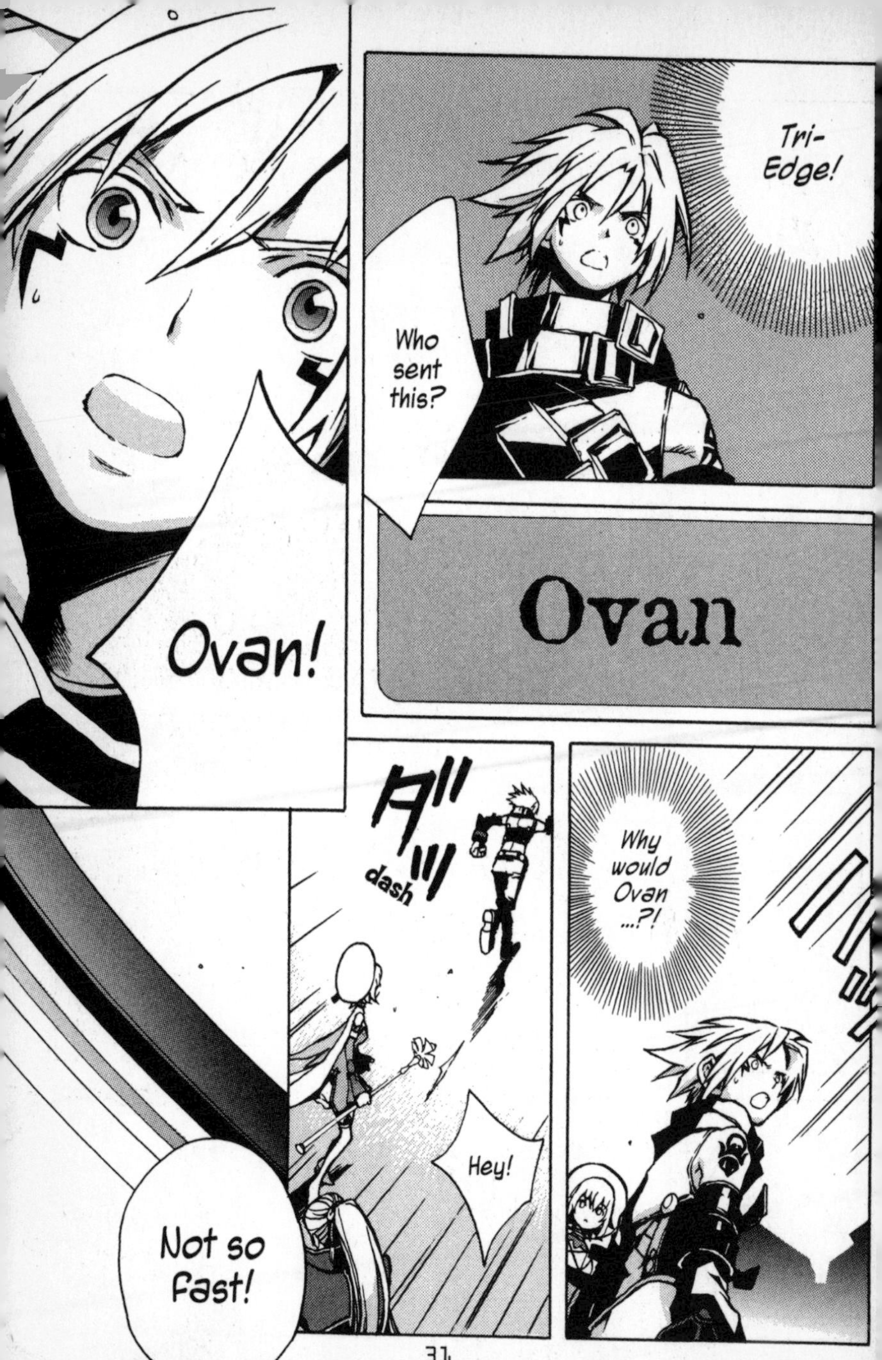
Tri-Edge!
Who sent this?
Ovan
Ovan!
Why would Ovan ...?!
dash
Hey!
Not so fast!

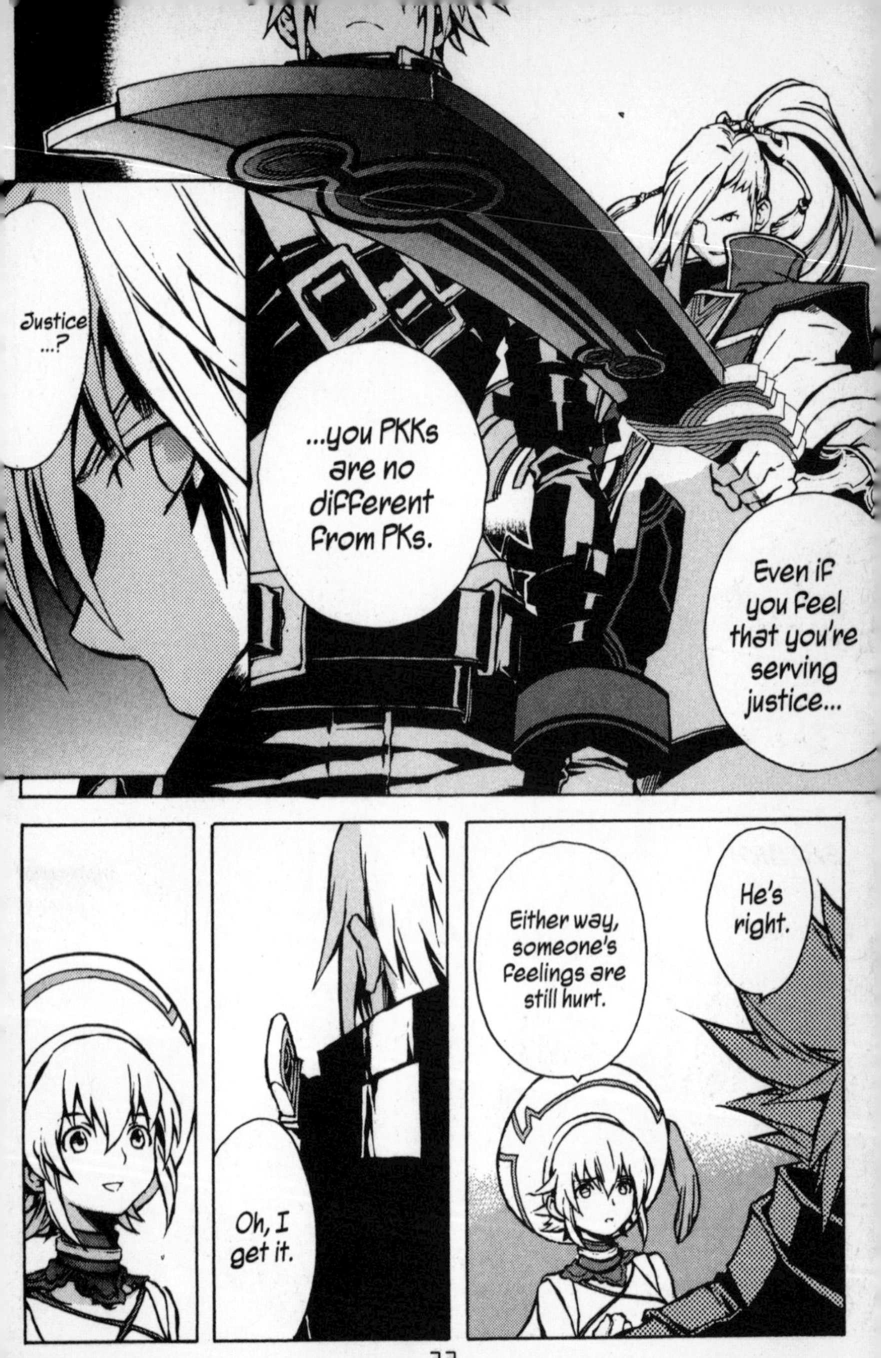
Even if you feel that you're serving justice...
...you PKKs are no different from PKs.
Justice ...?
He's right.
Either way, someone's feelings are still hurt.
Oh, I get it.

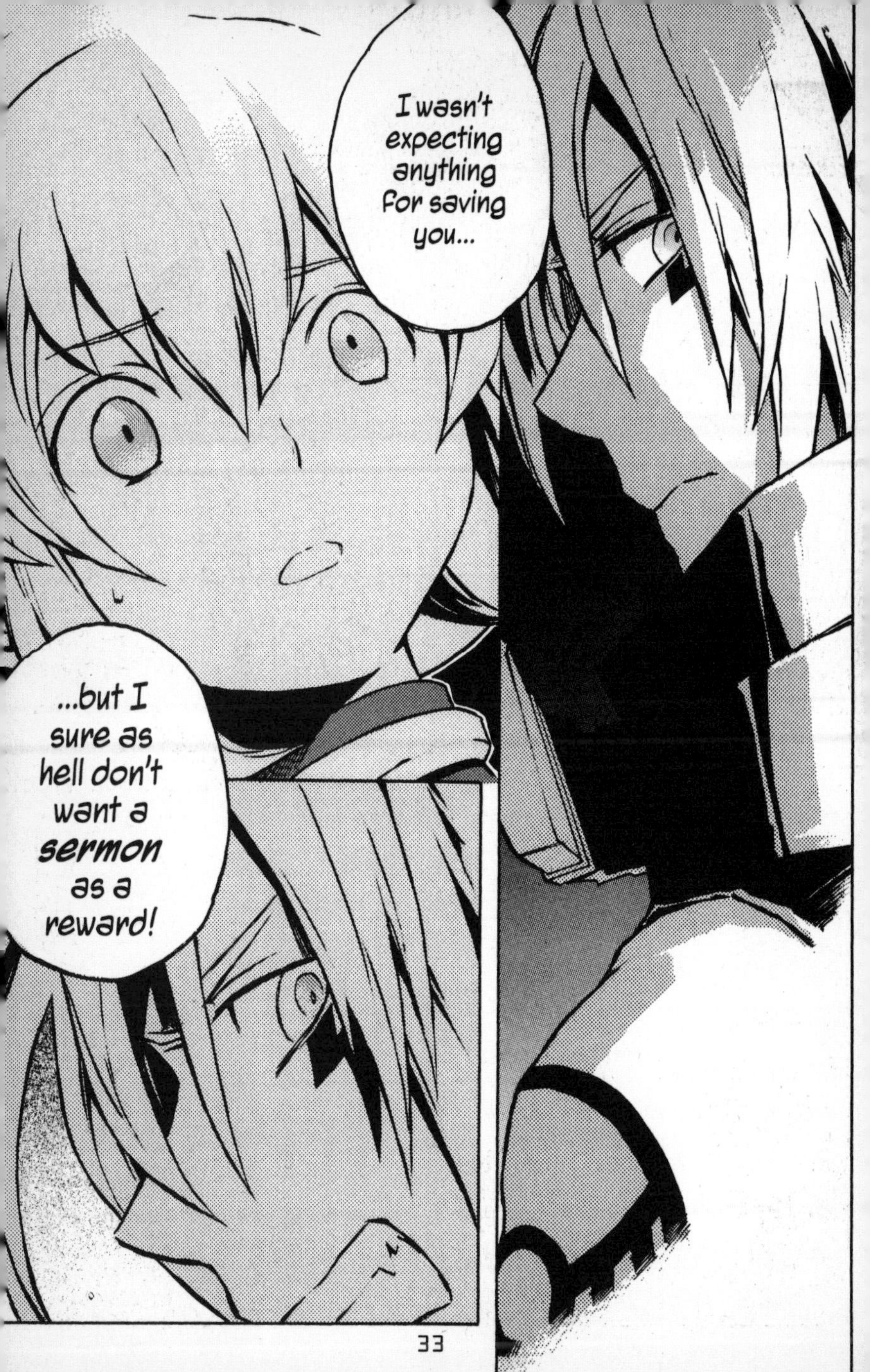
I wasn't expecting anything for saving you...
...but I sure as hell don't want a ***sermon*** as a reward!

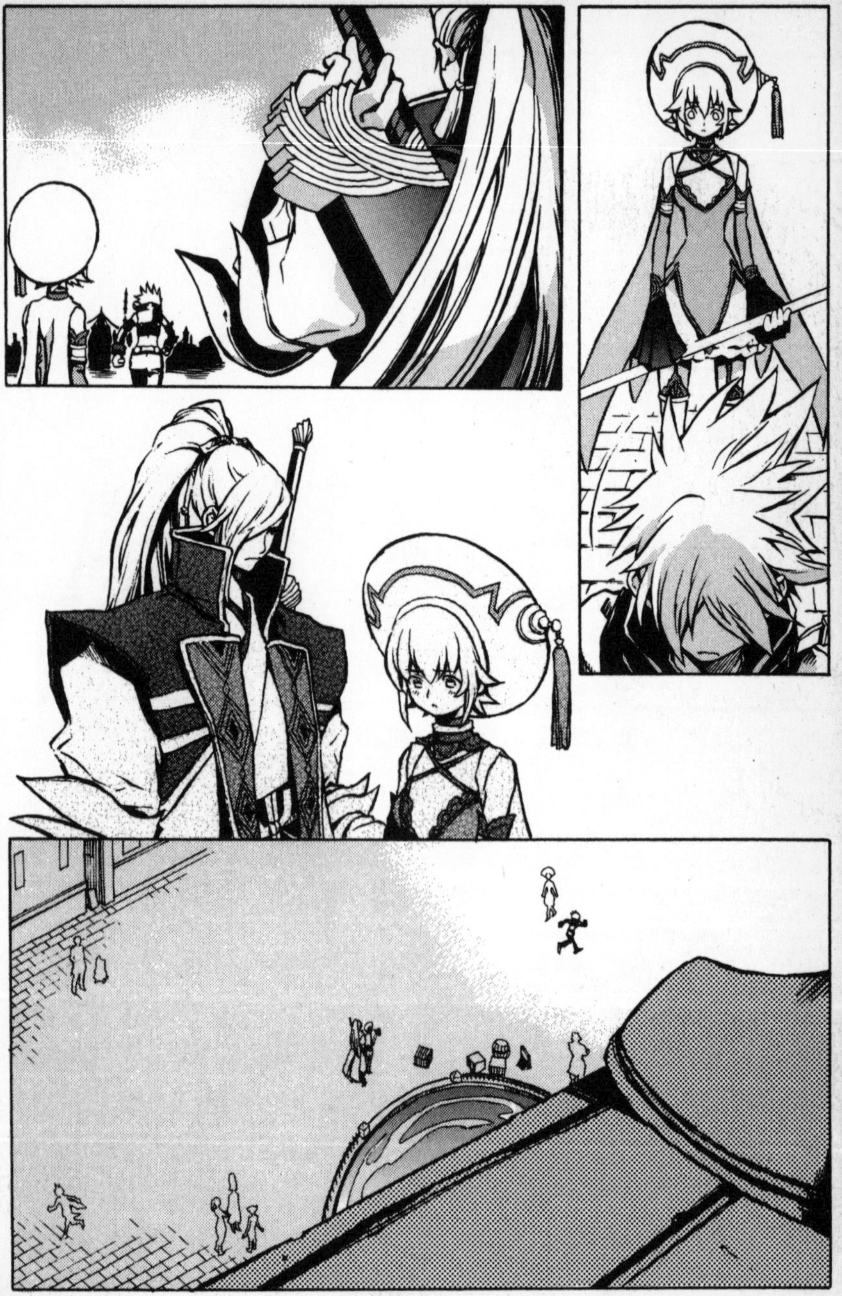

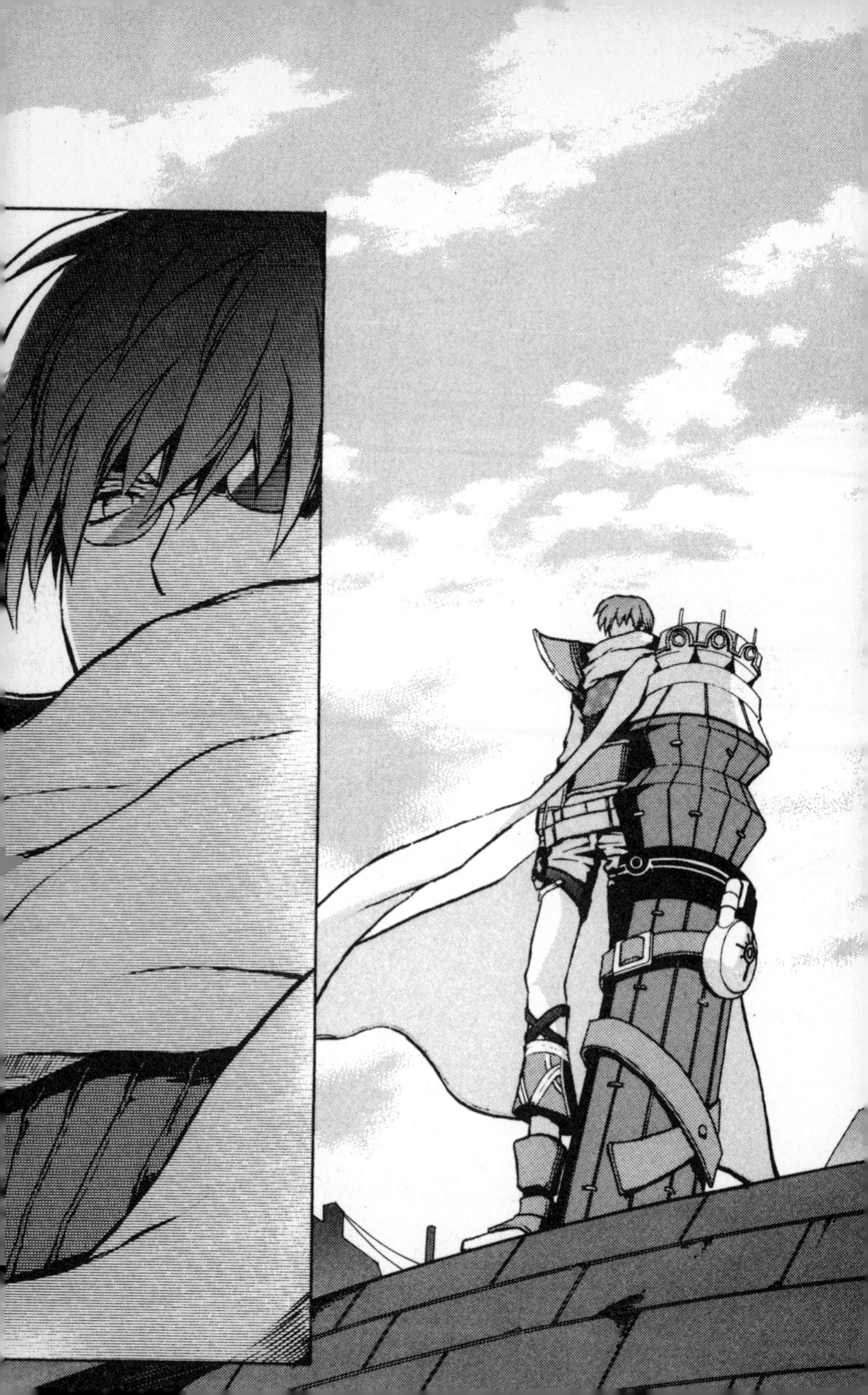

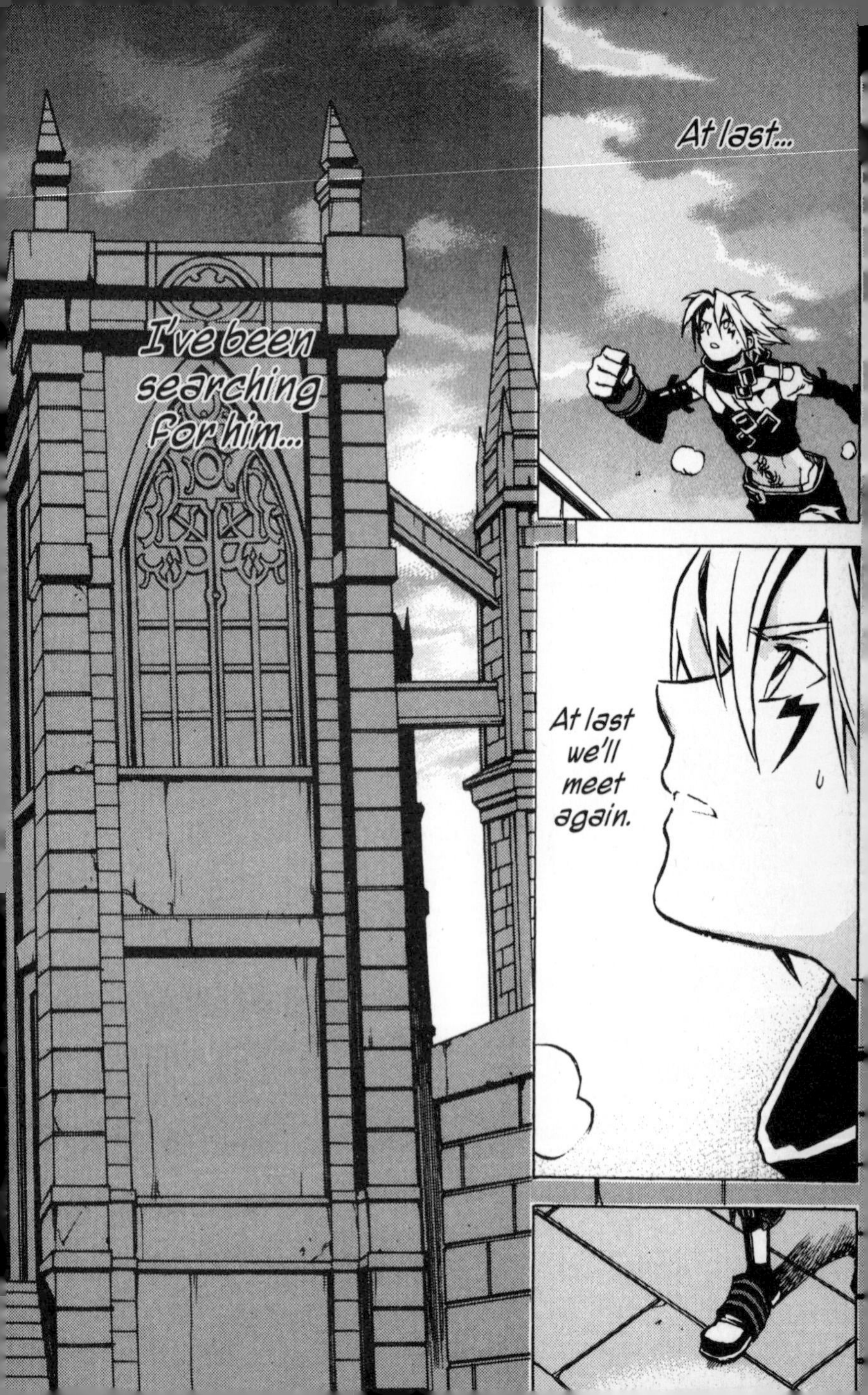
At last...
At last we'll meet again.
I've been searching for him...

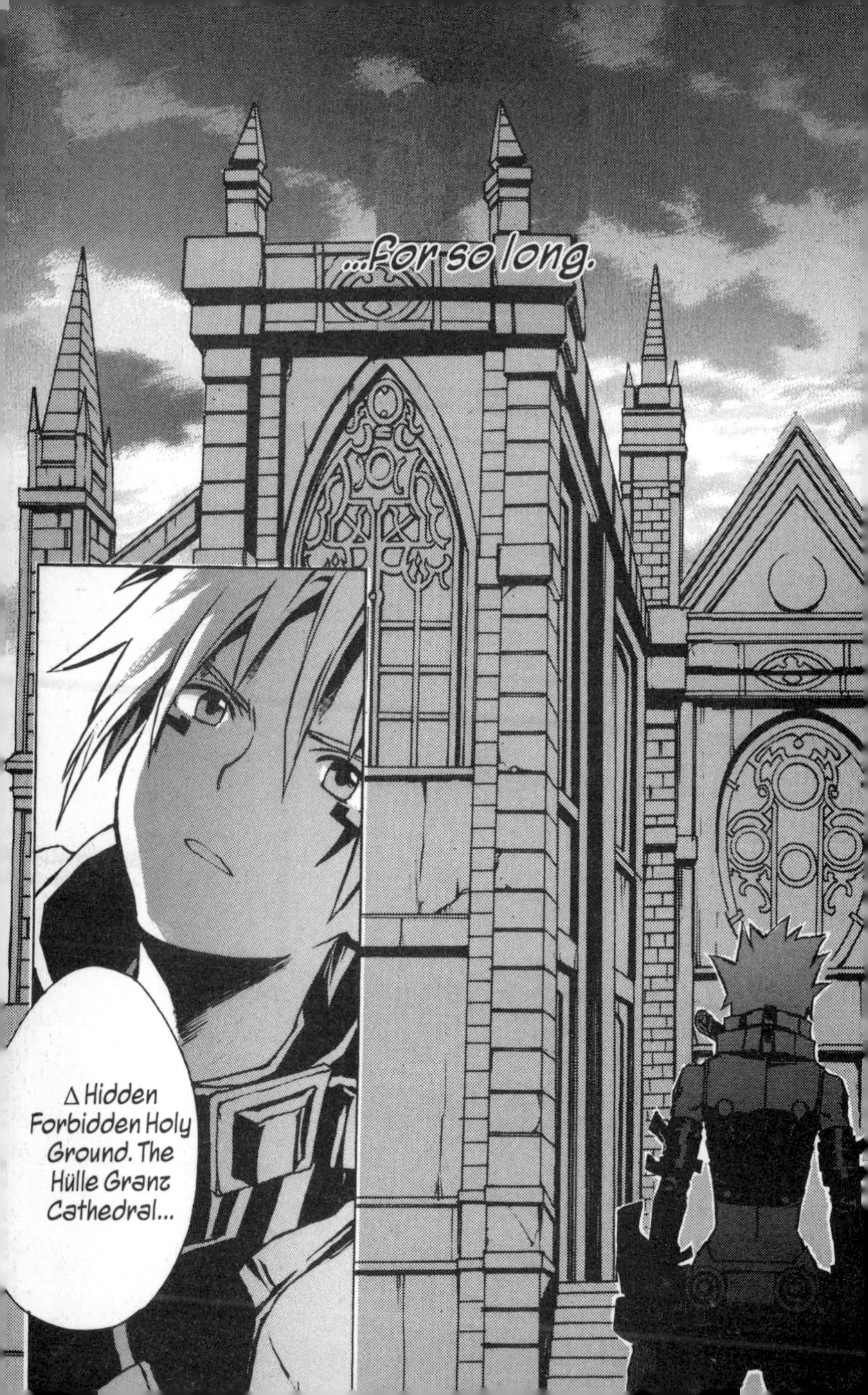
...for so long.
A Hidden Forbidden Holy Ground. The Hülle Granz Cathedral...

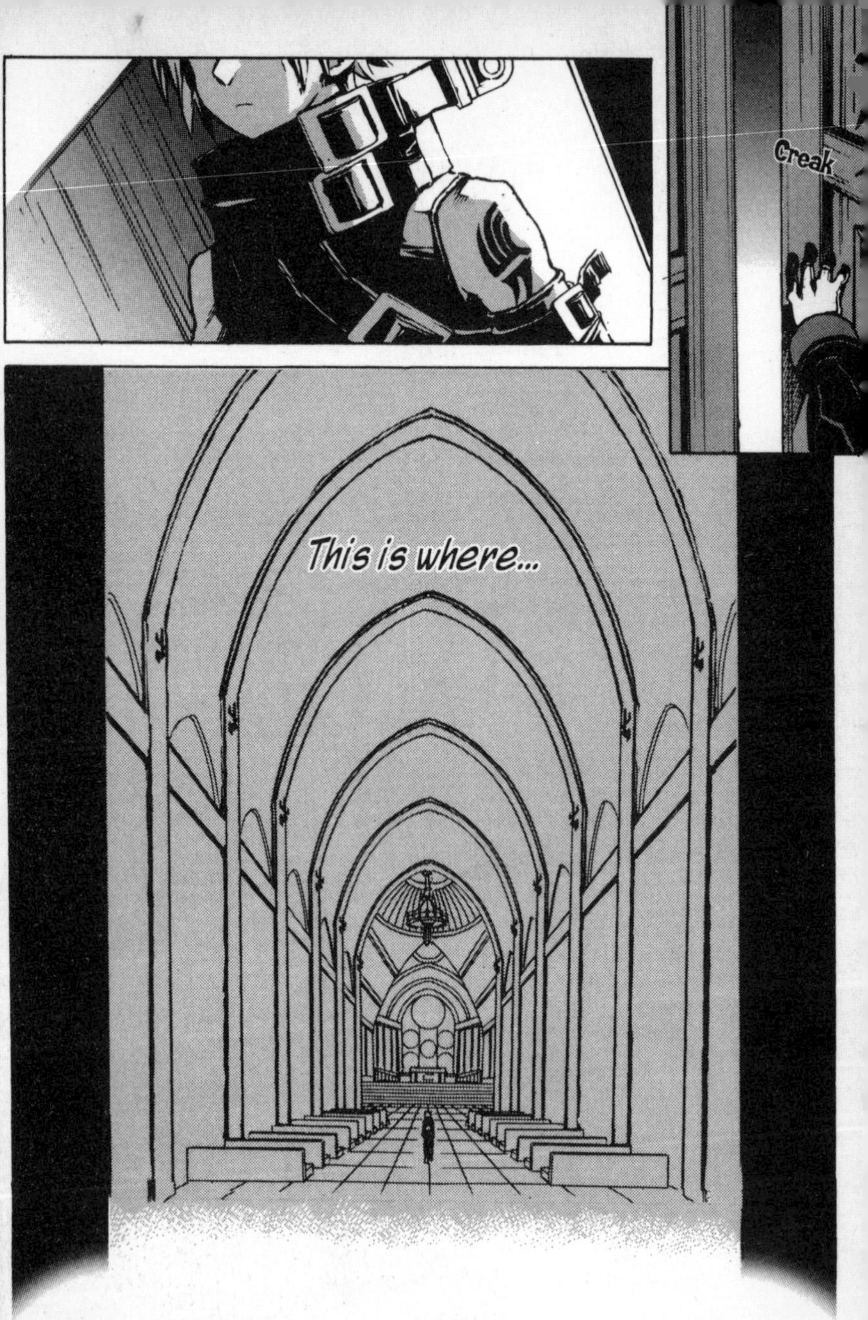
Creak
This is where...

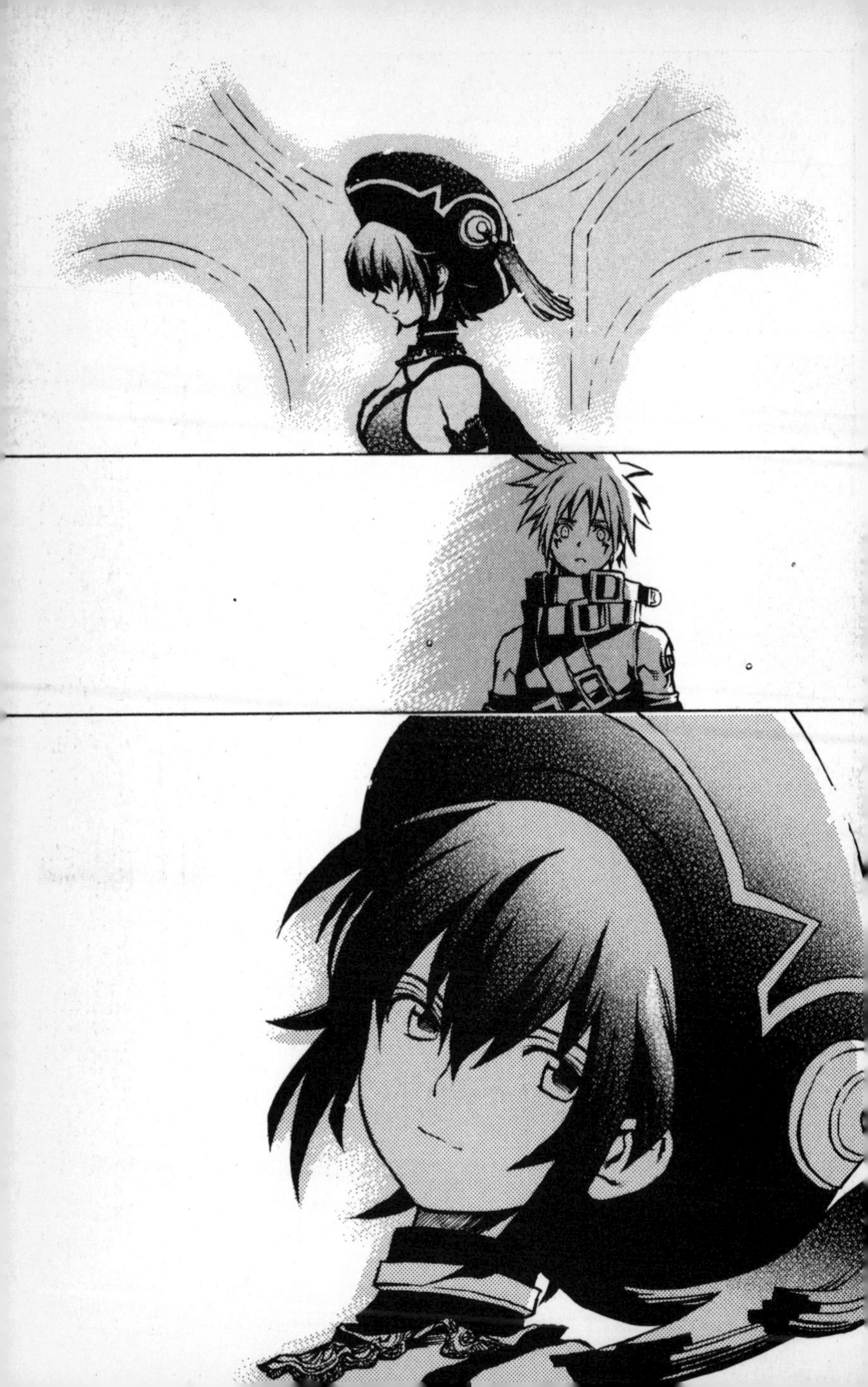

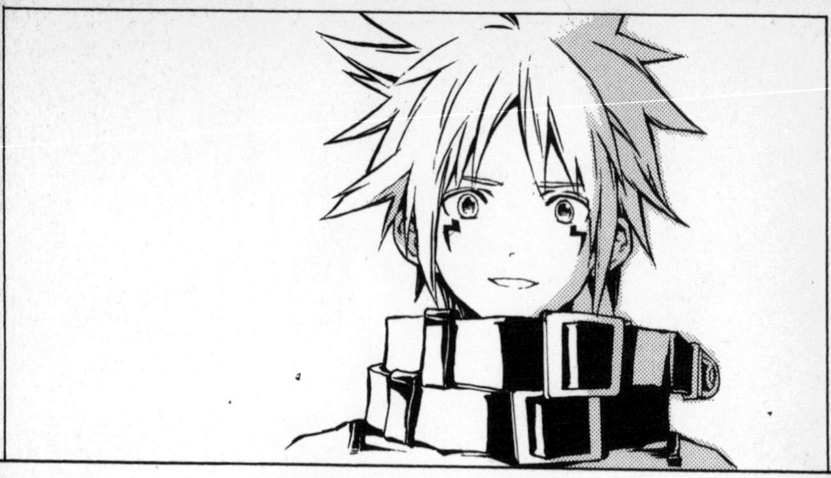
Shino!
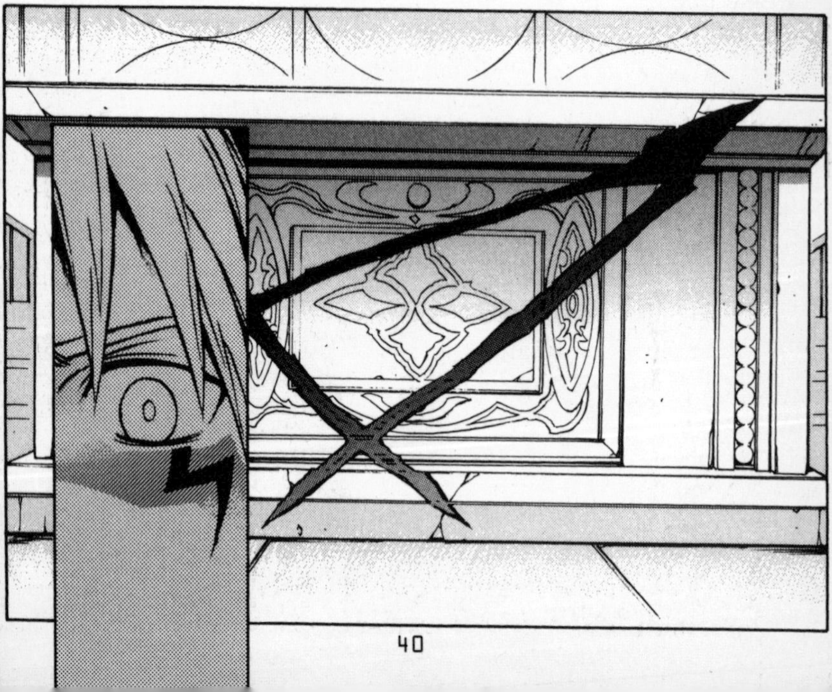

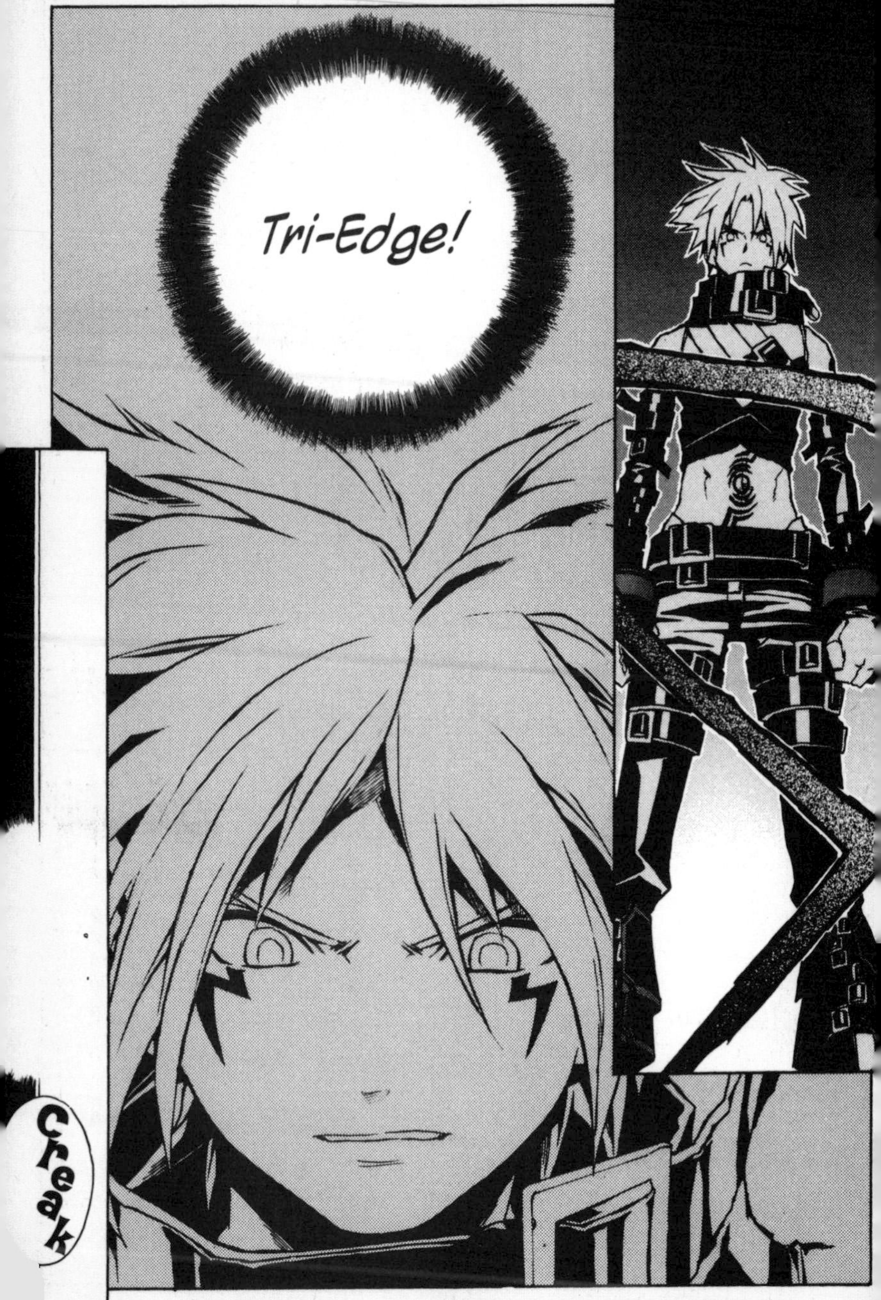
Tri-Edge!
Creak

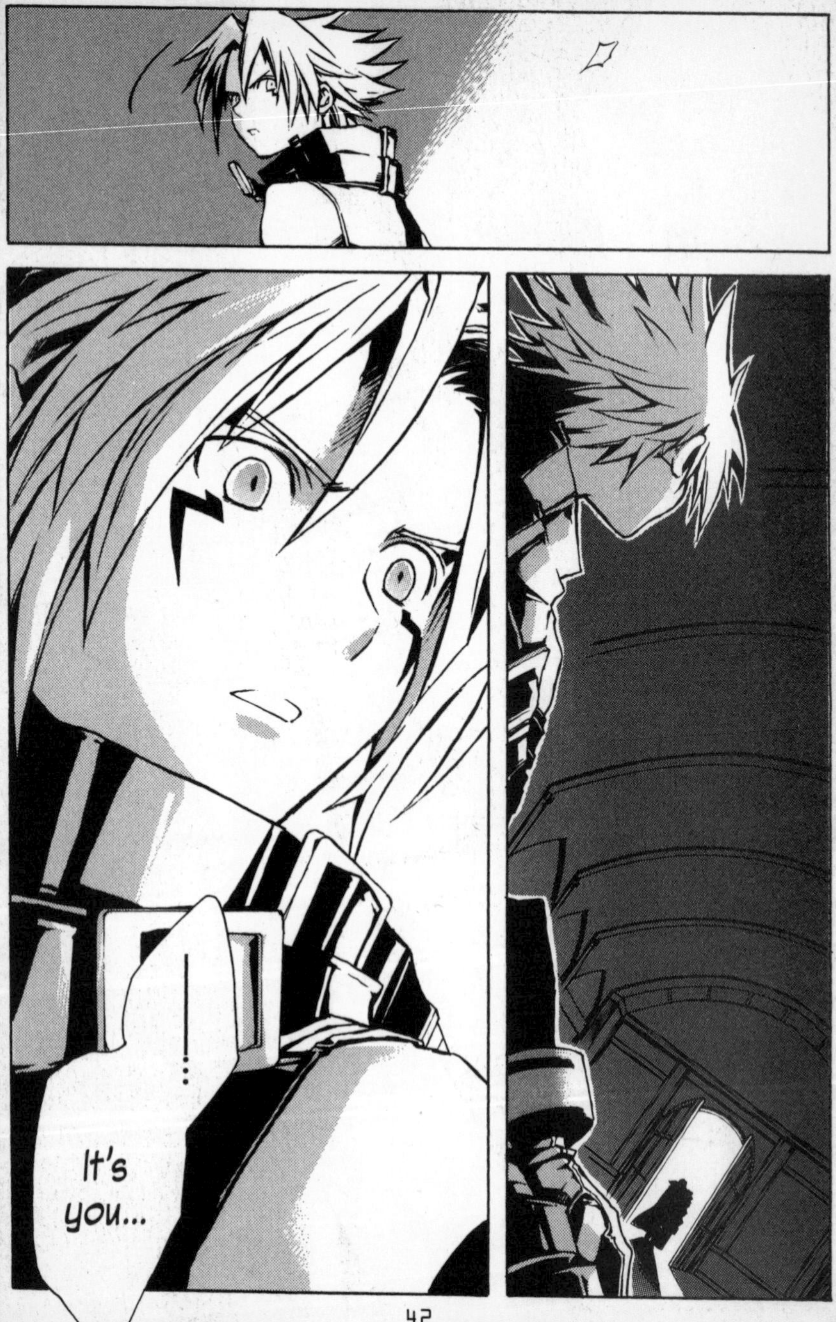
......
It's you...

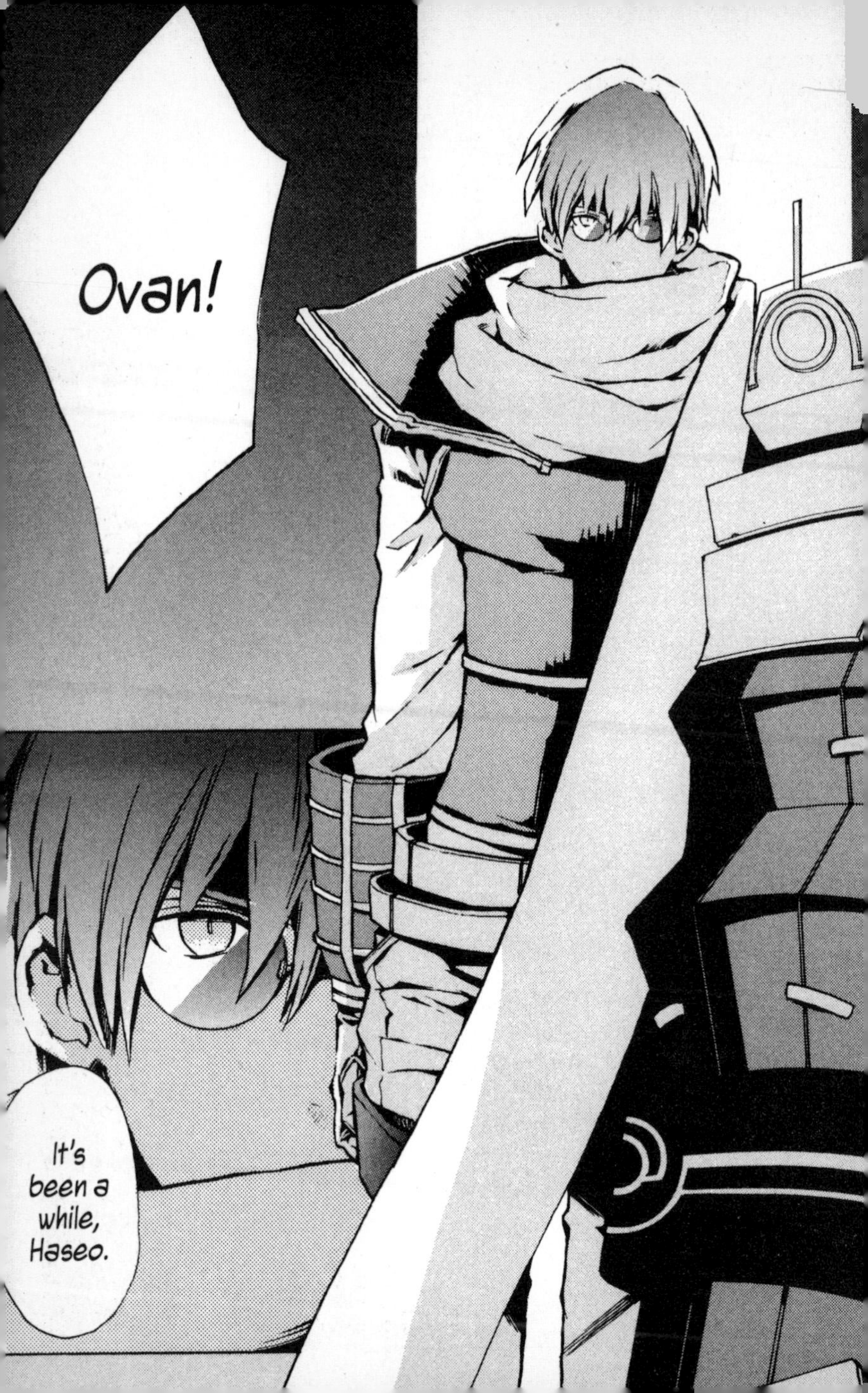
Ovan!
It's been a while, Haseo.

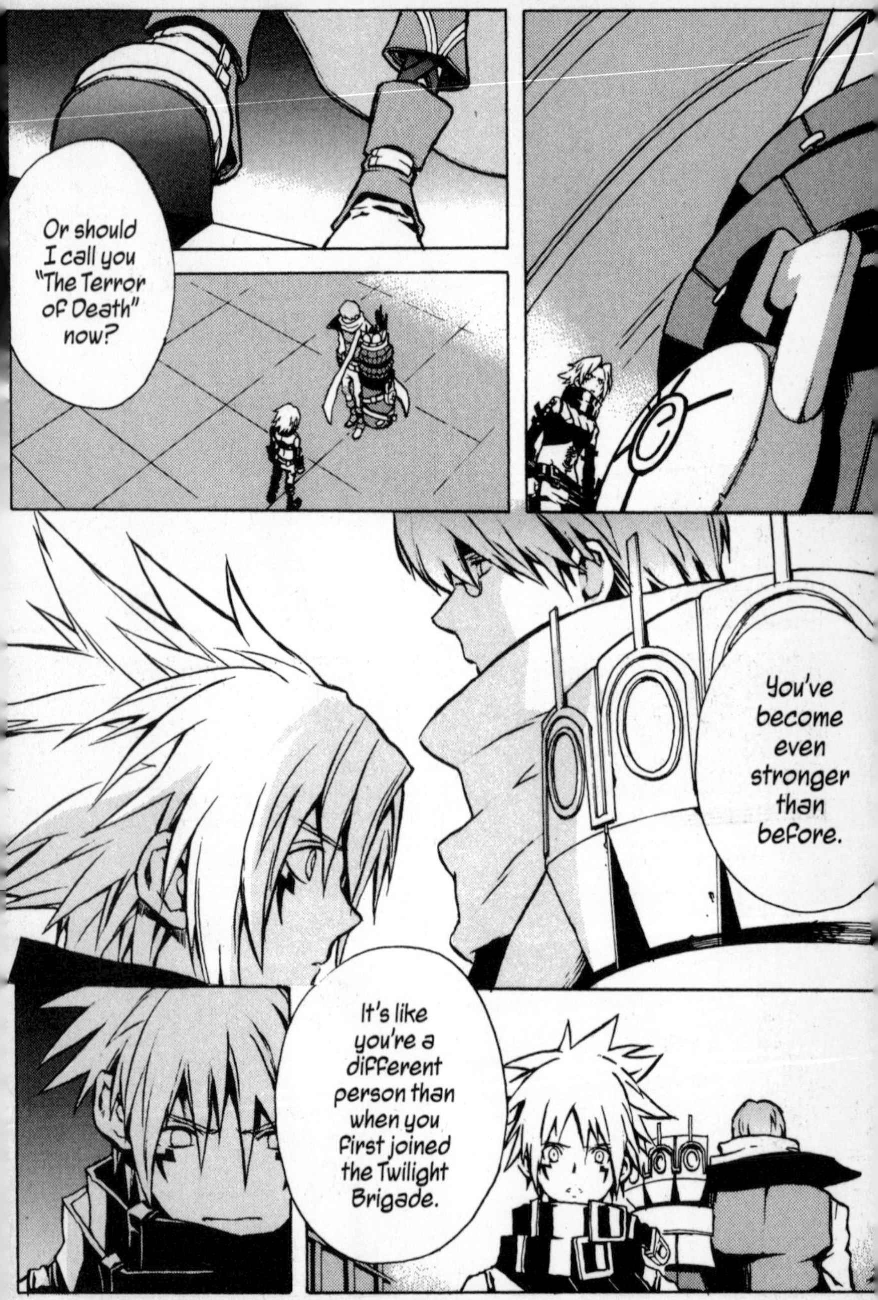
Or should I call you "The Terror of Death" now?
You've become even stronger than before.
It's like you're a different person than when you first joined the Twilight Brigade.

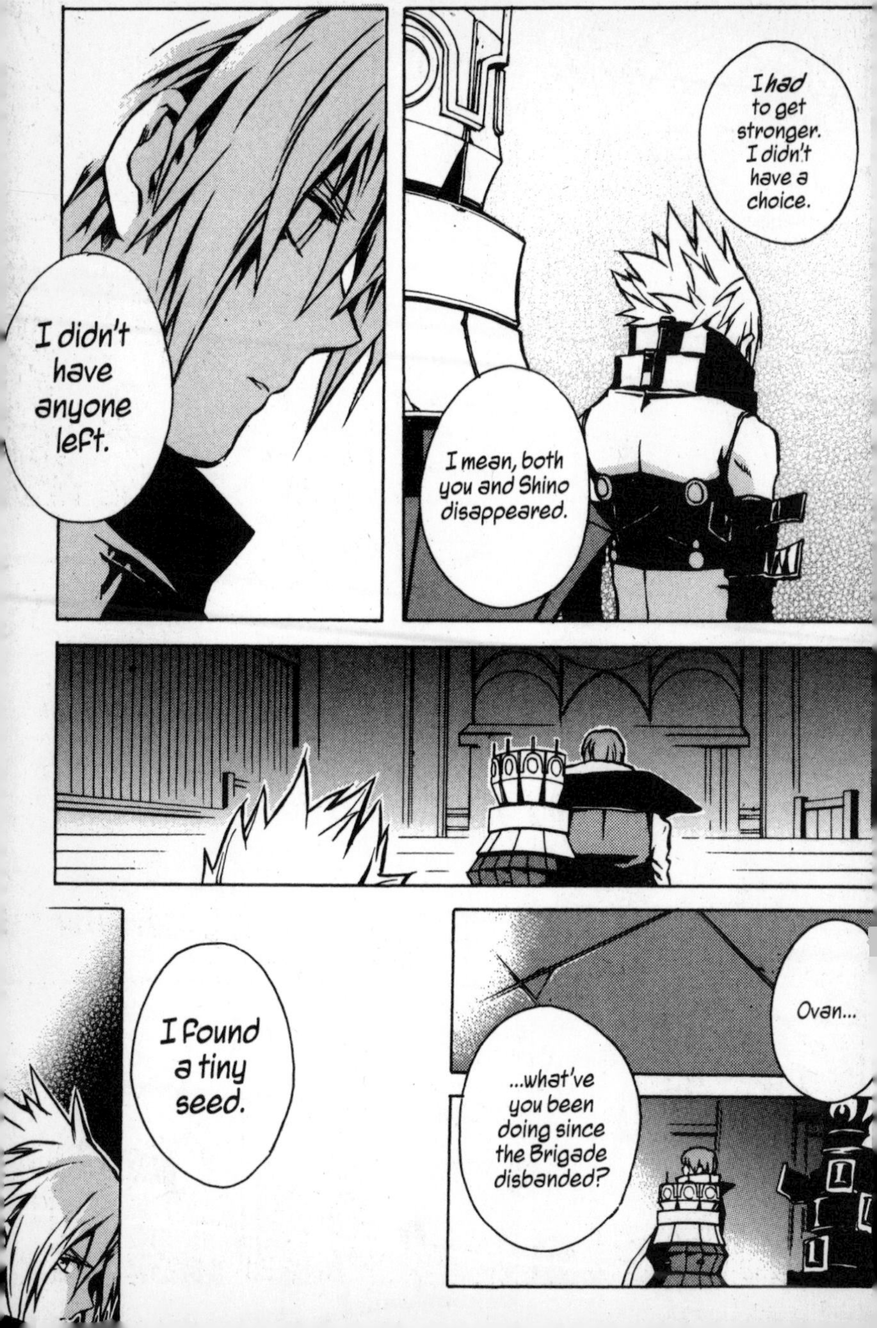
I had to get stronger. I didn't have a choice.
I mean, both you and Shino disappeared.
I didn't have anyone left.
Ovan...
...what've you been doing since the Brigade disbanded?
I found a tiny seed.

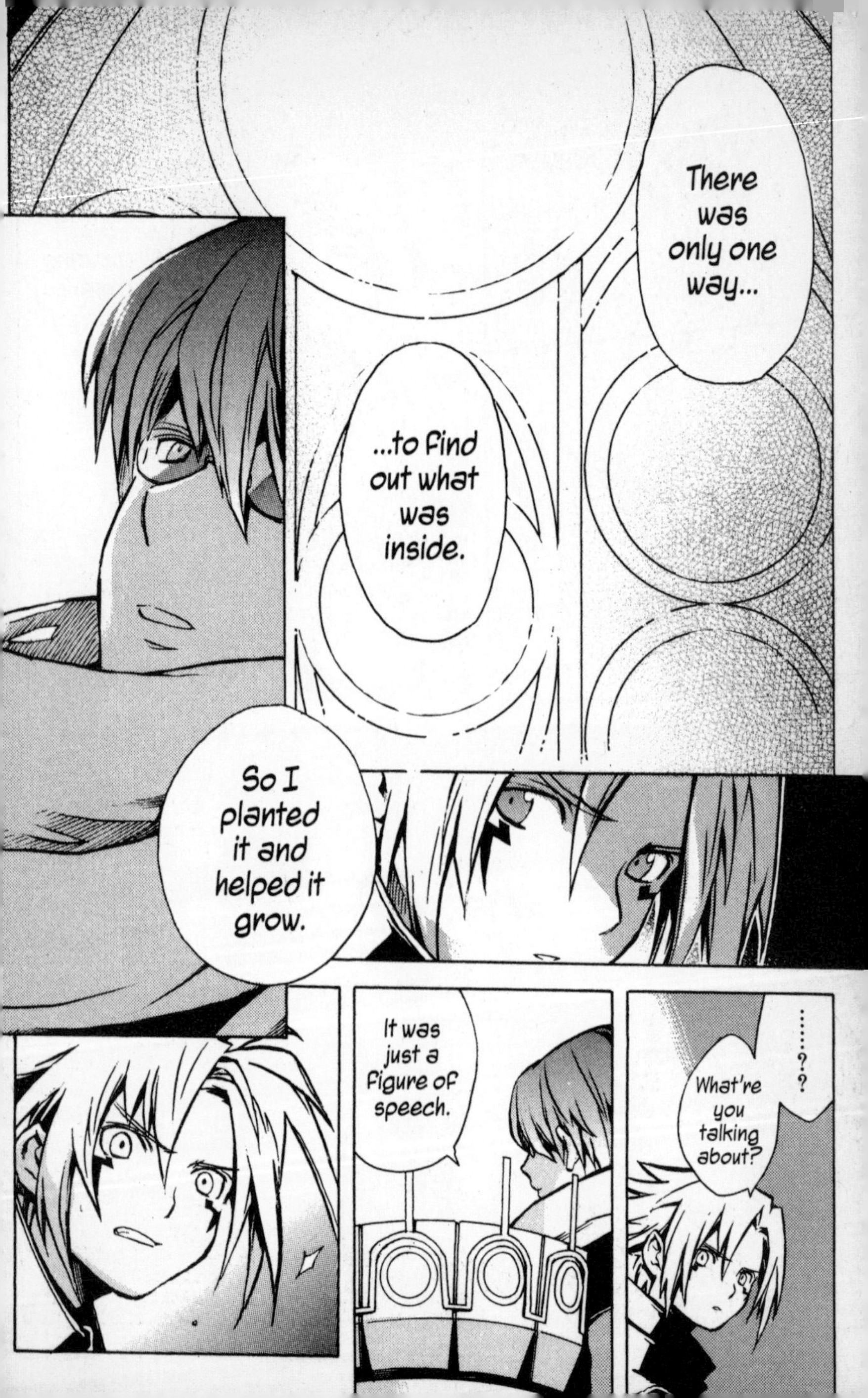
There was only one way...
...to find out what was inside.
So I planted it and helped it grow.
......??
What're you talking about?
It was just a figure of speech.

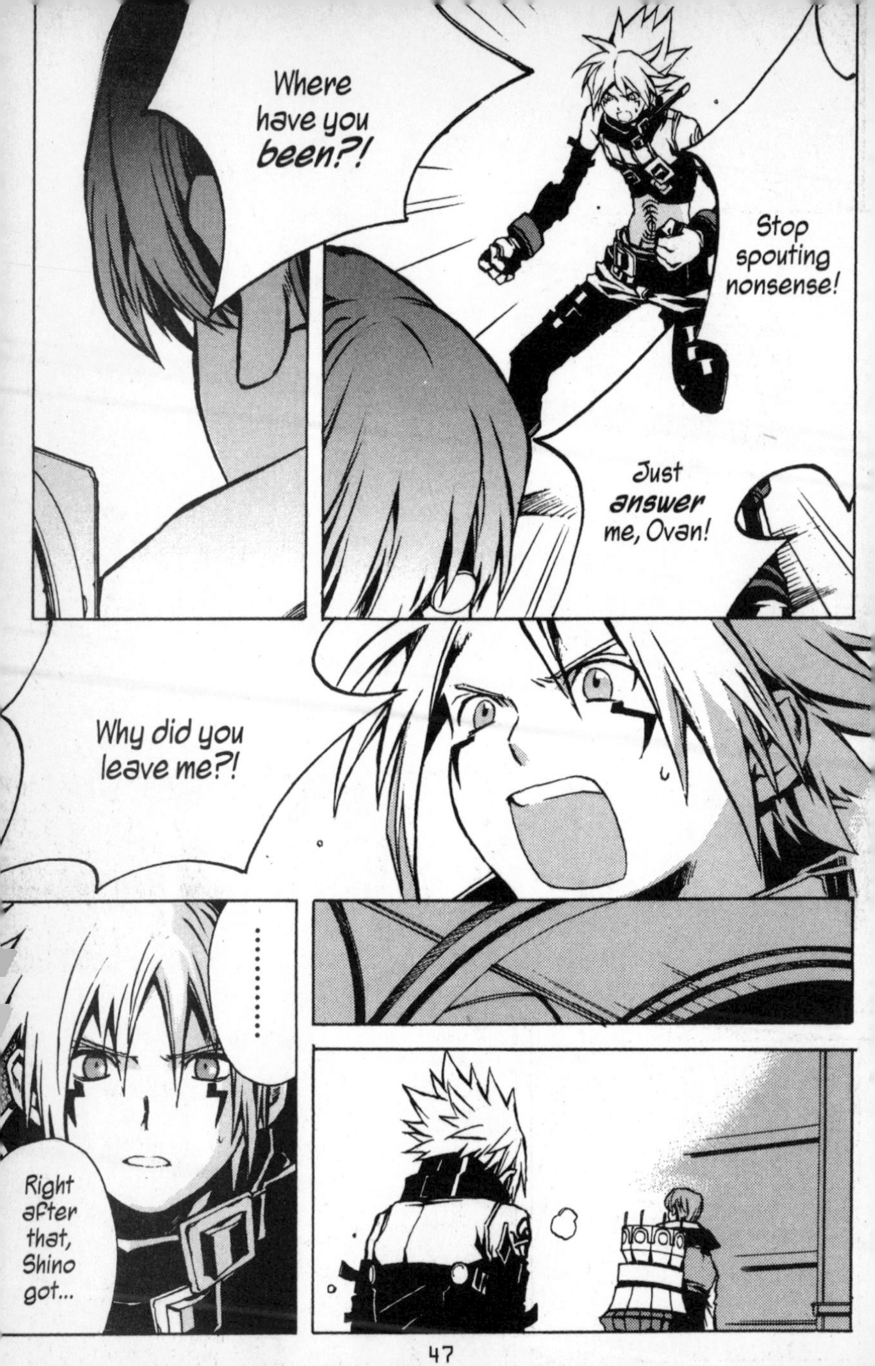
Stop spouting nonsense!
Just **answer** me, Ovan!
Where have you **been?!**
Why did you leave me?!
......
Right after that, Shino got...

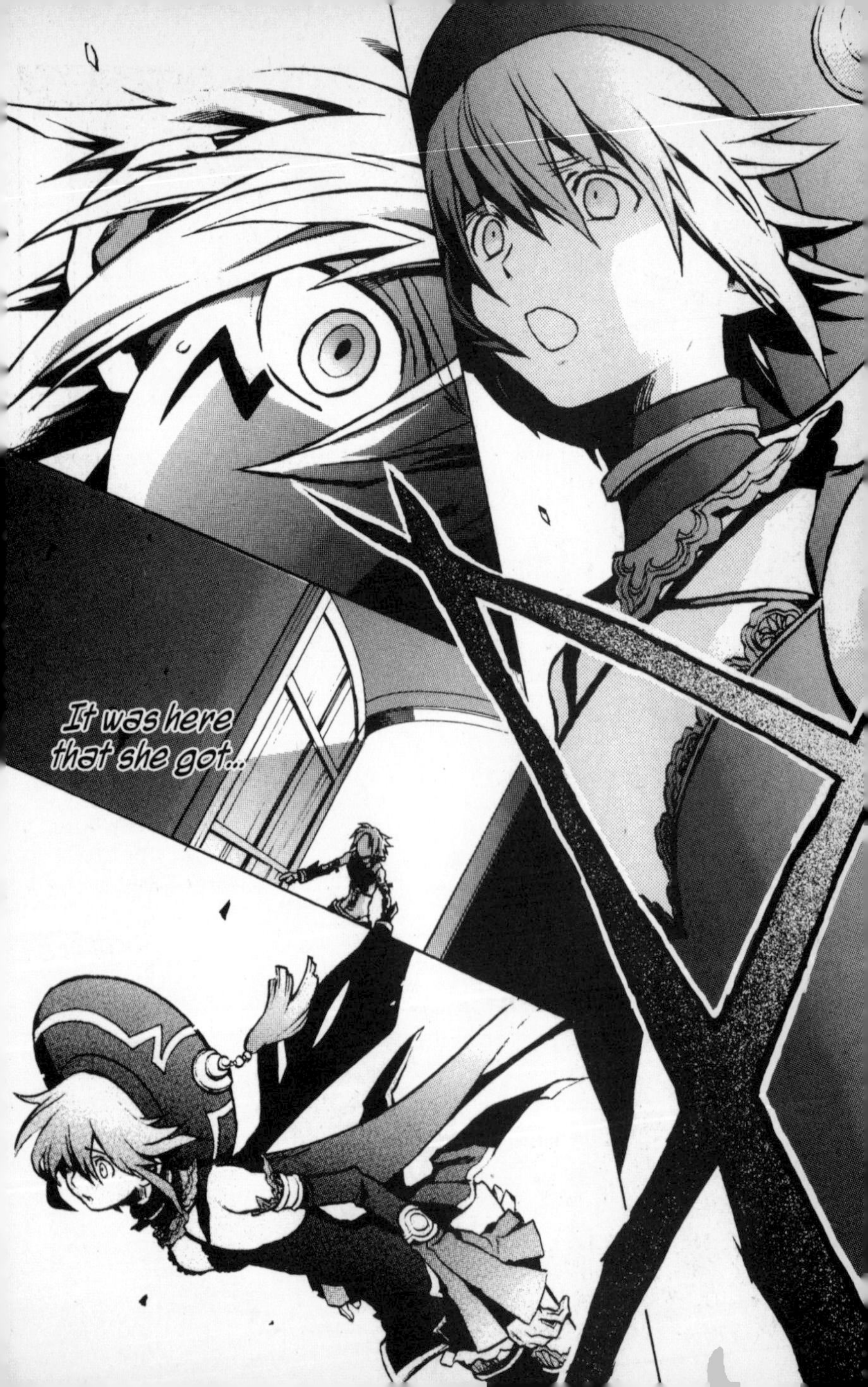
It was here that she got...

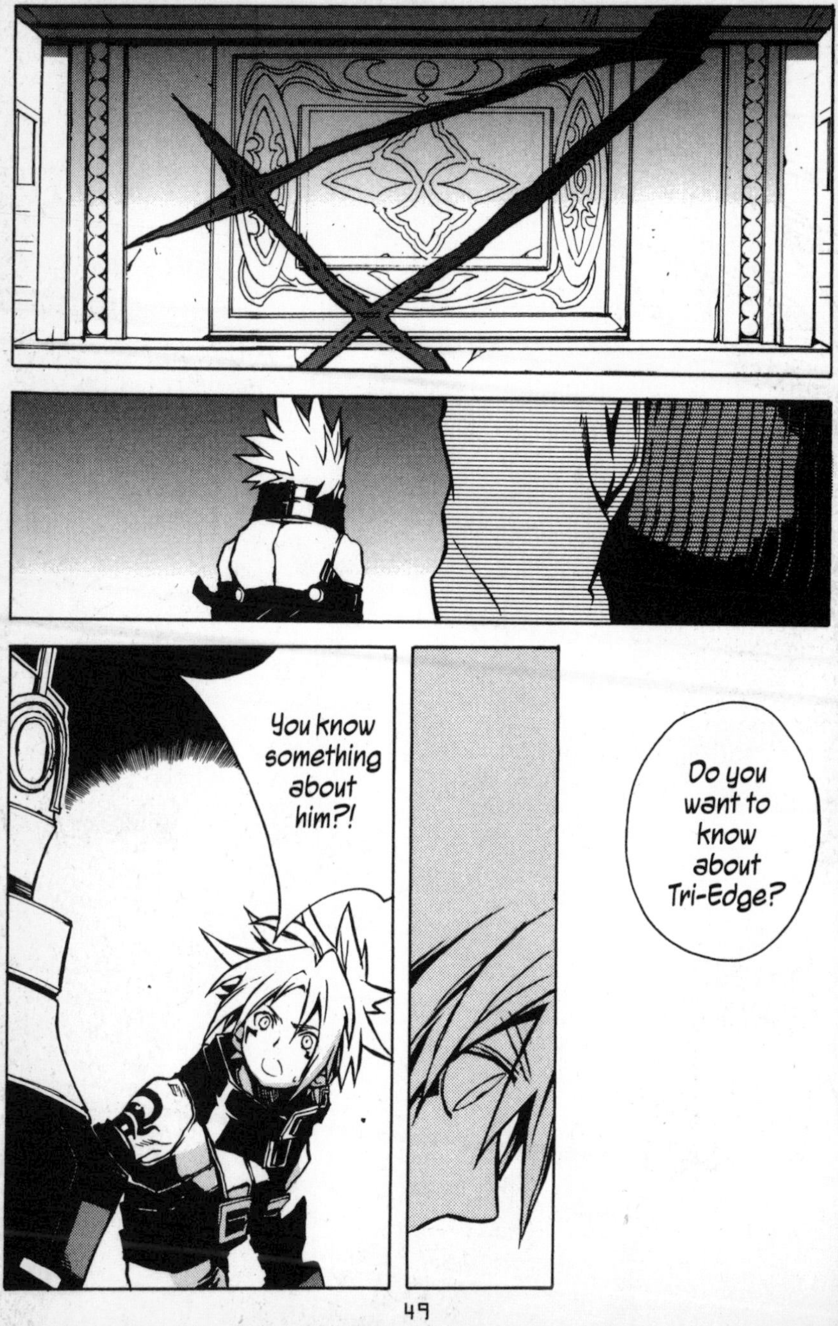
Do you want to know about Tri-Edge?
You know something about him?!

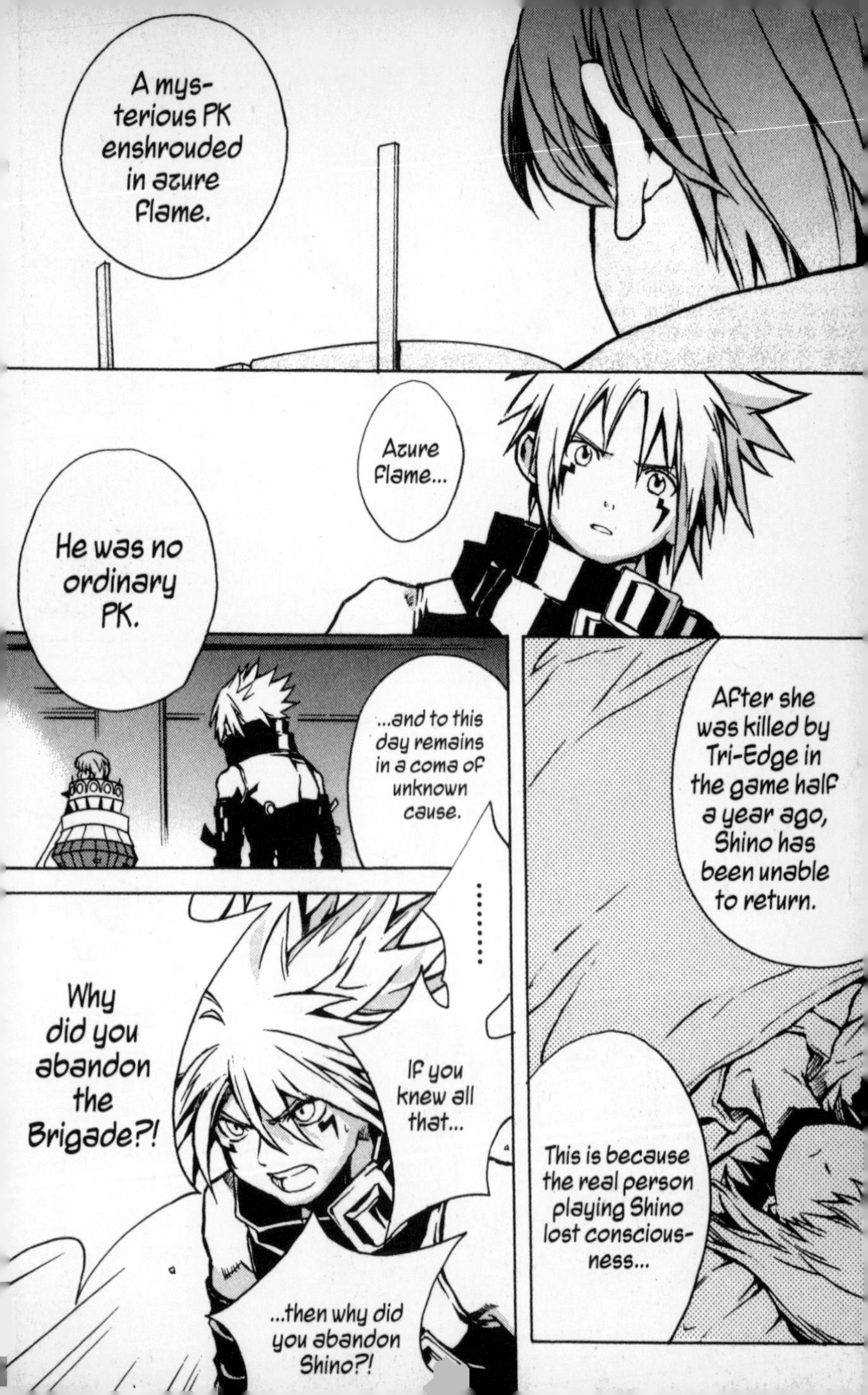
A mysterious PK enshrouded in azure flame.
Azure flame...
He was no ordinary PK.
After she was killed by Tri-Edge in the game half a year ago, Shino has been unable to return.
This is because the real person playing Shino lost consciousness...
...and to this day remains in a coma of unknown cause.
......
If you knew all that...
...then why did you abandon Shino?!
Why did you abandon the Brigade?!

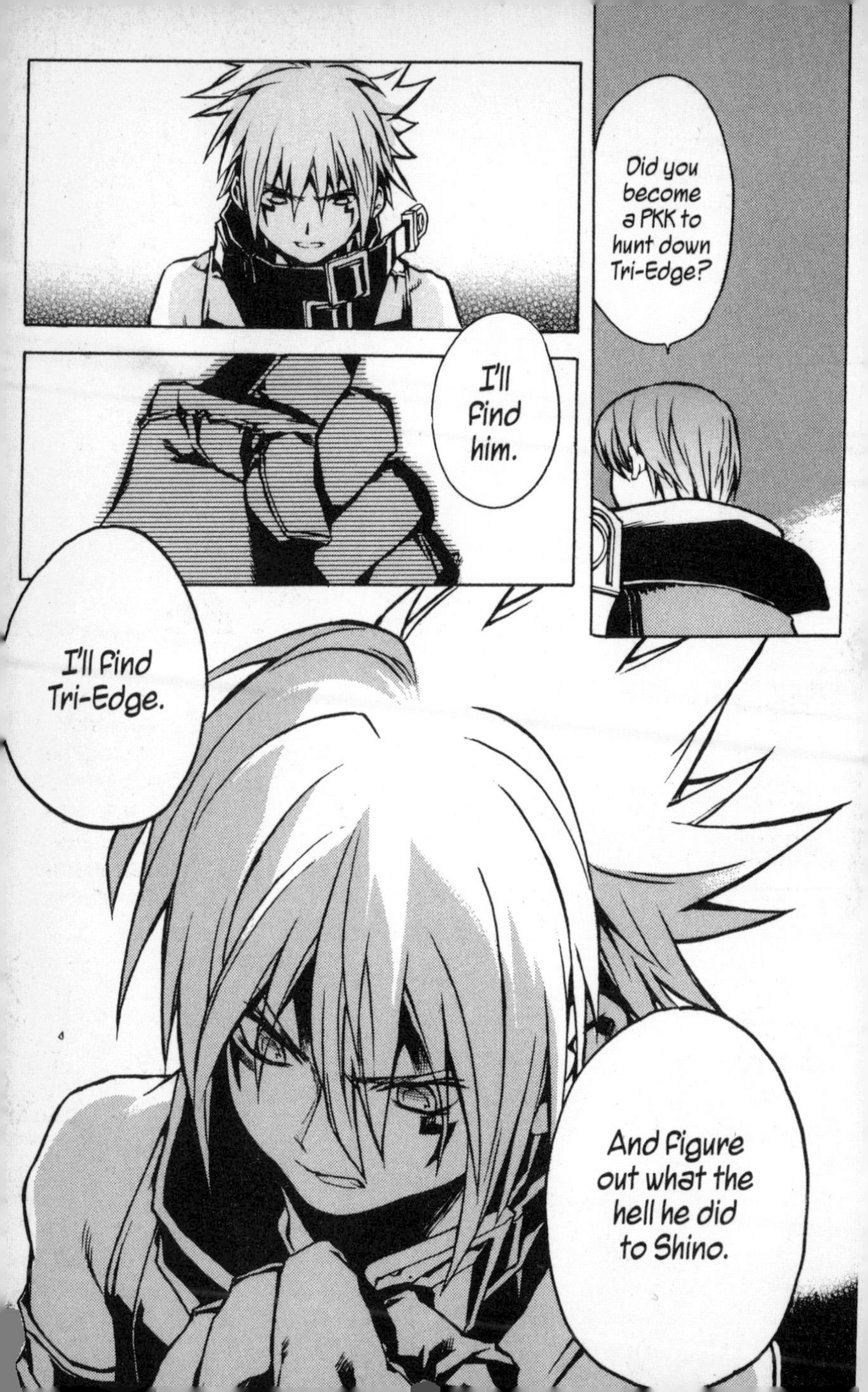
Did you become a PKK to hunt down Tri-Edge?
I'll find him.
I'll find Tri-Edge.
And figure out what the hell he did to Shino.

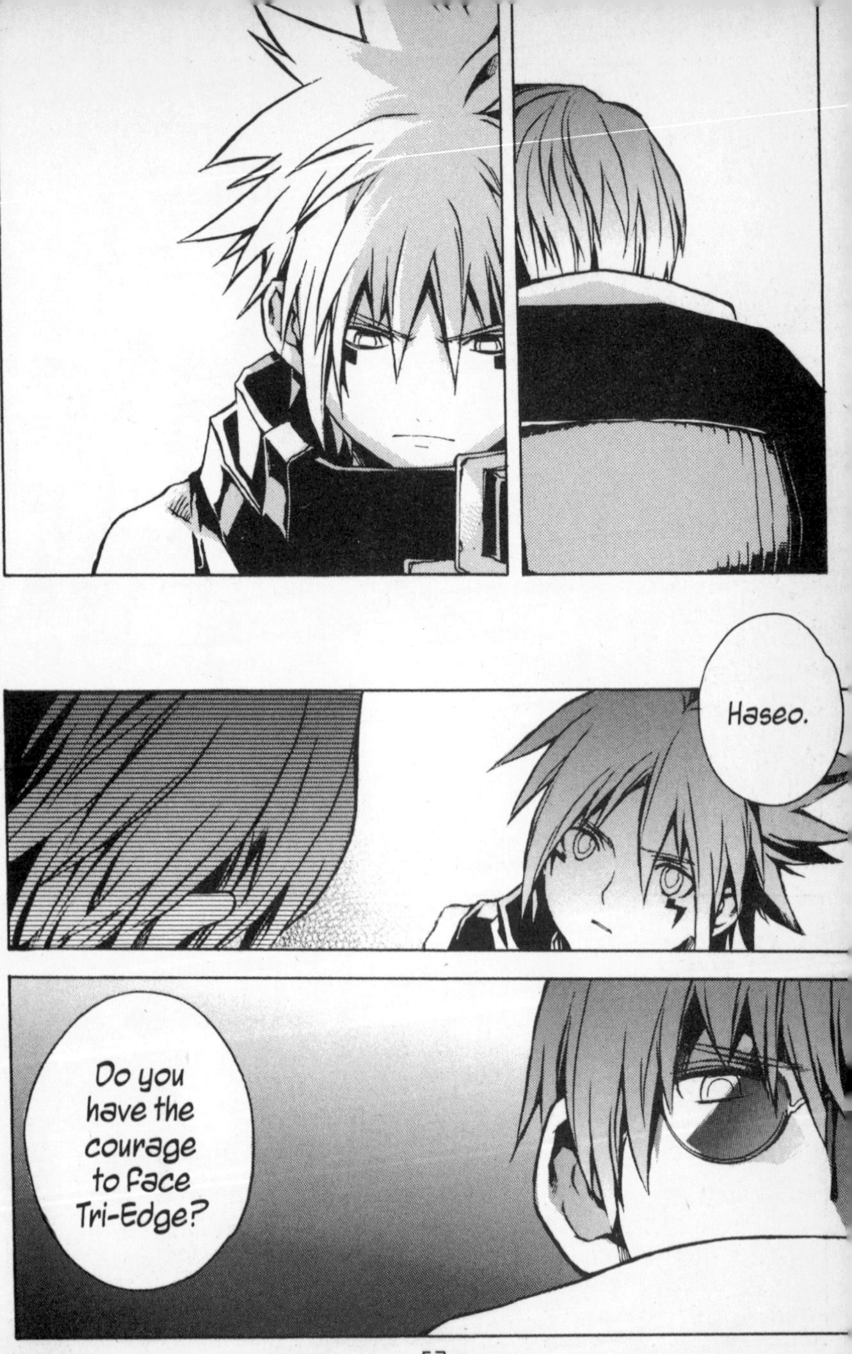
Haseo.
Do you have the courage to face Tri-Edge?

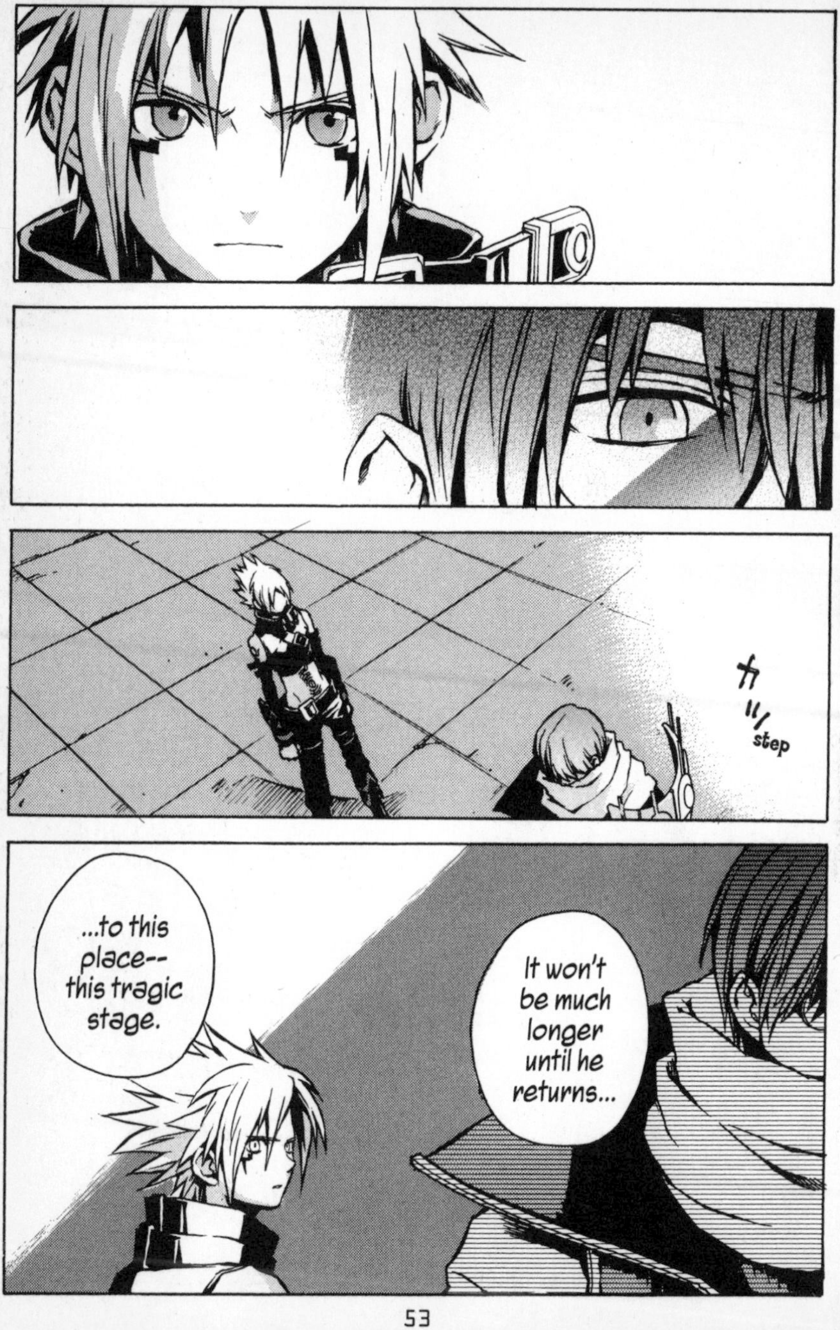
step
It won't be much longer until he returns...
...to this place--this tragic stage.

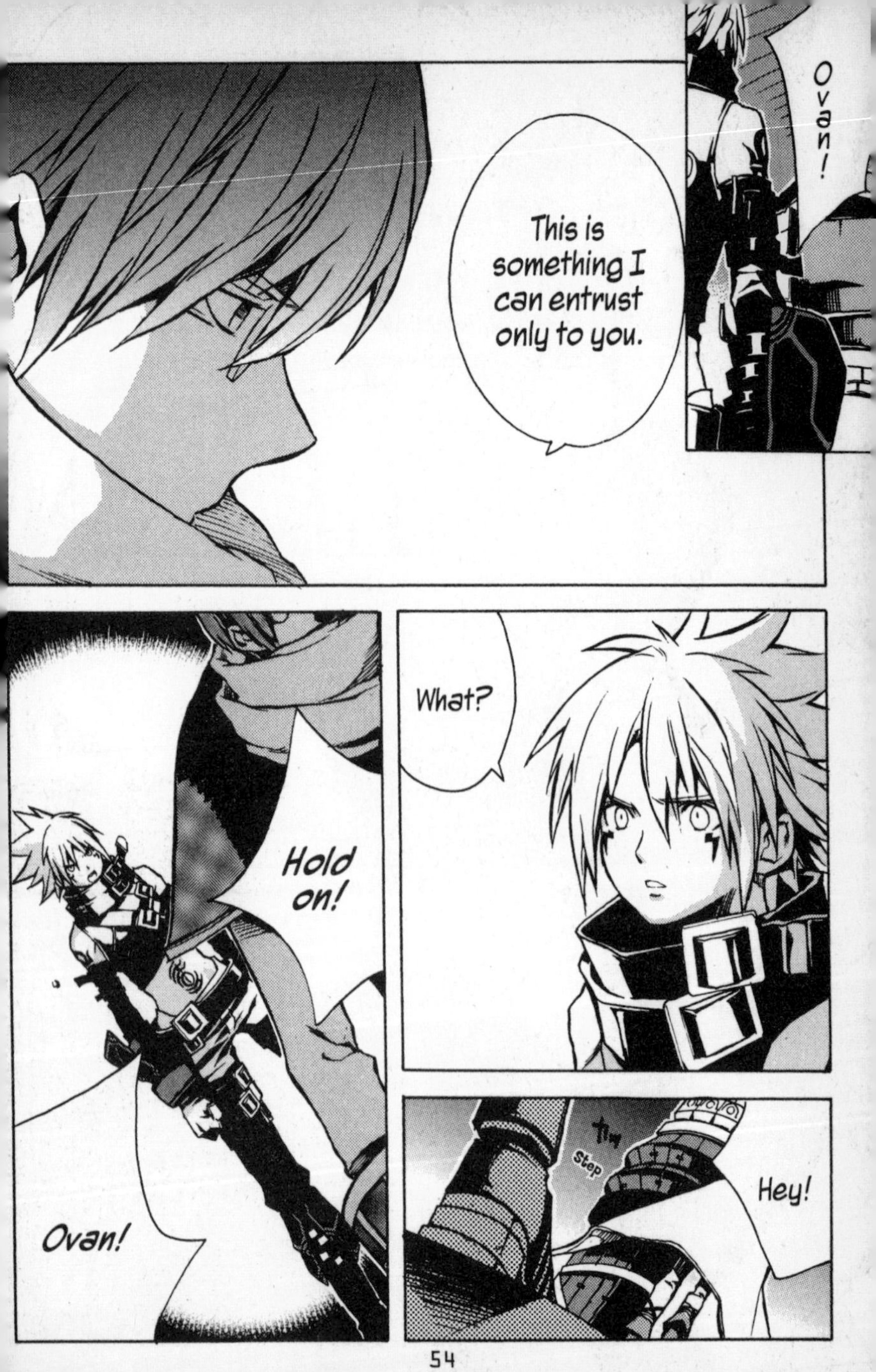
Ovan!
This is something I can entrust only to you.
What?
Step
Hey!
Hold on!
Ovan!

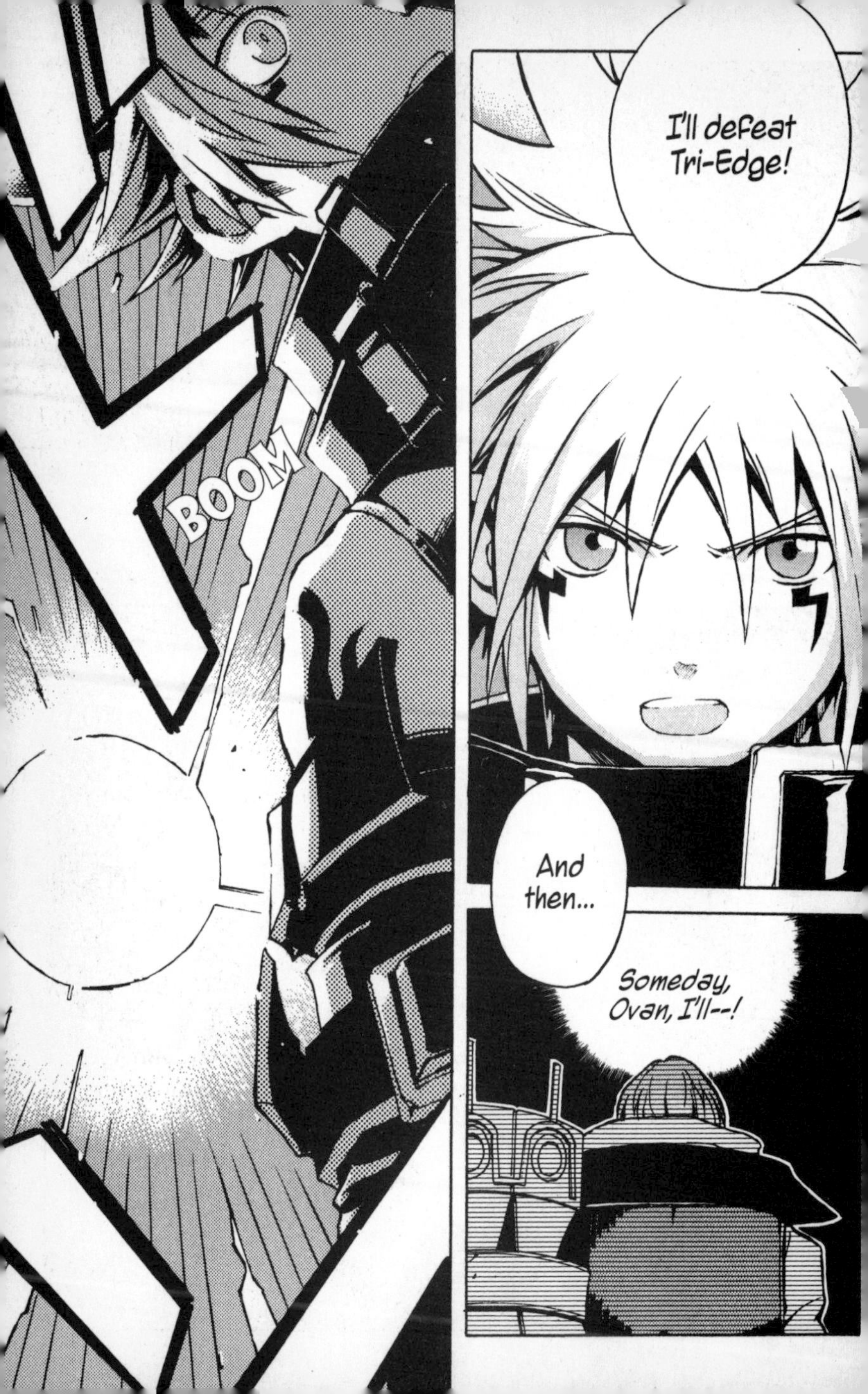
I'll defeat Tri-Edge!
And then...
Someday, Ovan, I'll--!
BOOM

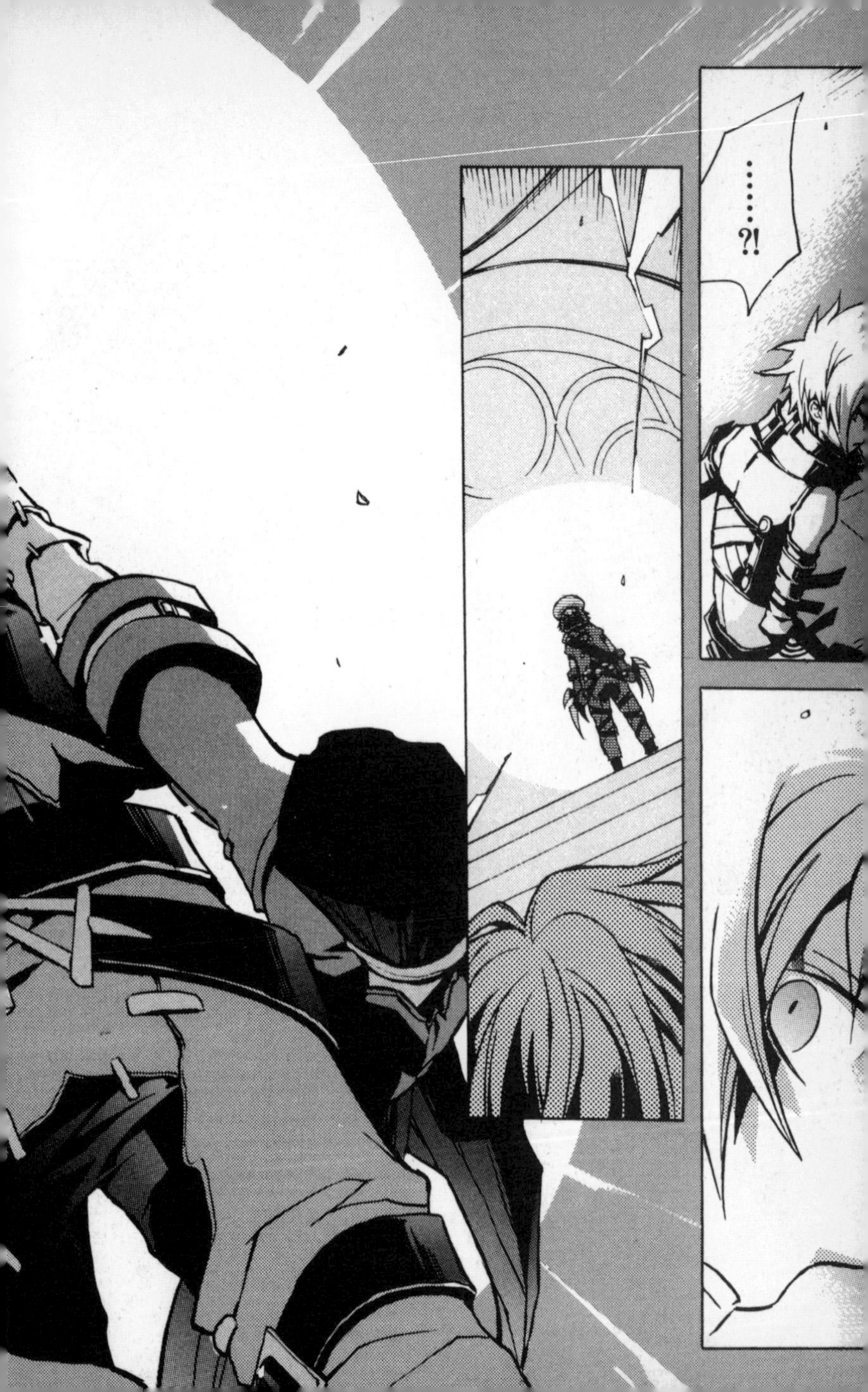
......?!

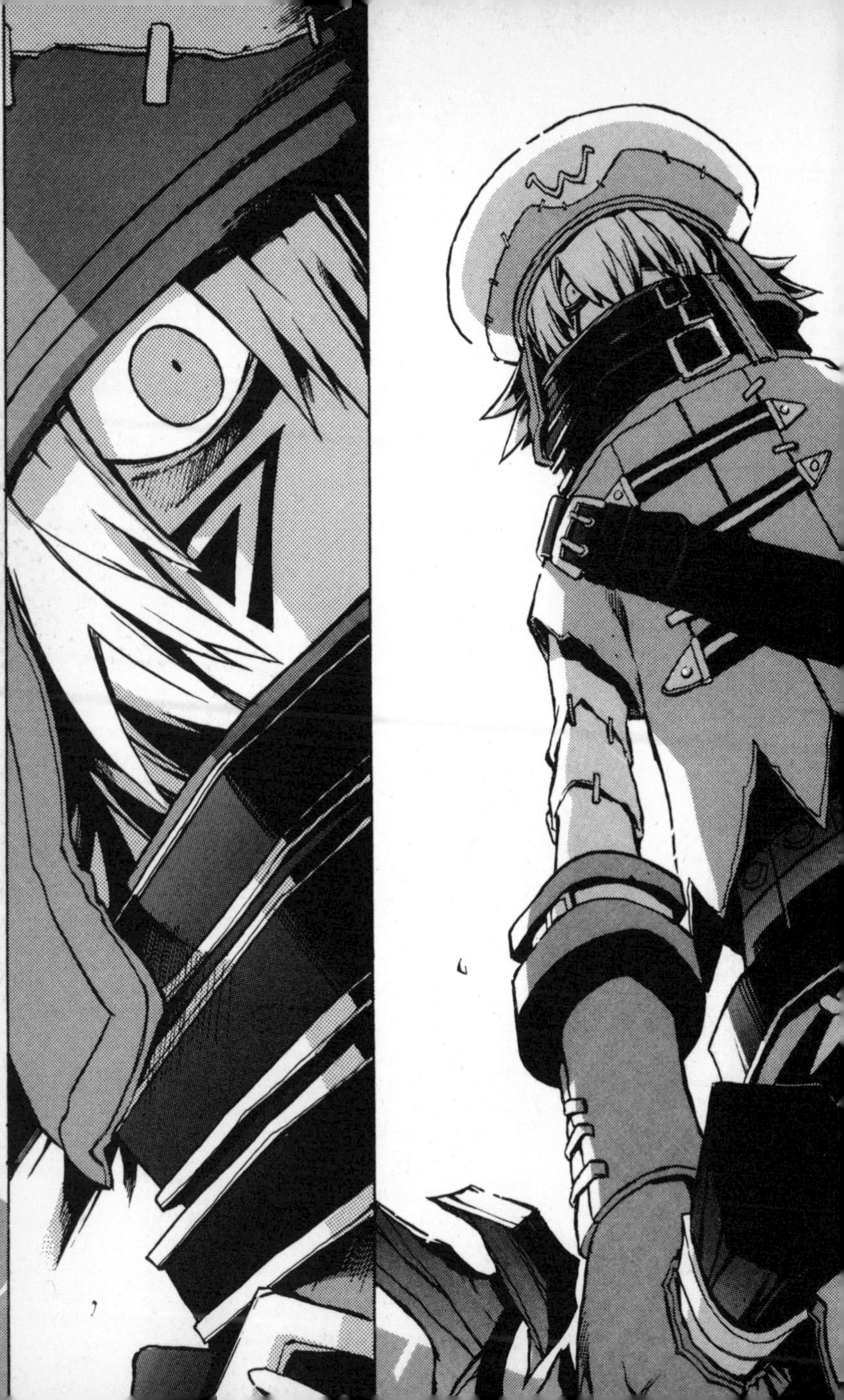

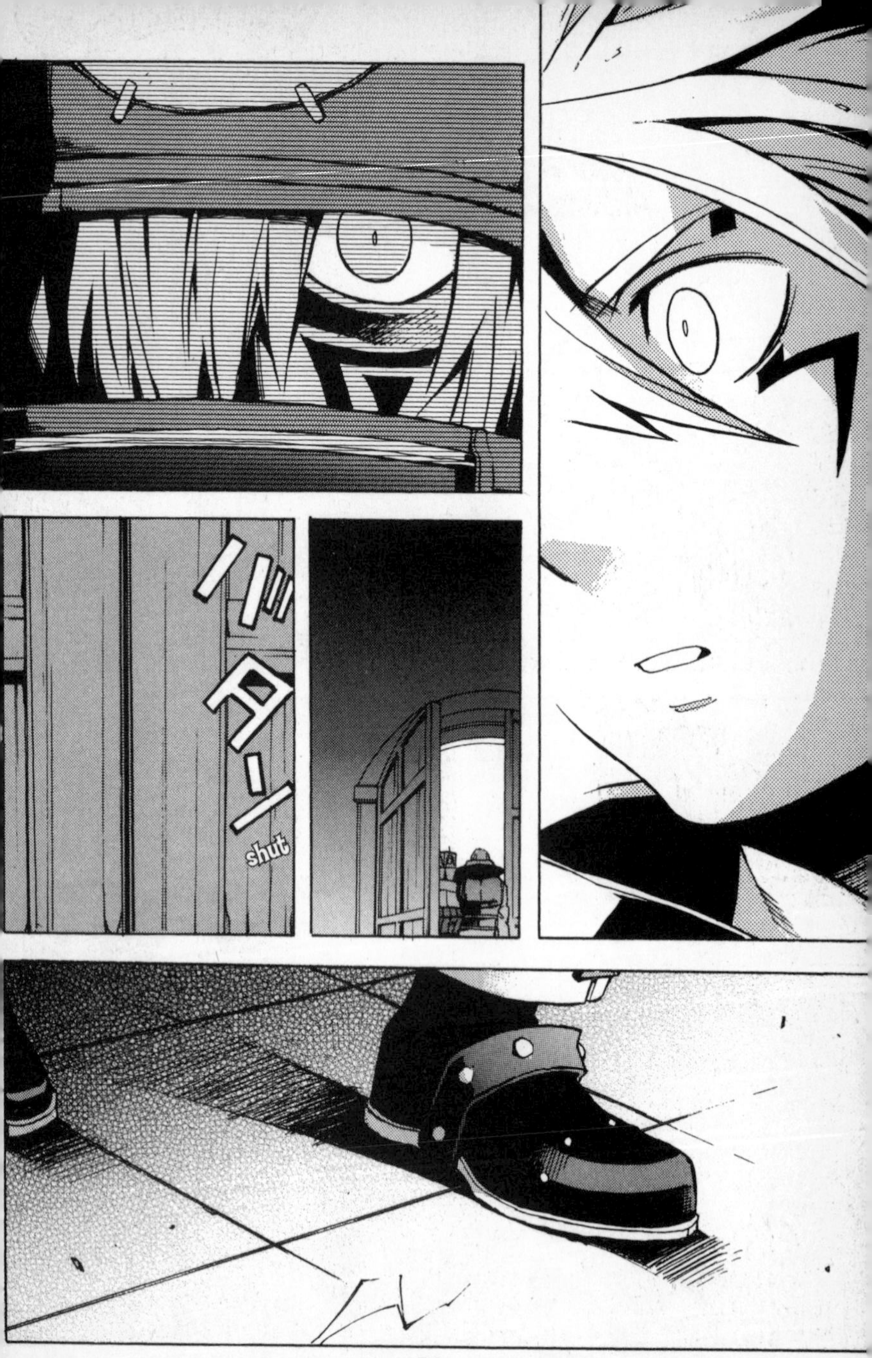
バタン
shut

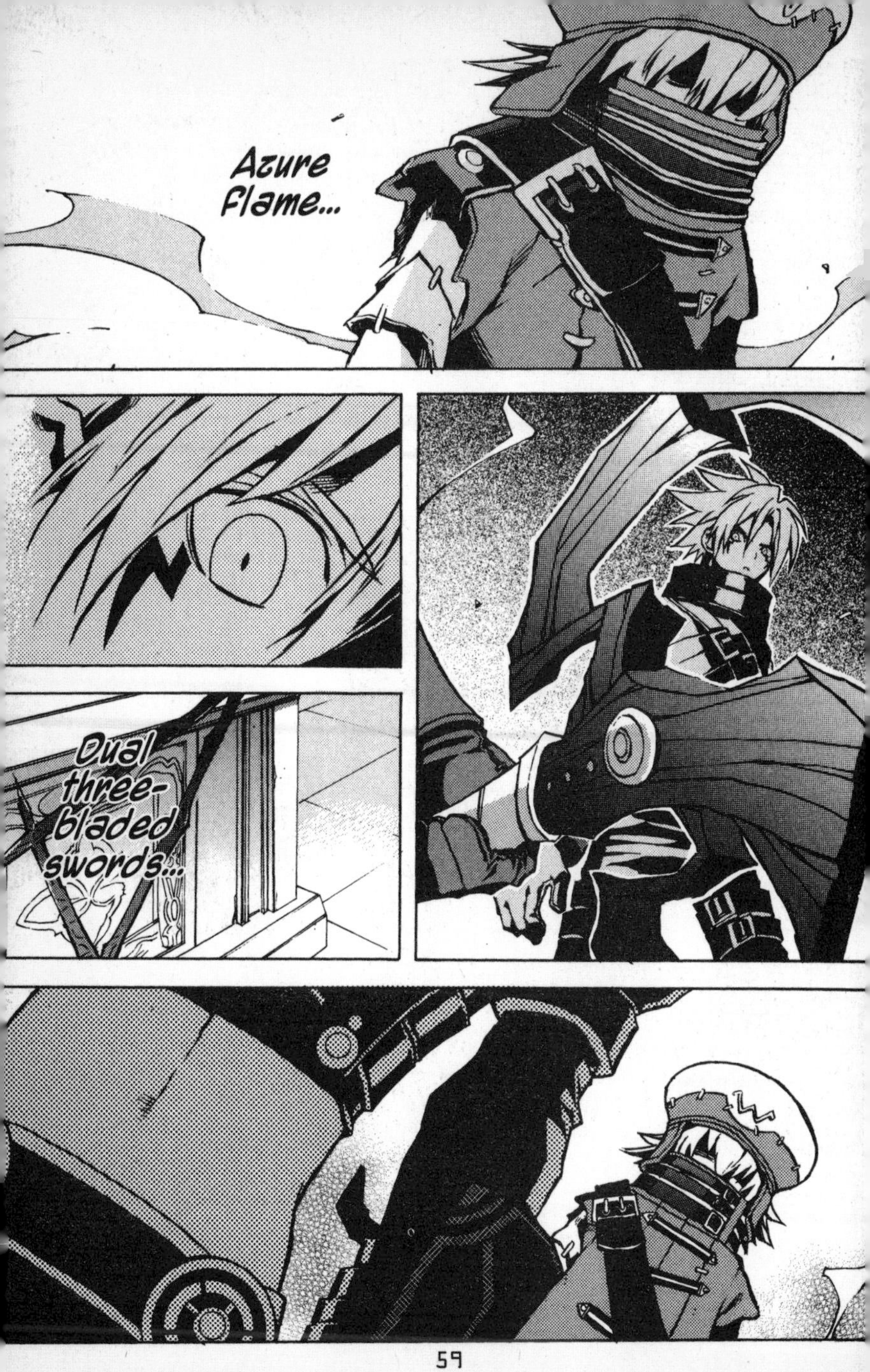
Azure flame...
Dual three-bladed swords...

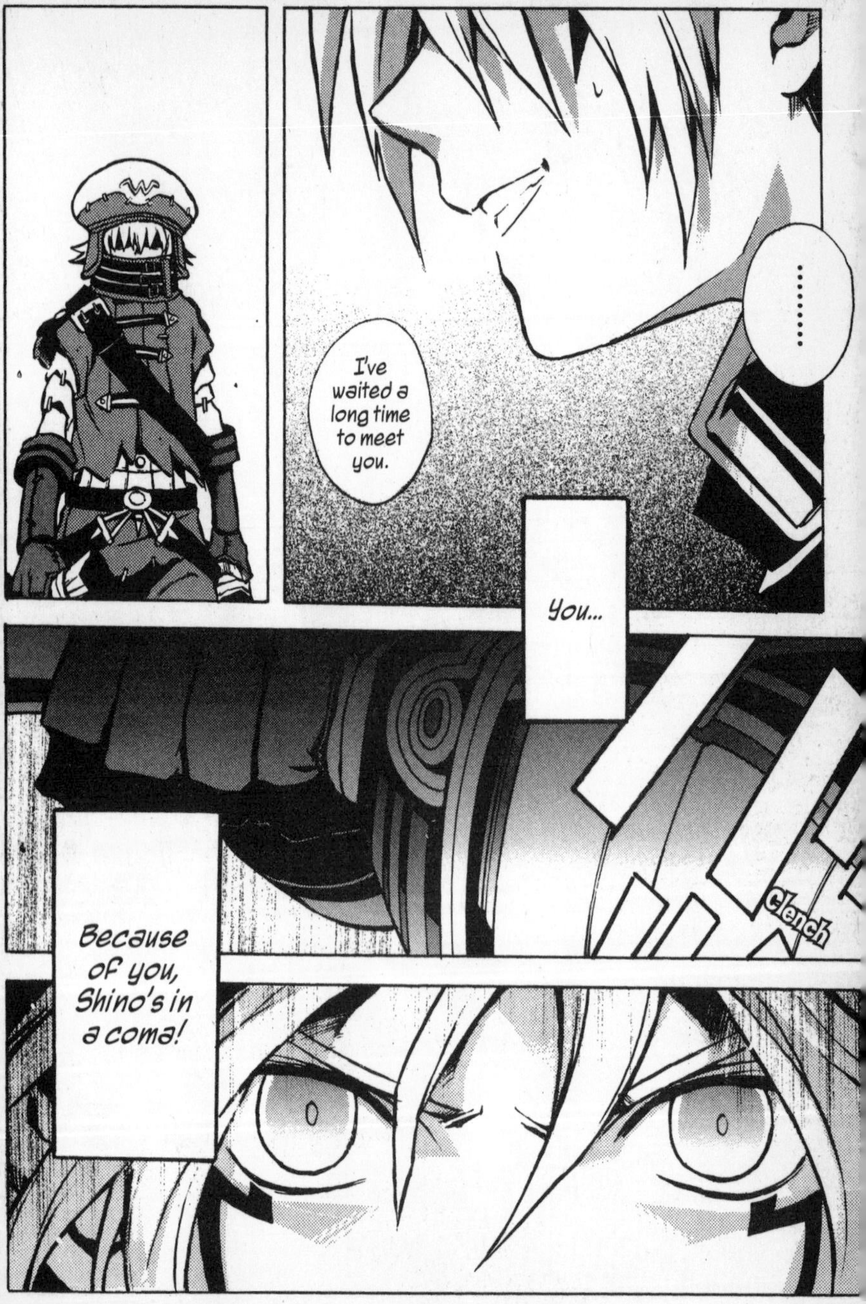

......
I've waited a long time to meet you.
You...
Clench
Because of you, Shino's in a coma!

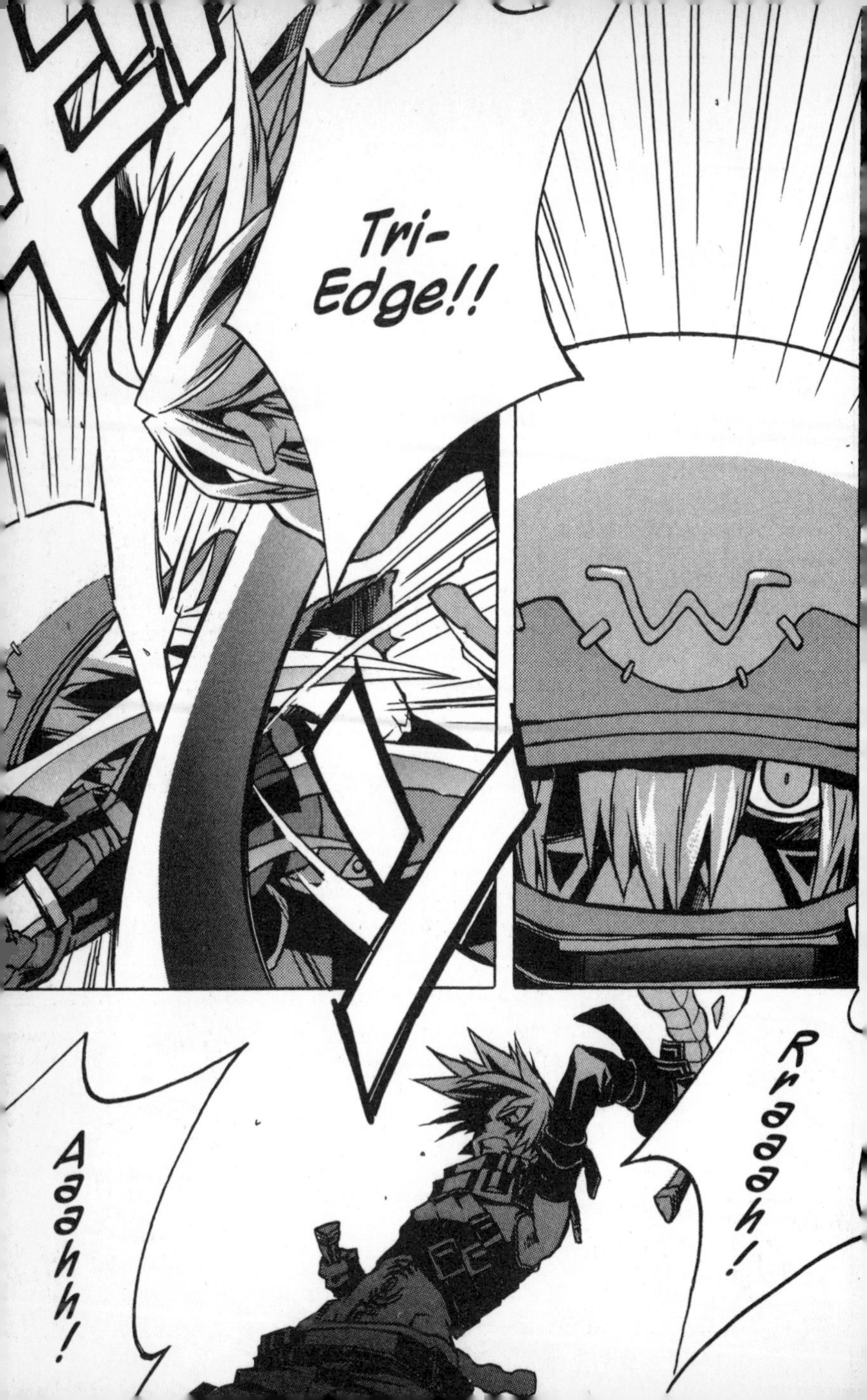
Tri-Edge!!
Rraaah!
Aaahh!

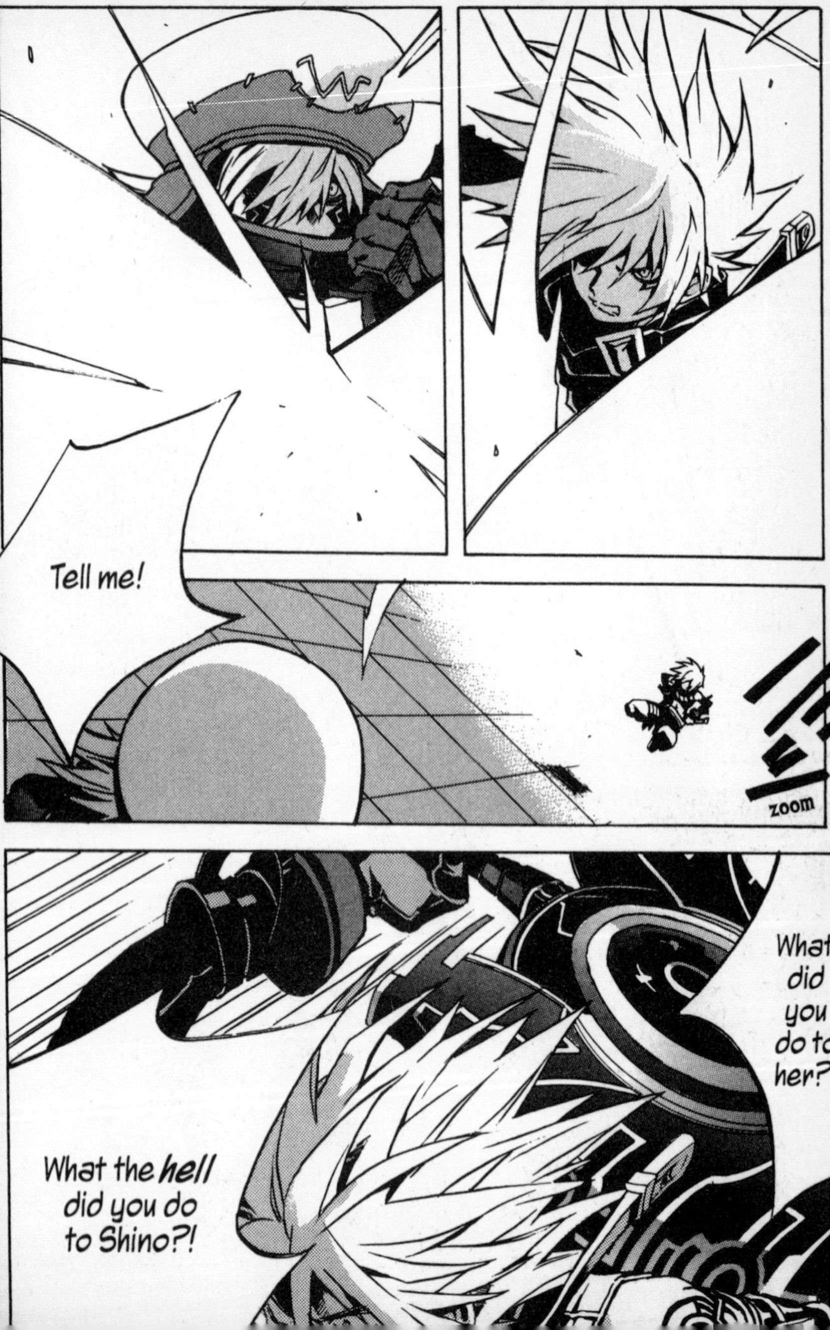
Tell me!
ZOOM
What did you do to her?!
What the ***hell*** did you do to Shino?!

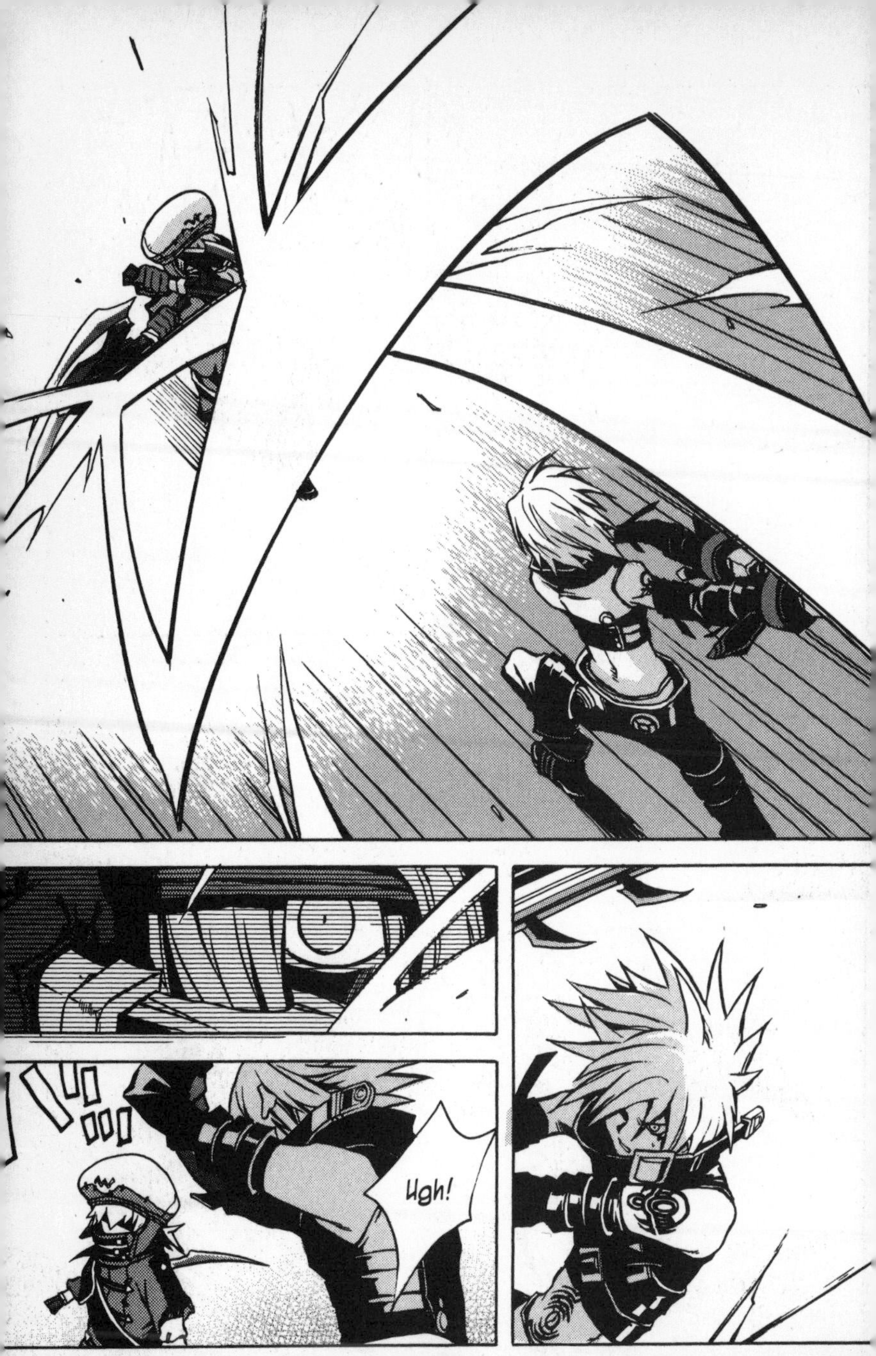
Ugh!

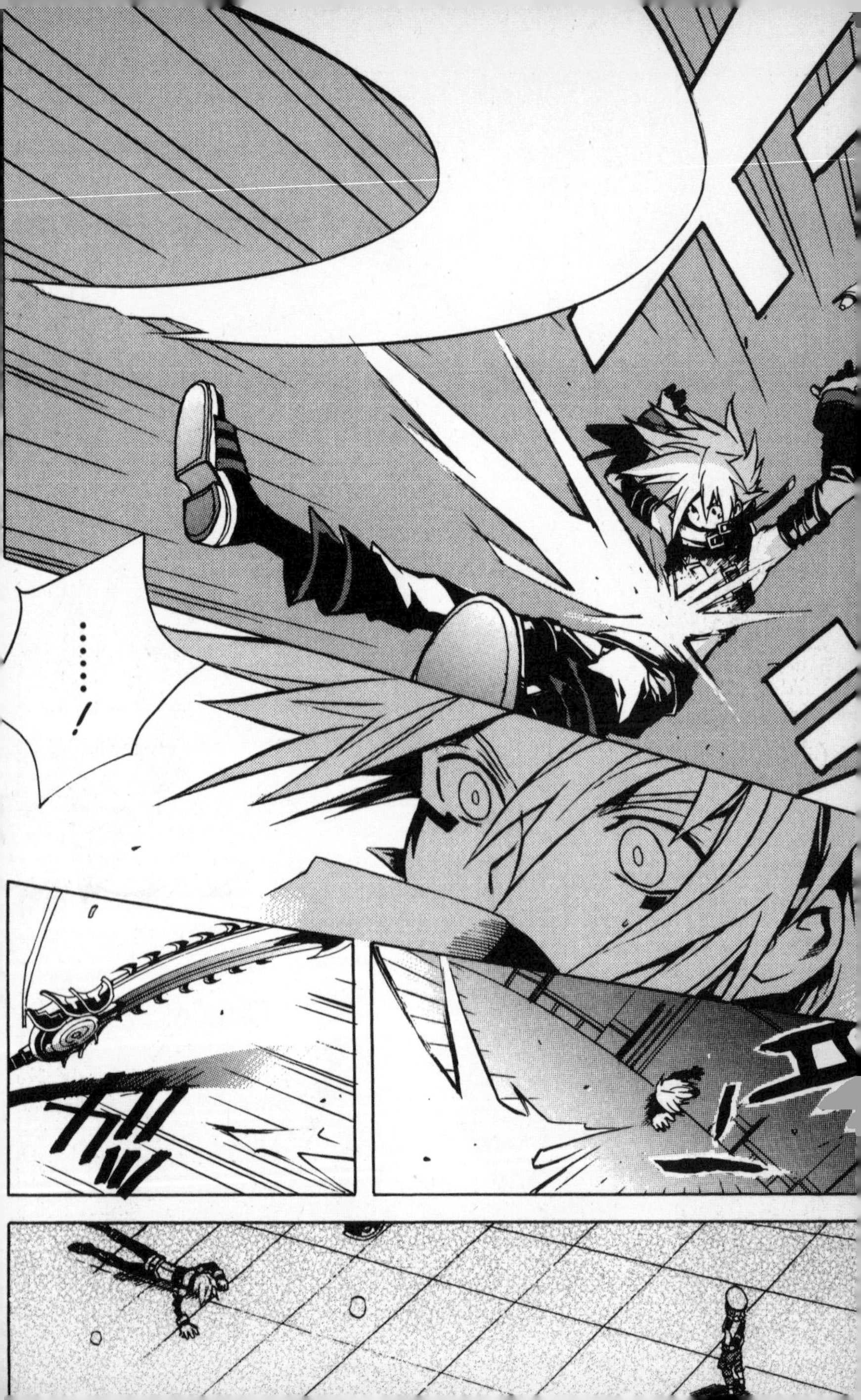
......!

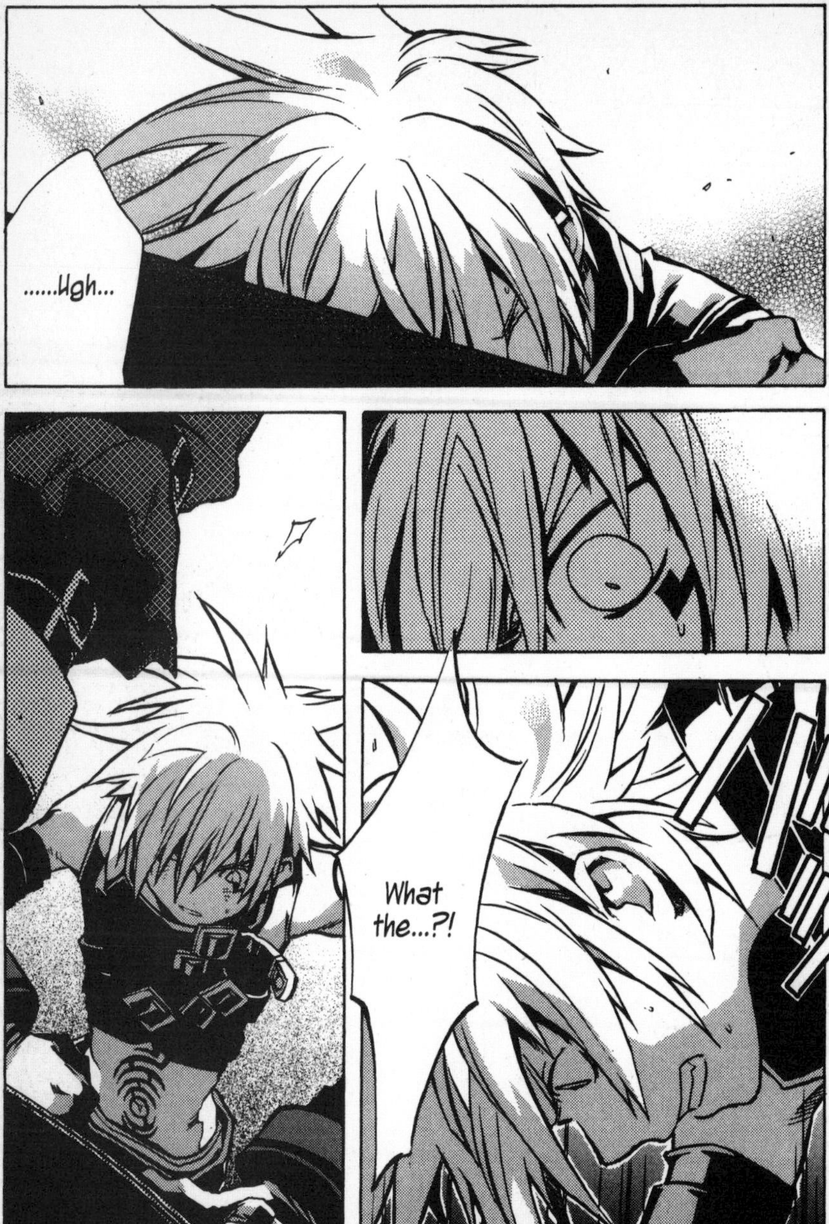
......Ugh...
What the...?!

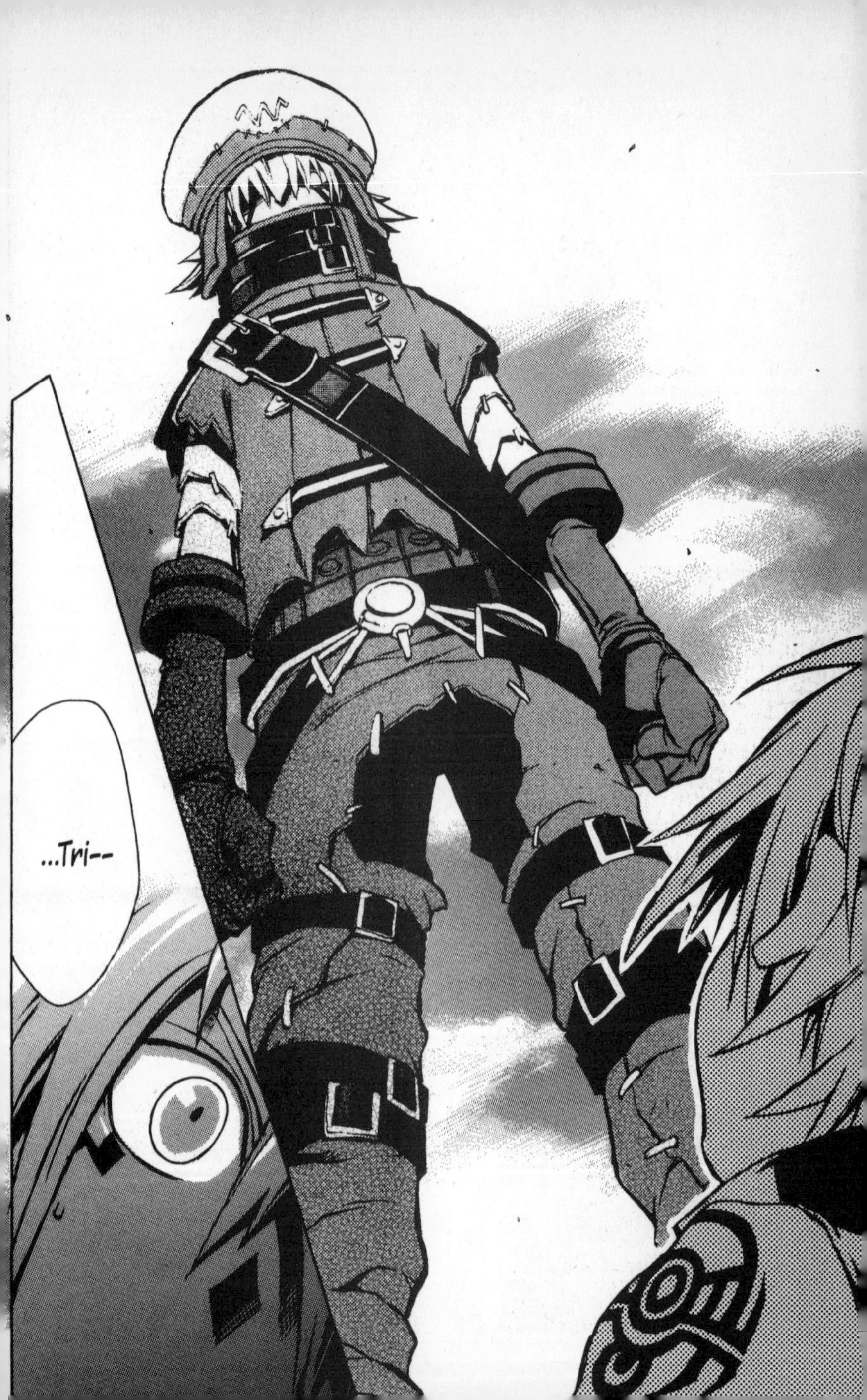
...Tri--

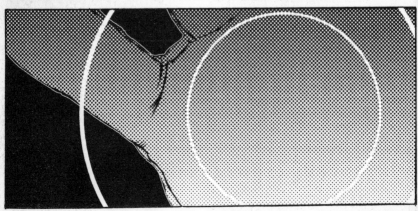

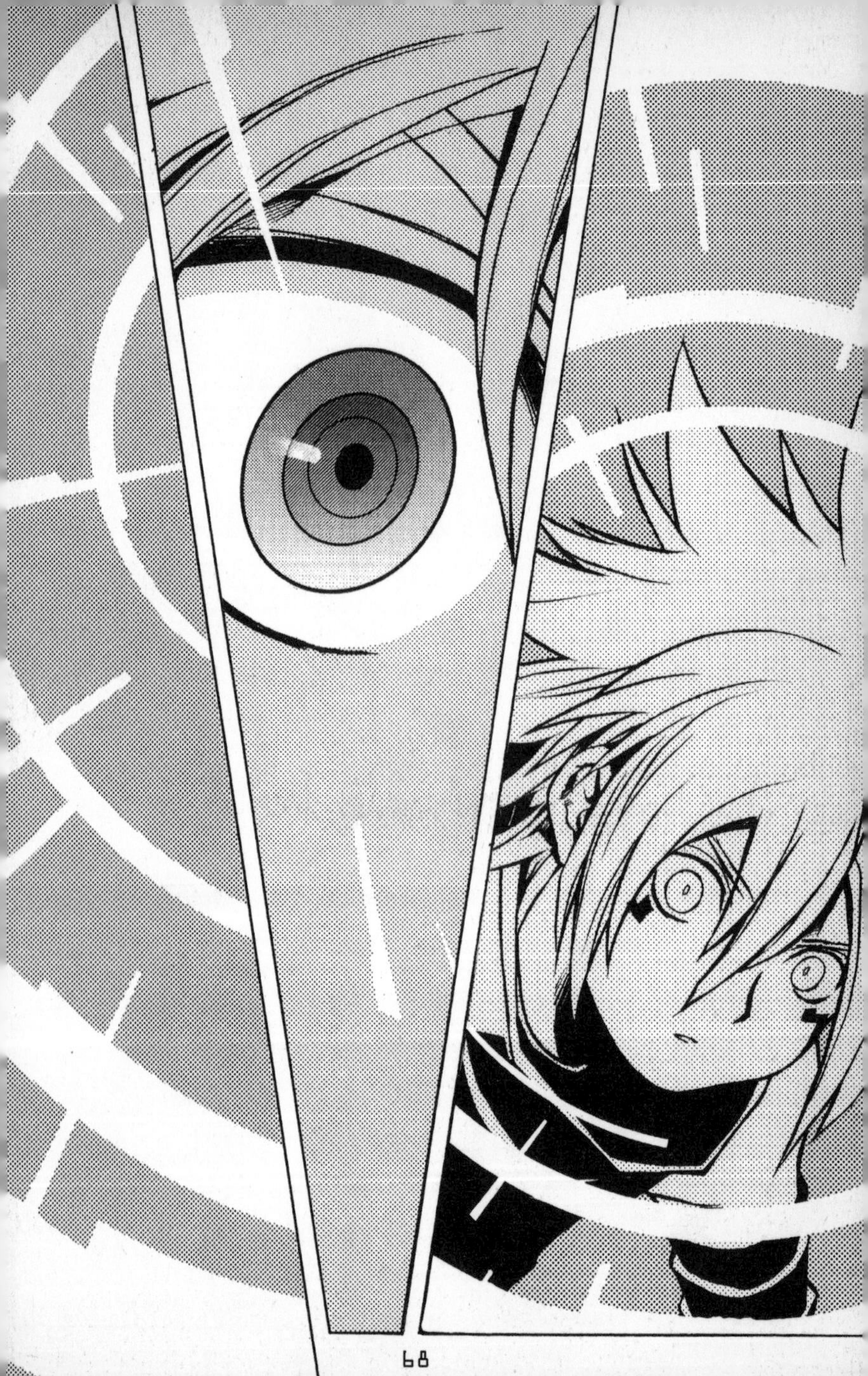

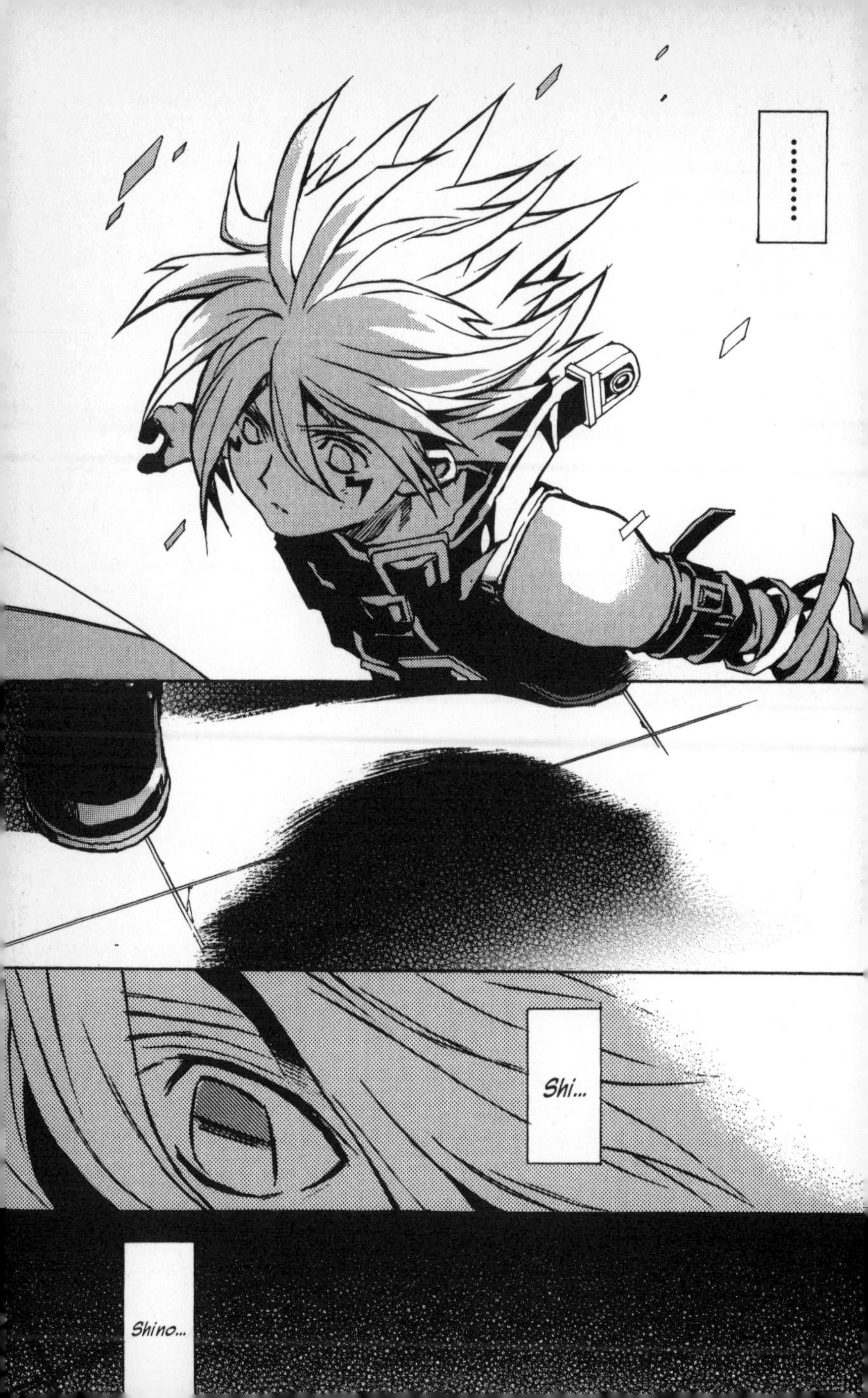
....
Shi...
Shino...

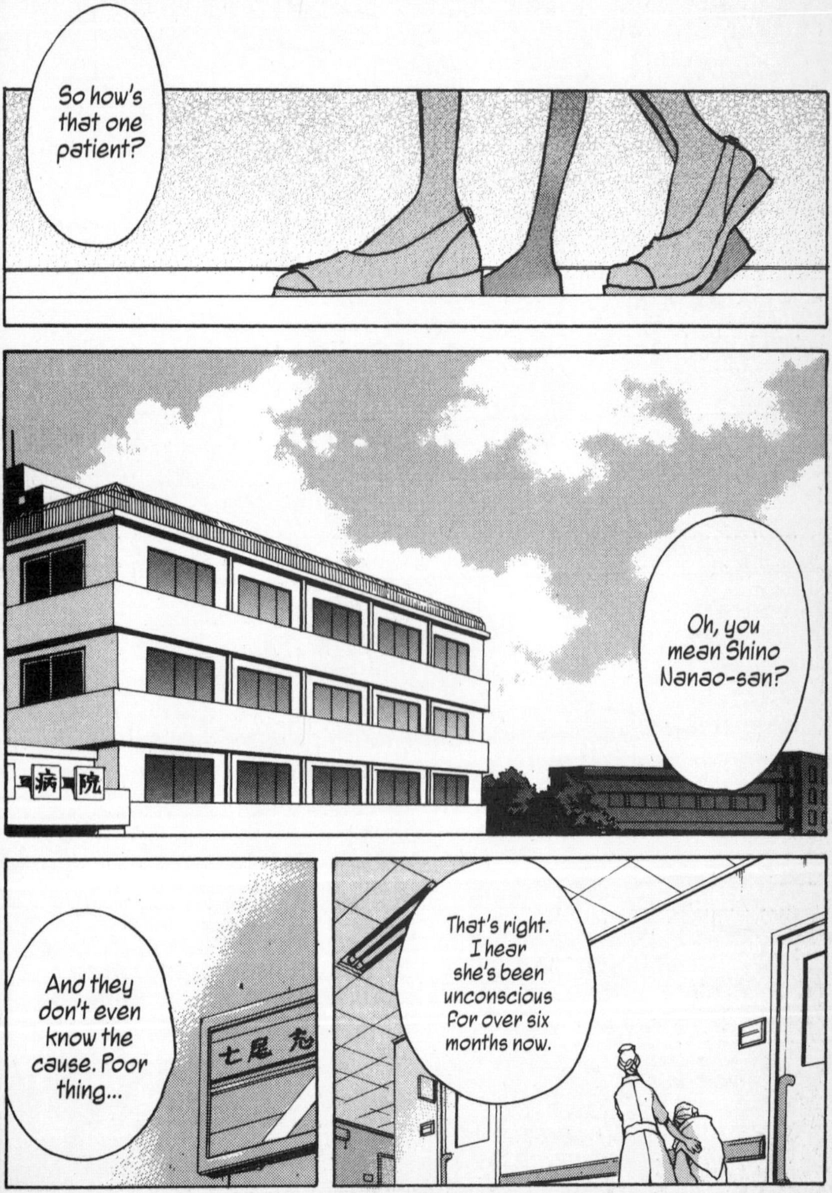
So how's that one patient?
Oh, you mean Shino Nanao-san?
That's right. I hear she's been unconscious for over six months now.
And they don't even know the cause. Poor thing...

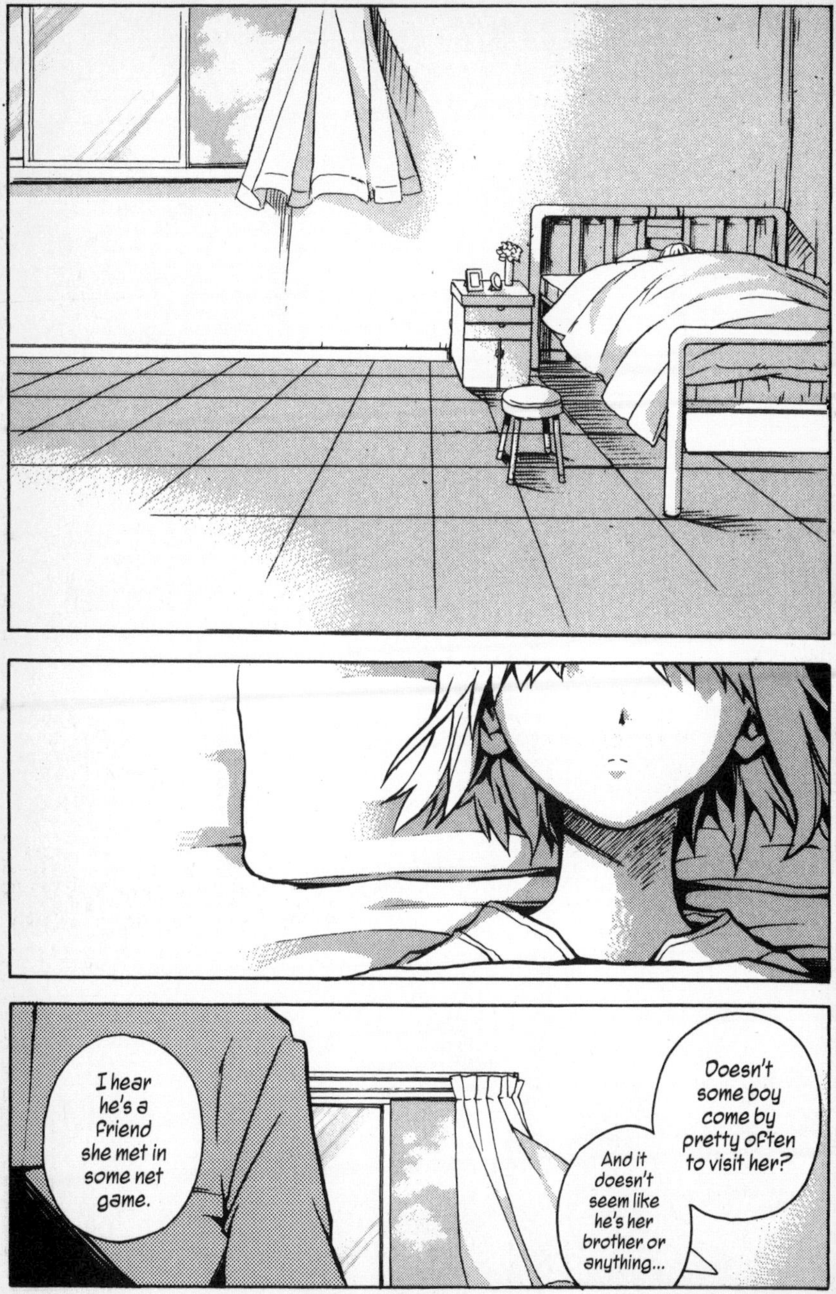
Doesn't some boy come by pretty often to visit her?
And it doesn't seem like he's her brother or anything...
I hear he's a friend she met in some net game.

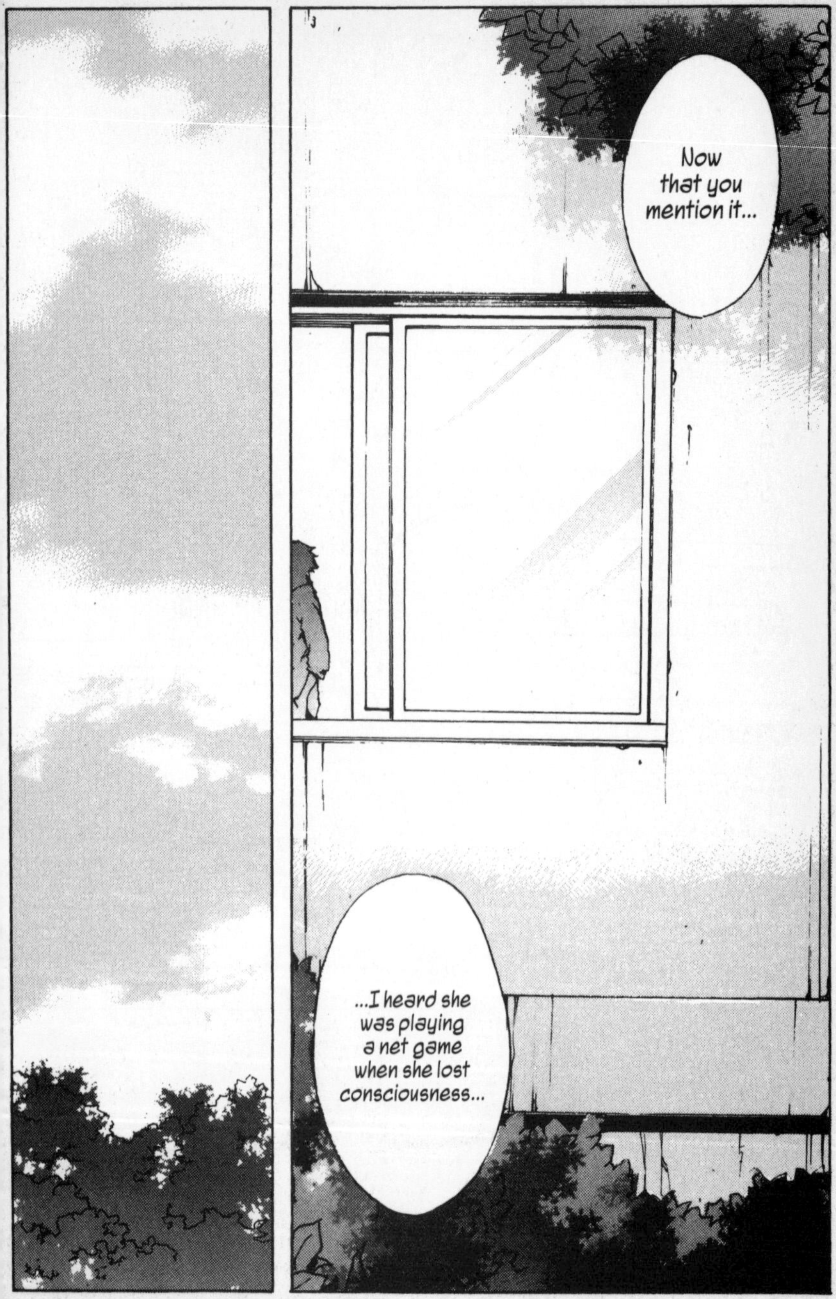
Now that you mention it...
...I heard she was playing a net game when she lost consciousness...

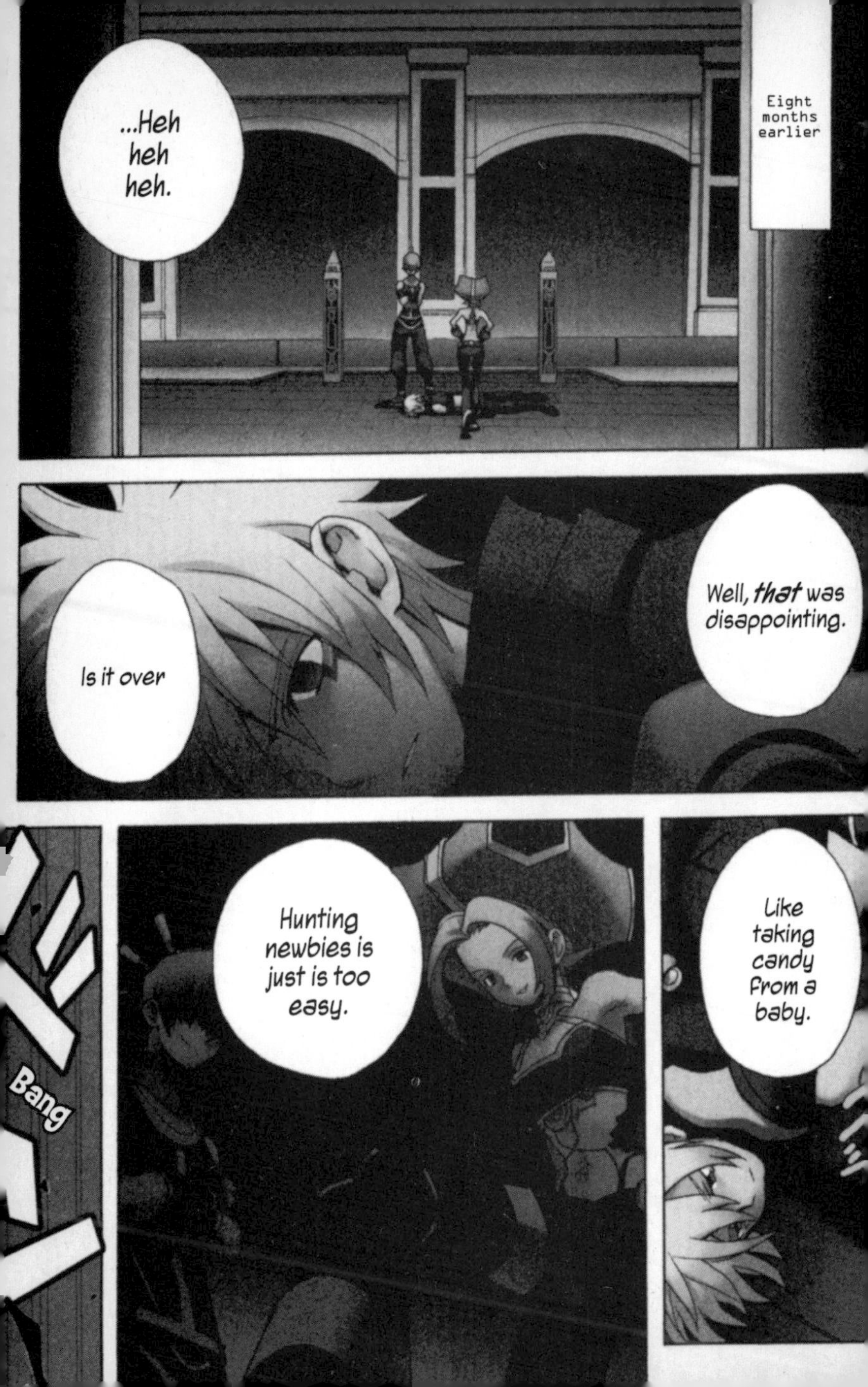
Eight months earlier
...Heh heh heh.
Well, *that* was disappointing.
Is it over
Like taking candy from a baby.
Hunting newbies is just is too easy.
Bang

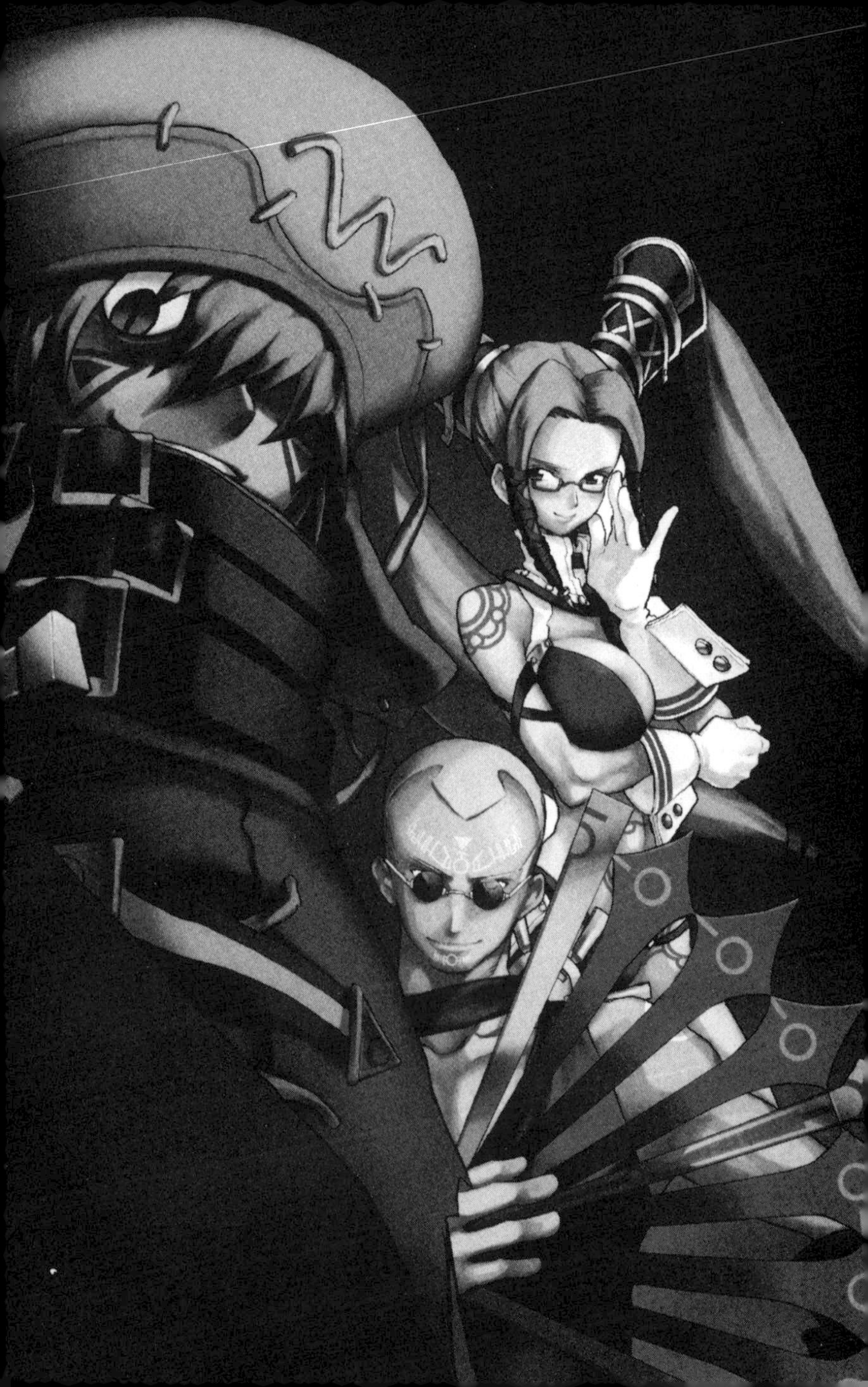

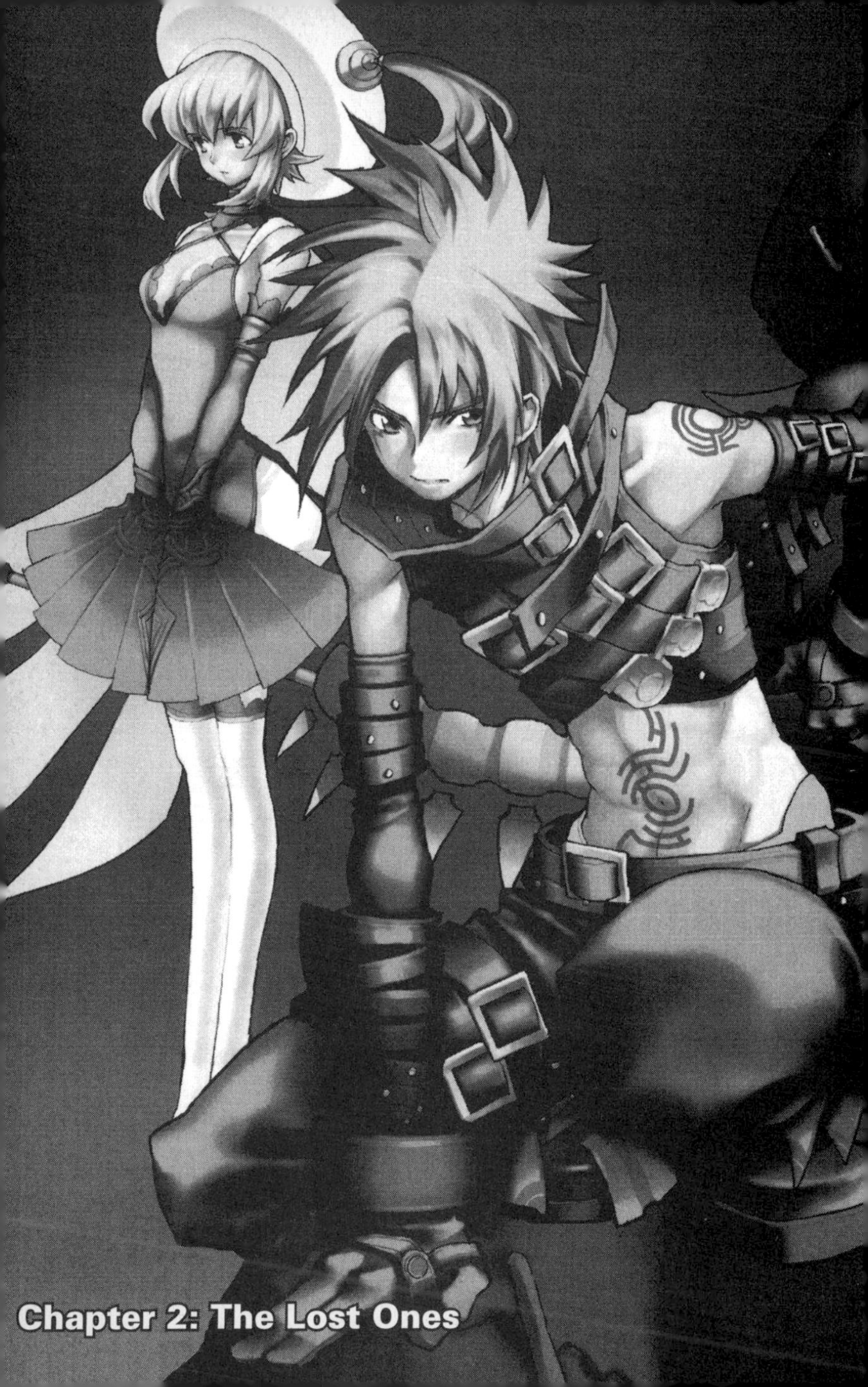
Chapter 2: The Lost Ones

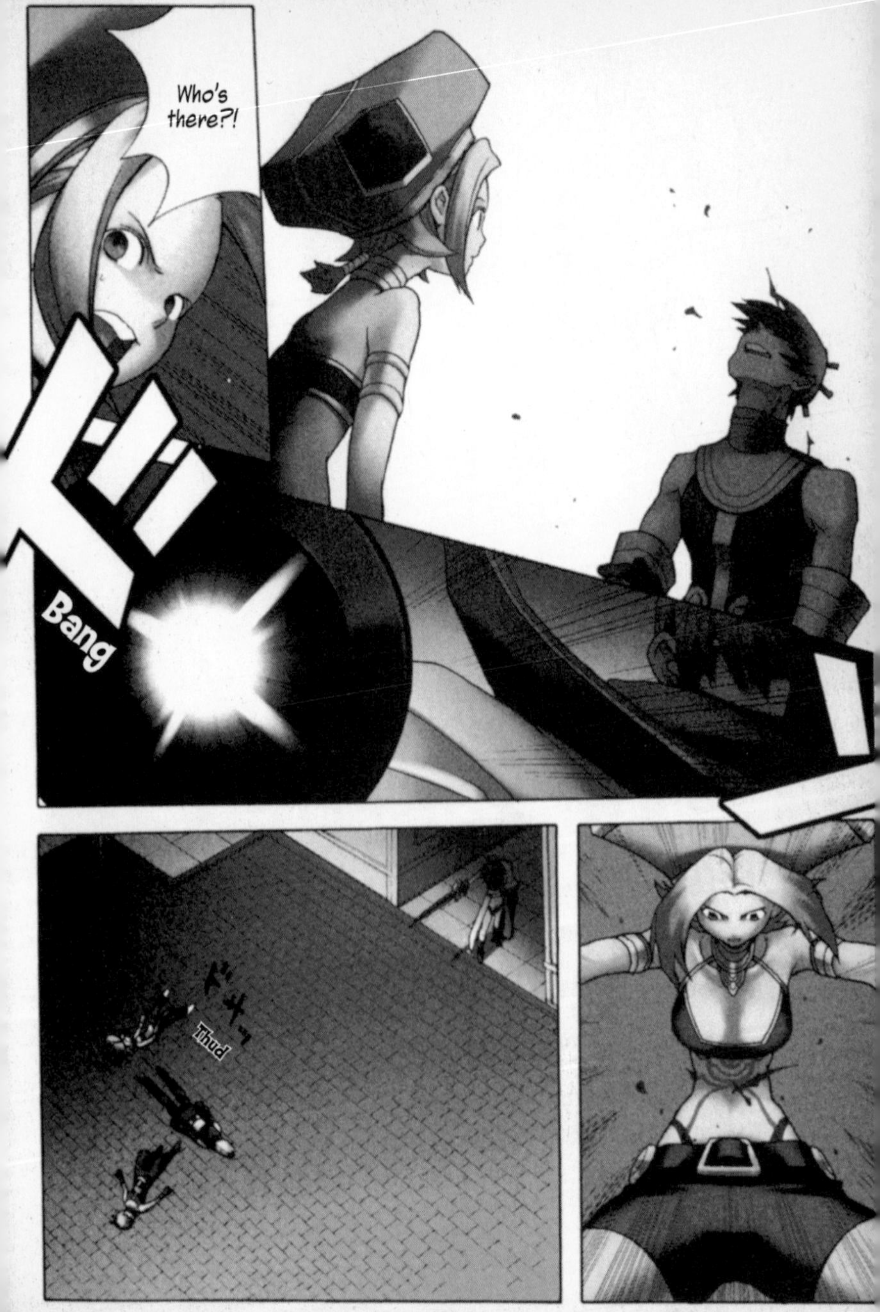

Who's there?!
Bang
Thud

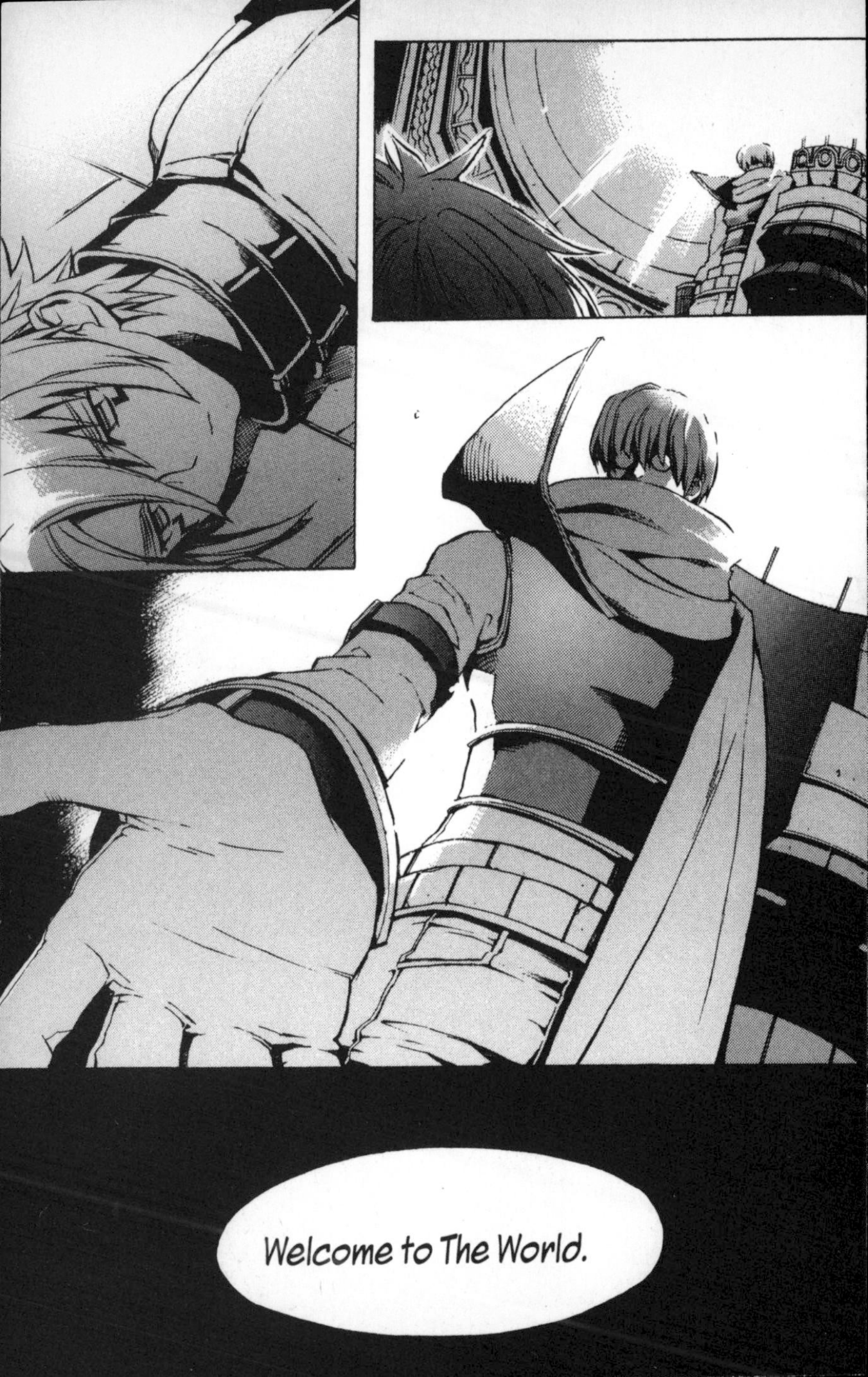
Welcome to The World.

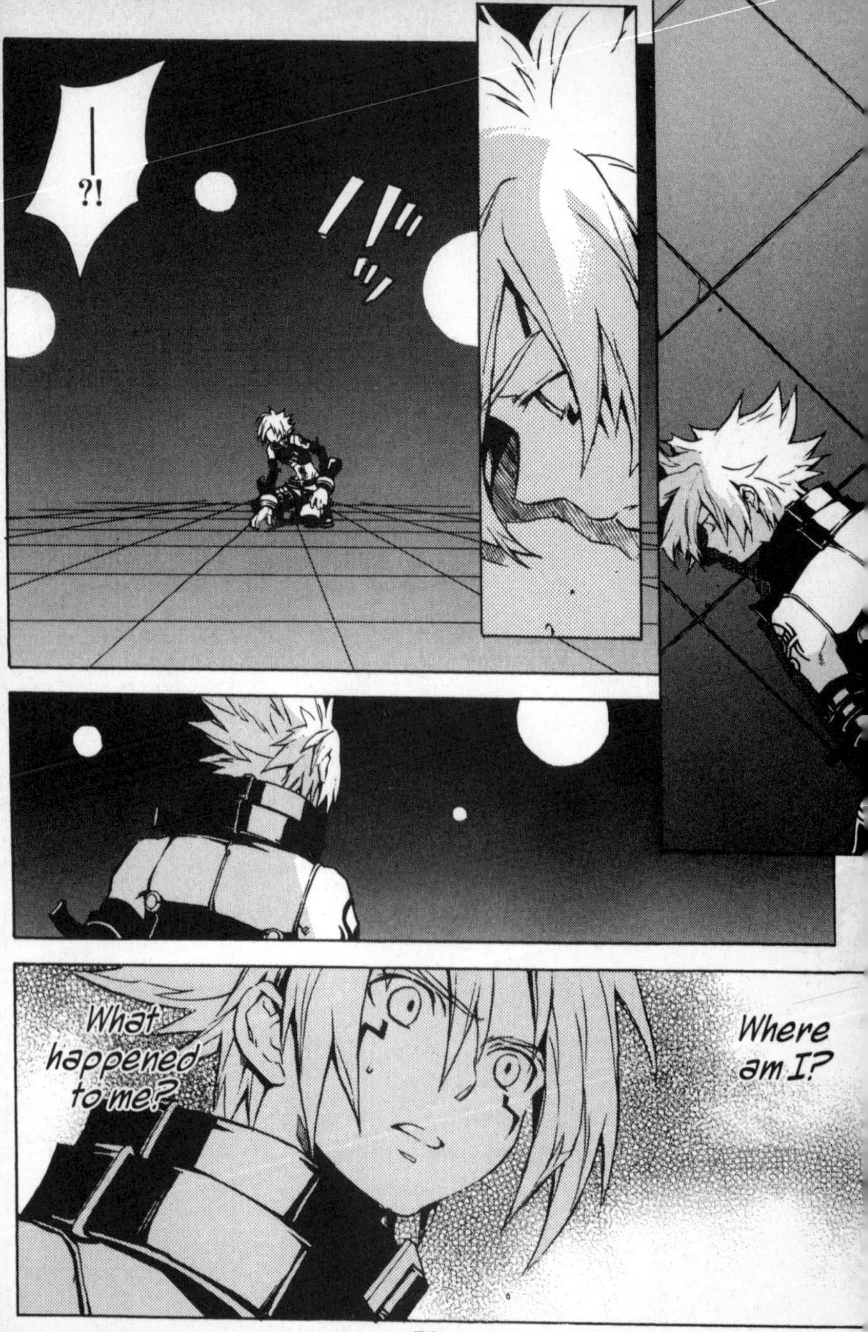
—?!
Where am I?
What happened to me?

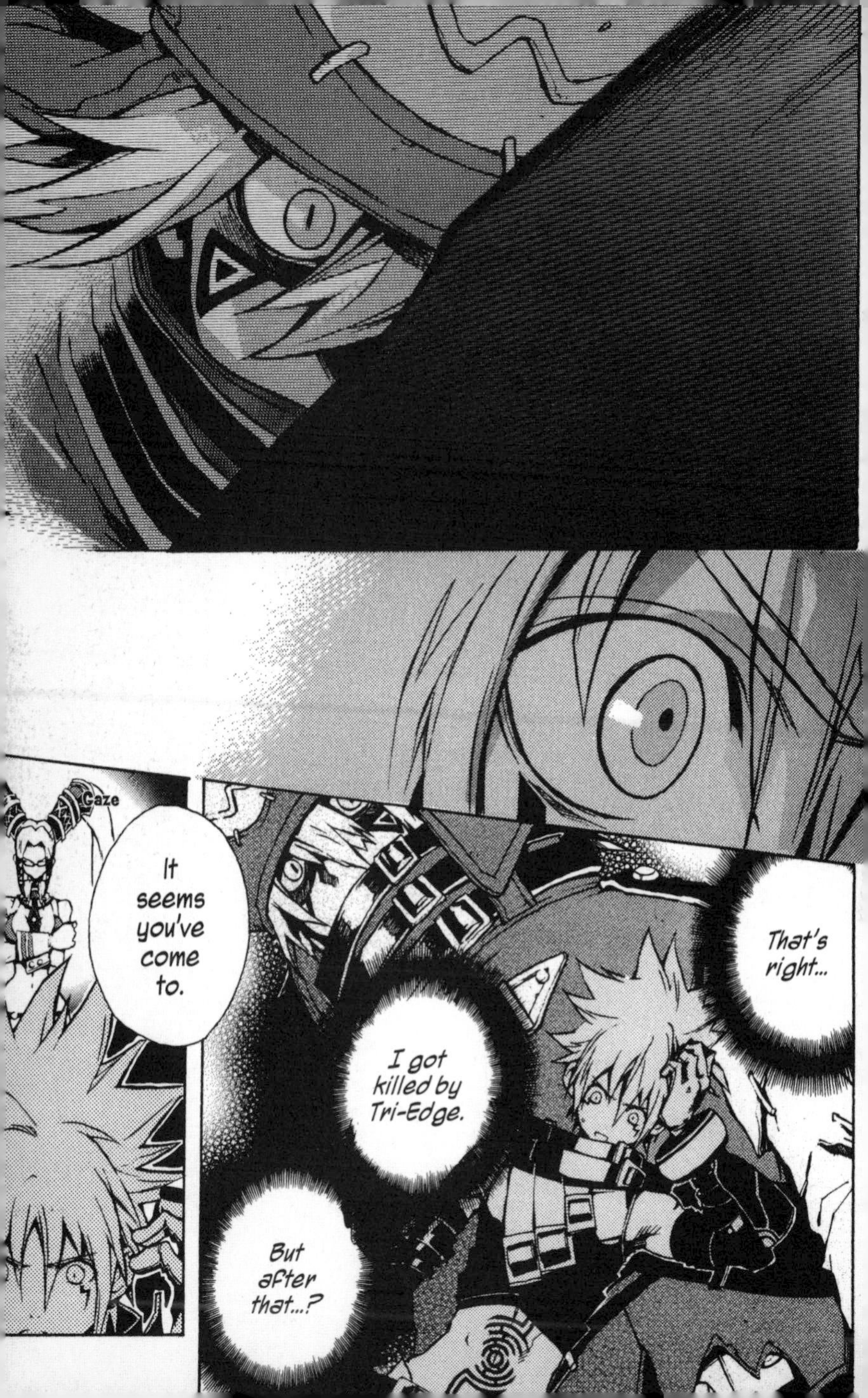
That's right...
I got killed by Tri-Edge.
But after that...?
Gaze
It seems you've come to.

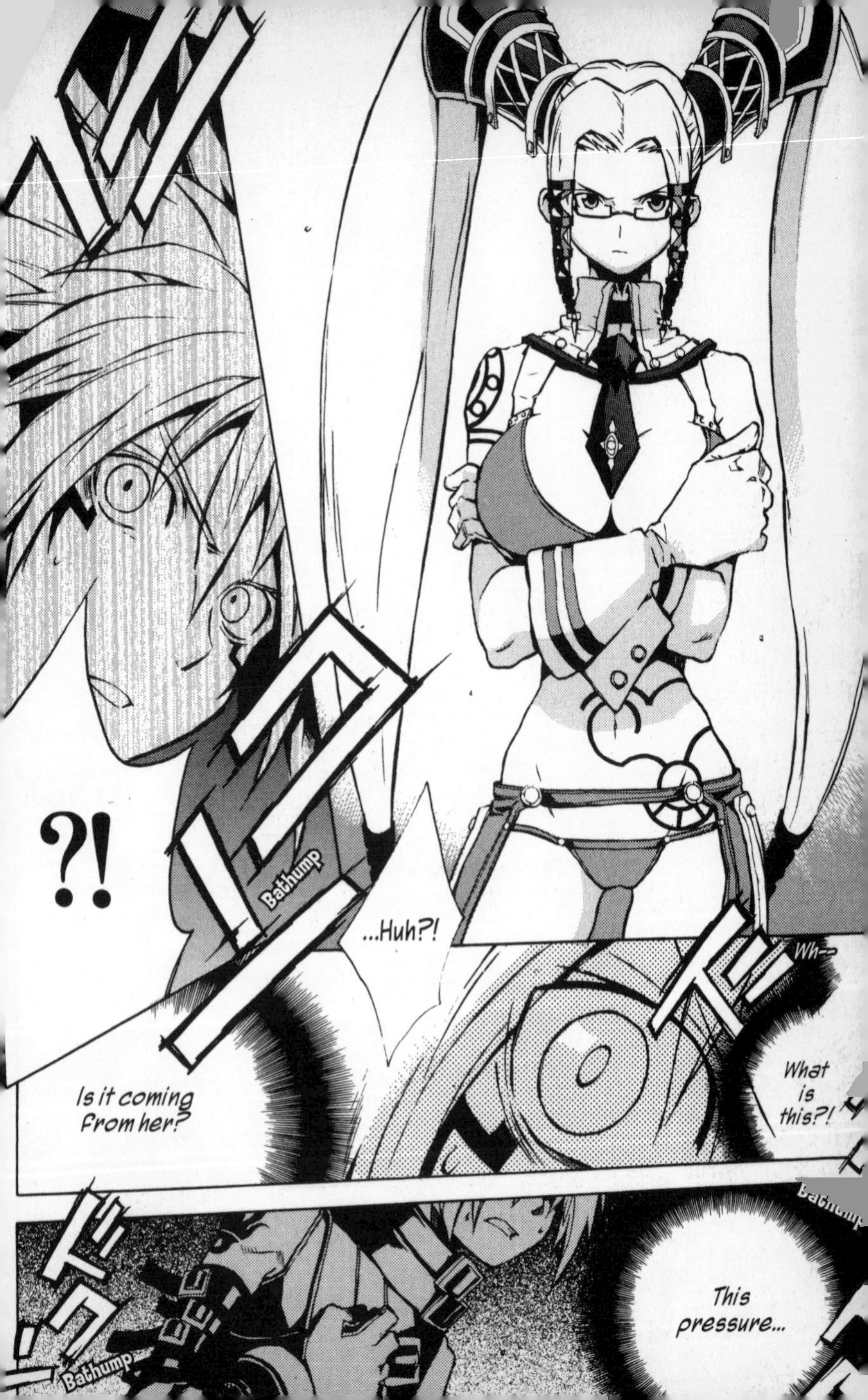

?!
Bathump
...Huh?!
Wh-
What is this?!
Is it coming from her?
This pressure...
Bathump

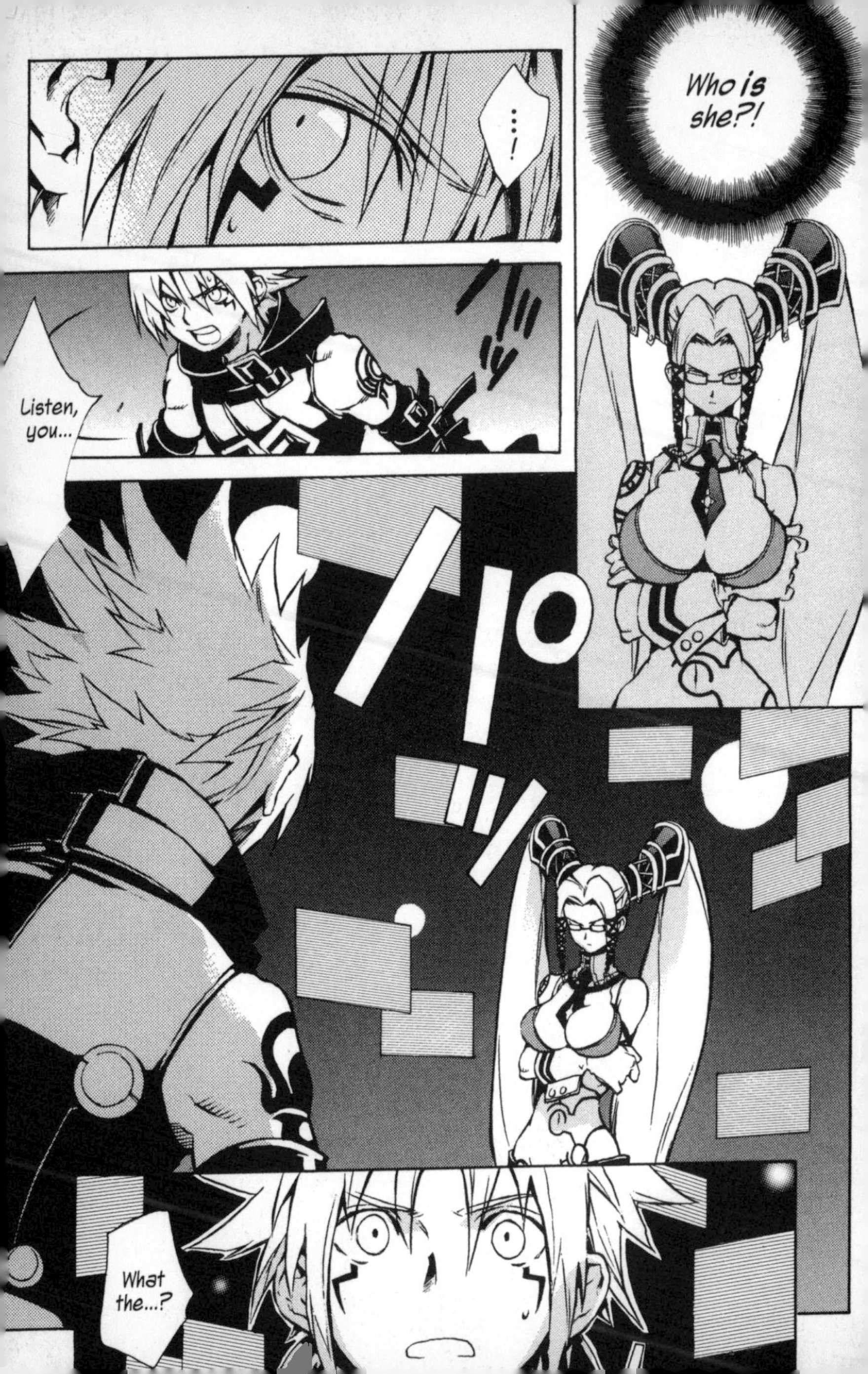
Who is she?!
...!
Listen, you...
What the...?

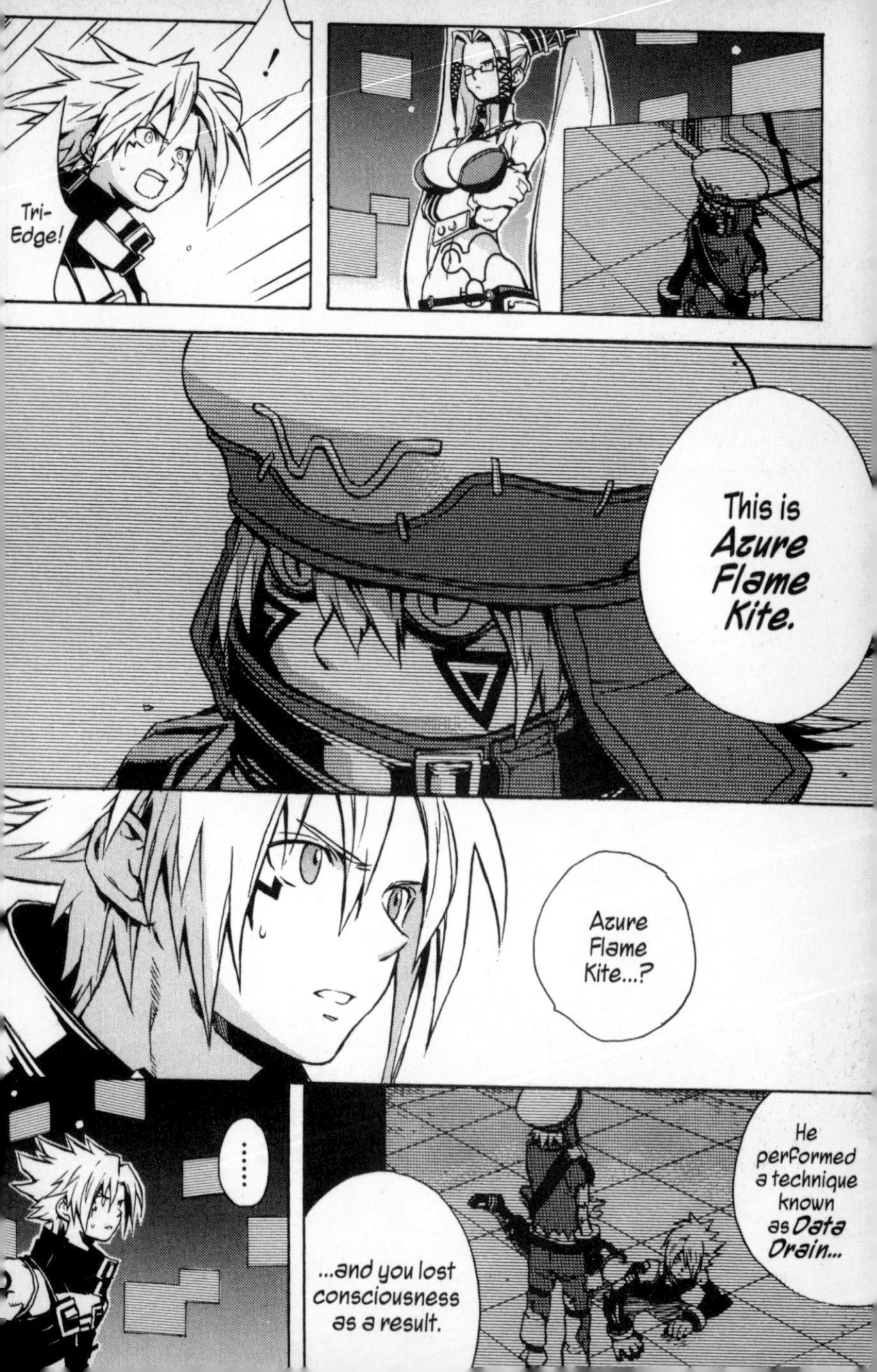
!
Tri-Edge!
This is Azure Flame Kite.
Azure Flame Kite...?
He performed a technique known as Data Drain...
...and you lost consciousness as a result.
......

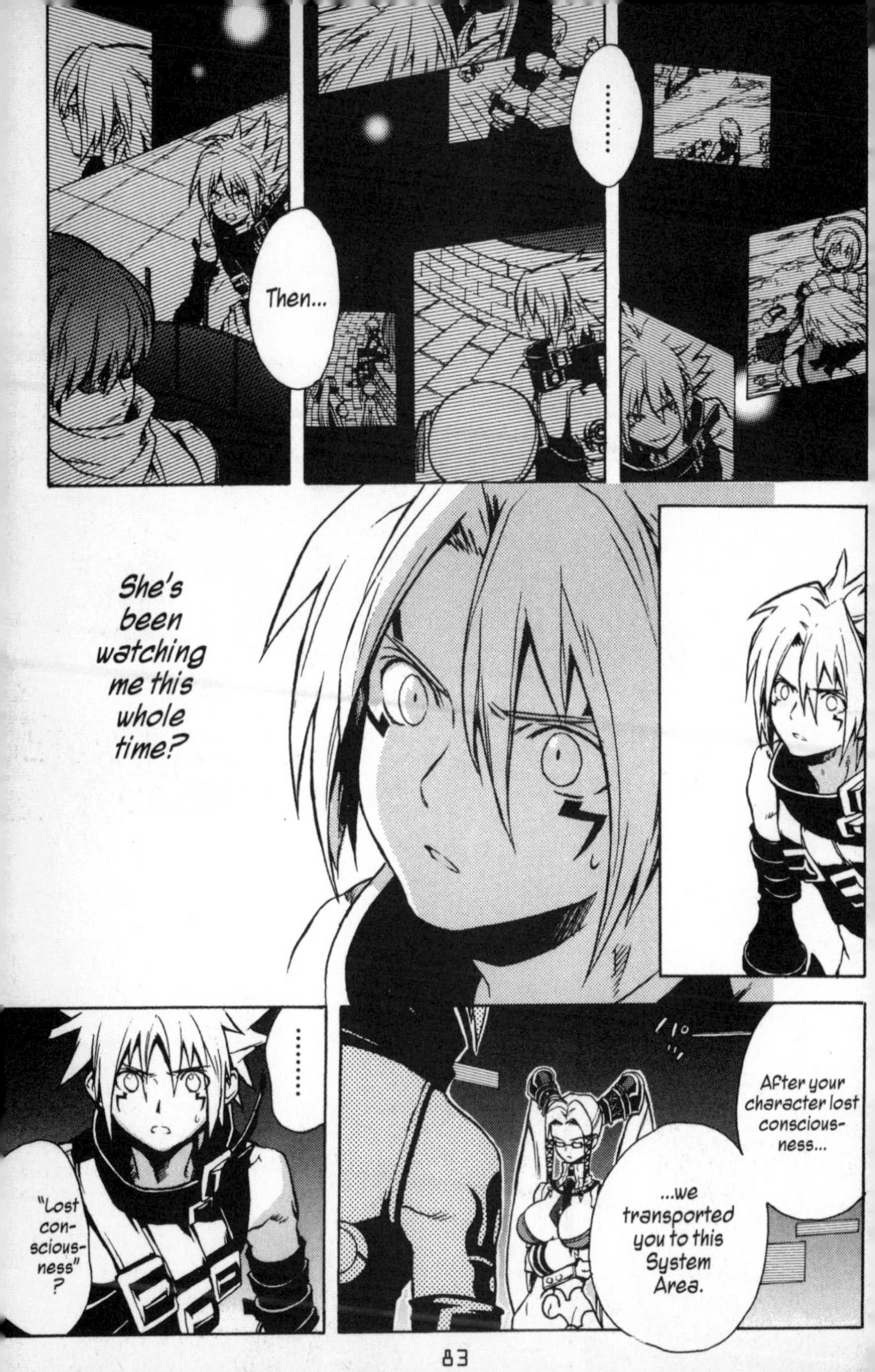
......
Then...
She's been watching me this whole time?
After your character lost conscious-ness...
...we transported you to this System Area.
......
"Lost con-scious-ness"?

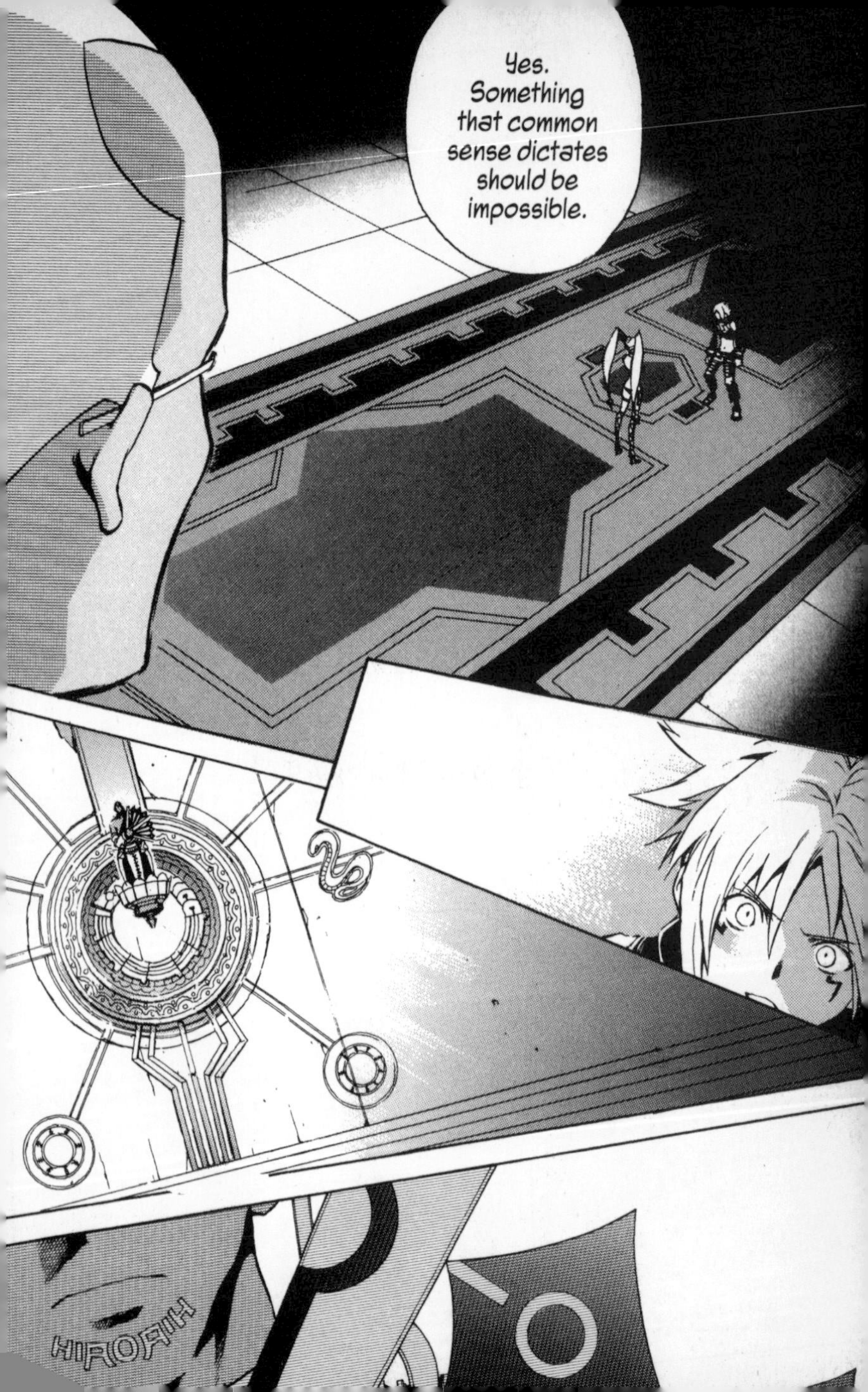
Yes. Something that common sense dictates should be impossible.

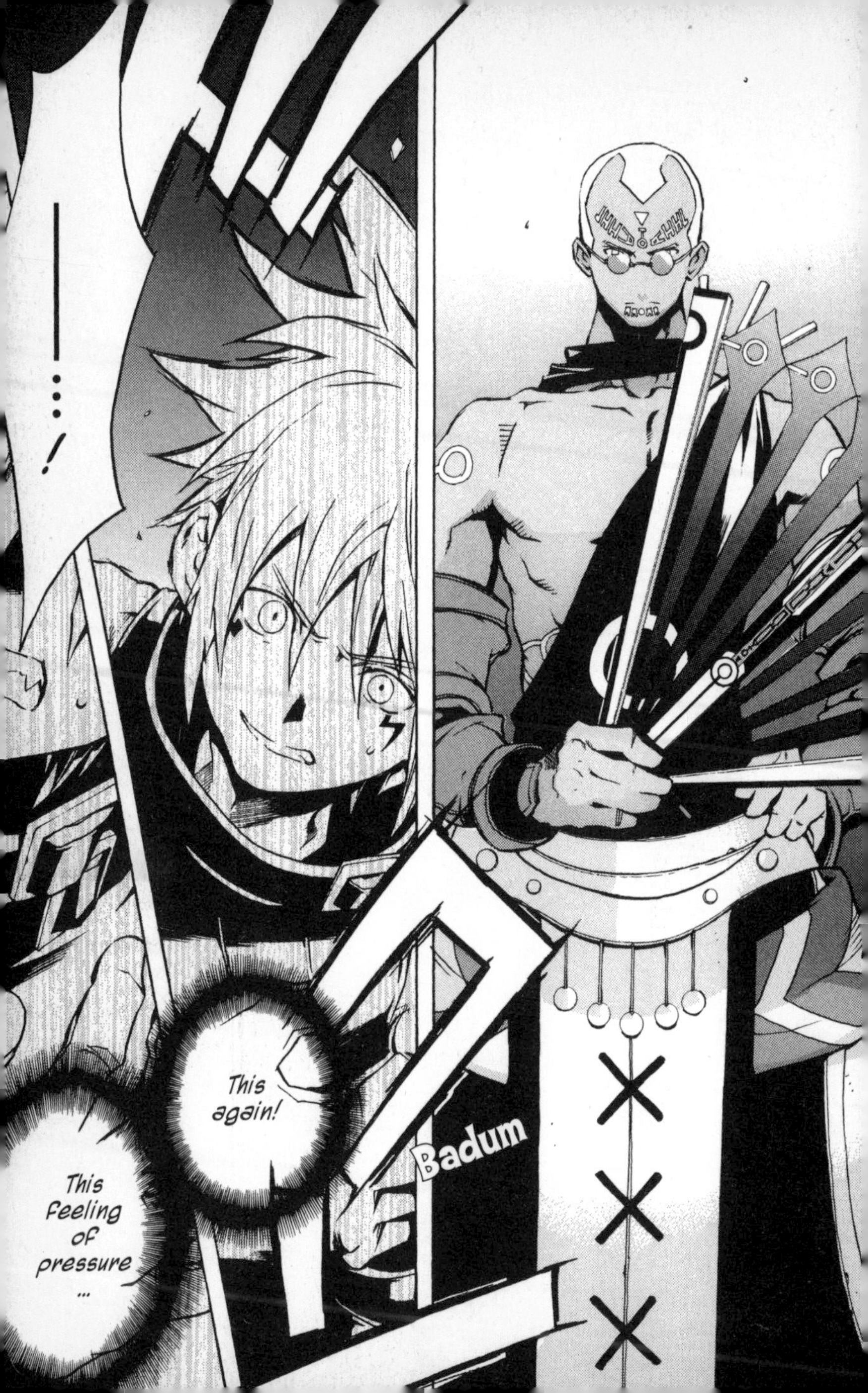

——…!
Badum
This again!
This feeling of pressure ...

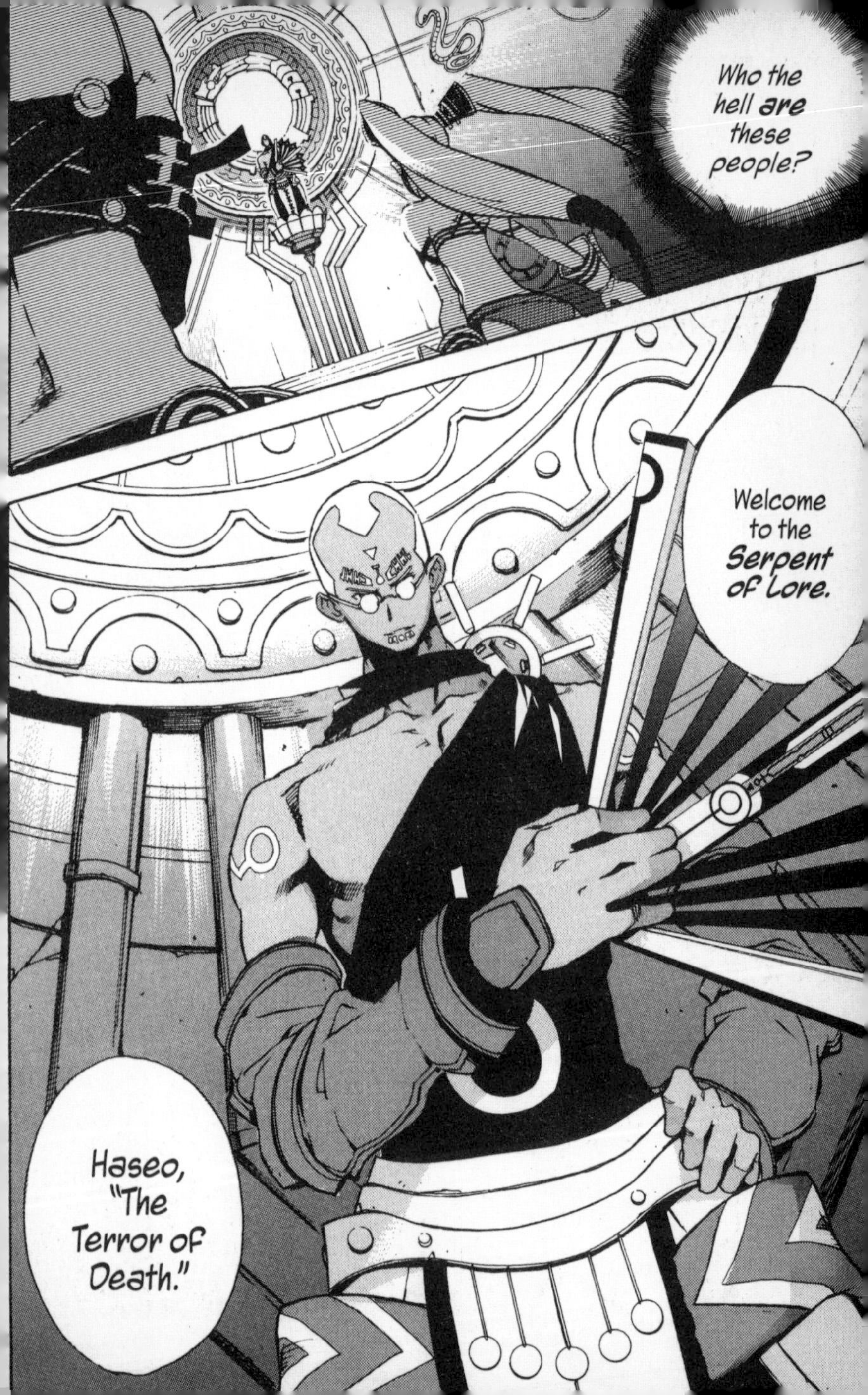

Who the hell are these people?
Welcome to the Serpent of Lore.
Haseo, "The Terror of Death."

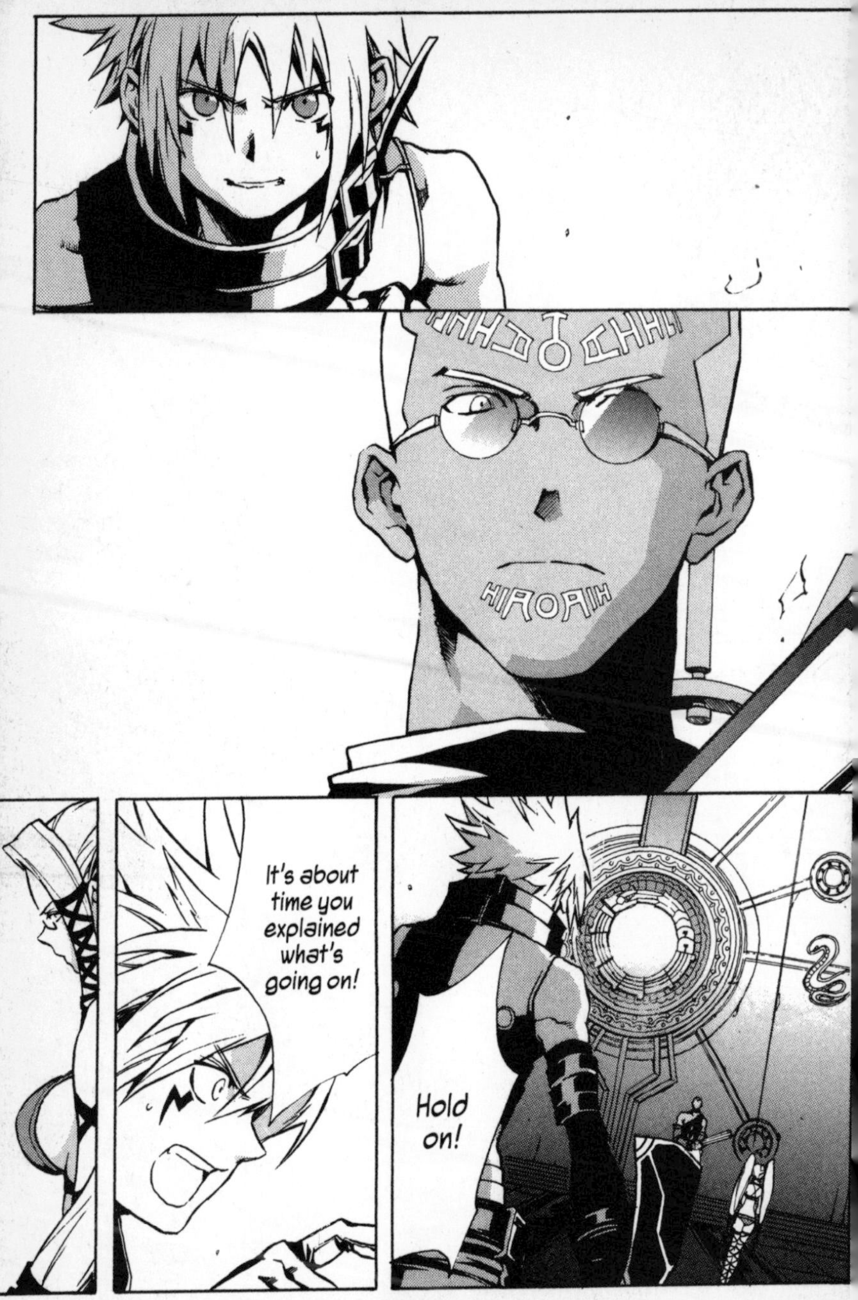
Hold on!
It's about time you explained what's going on!

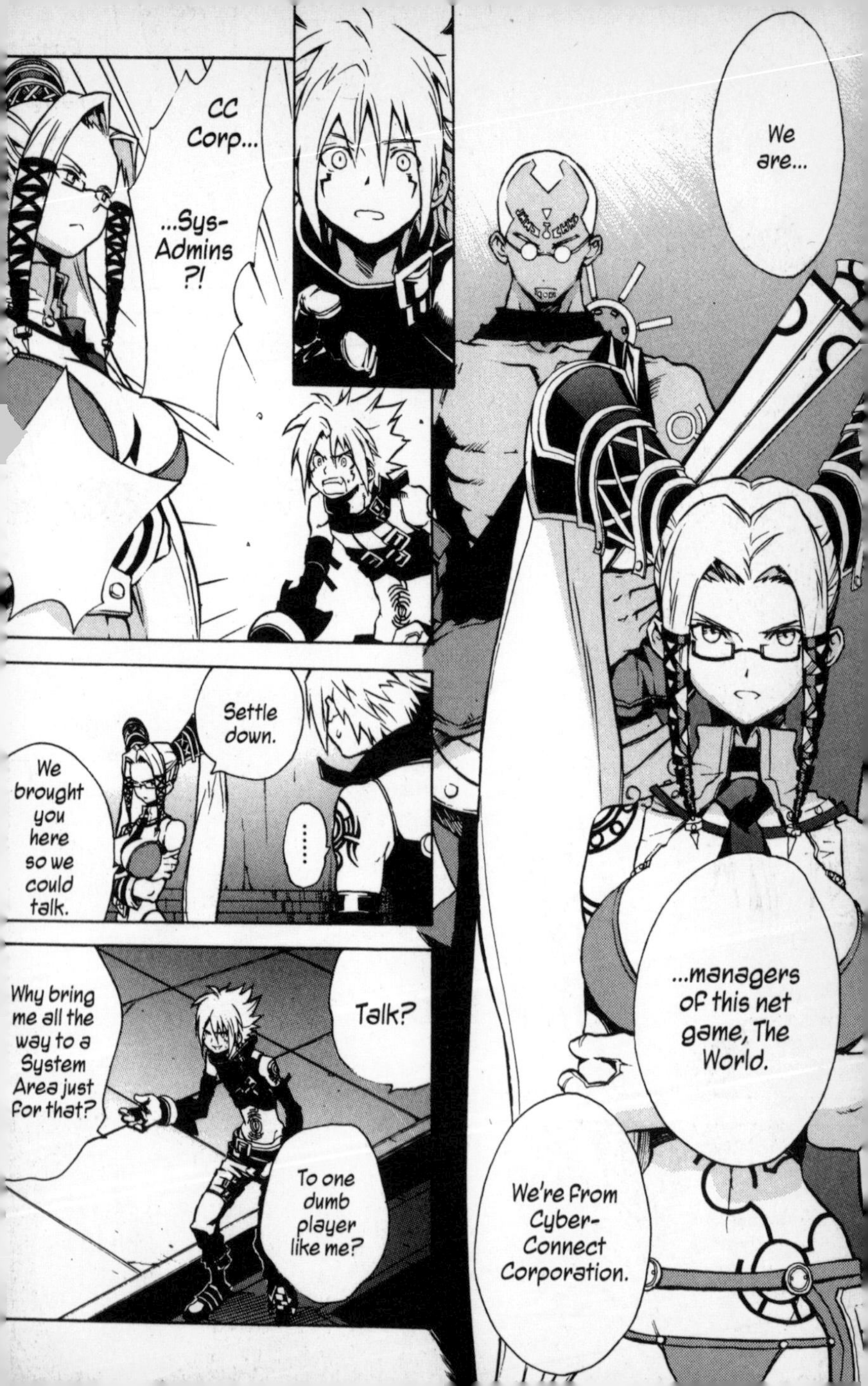
We are...
...managers of this net game, The World.
We're from Cyber-Connect Corporation.
CC Corp...
...Sys-Admins ?!
Settle down.
......
We brought you here so we could talk.
Talk?
Why bring me all the way to a System Area just for that?
To one dumb player like me?

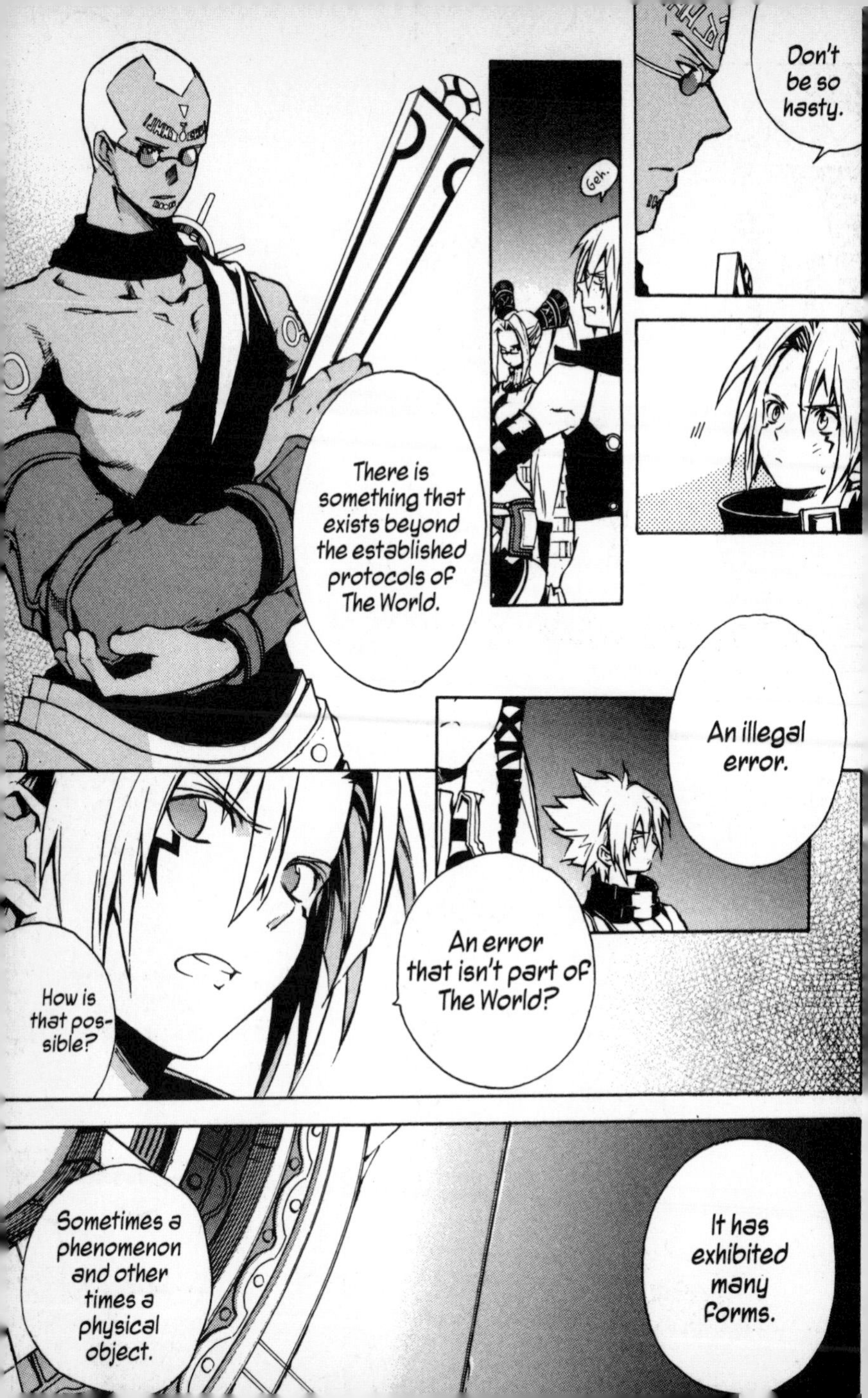
Don't be so hasty.
Geh.
There is something that exists beyond the established protocols of The World.
An illegal error.
An error that isn't part of The World?
How is that possible?
It has exhibited many forms.
Sometimes a phenomenon and other times a physical object.

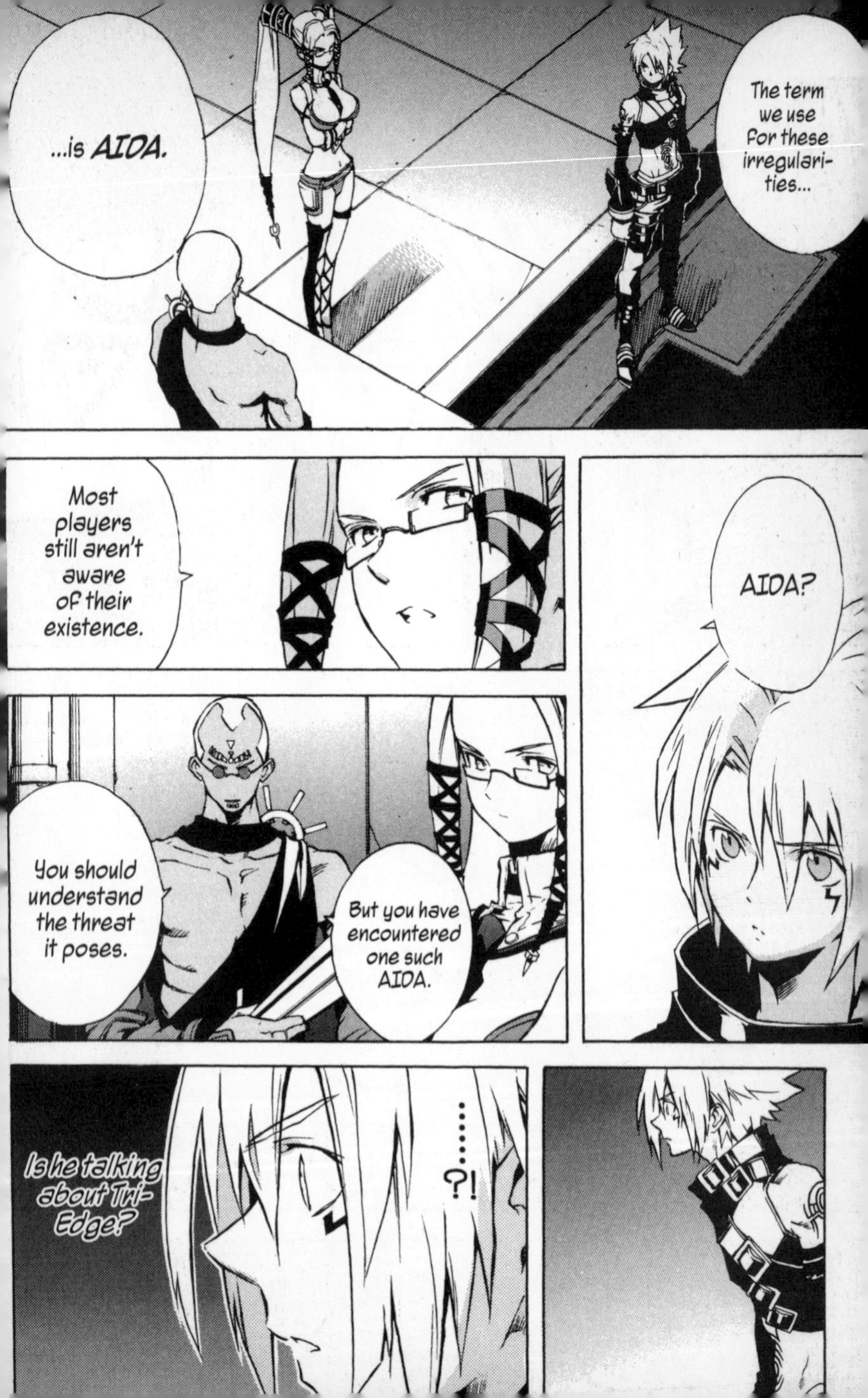

The term we use for these irregularities...
...is AIDA.
AIDA?
Most players still aren't aware of their existence.
But you have encountered one such AIDA.
You should understand the threat it poses.
......?!
Is he talking about Tri-Edge?

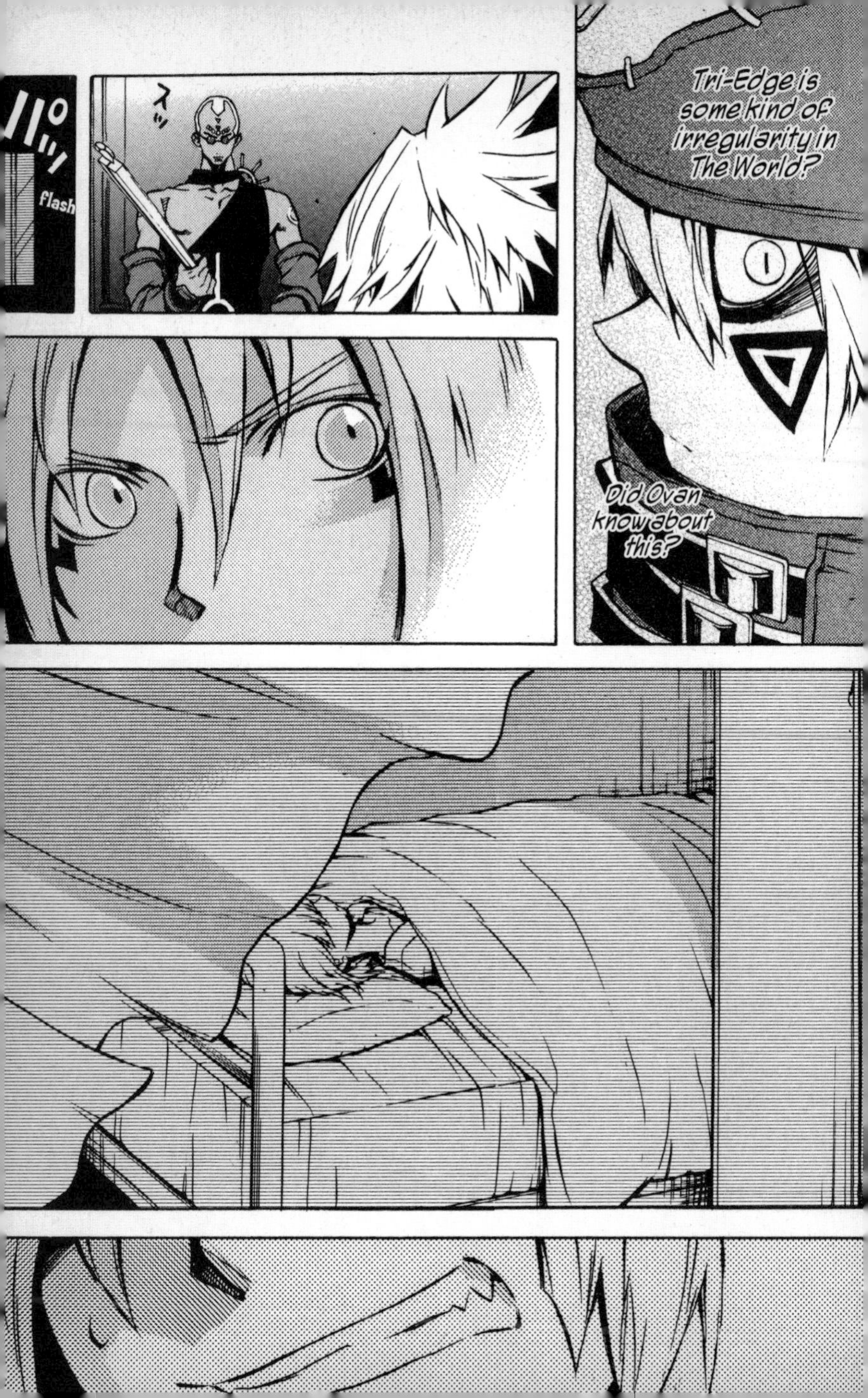
Tri-Edge is some kind of irregularity in The World?
Did Ovan know about this?
スッ
flash

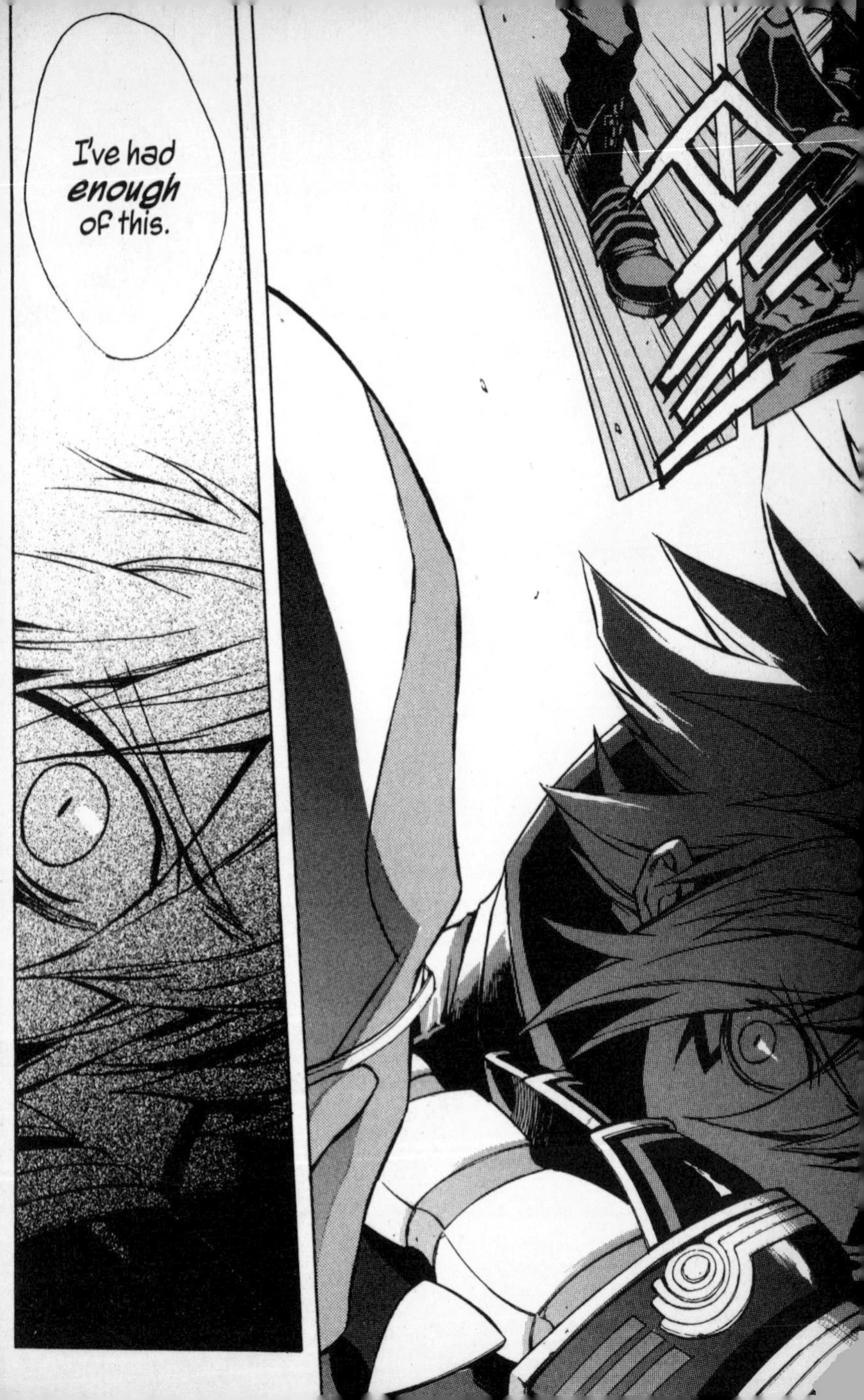
I've had enough of this.

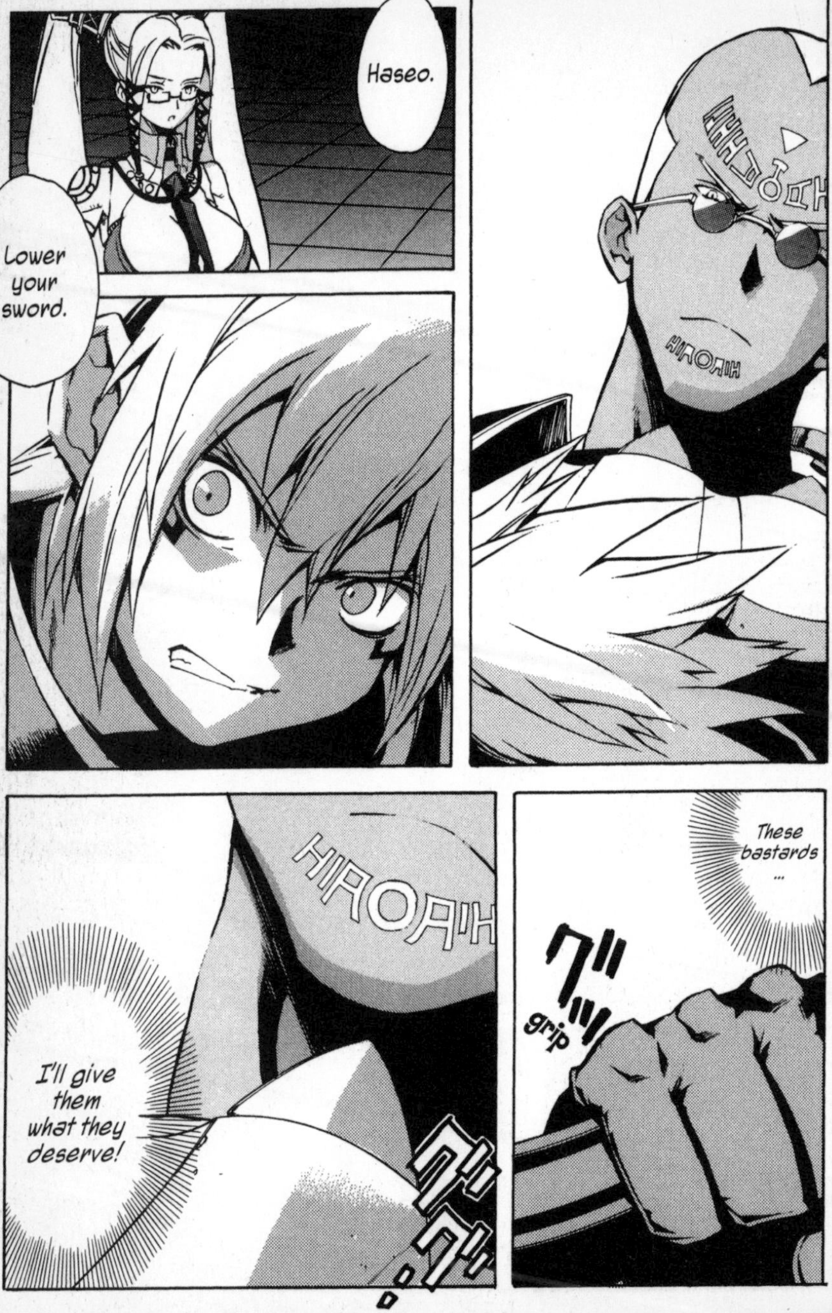
Haseo.
Lower your sword.
These bastards ...
grip
I'll give them what they deserve!

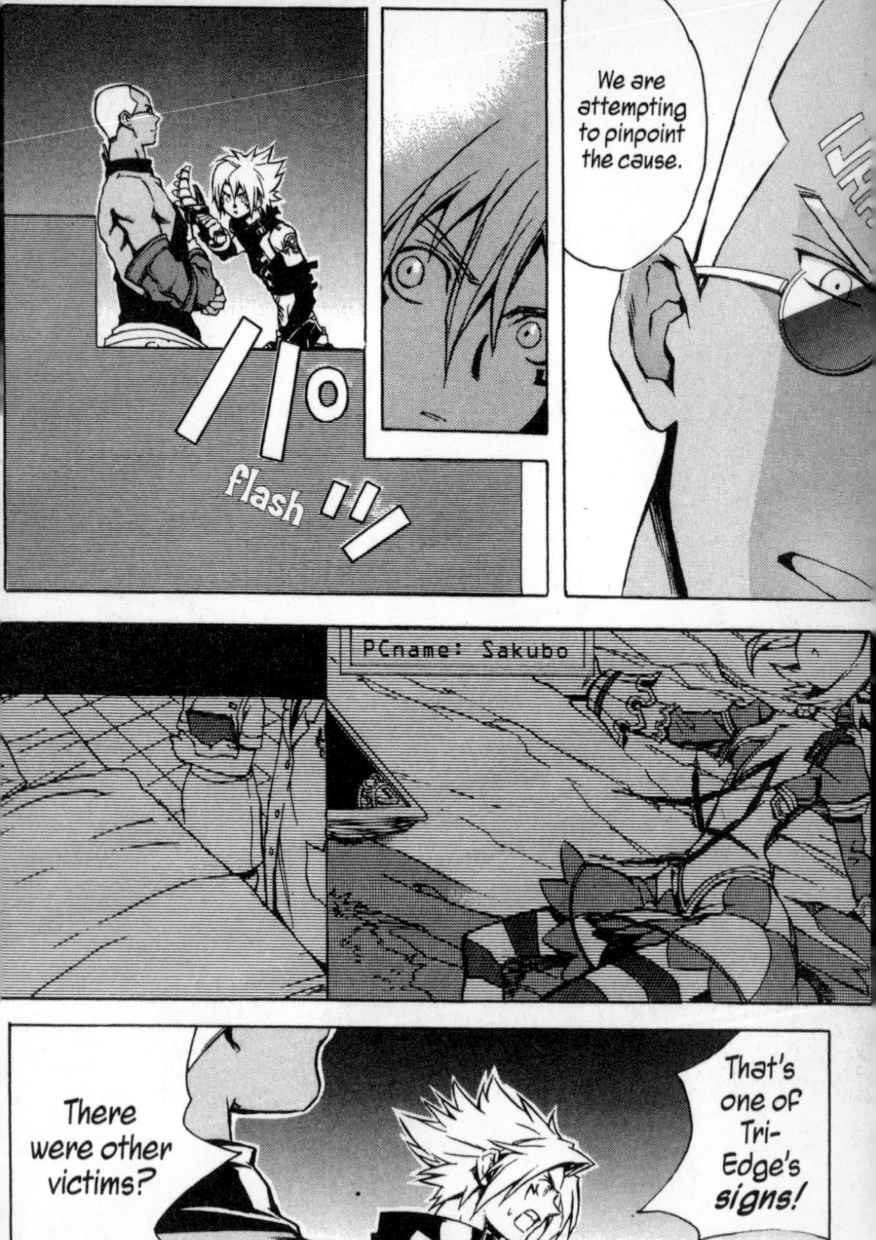
We are attempting to pinpoint the cause.
flash
PCname: Sakubo
That's one of Tri-Edge's signs!
There were other victims?

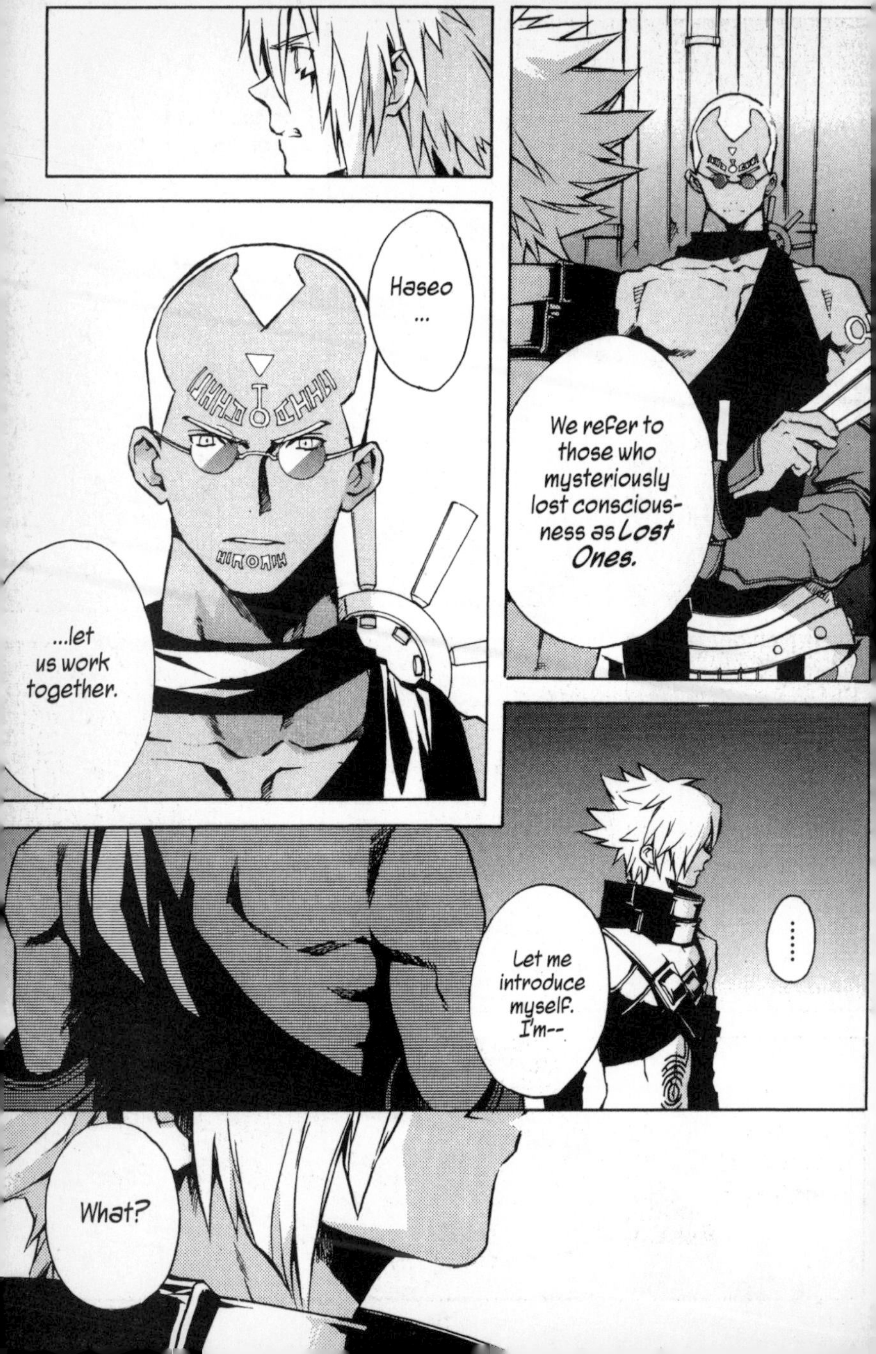

We refer to those who mysteriously lost conscious-ness as *Lost Ones.*
Haseo ...
...let us work together.
......
Let me introduce myself. I'm--
What?

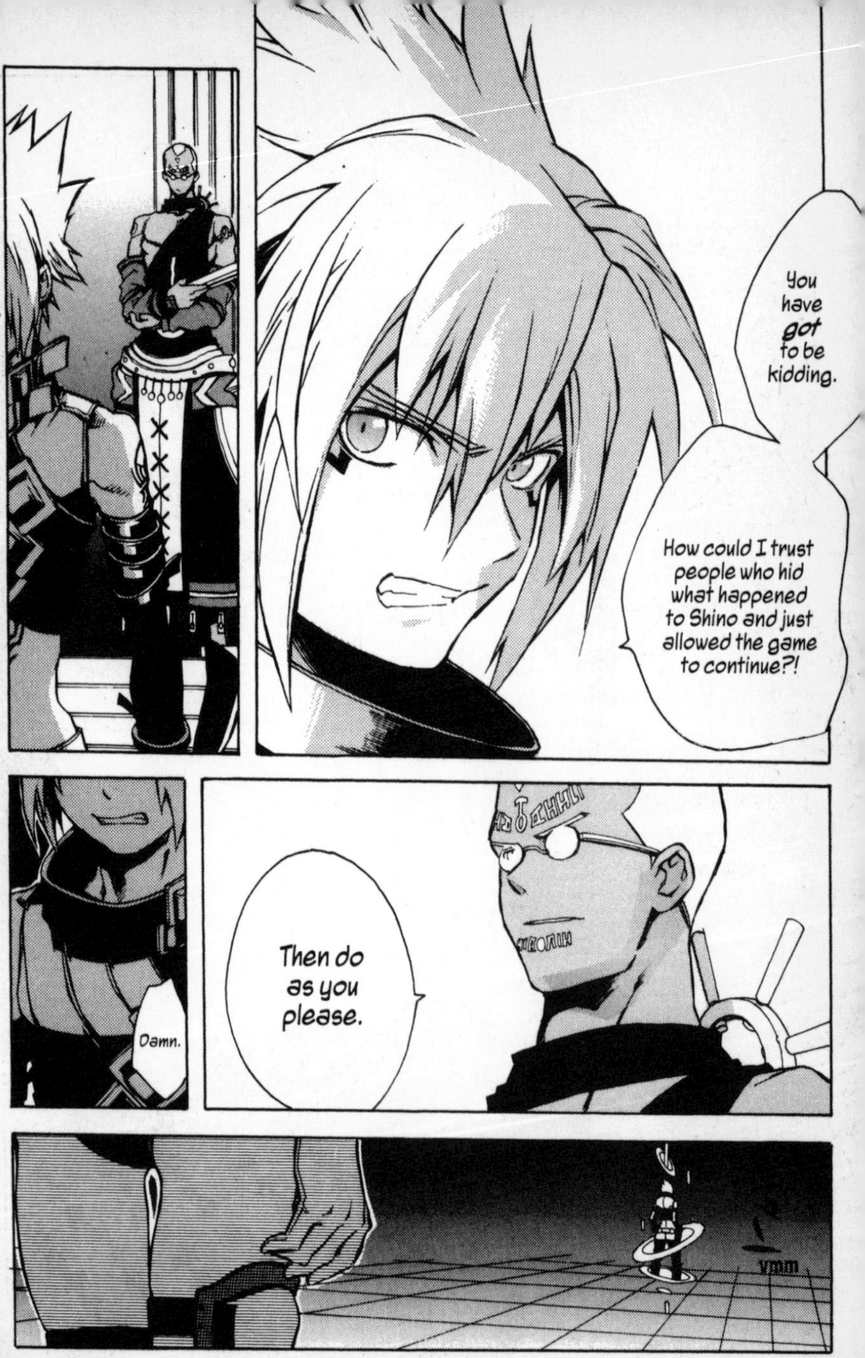
You have got to be kidding.
How could I trust people who hid what happened to Shino and just allowed the game to continue?!
Then do as you please.
Damn.
vmm

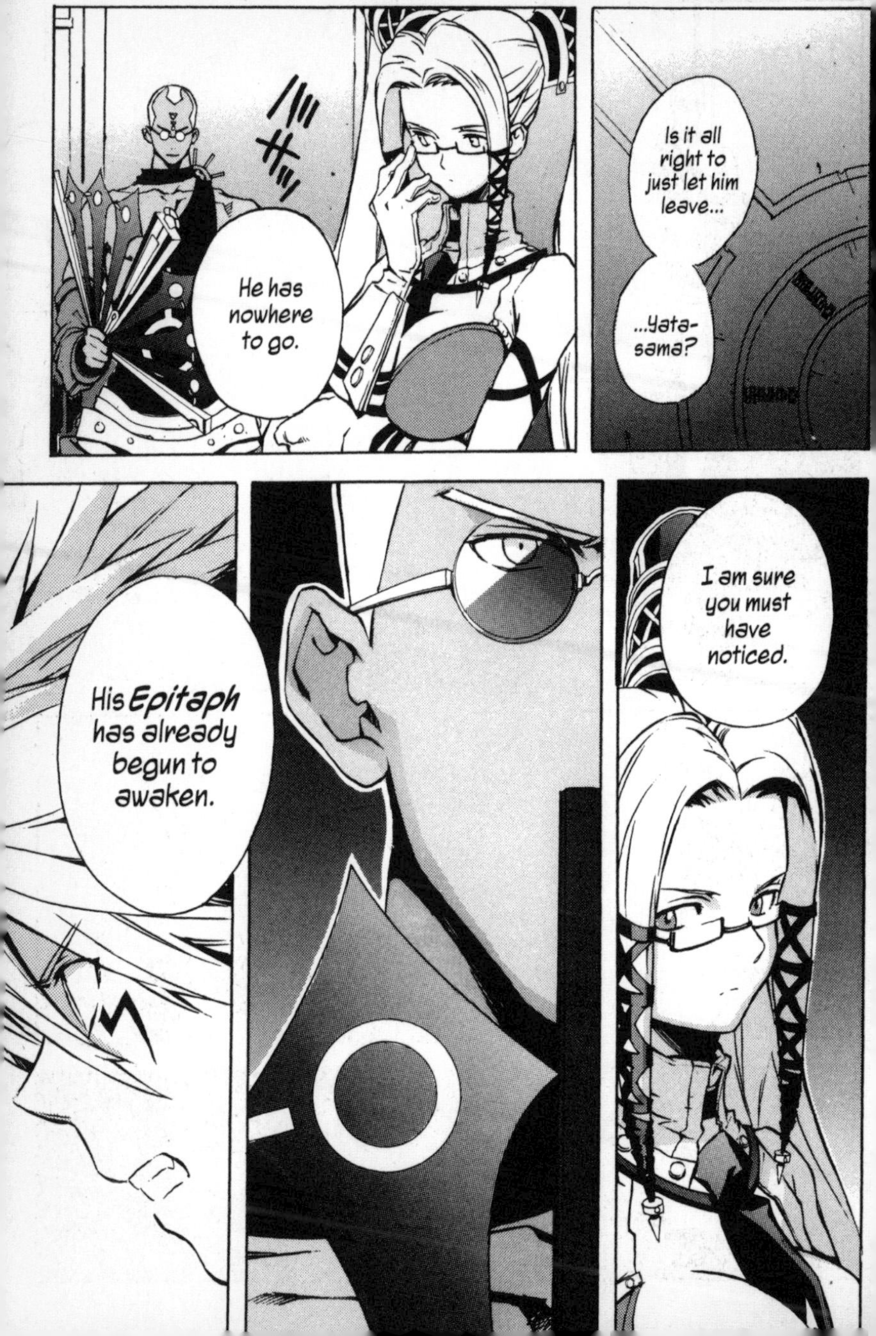
Is it all right to just let him leave...
...Yata-sama?
He has nowhere to go.
I am sure you must have noticed.
His *Epitaph* has already begun to awaken.

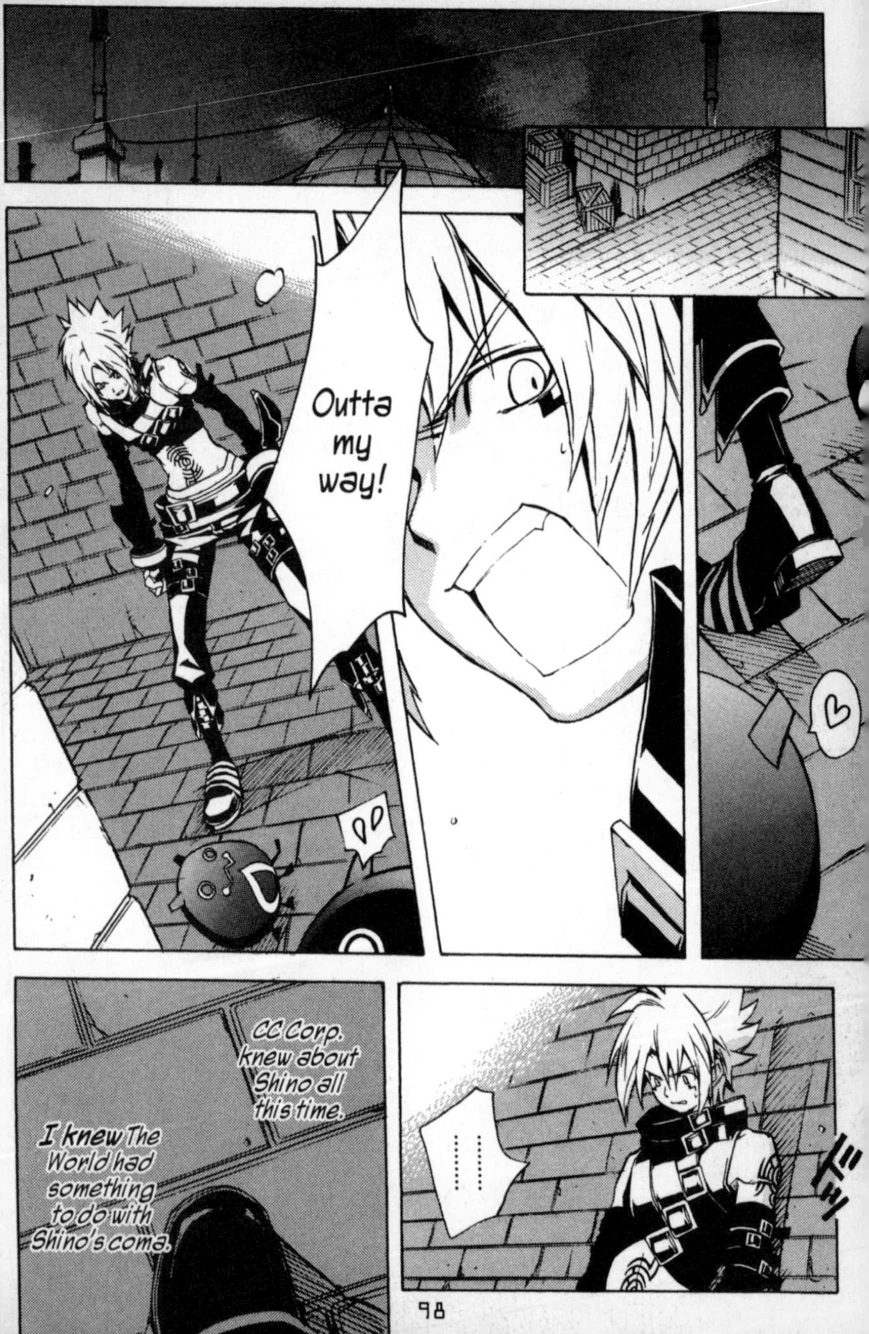
Outta my way!
......
CC Corp. knew about Shino all this time.
I knew The World had something to do with Shino's coma.

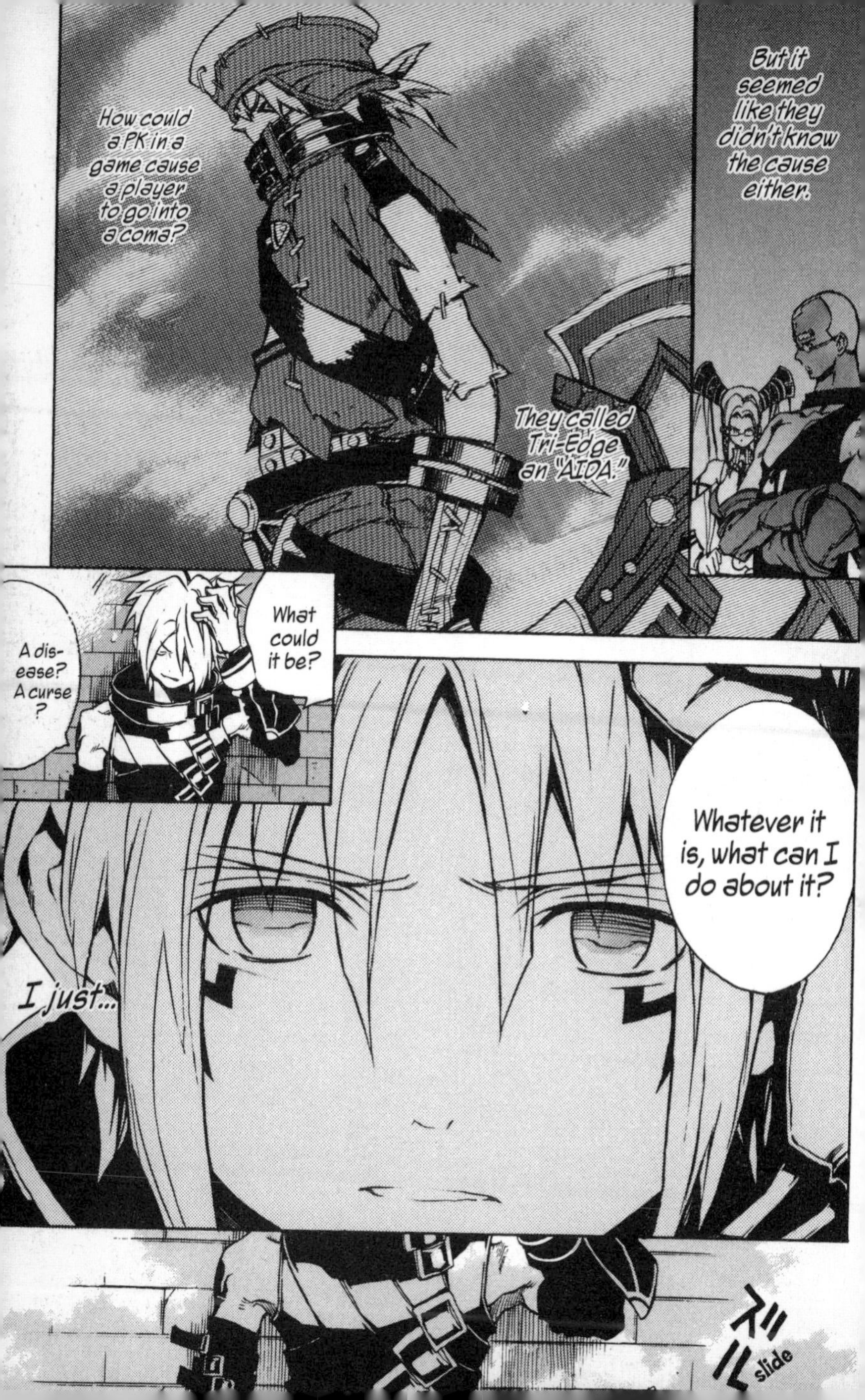

But it seemed like they didn't know the cause either.
How could a PK in a game cause a player to go into a coma?
They called Tri-Edge an "AIDA."
What could it be?
A dis-ease? A curse ?
Whatever it is, what can I do about it?
I just...
slide

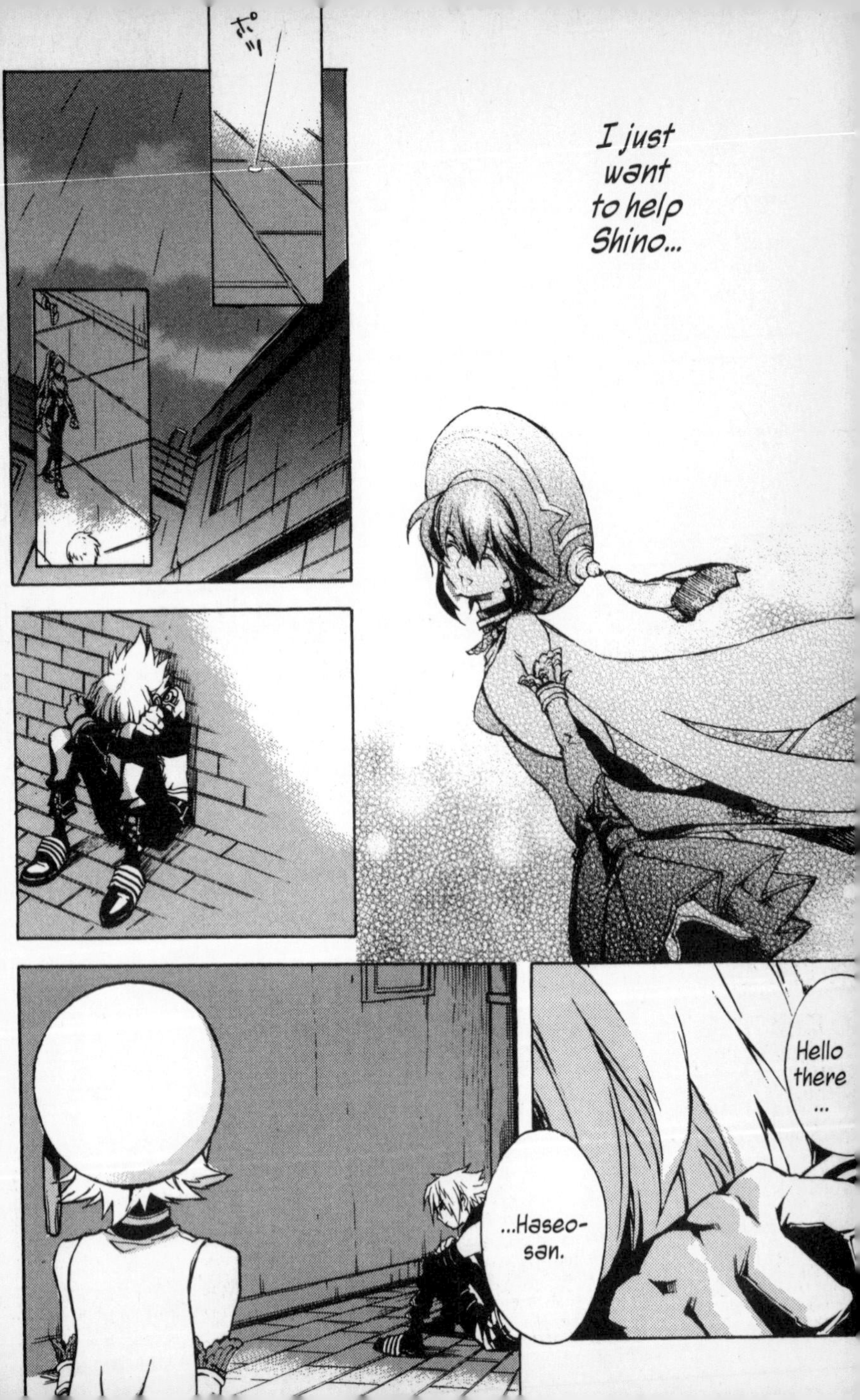
I just want to help Shino...
ポツ
Hello there ...
...Haseo-san.

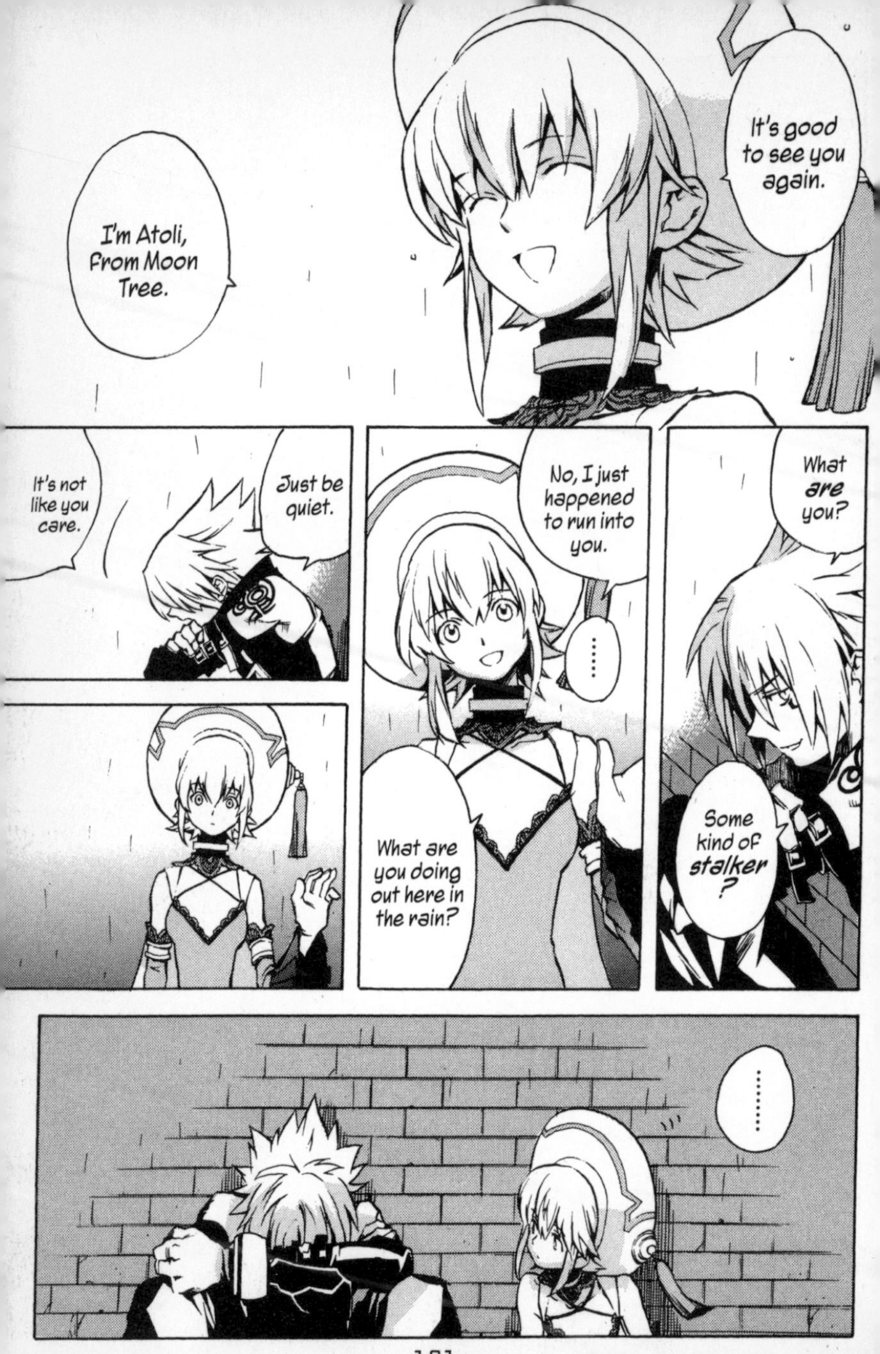
It's good to see you again.
I'm Atoli, from Moon Tree.
What *are* you?
Some kind of **stalker**?
No, I just happened to run into you.
......
What are you doing out here in the rain?
Just be quiet.
It's not like you care.
....

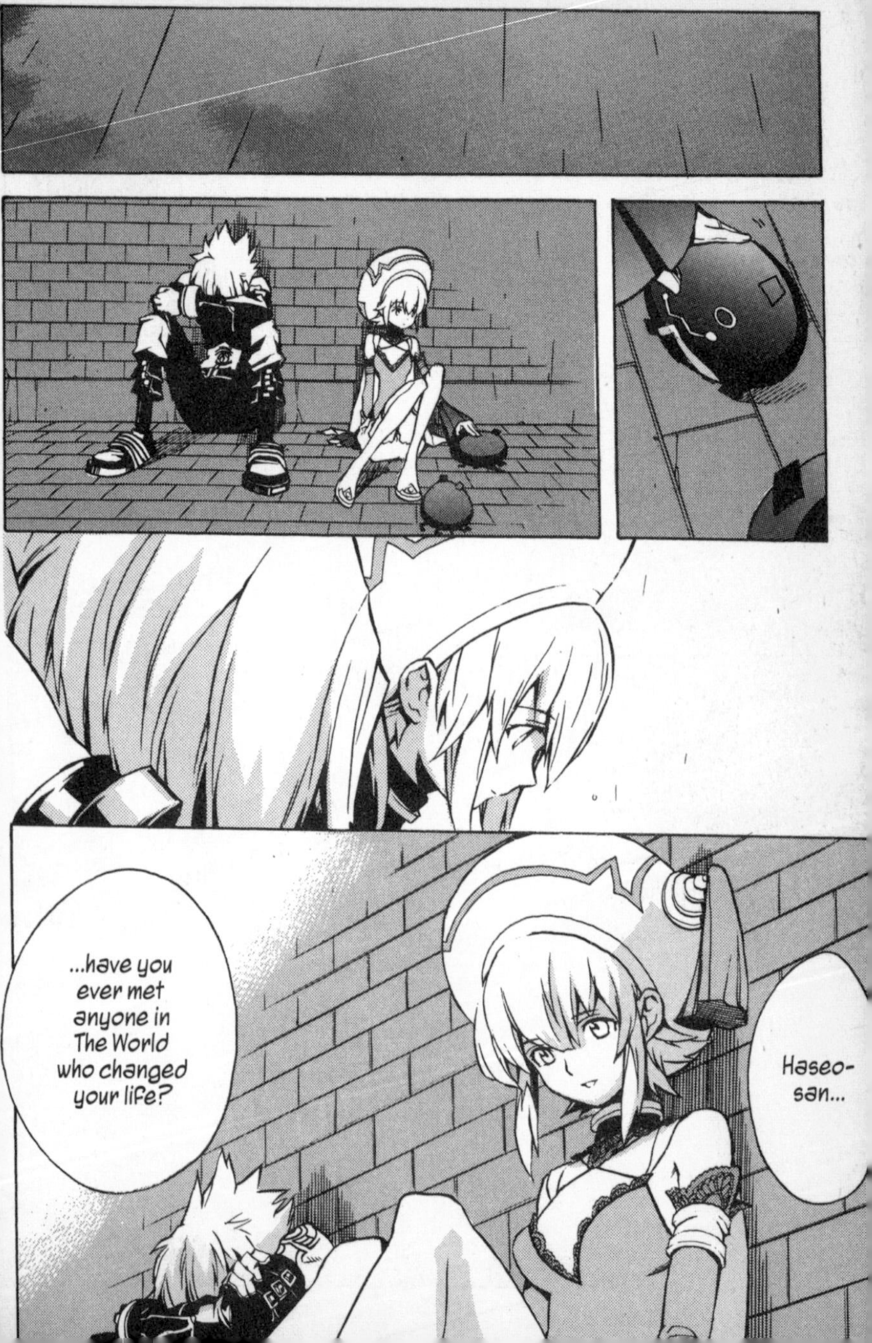
Haseo-san...
...have you ever met anyone in The World who changed your life?

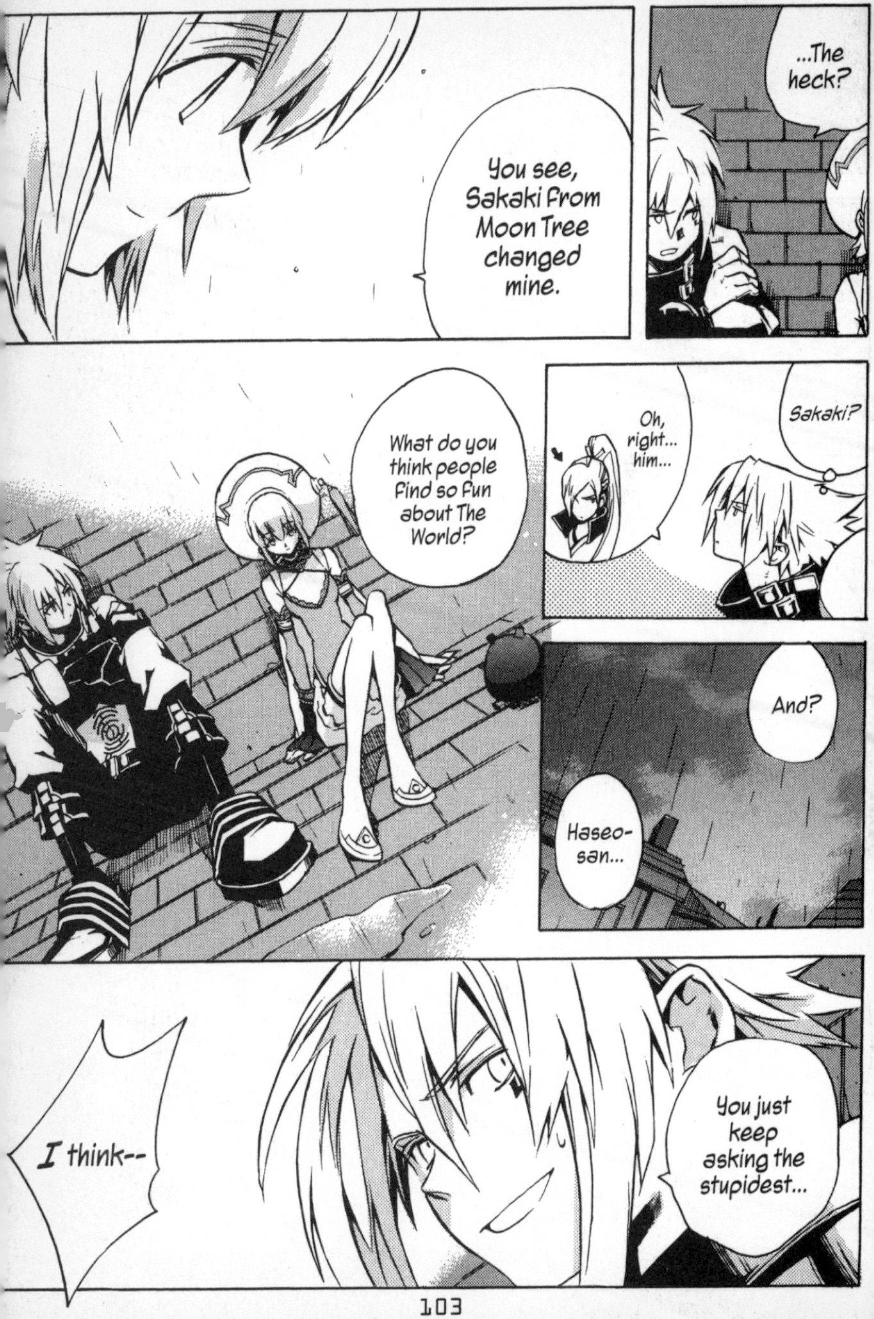
...The heck?
You see, Sakaki from Moon Tree changed mine.
Sakaki?
Oh, right... him...
And?
Haseo-san...
What do you think people find so fun about The World?
You just keep asking the stupidest...
I think--

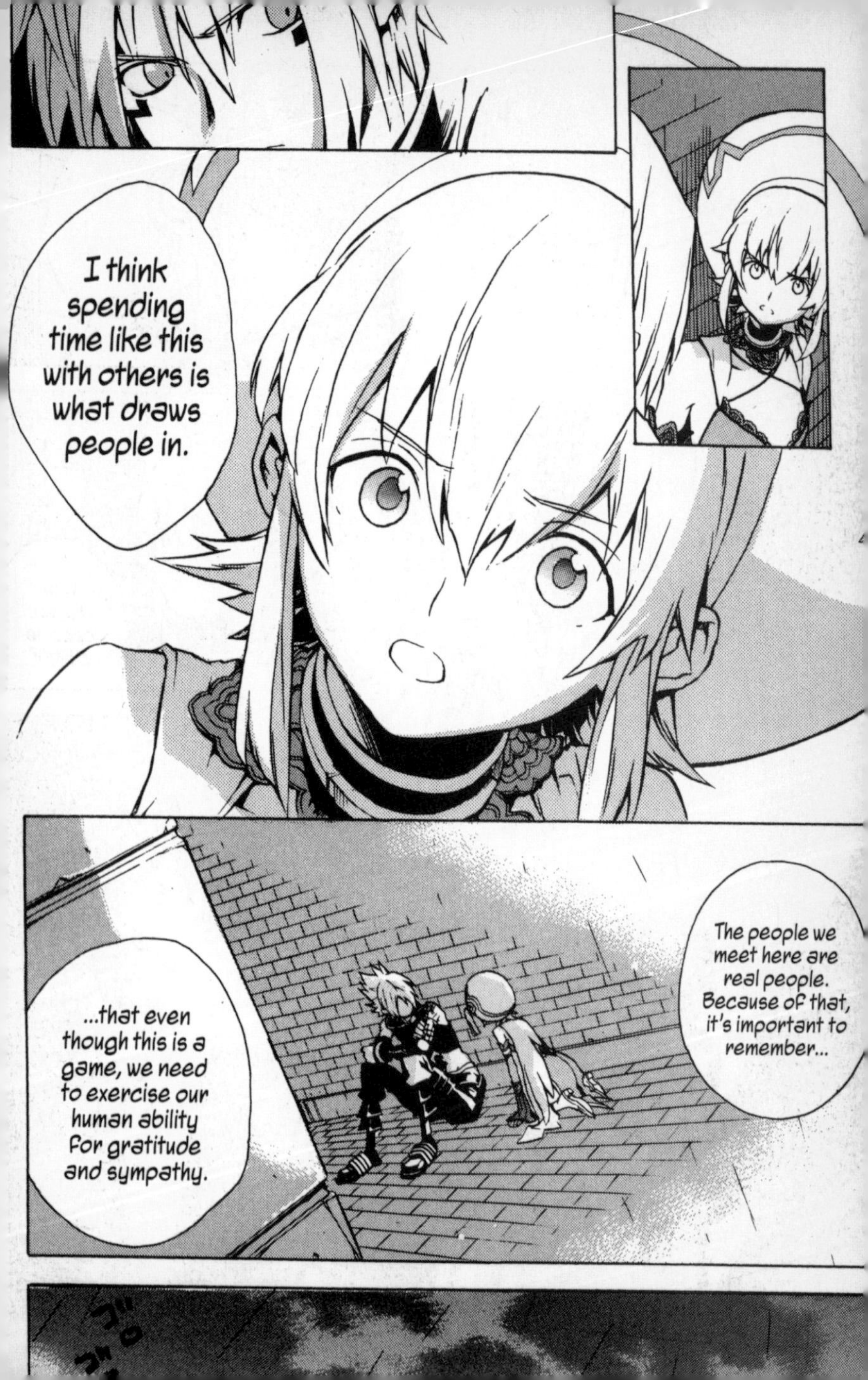
I think spending time like this with others is what draws people in.
The people we meet here are real people. Because of that, it's important to remember...
...that even though this is a game, we need to exercise our human ability for gratitude and sympathy.

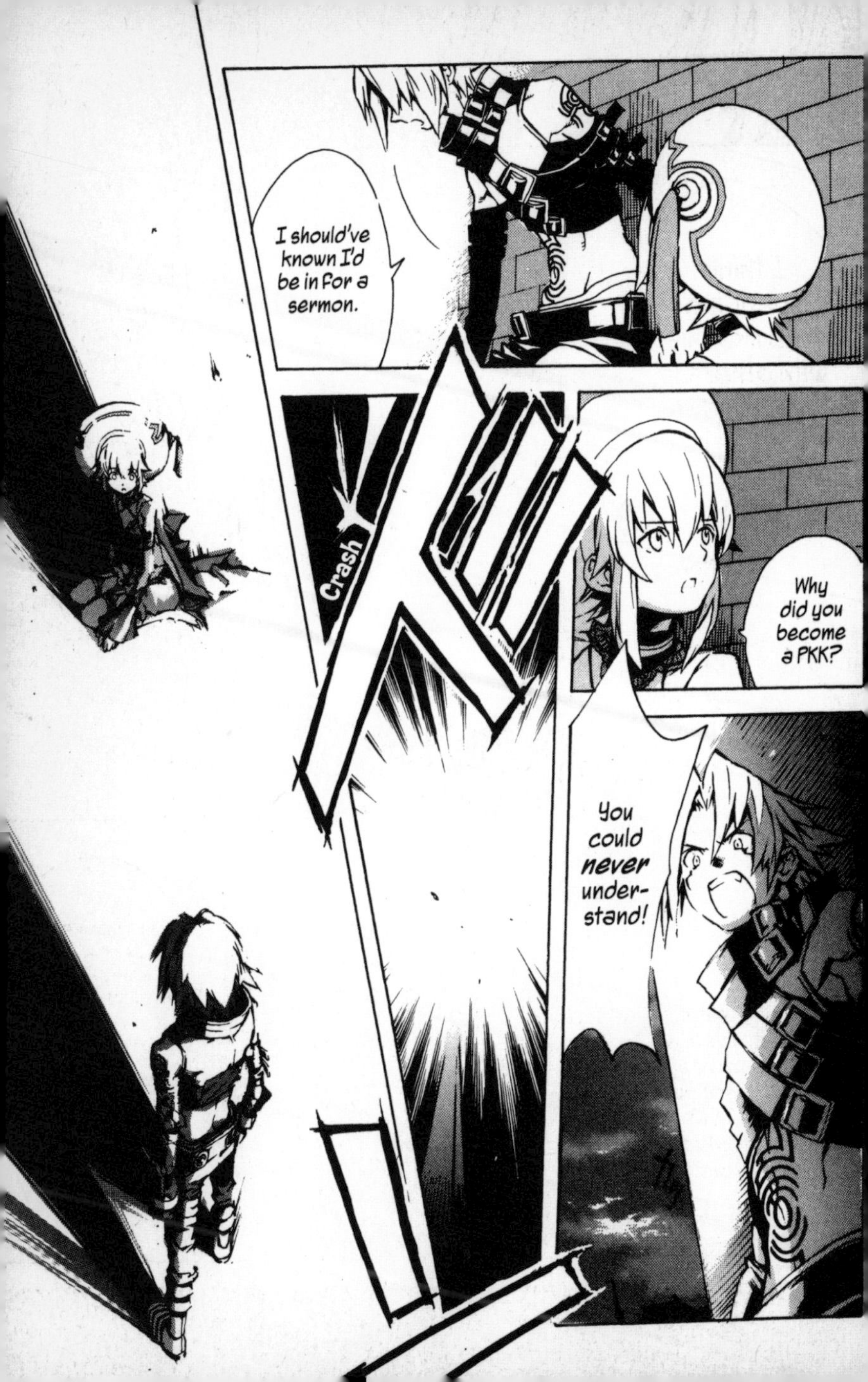
I should've known I'd be in for a sermon.
Why did you become a PKK?
Crash
You could never under-stand!

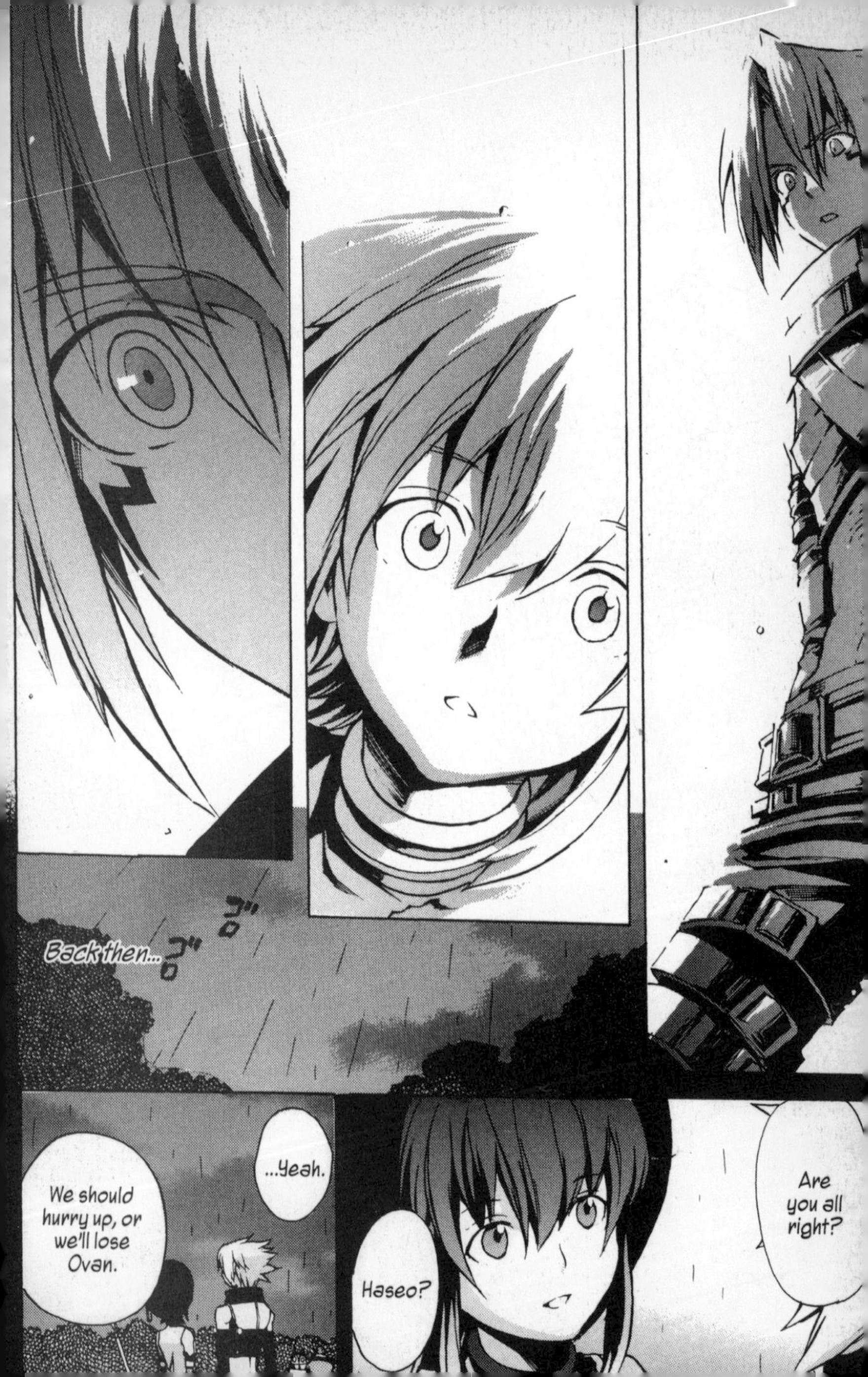
ゴゴ
Back then...
Are you all right?
Haseo?
...Yeah.
We should hurry up, or we'll lose Ovan.

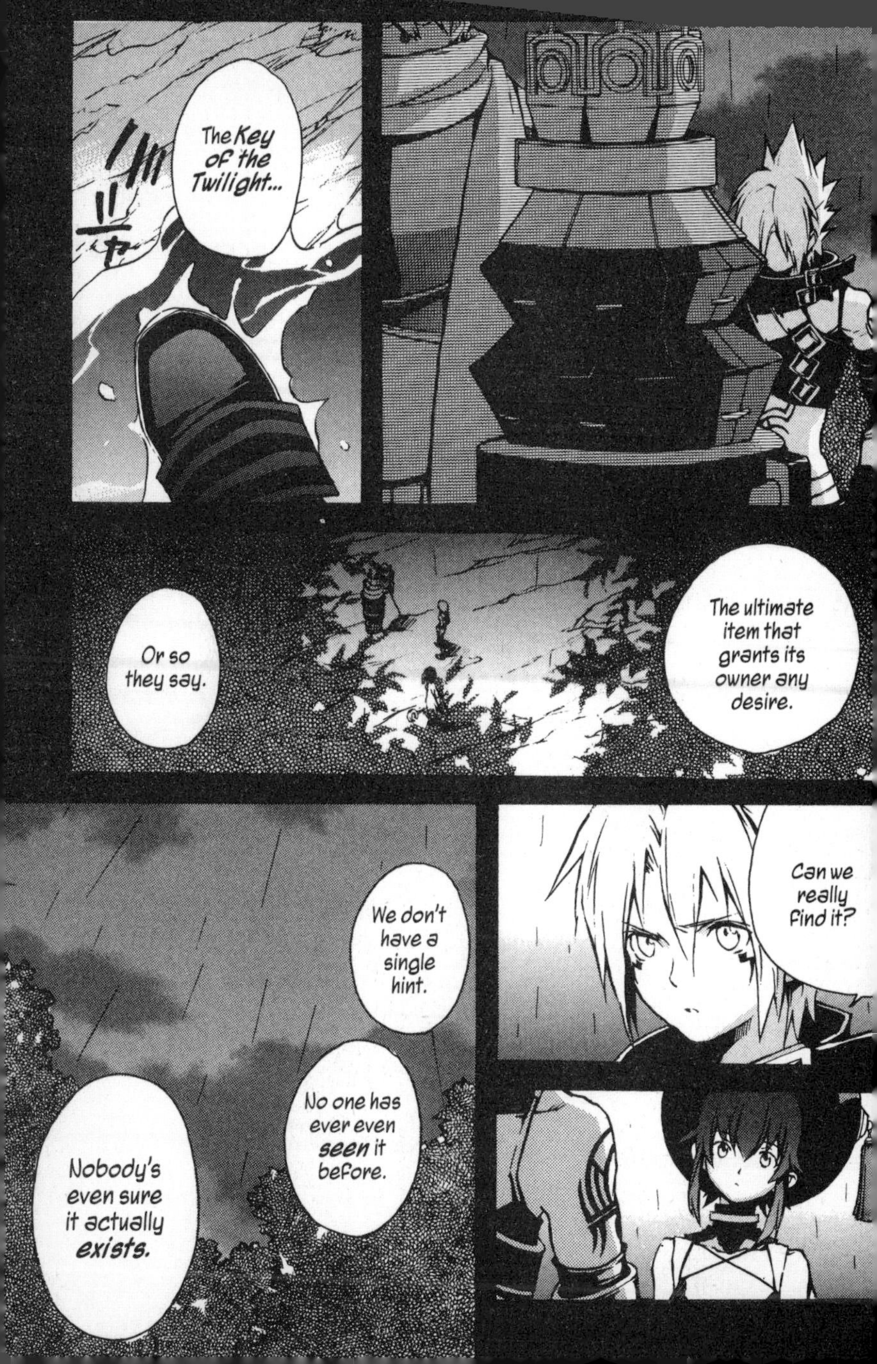
The Key of the Twilight...
The ultimate item that grants its owner any desire.
Or so they say.
Can we really find it?
We don't have a single hint.
No one has ever even *seen* it before.
Nobody's even sure it actually *exists.*

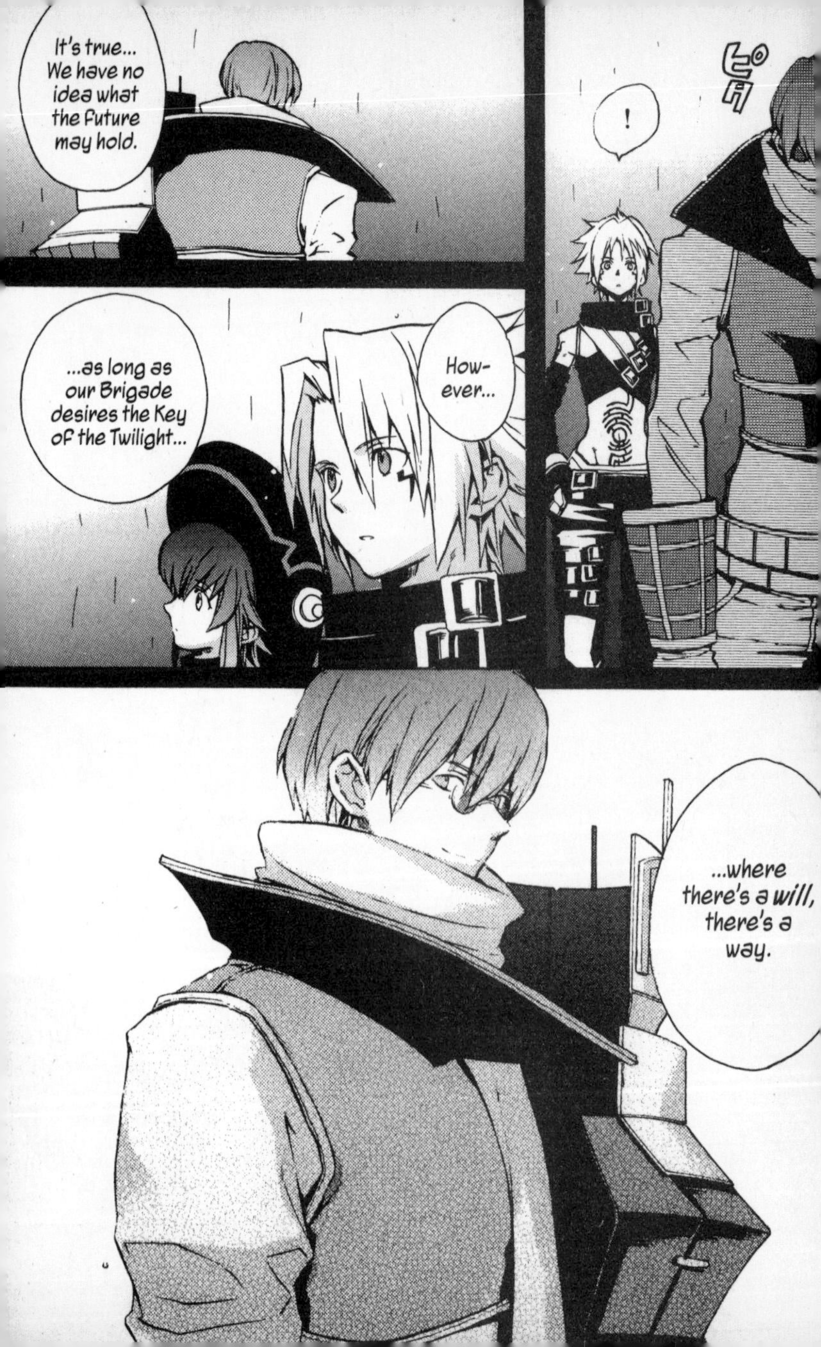

!
ピク
It's true... We have no idea what the future may hold.
How-ever...
...as long as our Brigade desires the Key of the Twilight...
...where there's a *will*, there's a way.

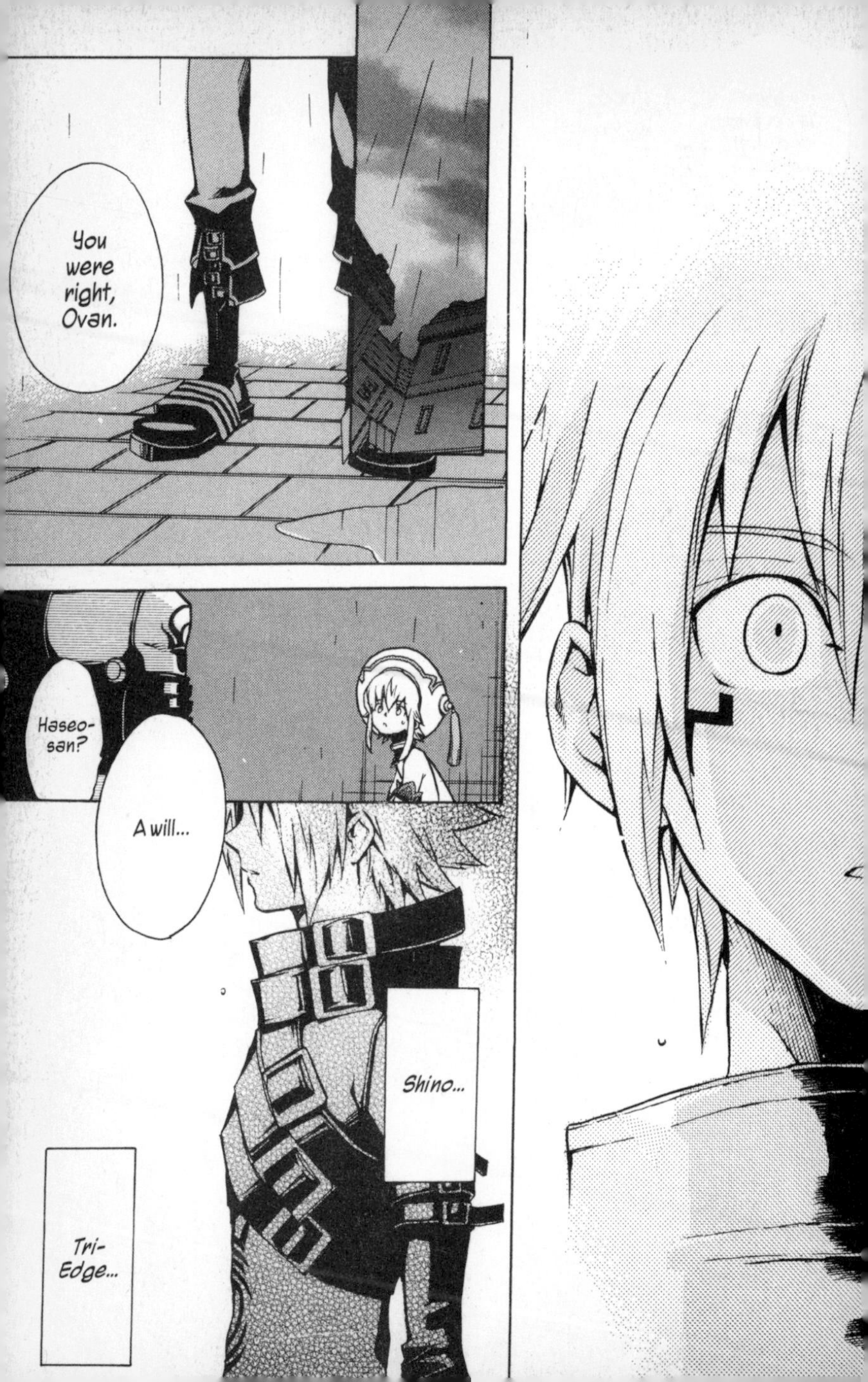
You were right, Ovan.
Haseo-san?
A will...
Shino...
Tri-Edge...

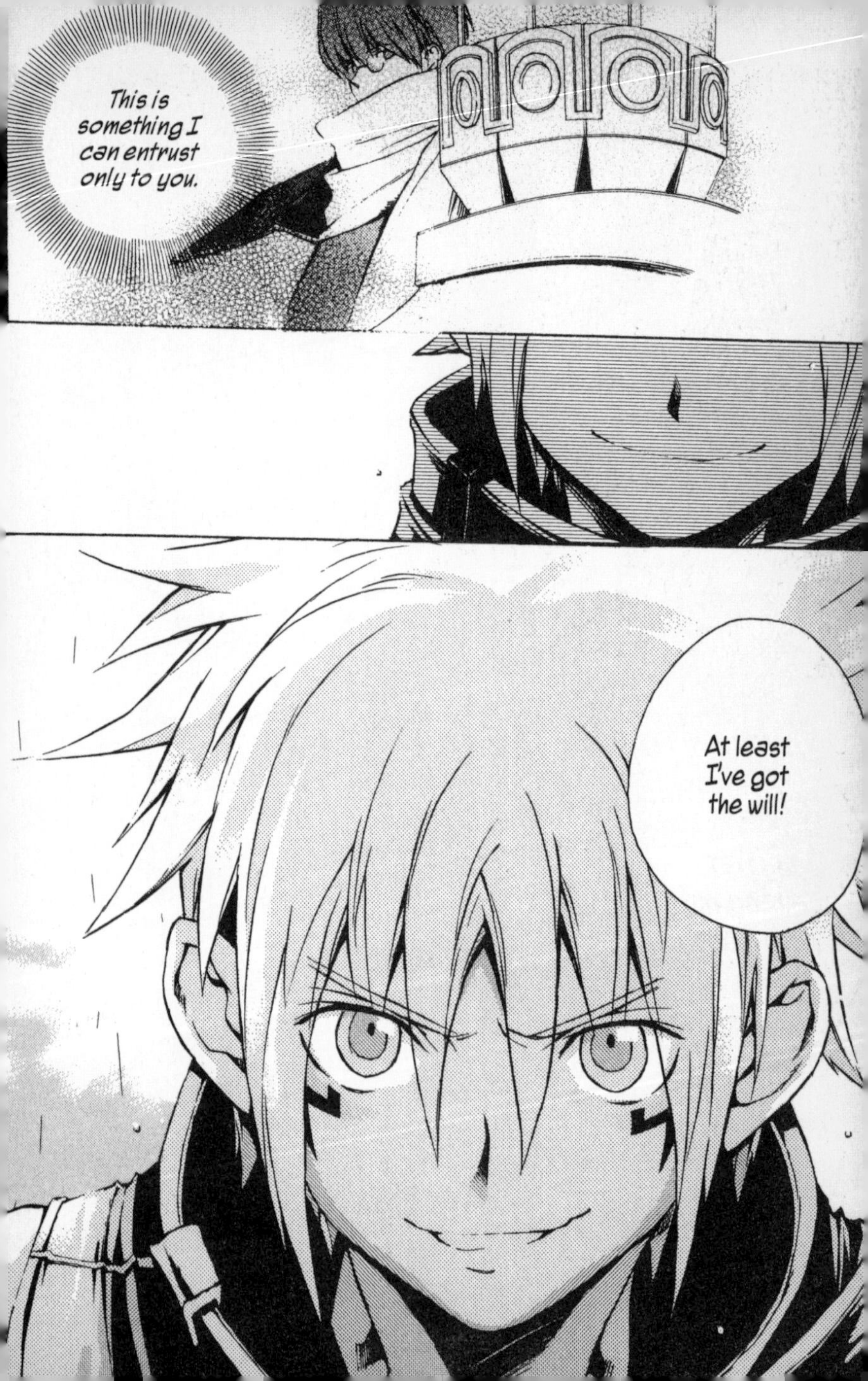
This is something I can entrust only to you.
At least I've got the will!

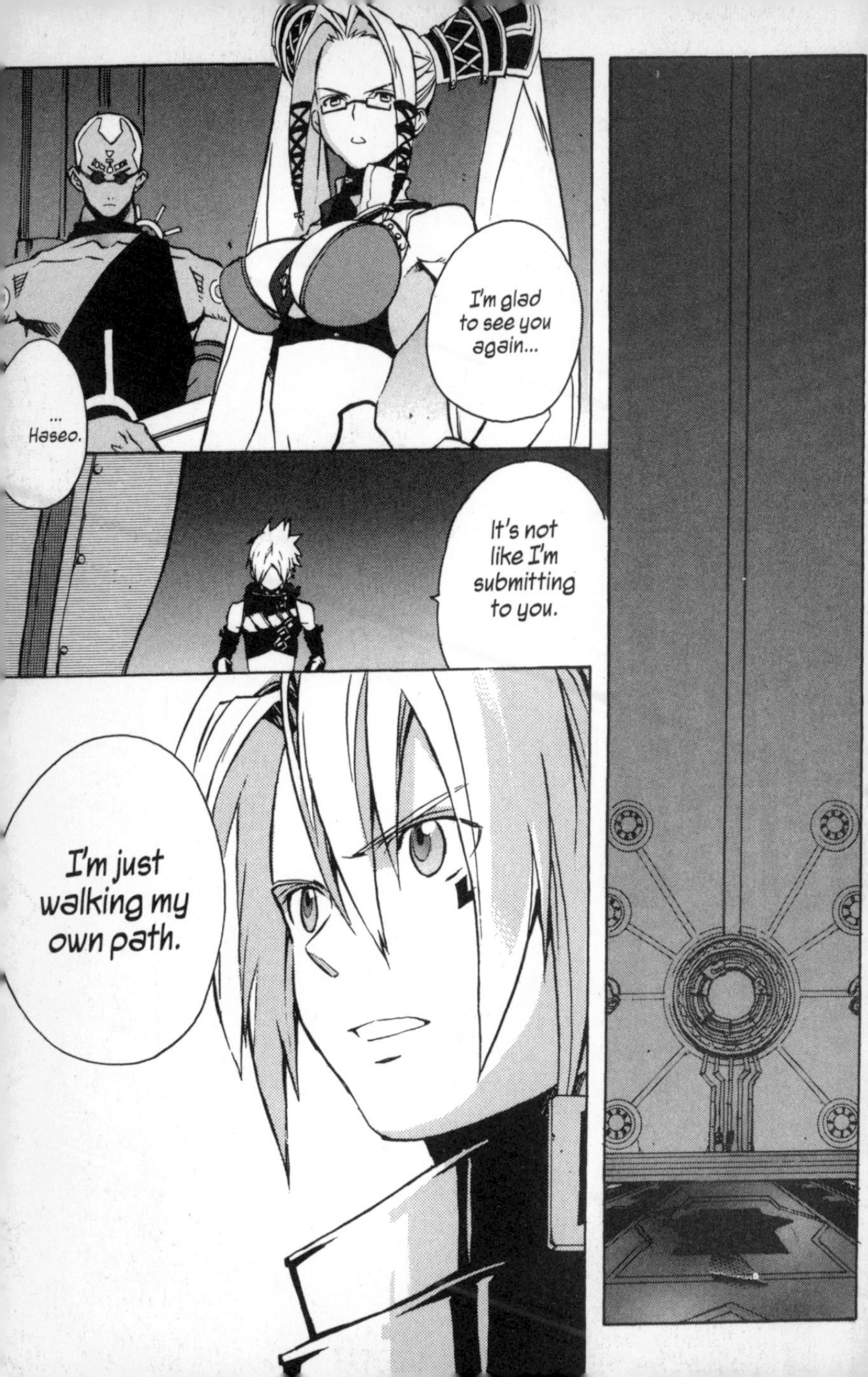
I'm glad to see you again...
... Haseo.
It's not like I'm submitting to you.
I'm just walking my own path.

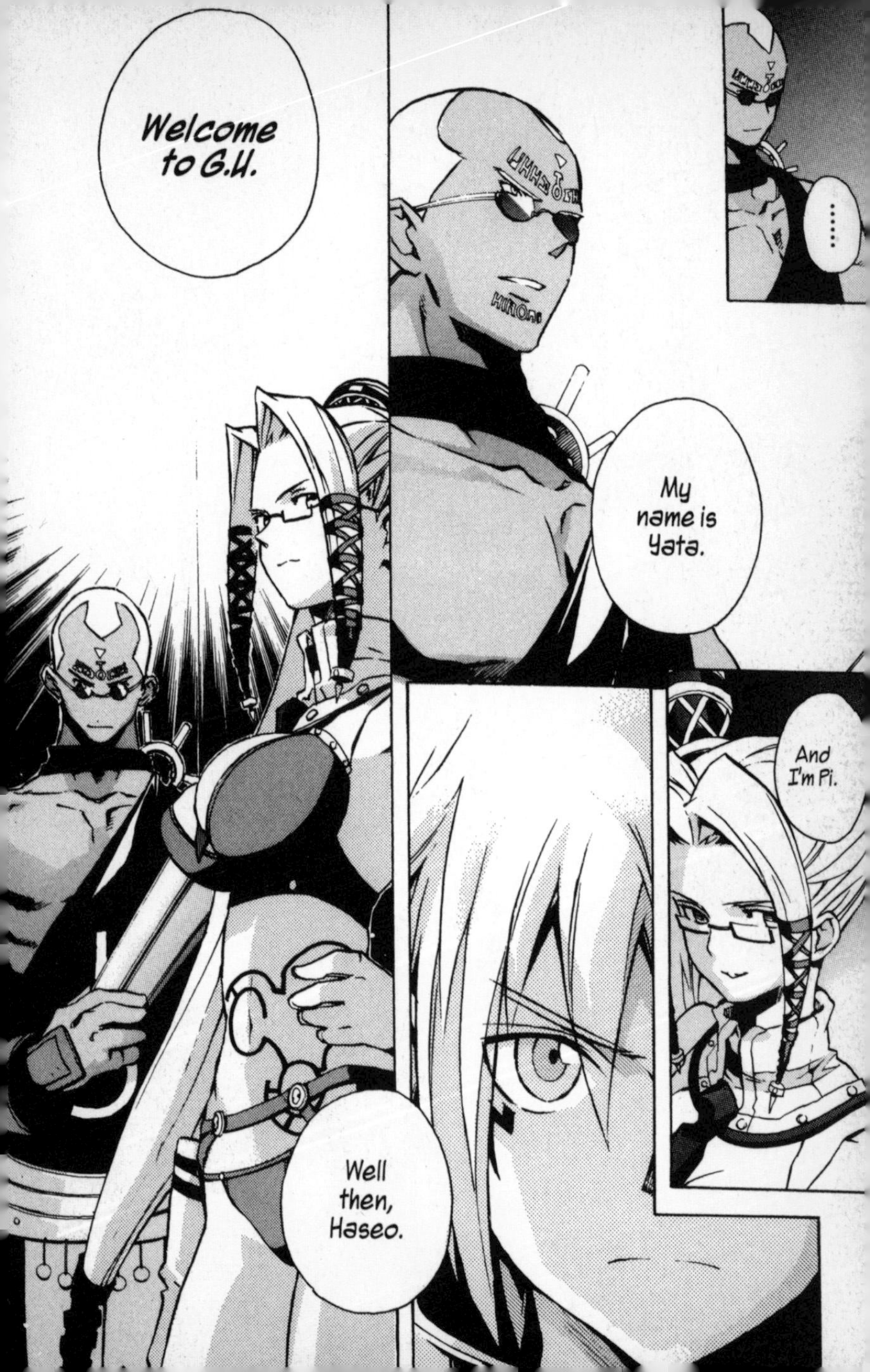
......
Welcome to G.U.
My name is Yata.
And I'm Pi.
Well then, Haseo.

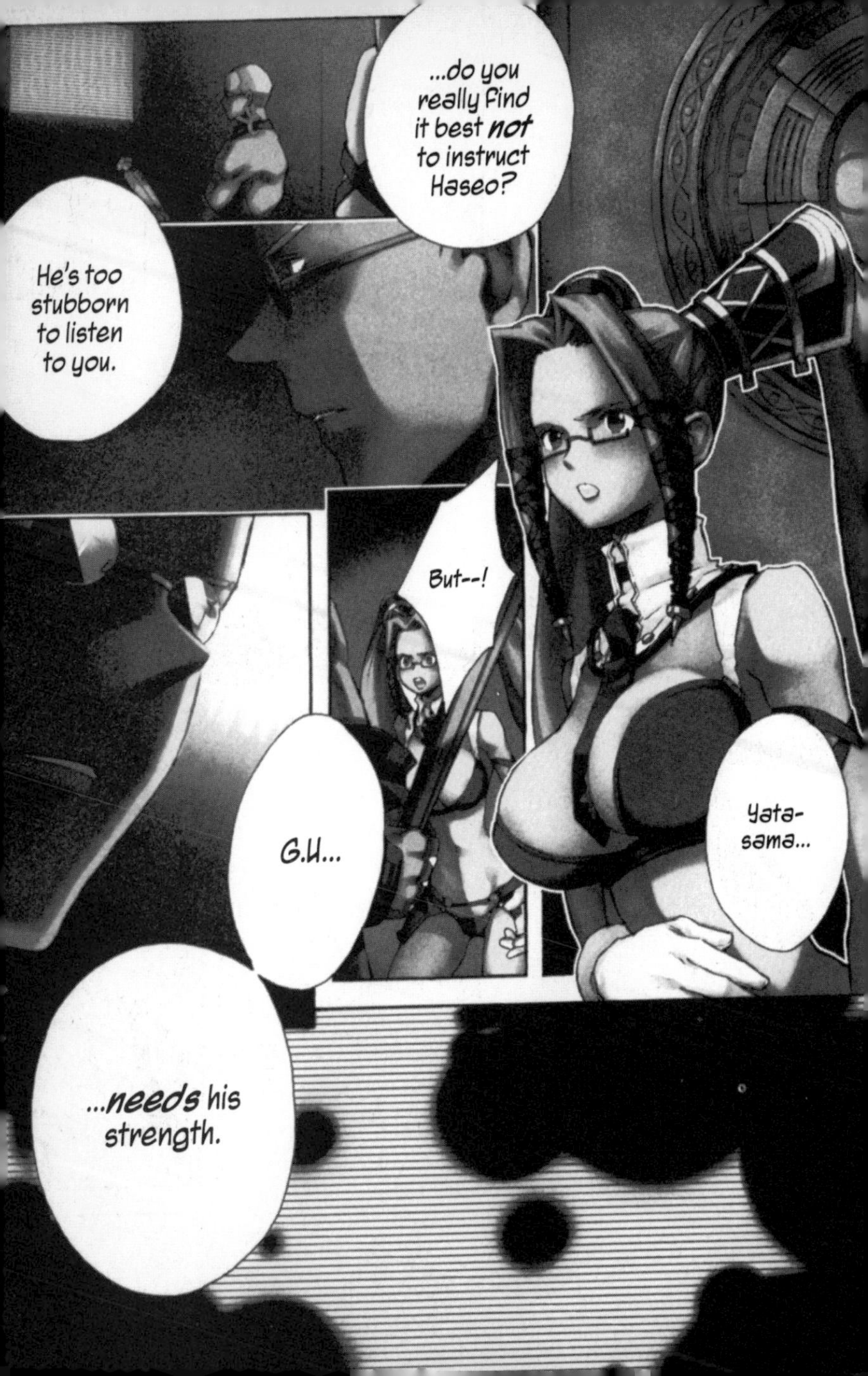
...do you really find it best *not* to instruct Haseo?
He's too stubborn to listen to you.
But--!
Yata-sama...
G.U...
...*needs* his strength.

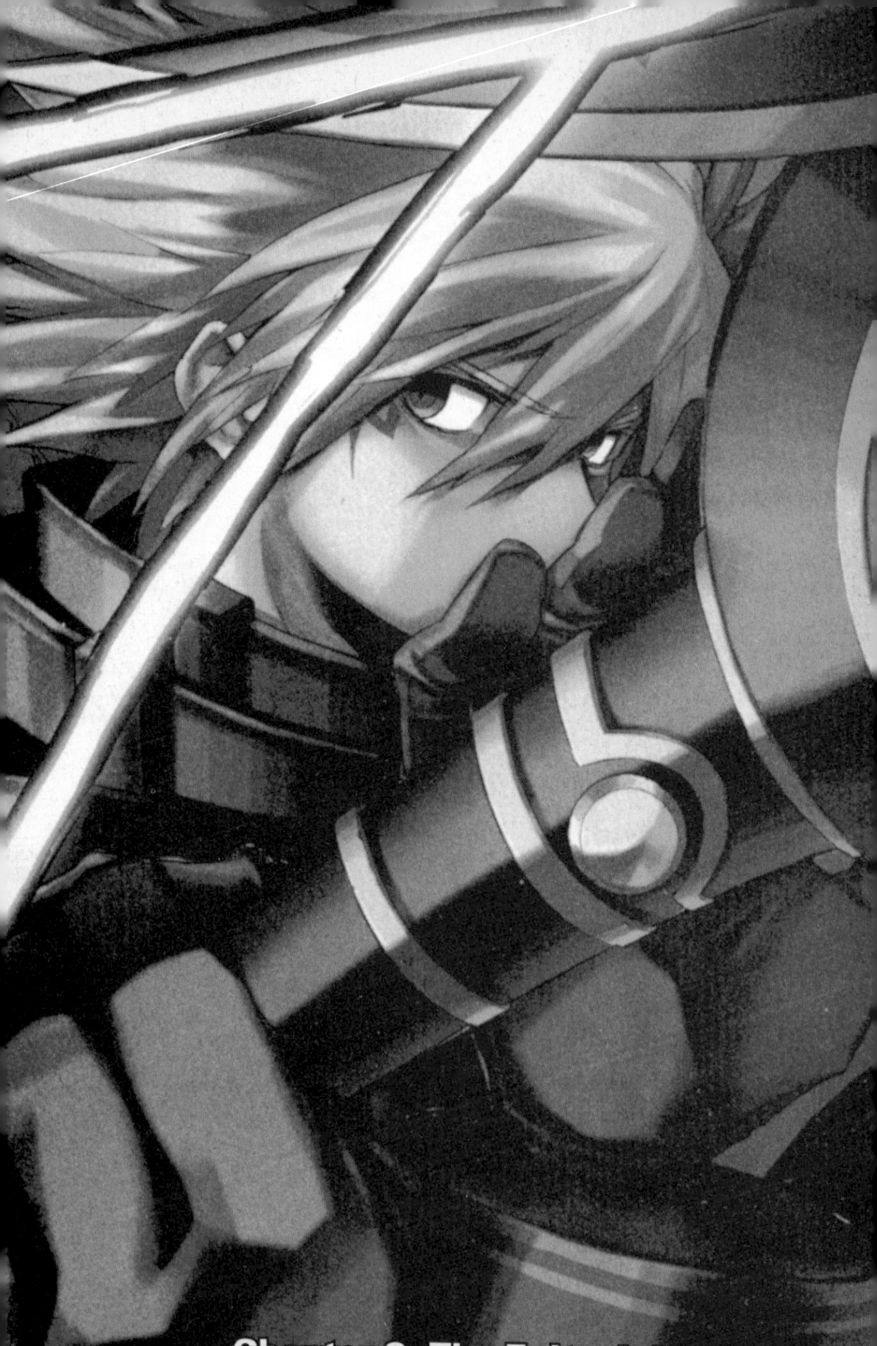

Chapter 3: The Epitaph Users

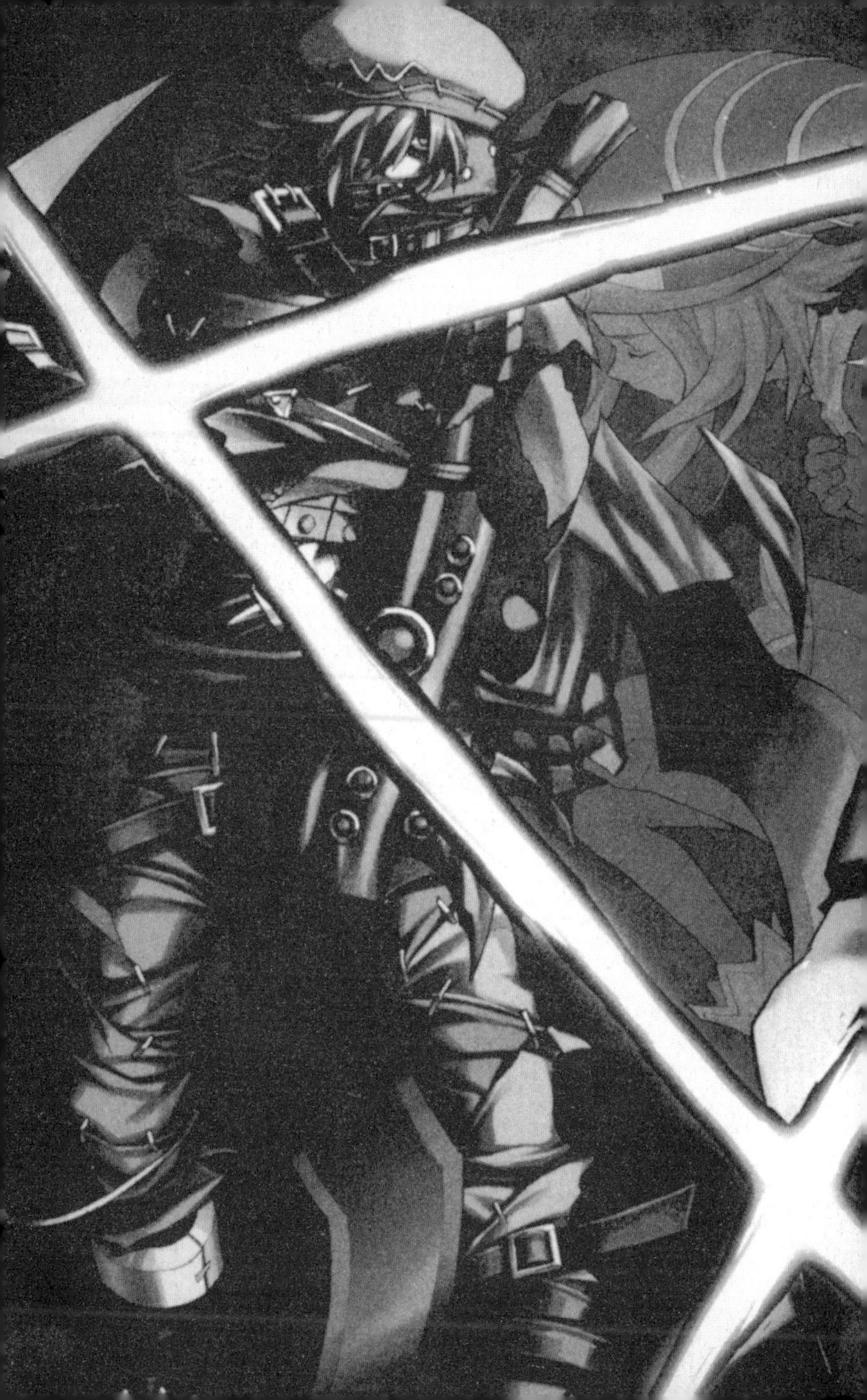

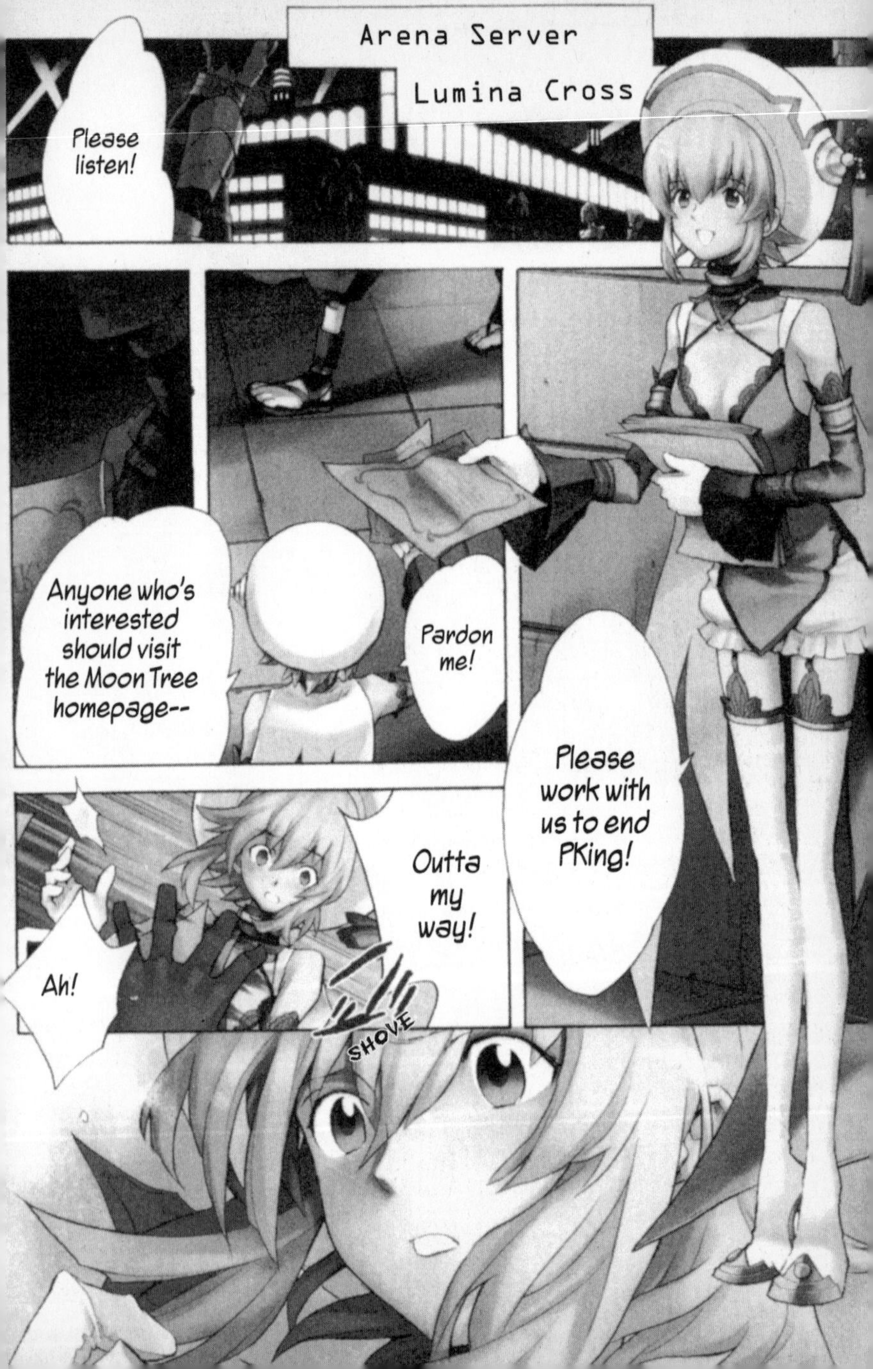
Arena Server
Lumina Cross
Please listen!
Please work with us to end PKing!
Anyone who's interested should visit the Moon Tree homepage--
Pardon me!
Outta my way!
SHOVE
Ah!

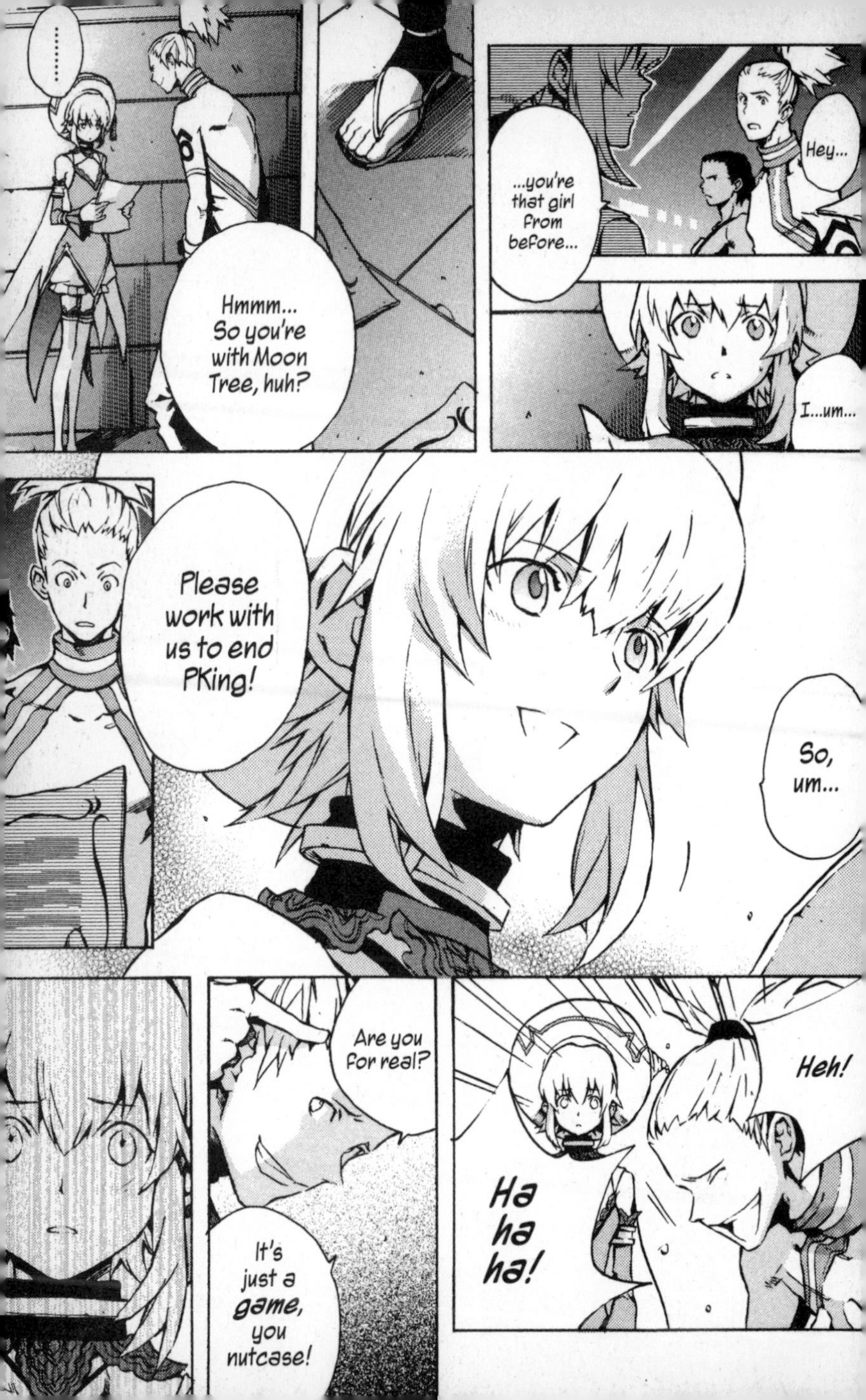
Hey...
...you're that girl from before...
I...um...
......
Hmmm... So you're with Moon Tree, huh?
So, um...
Please work with us to end PKing!
Heh!
Ha ha ha!
Are you for real?
It's just a *game*, you nutcase!

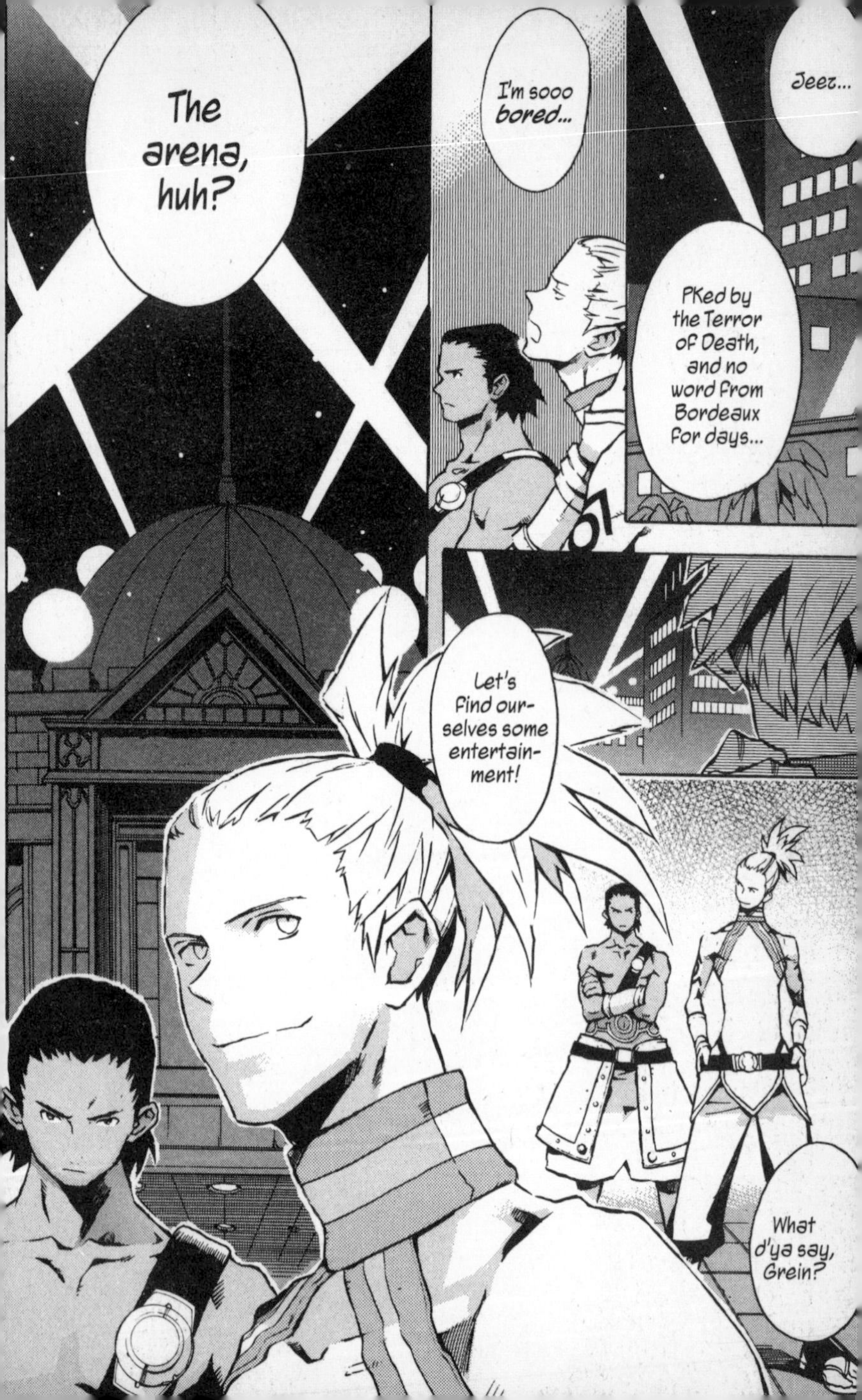
Jeez...
PKed by the Terror of Death, and no word from Bordeaux for days...
I'm sooo bored...
Let's find our-selves some entertain-ment!
What d'ya say, Grein?
The arena, huh?

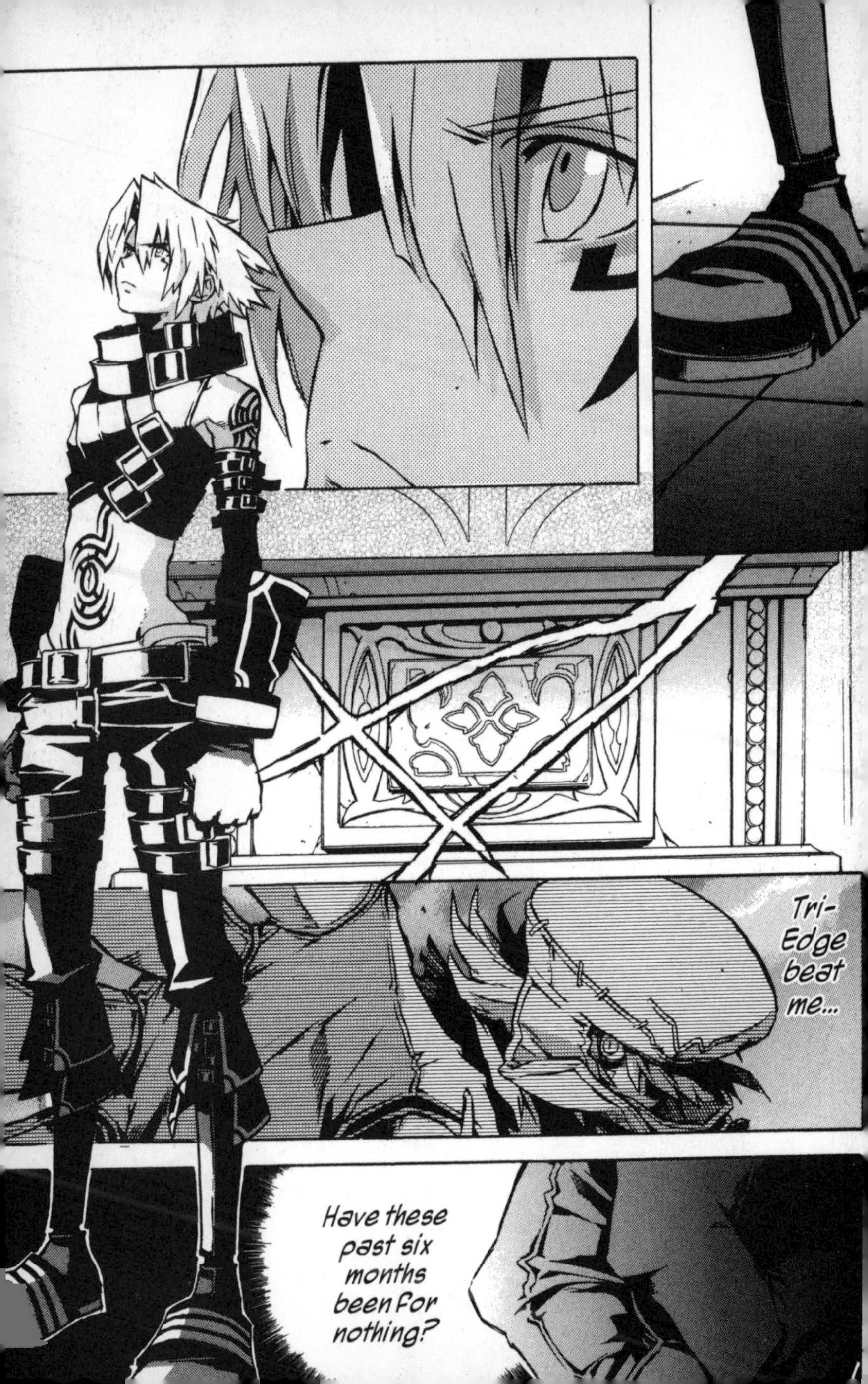
Tri-Edge beat me...
Have these past six months been for nothing?

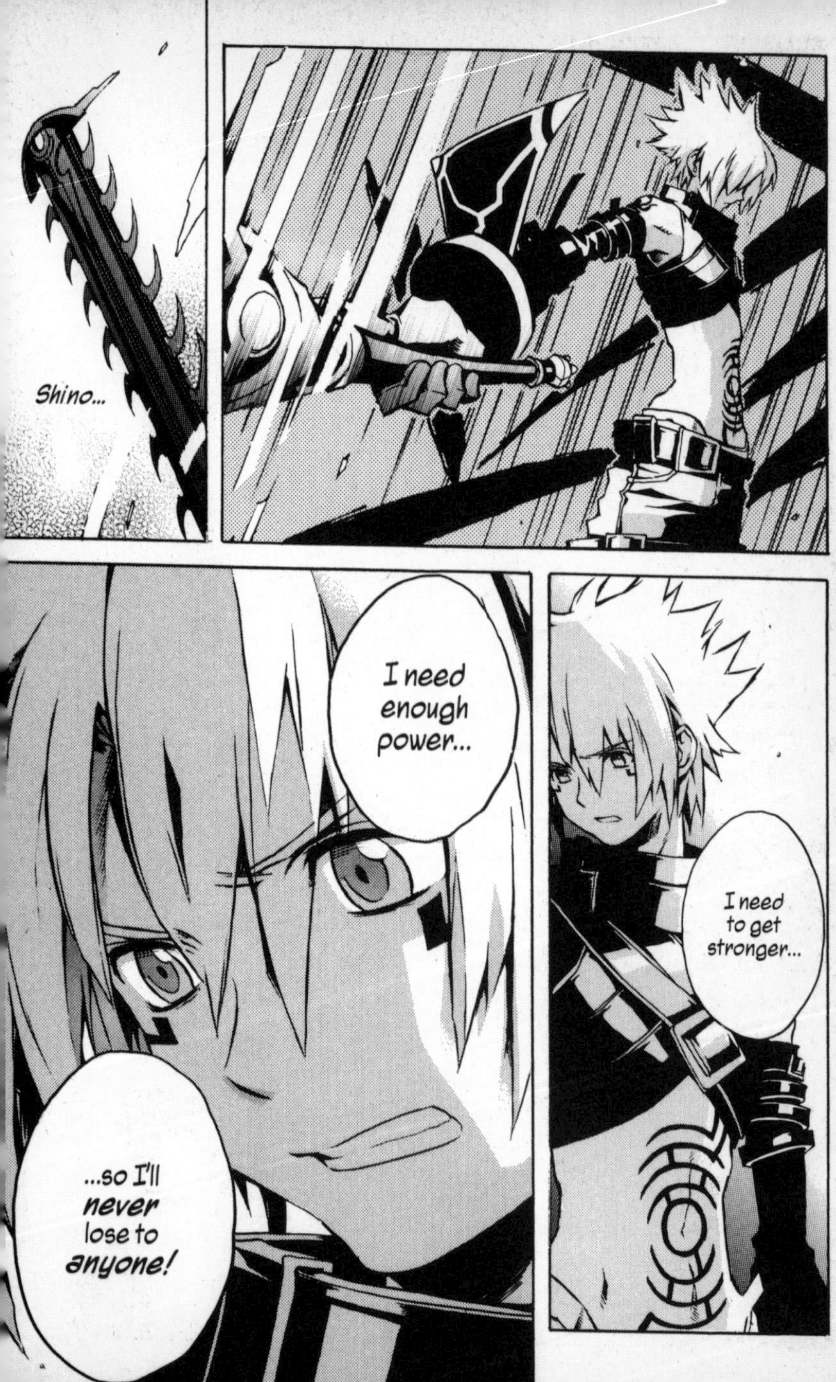
Shino...
I need to get stronger...
I need enough power...
...so I'll **never** lose to **anyone!**

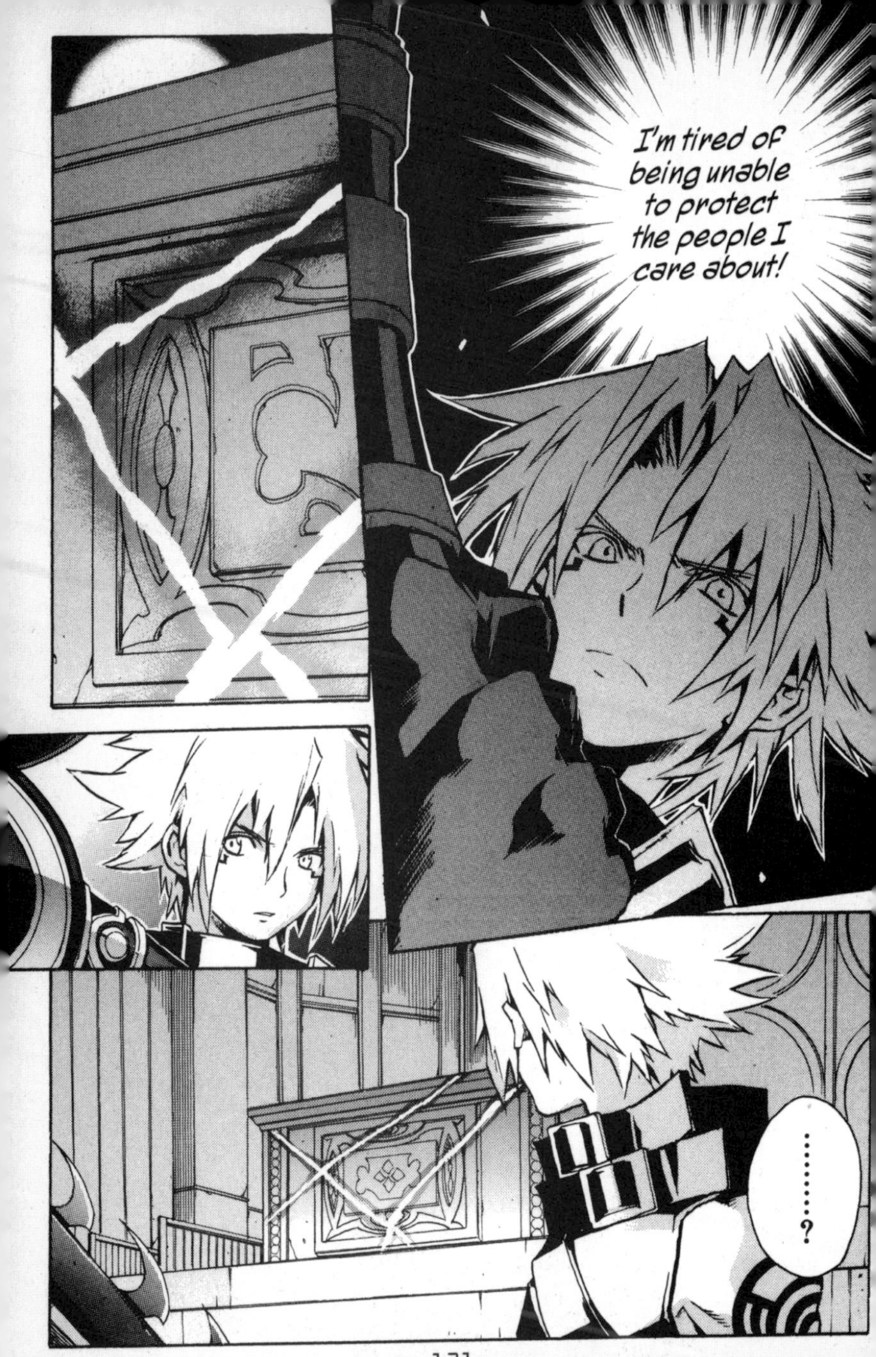
I'm tired of being unable to protect the people I care about!
.........?

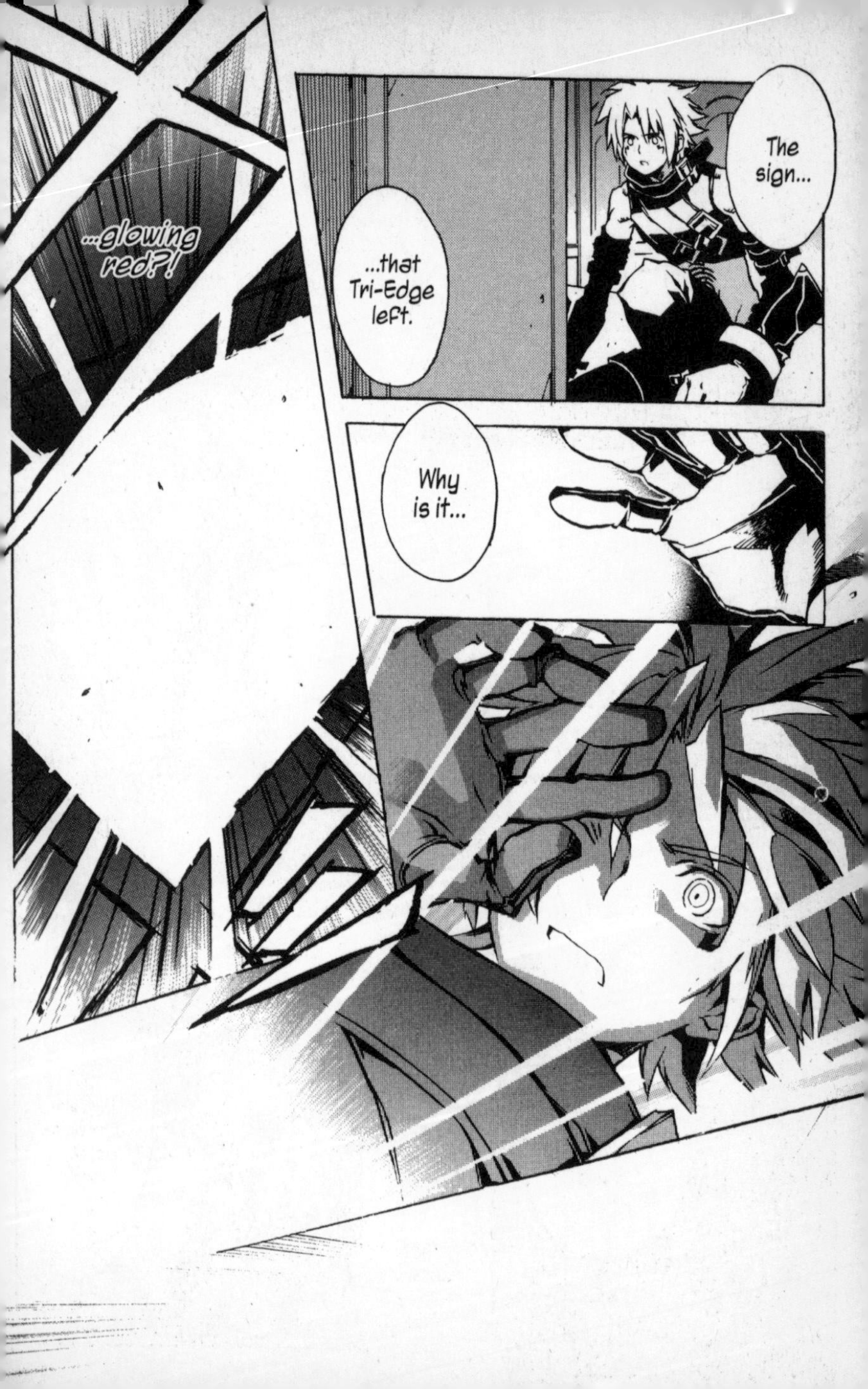
The sign...
...that Tri-Edge left.
Why is it...
...glowing red?!

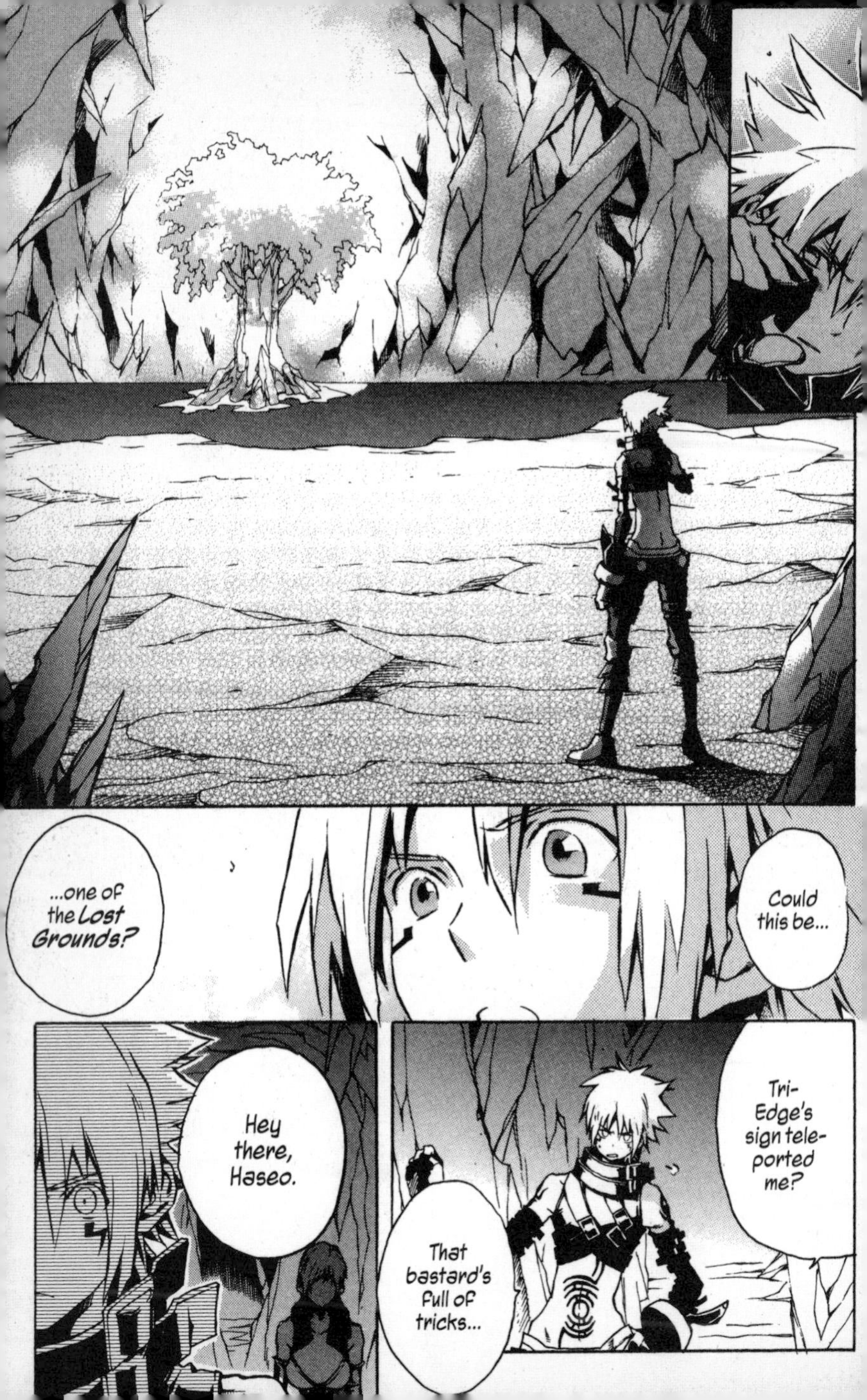
Could this be...
...one of the *Lost Grounds?*
Tri-Edge's sign teleported me?
That bastard's full of tricks...
Hey there, Haseo.

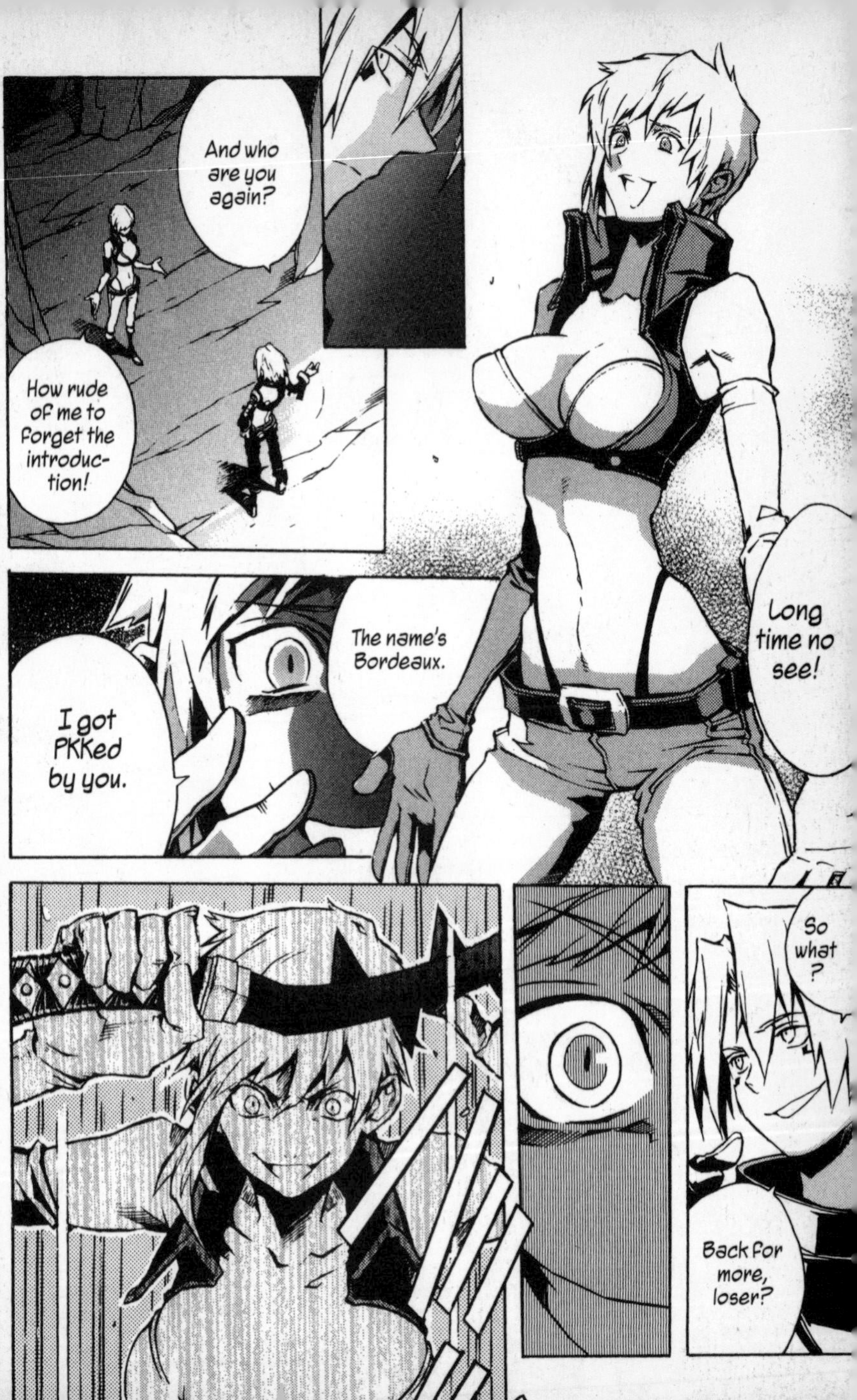
Long time no see!
And who are you again?
How rude of me to forget the introduction!
The name's Bordeaux.
I got PKKed by you.
So what?
Back for more, loser?

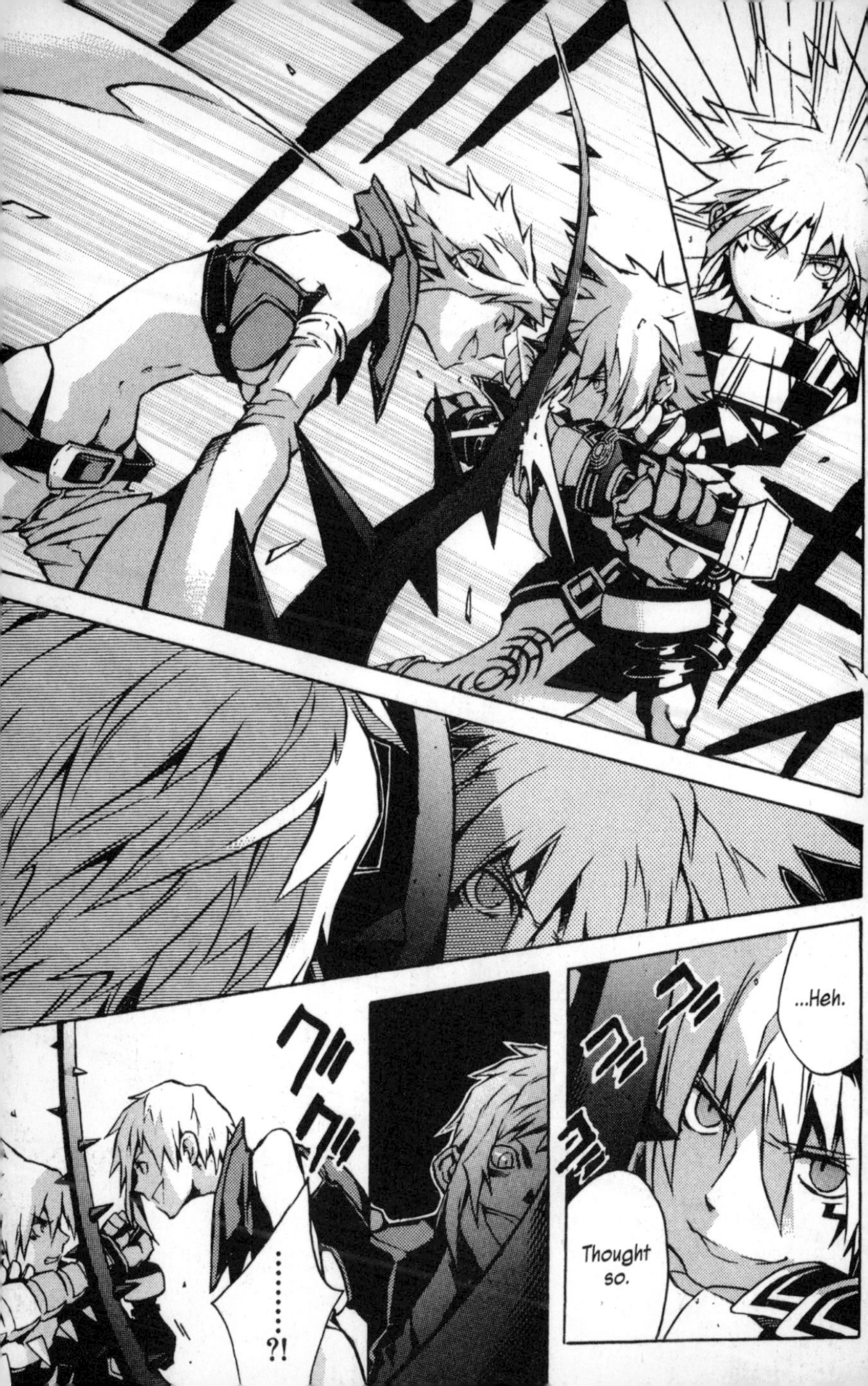
...Heh.
Thought so.
......?!

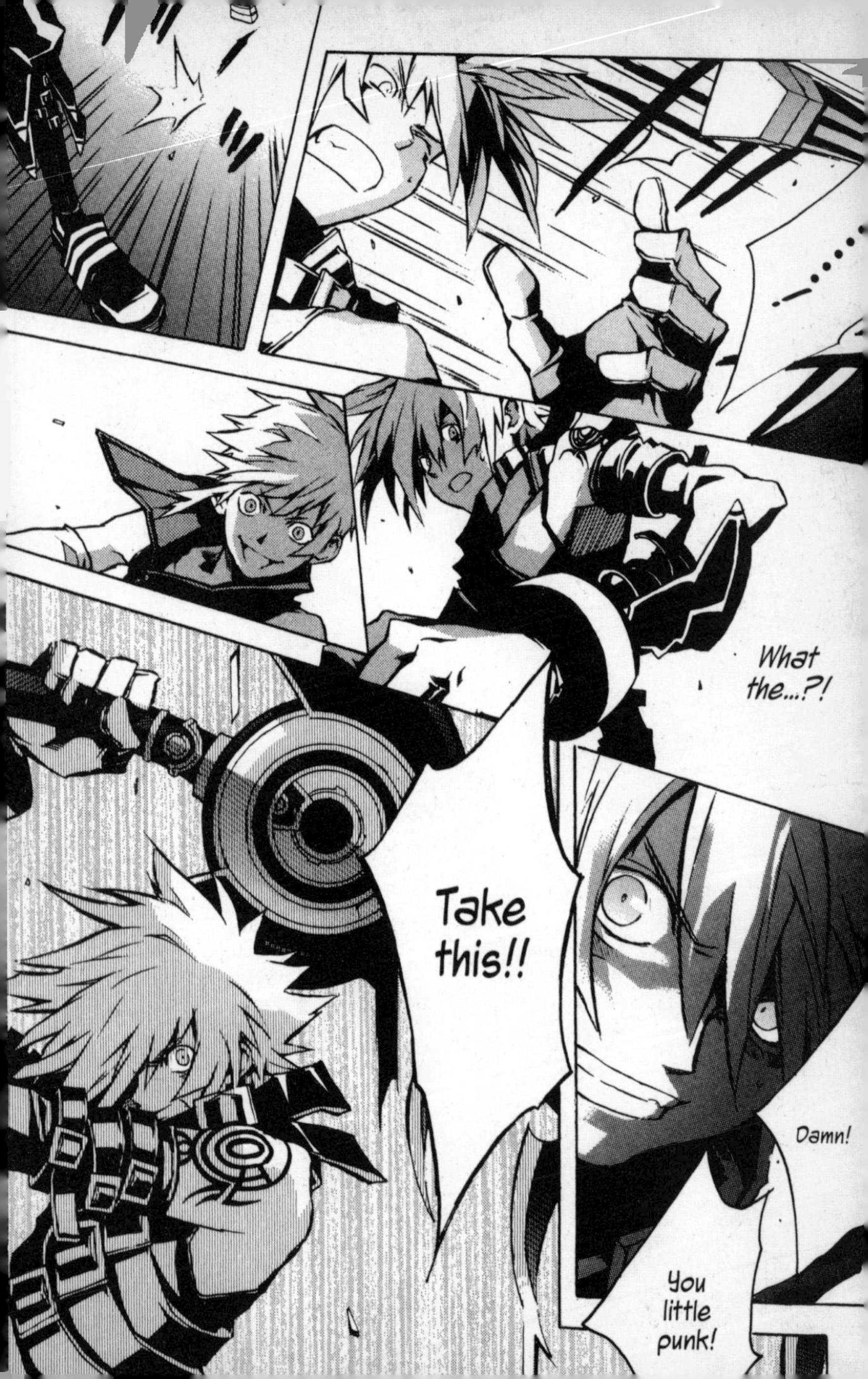
What the...?!
Damn!
You little punk!
Take this!!

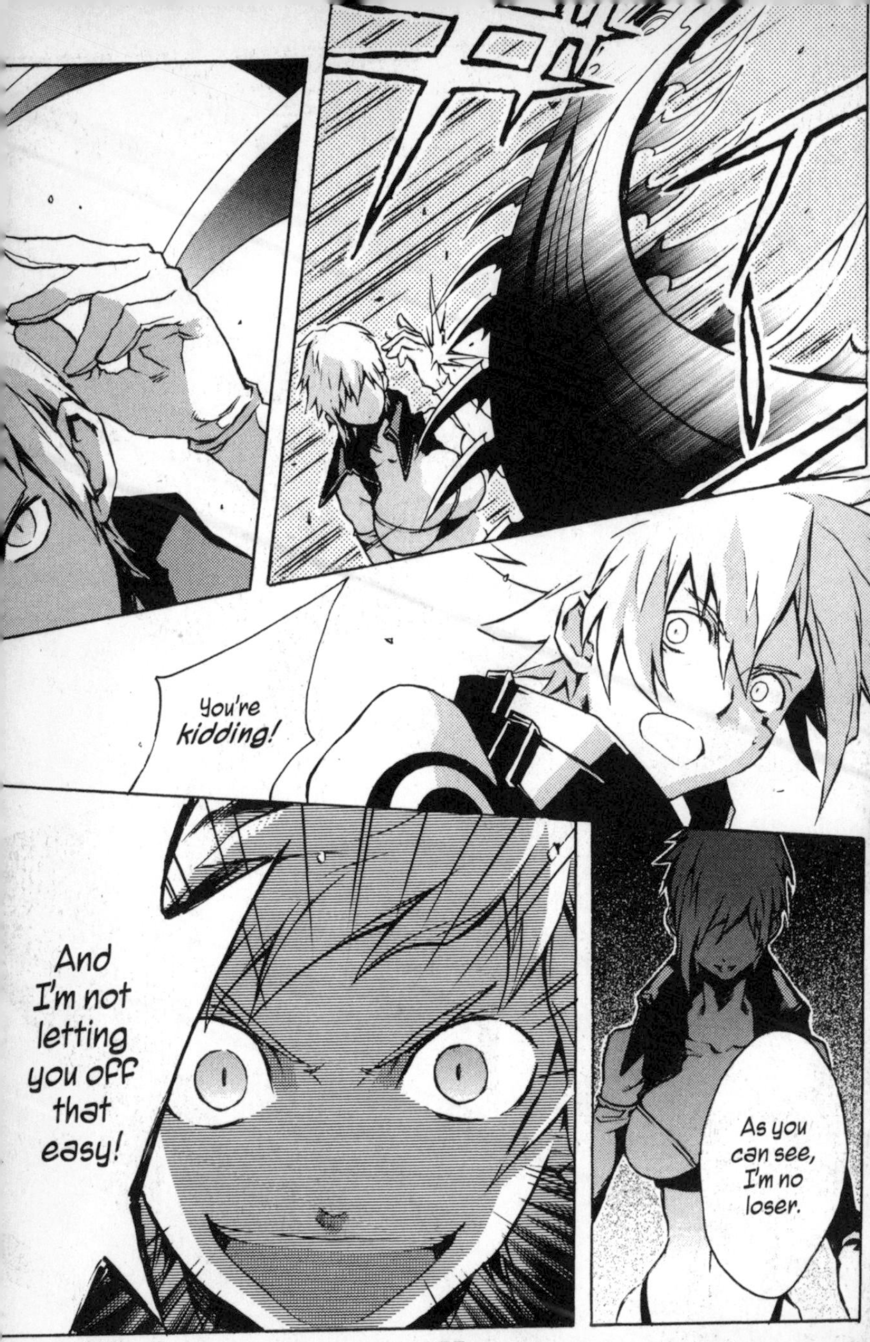
You're kidding!
As you can see, I'm no loser.
And I'm not letting you off that easy!

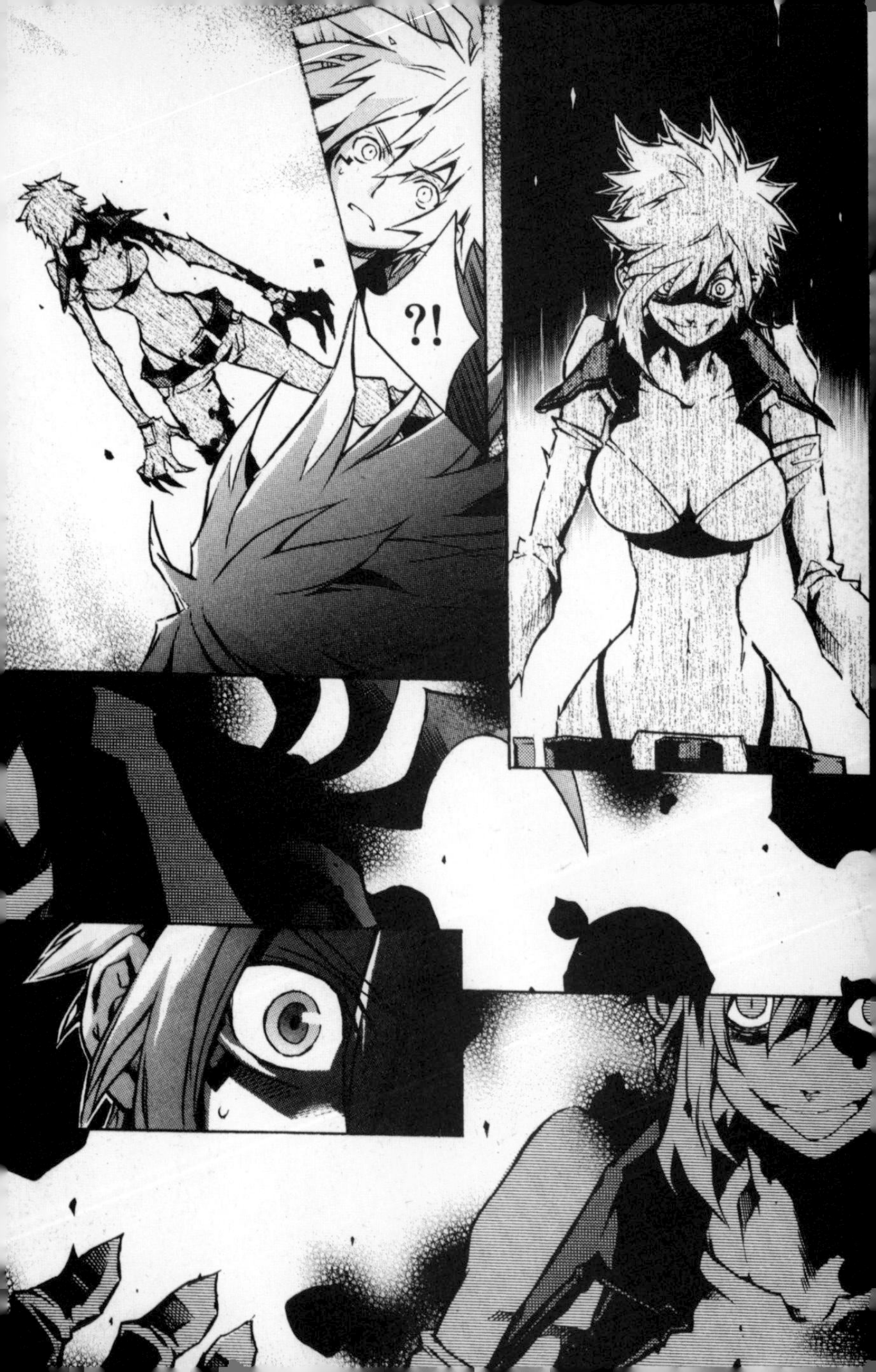
?!

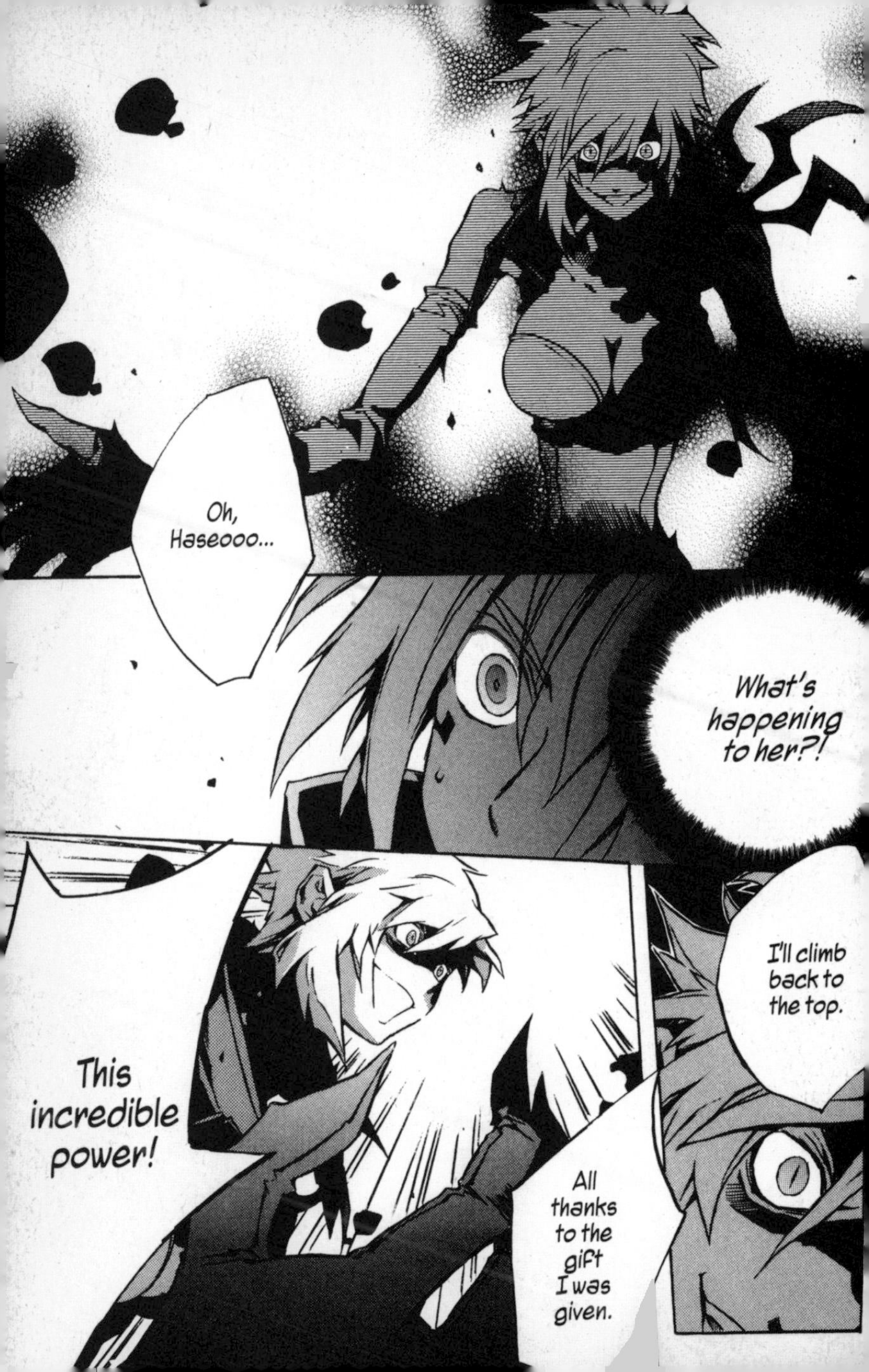
Oh, Haseooo...
What's happening to her?!
I'll climb back to the top.
This incredible power!
All thanks to the gift I was given.

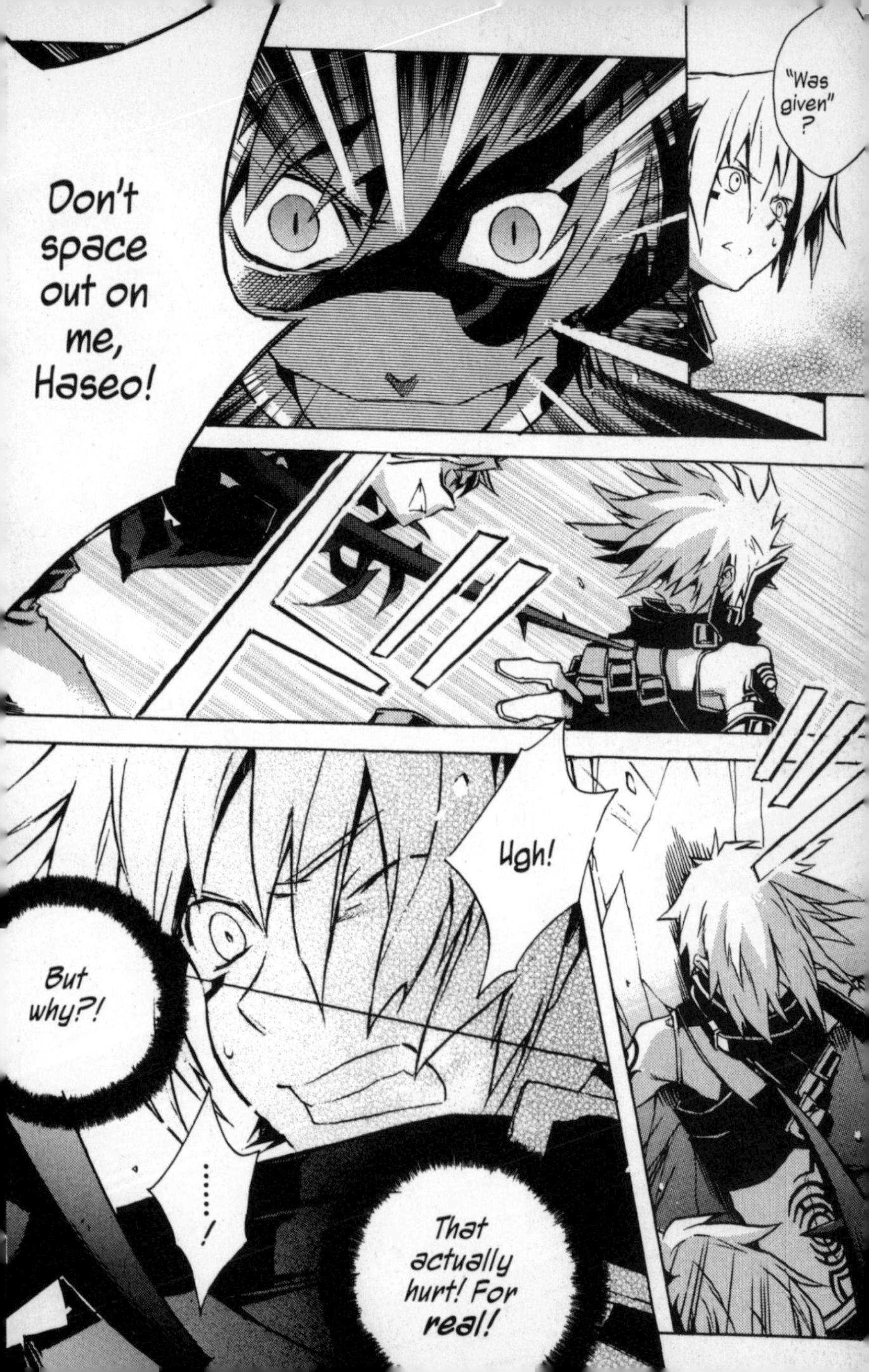
"Was given"?
Don't space out on me, Haseo!
Ugh!
But why?!
......!
That actually hurt! For real!

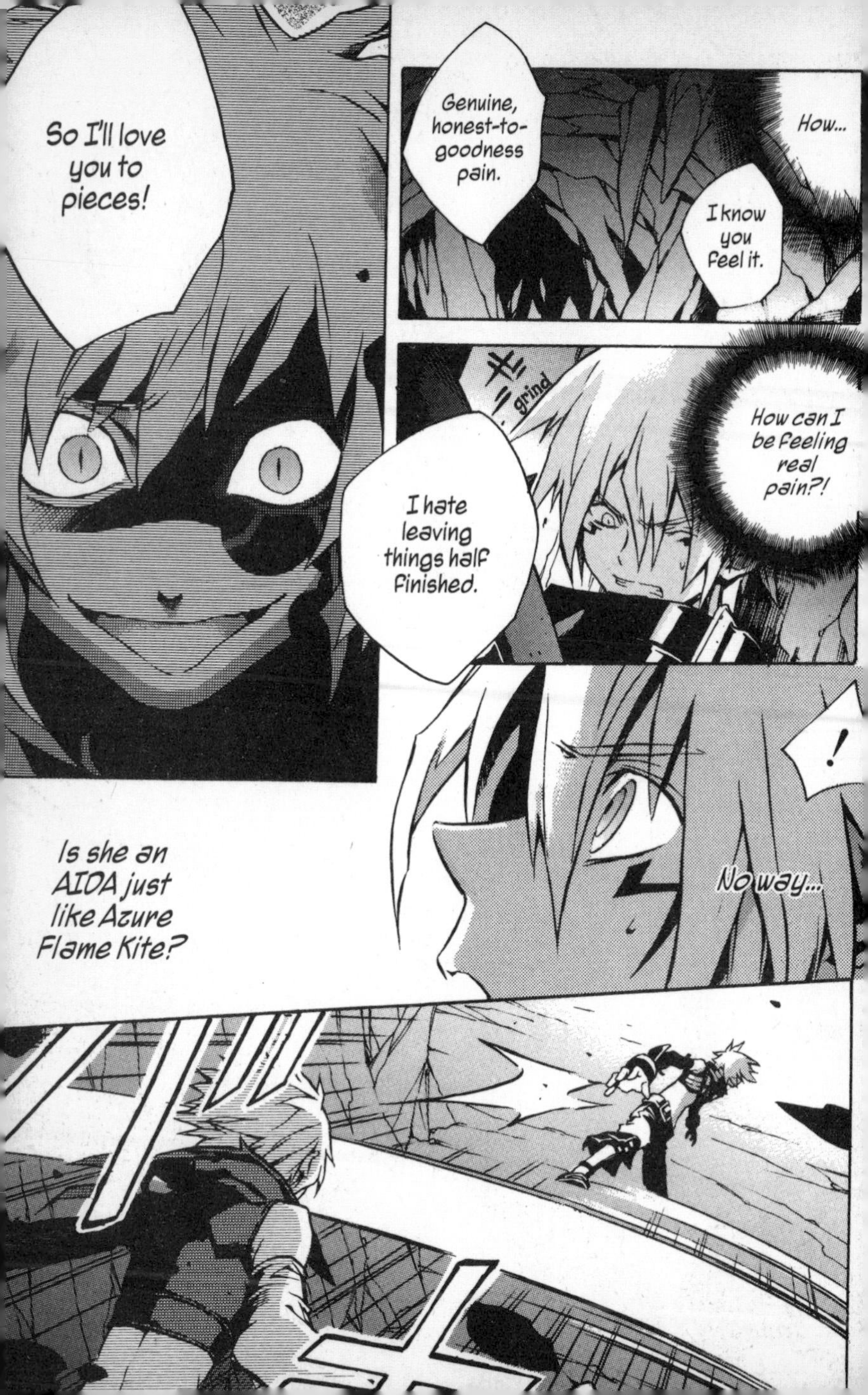
How...
Genuine, honest-to-goodness pain.
I know you feel it.
How can I be feeling real pain?!
grind
I hate leaving things half finished.
So I'll love you to pieces!
!
No way...
Is she an AIDA just like Azure Flame Kite?

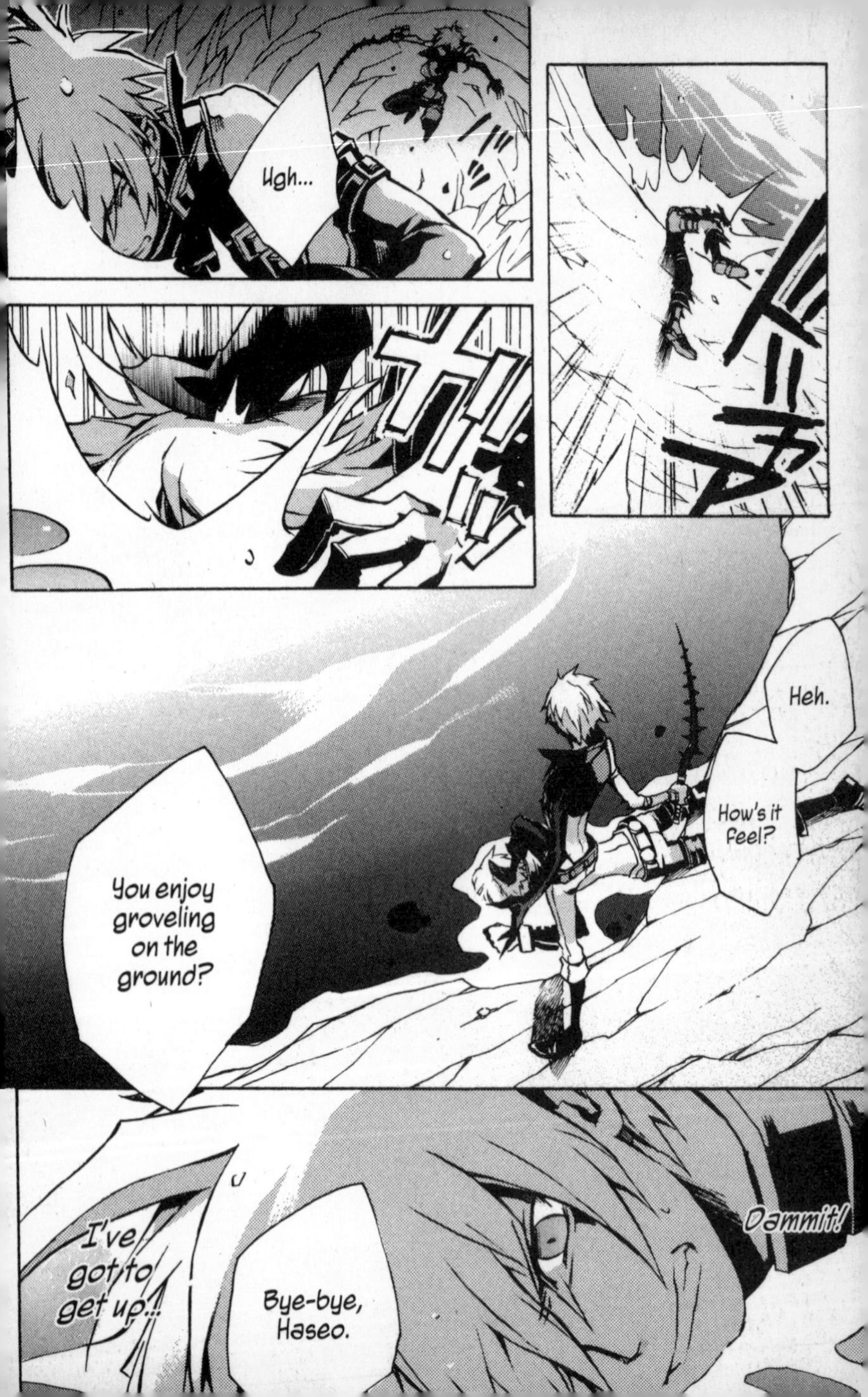
Ugh...
Heh.
How's it feel?
You enjoy groveling on the ground?
Dammit!
Bye-bye, Haseo.
I've got to get up...

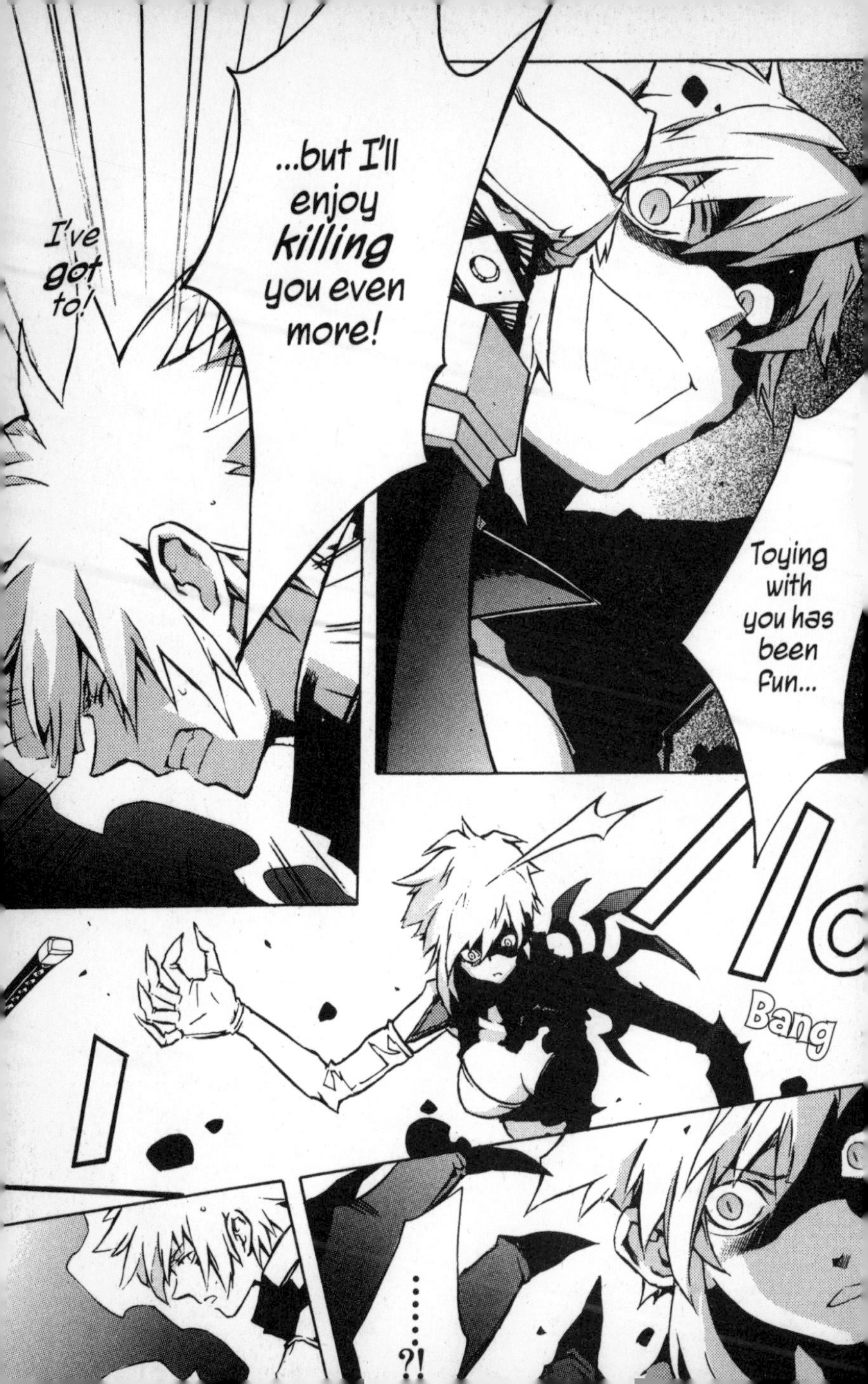
Toying with you has been fun...
...but I'll enjoy killing you even more!
I've got to!
Bang
......
?!

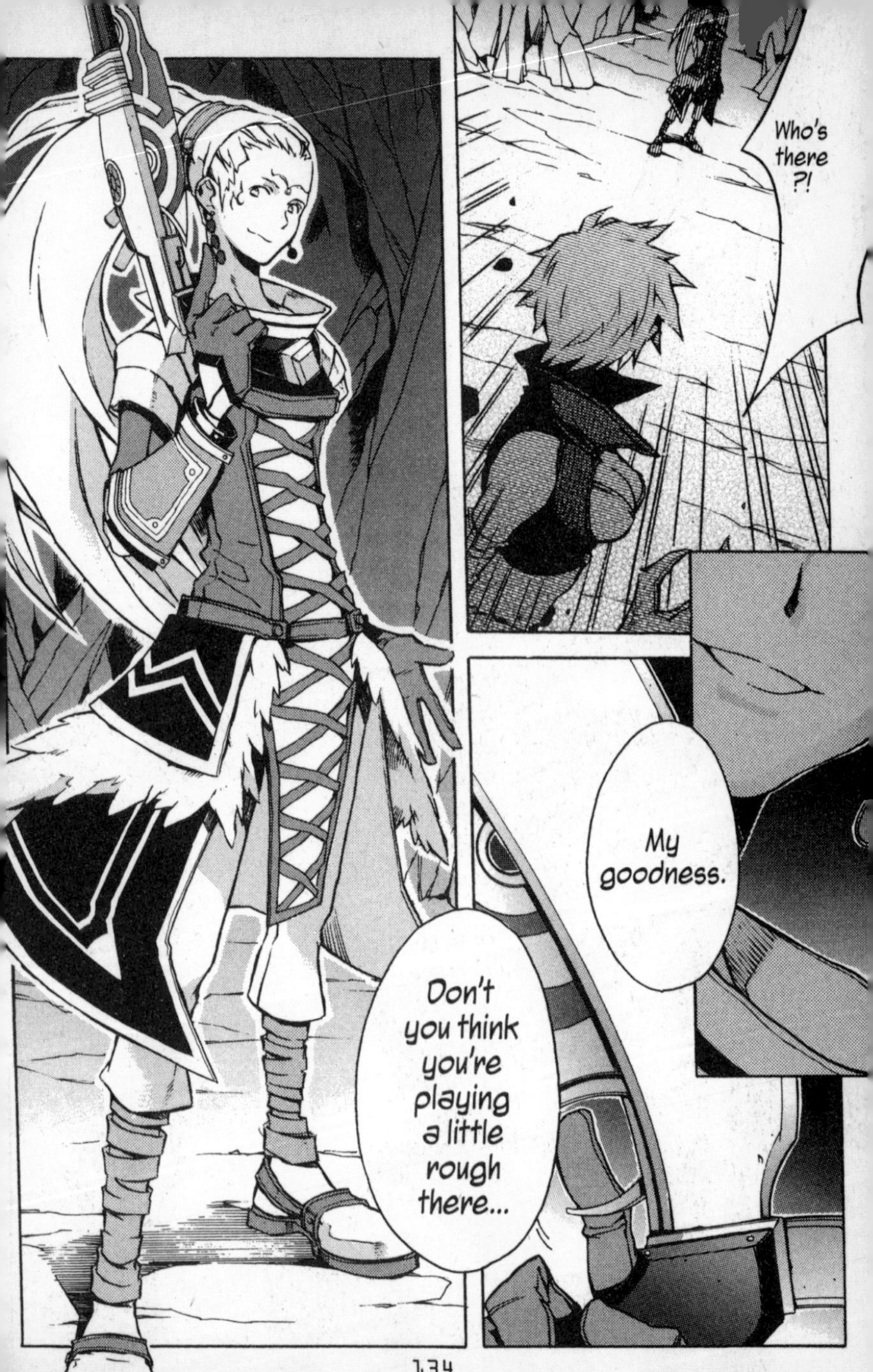
Who's there ?!
My goodness.
Don't you think you're playing a little rough there...

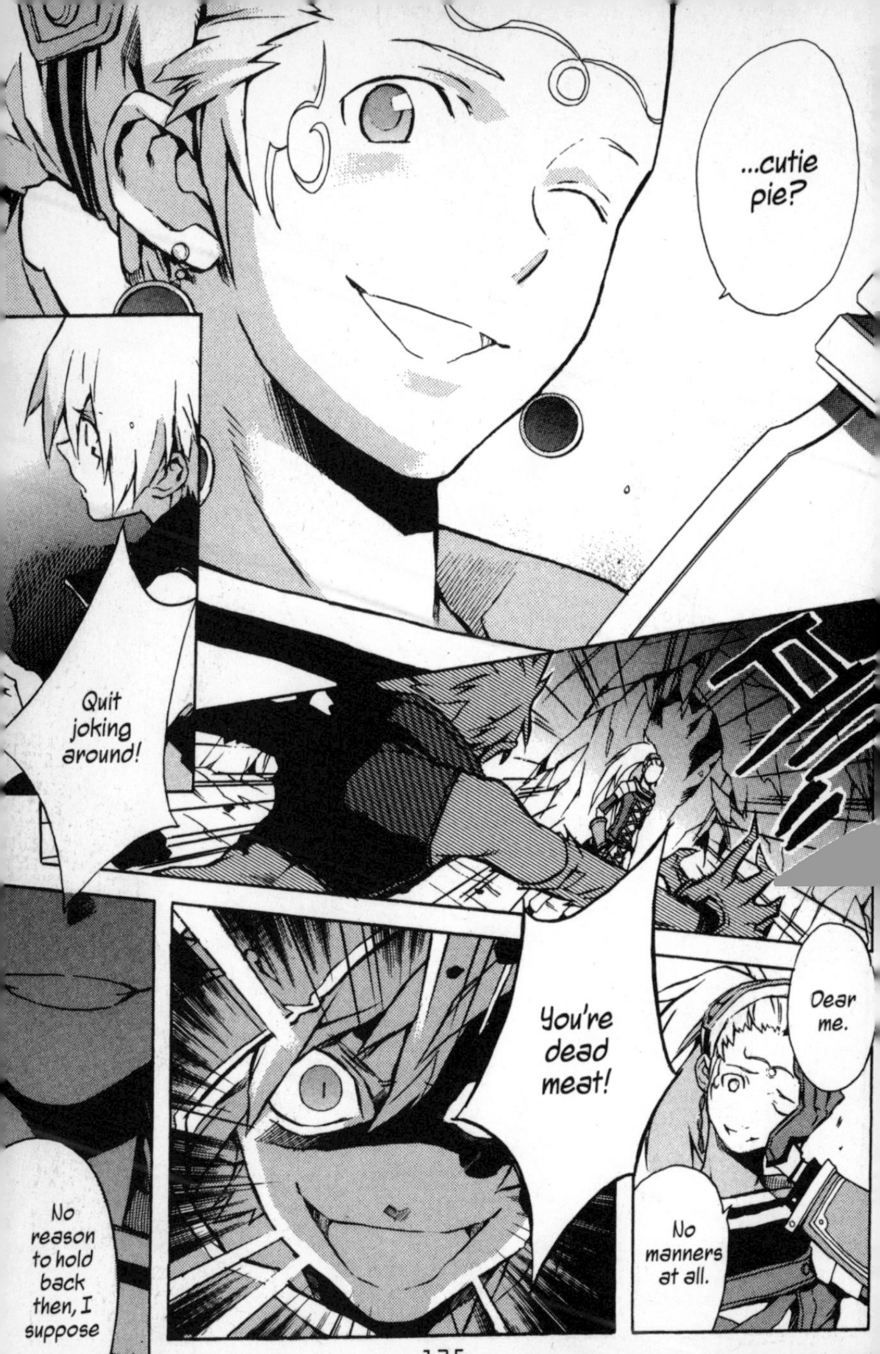
...cutie pie?
Quit joking around!
Dear me.
No manners at all.
You're dead meat!
No reason to hold back then, I suppose ...

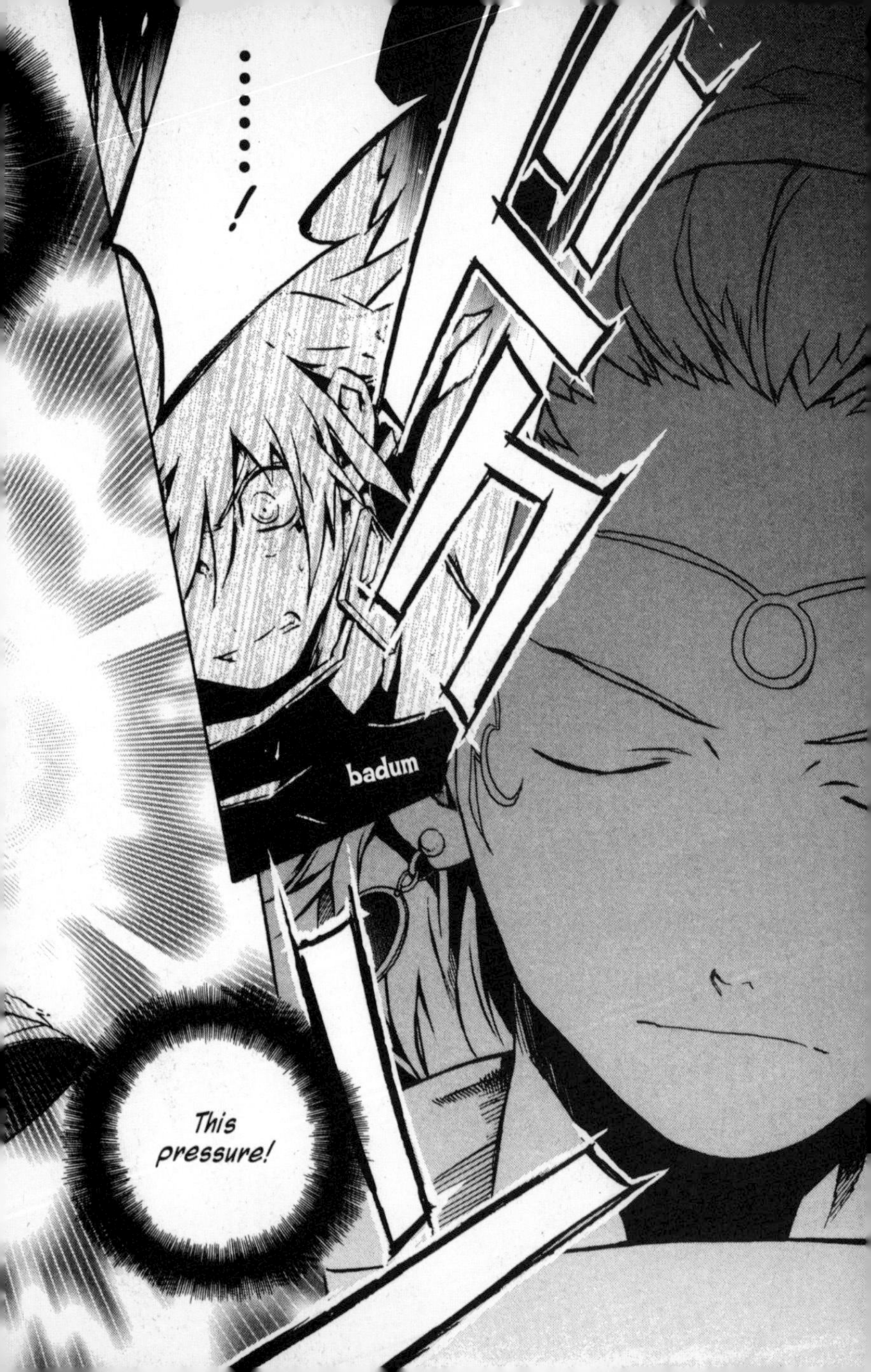
......!
badum
This pressure!

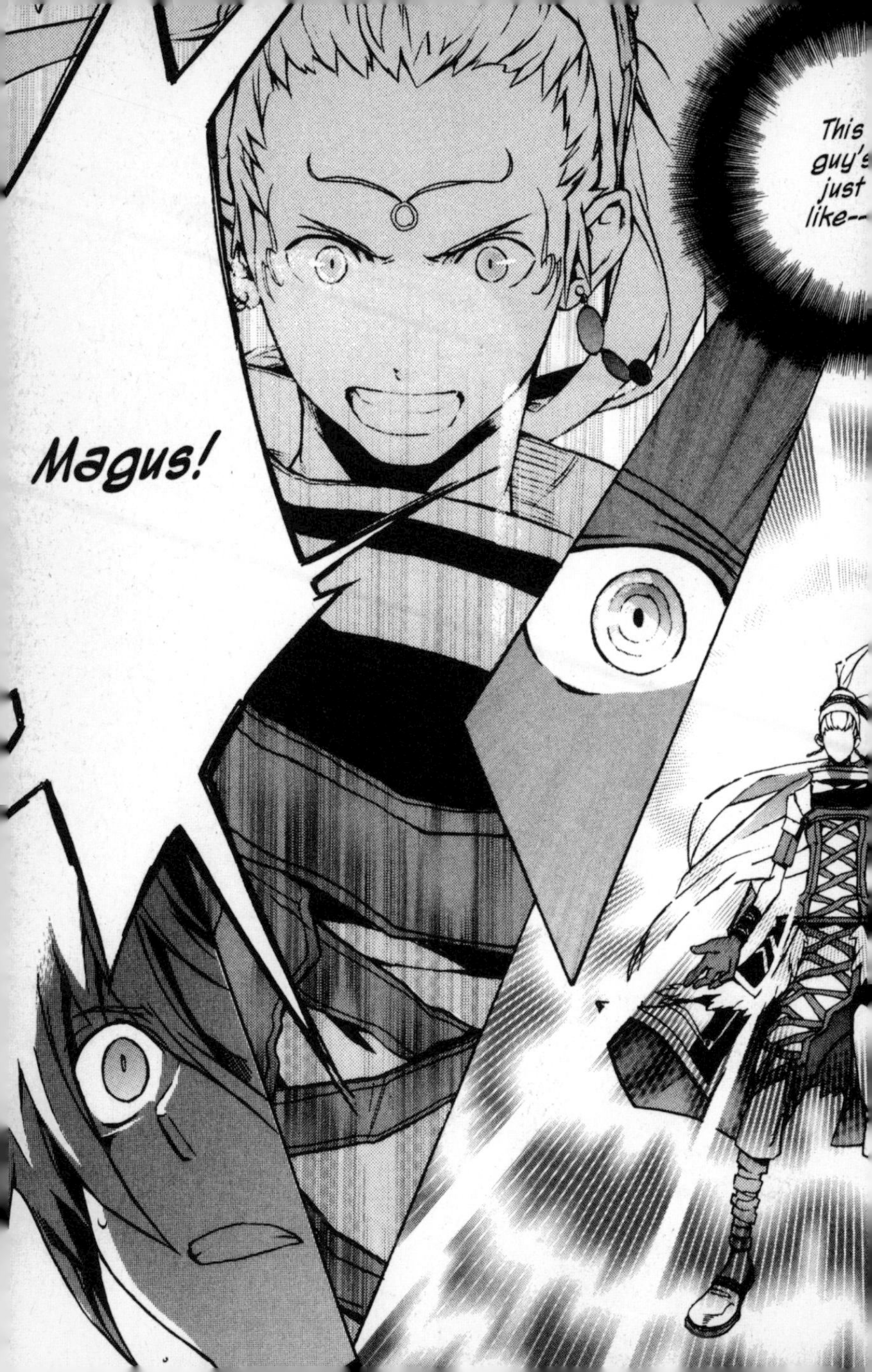
This guy's just like--
Magus!

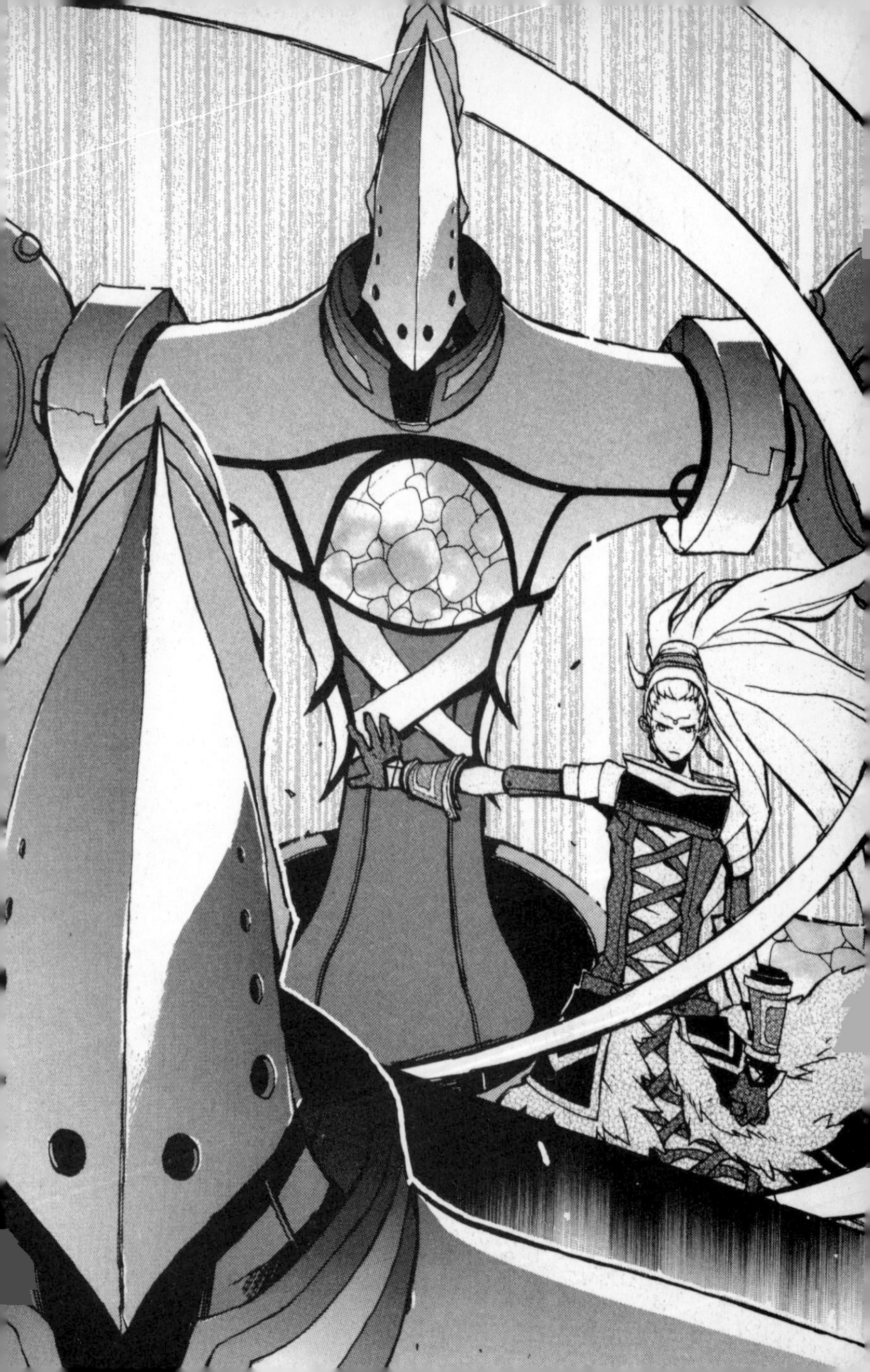

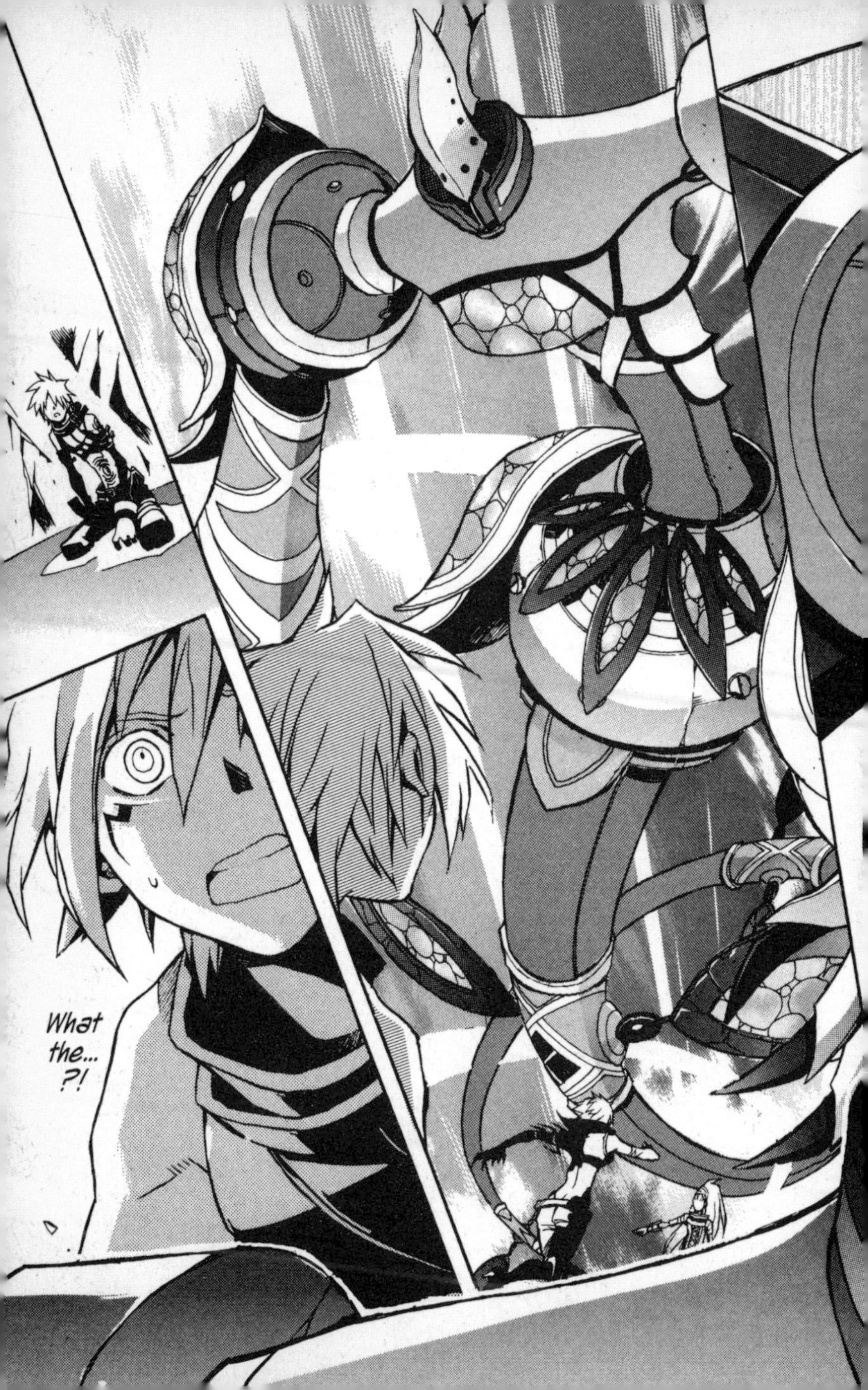
What the... ?!

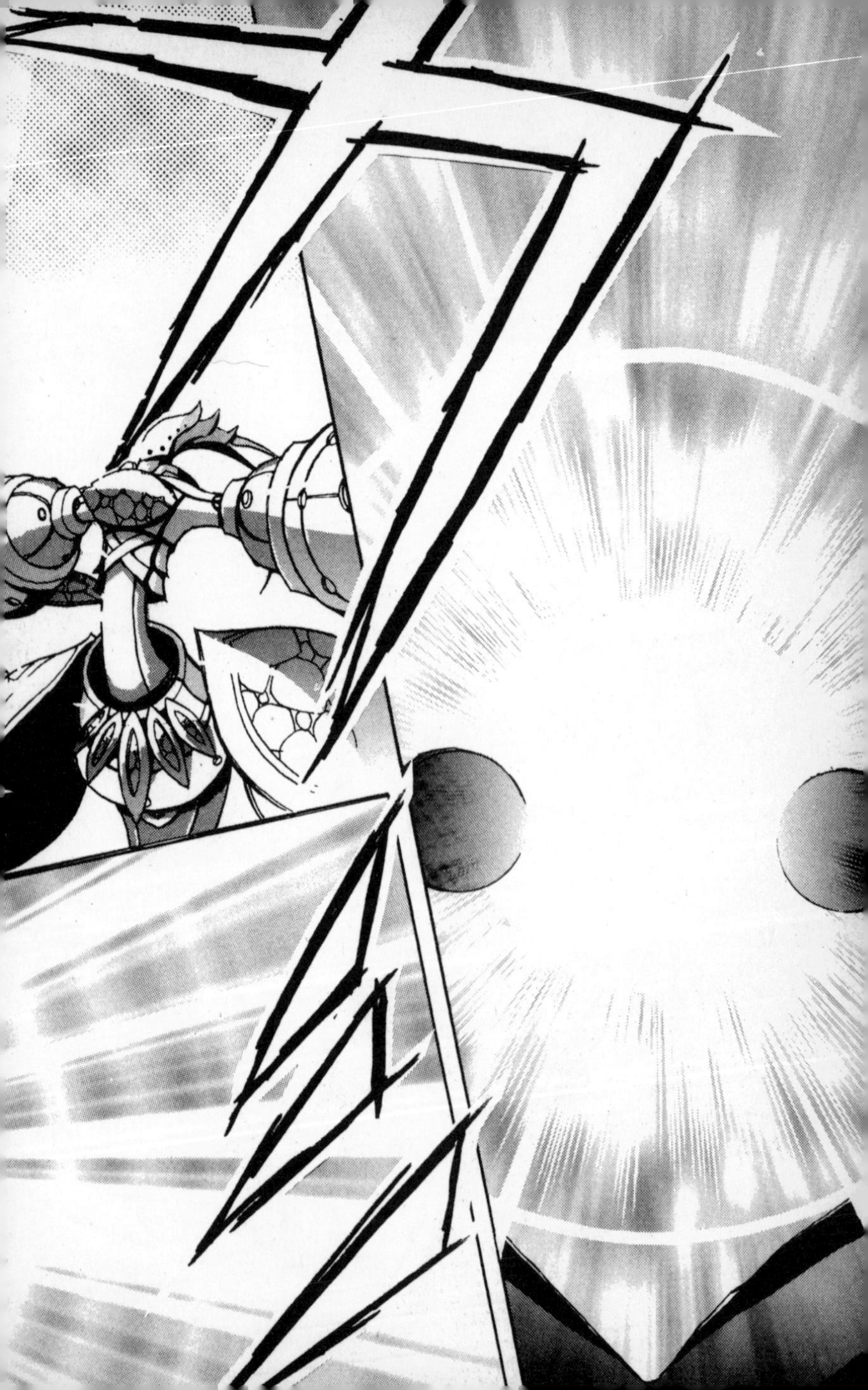

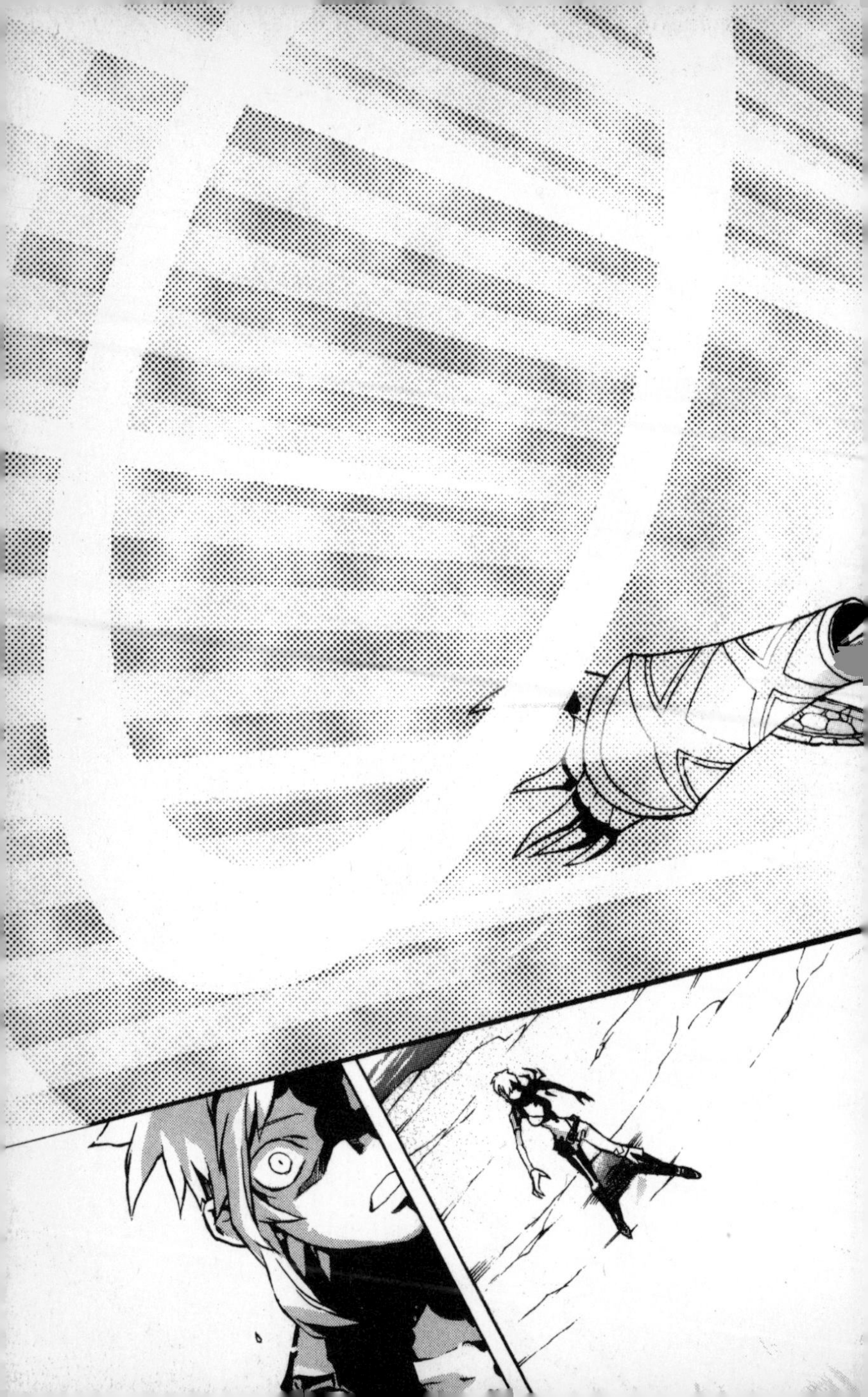

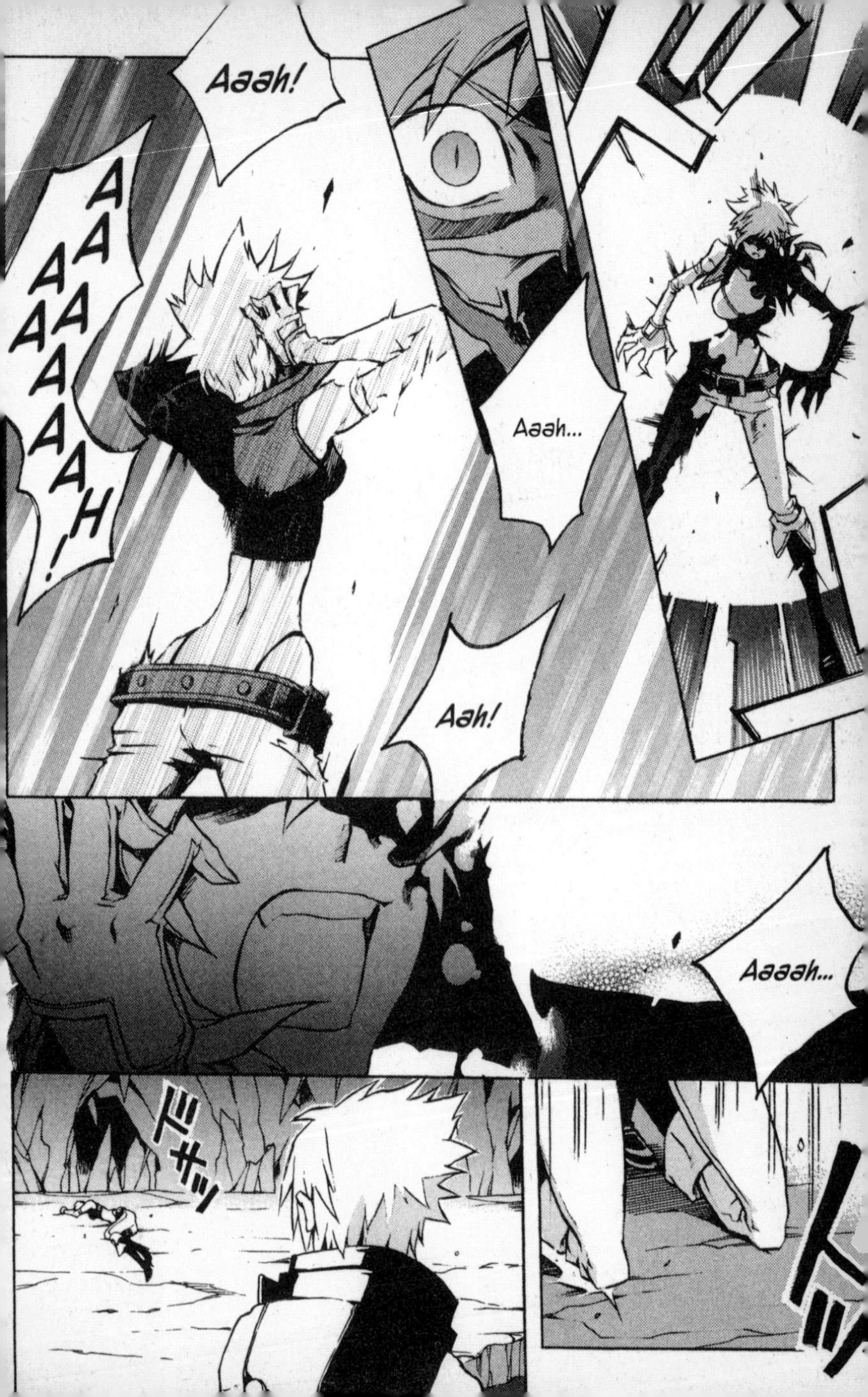
Aaah...
Aah!
Aaah!
AAAAAAAAH!
Aaaah...

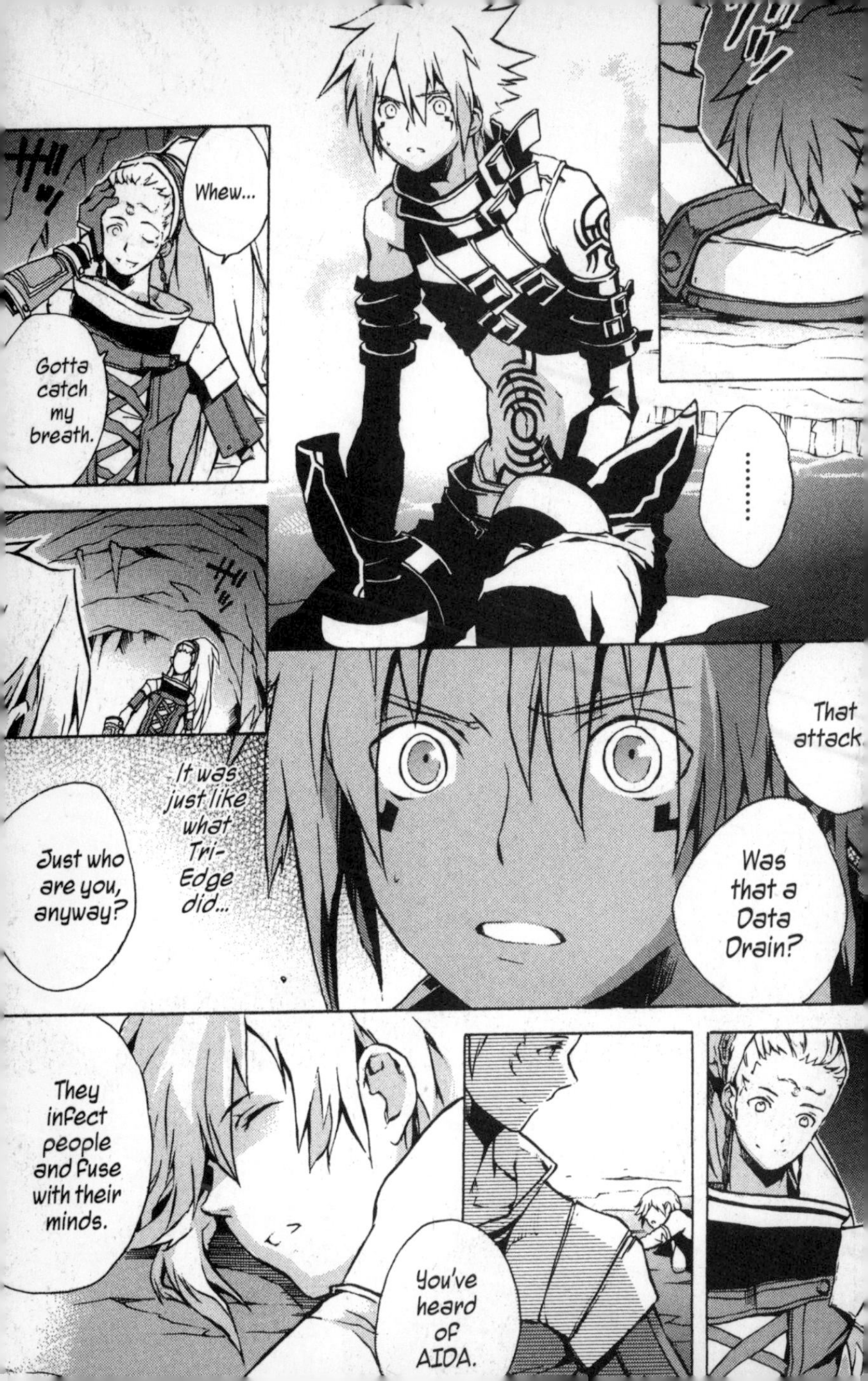
......
Whew...
Gotta catch my breath.
That attack.
Was that a Data Drain?
It was just like what Tri-Edge did...
Just who are you, anyway?
You've heard of AIDA.
They infect people and fuse with their minds.

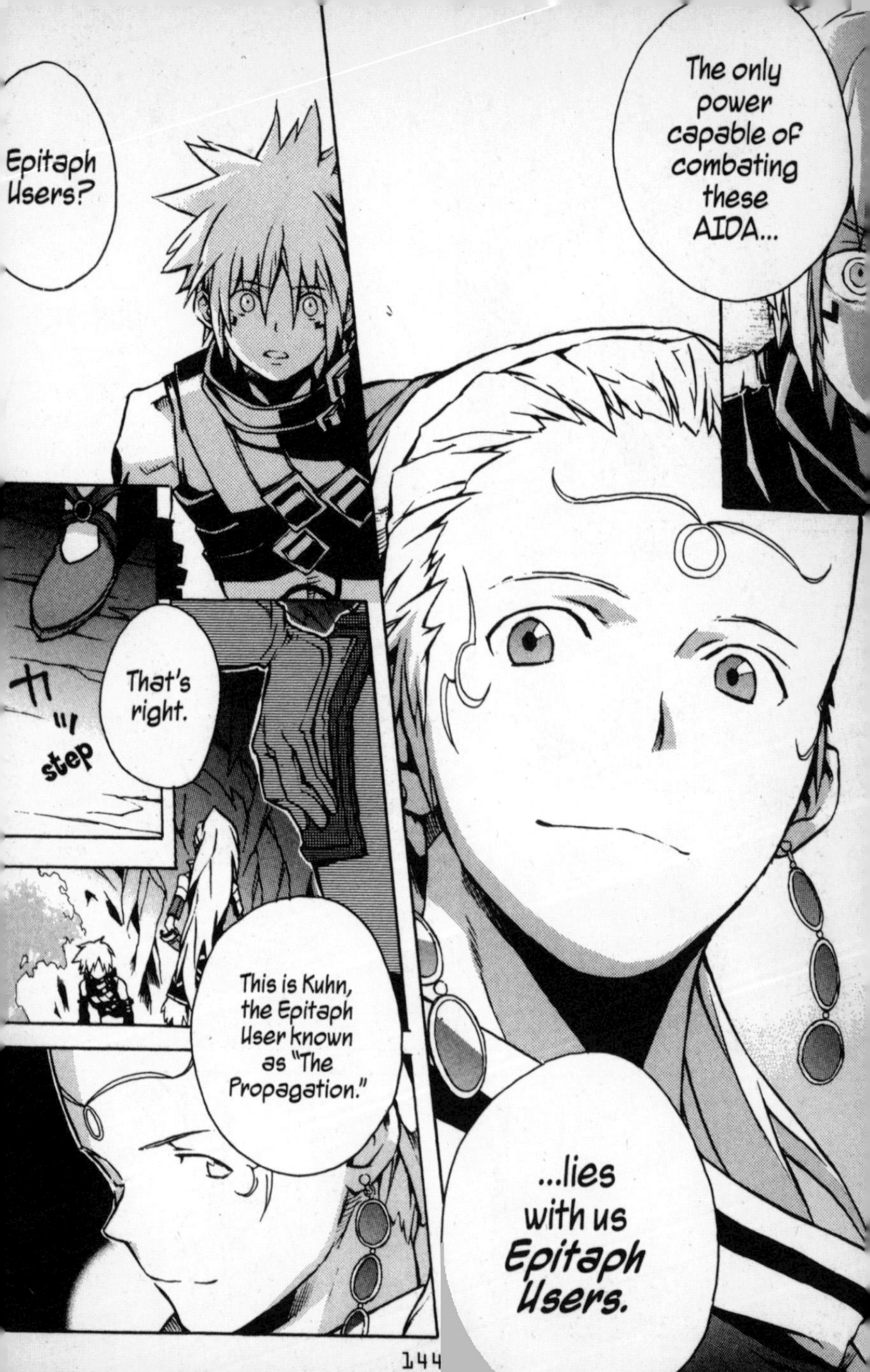

The only power capable of combating these AIDA...
...lies with us Epitaph Users.
Epitaph Users?
That's right.
step
This is Kuhn, the Epitaph User known as "The Propagation."

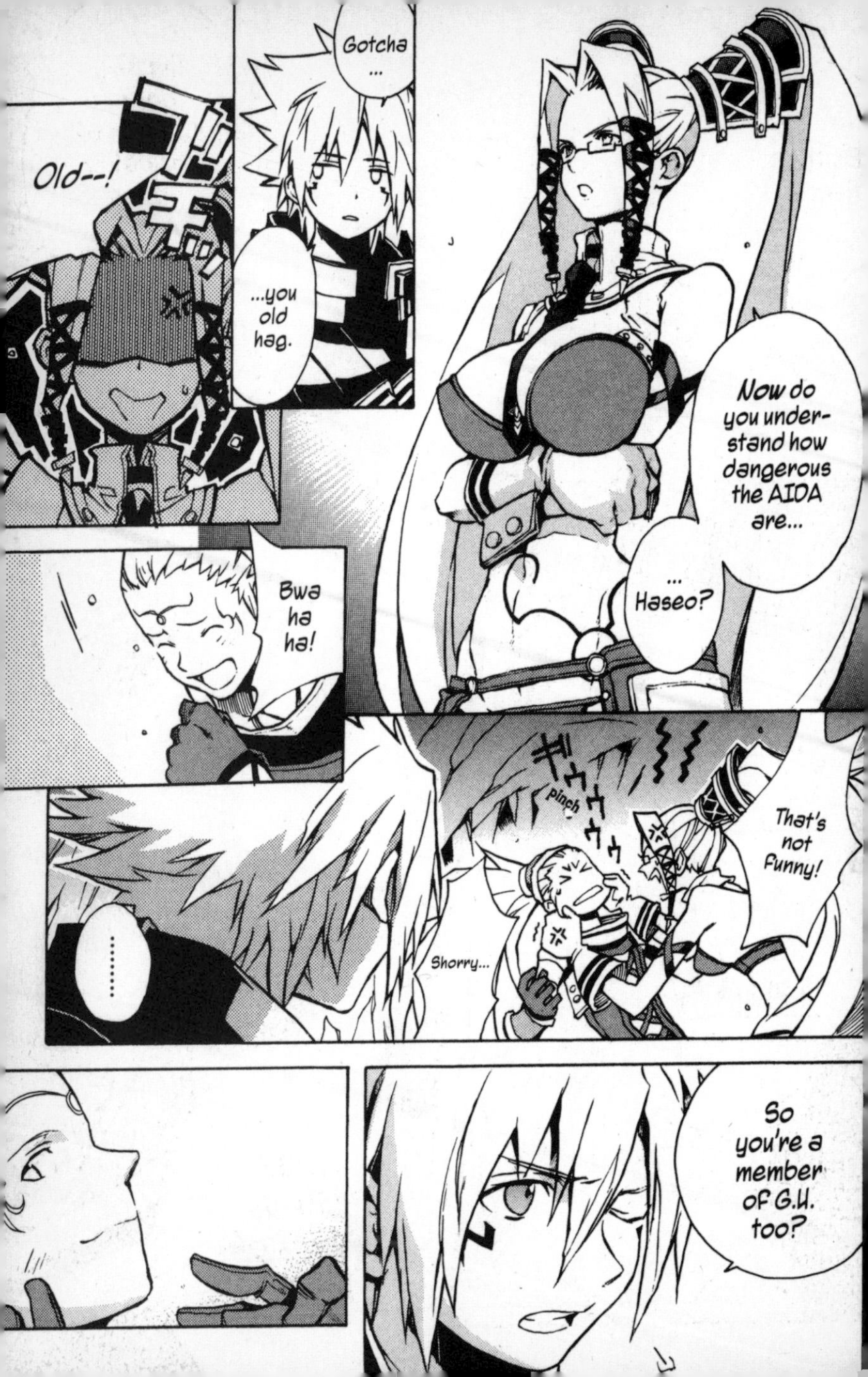
Now do you under-stand how dangerous the AIDA are...
... Haseo?
Gotcha ...
...you old hag.
Old--!
Bwa ha ha!
That's not funny!
pinch
Shorry...
....
So you're a member of G.U. too?

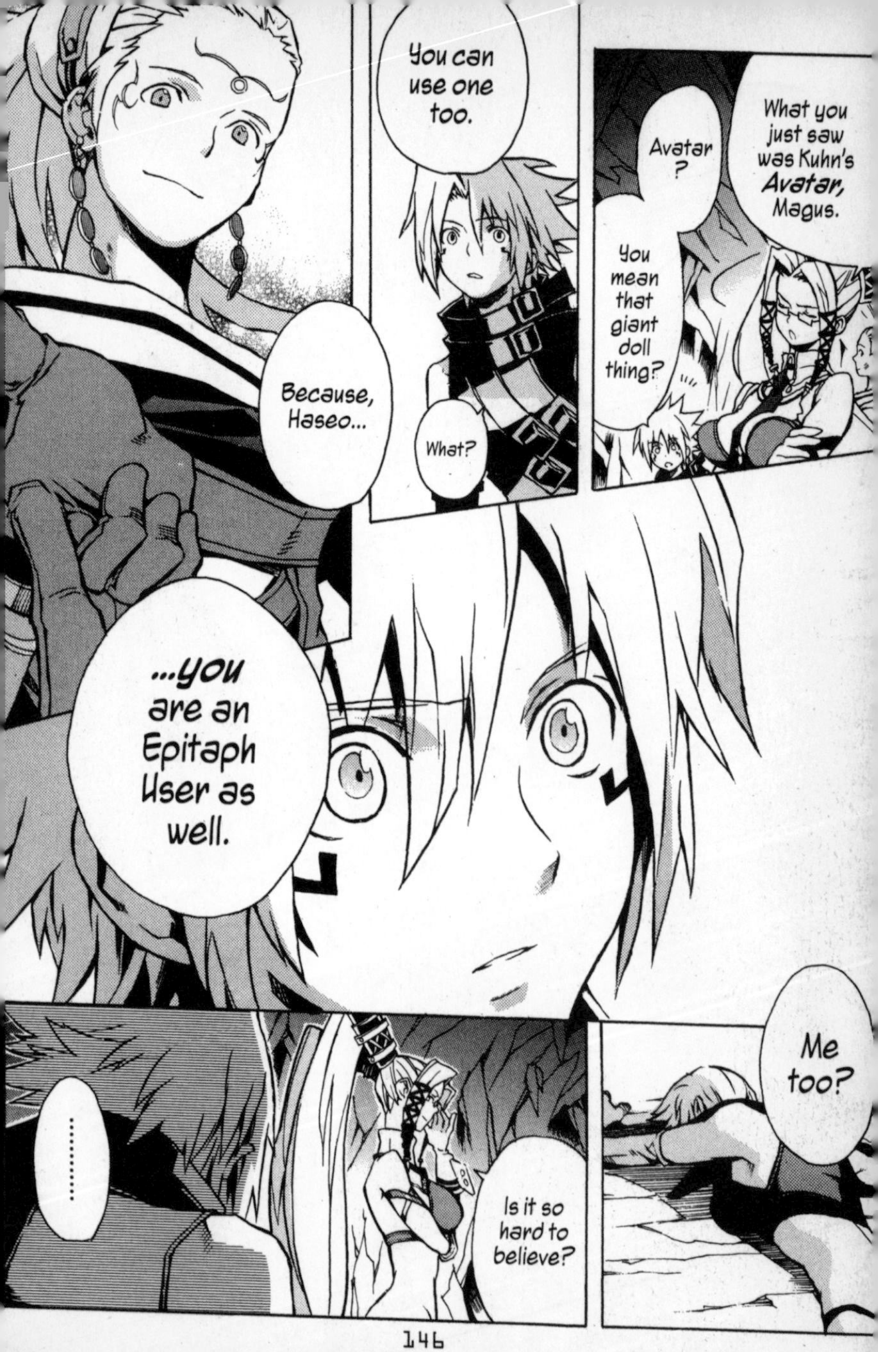
What you just saw was Kuhn's *Avatar,* Magus.
Avatar?
You mean that giant doll thing?
You can use one too.
What?
Because, Haseo...
...you are an Epitaph User as well.
Me too?
Is it so hard to believe?
....

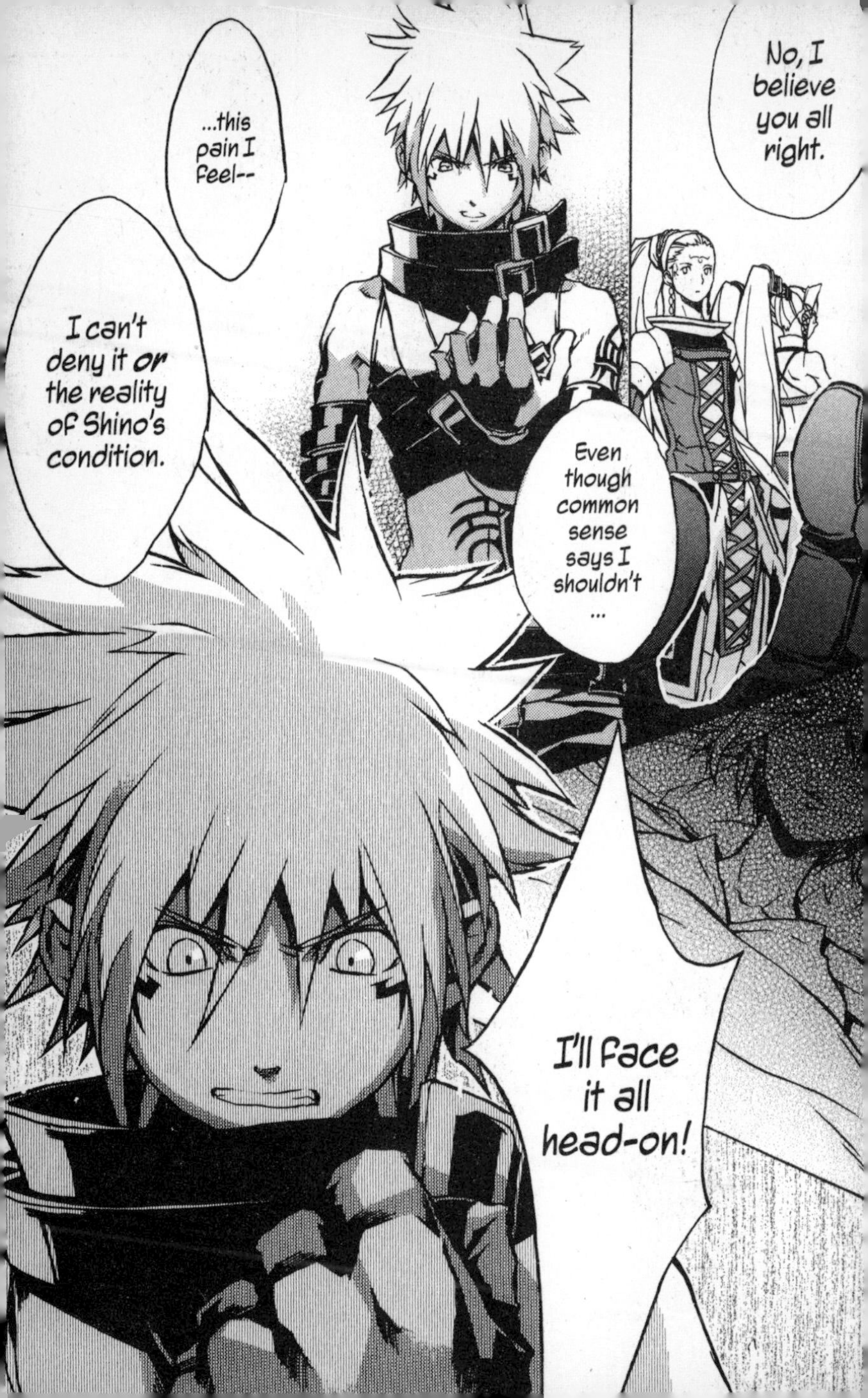
No, I believe you all right.
...this pain I feel--
I can't deny it **or** the reality of Shino's condition.
Even though common sense says I shouldn't ...
I'll face it all head-on!

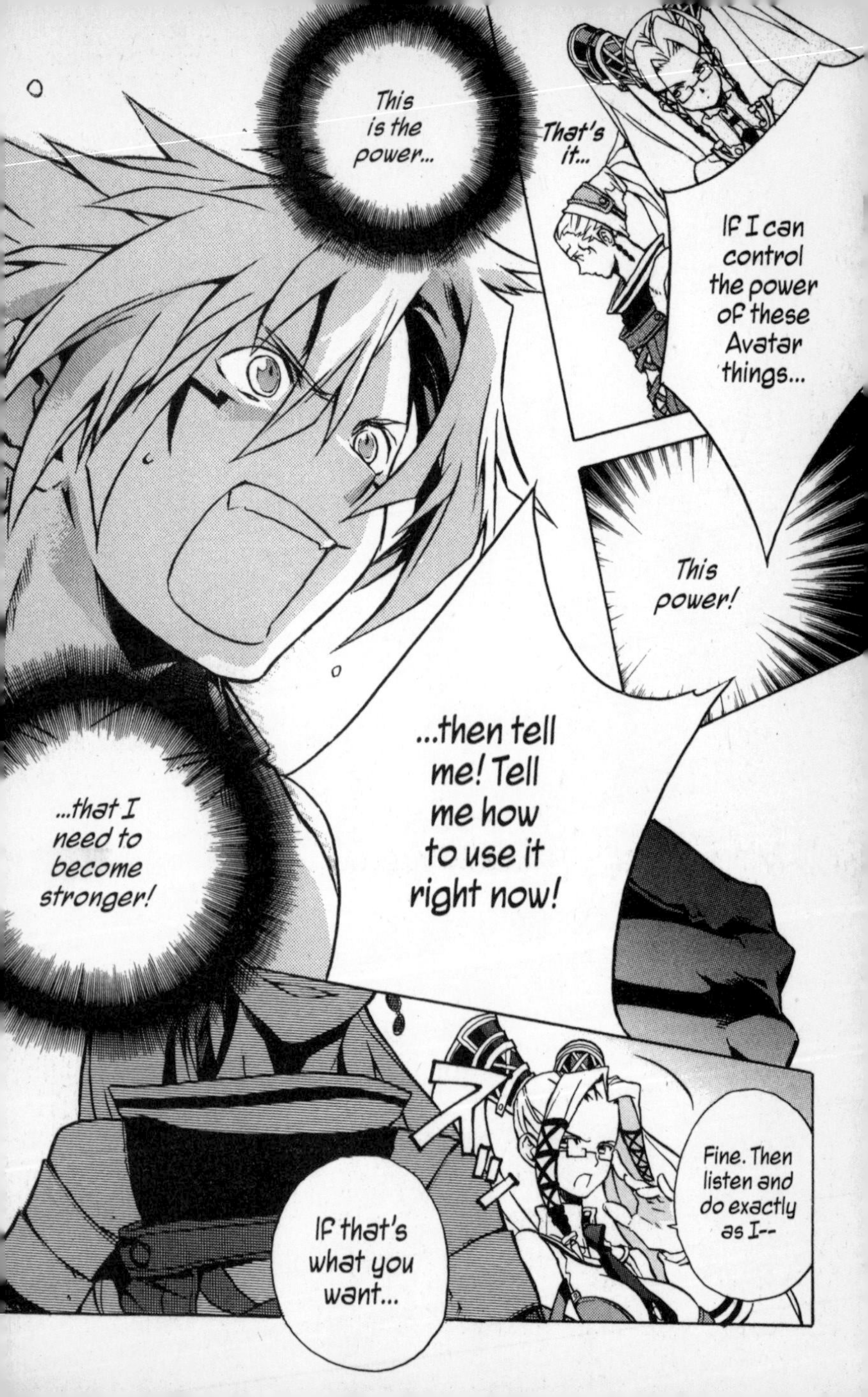
That's it...
If I can control the power of these Avatar things...
This power!
This is the power...
...that I need to become stronger!
...then tell me! Tell me how to use it right now!
Fine. Then listen and do exactly as I--
If that's what you want...

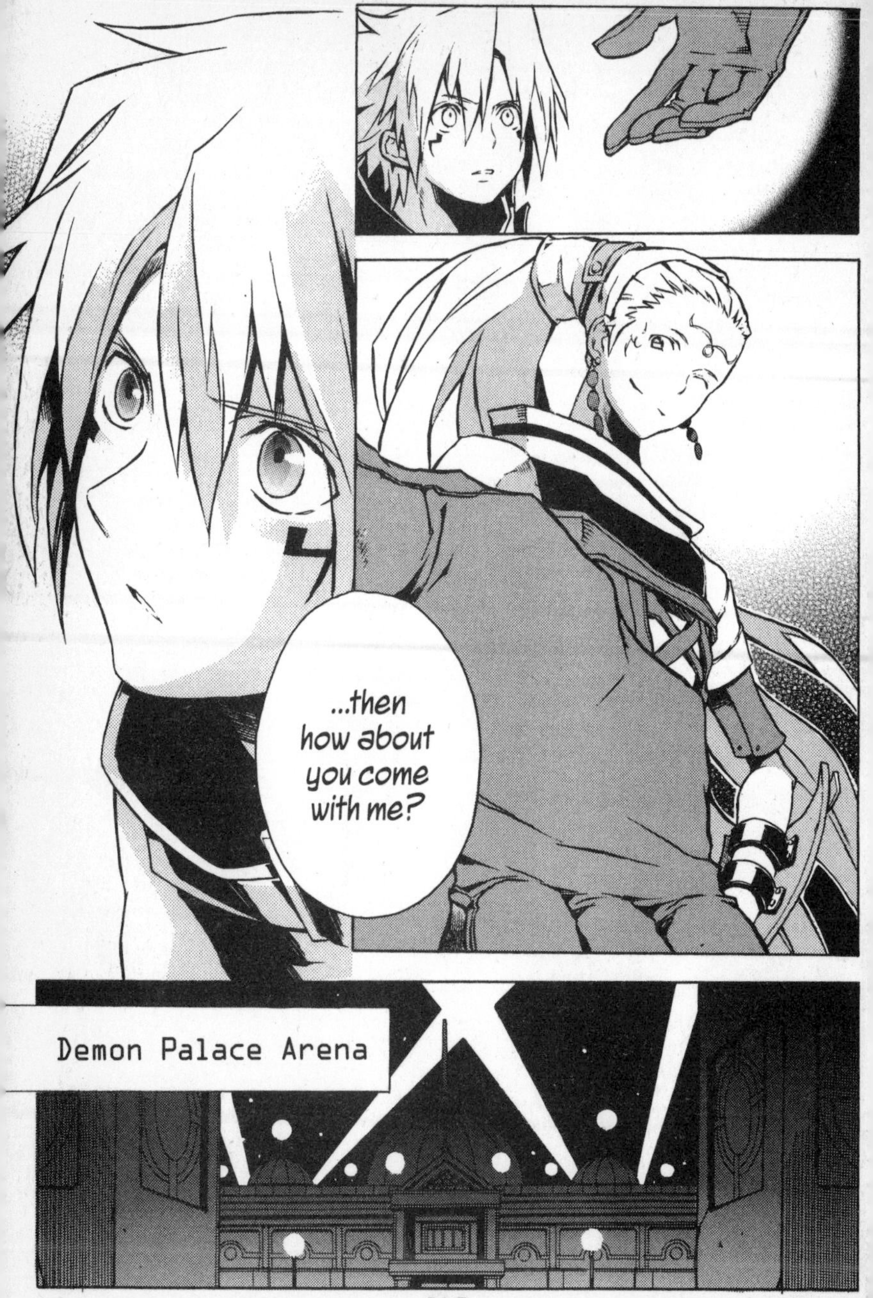
...then how about you come with me?
Demon Palace Arena

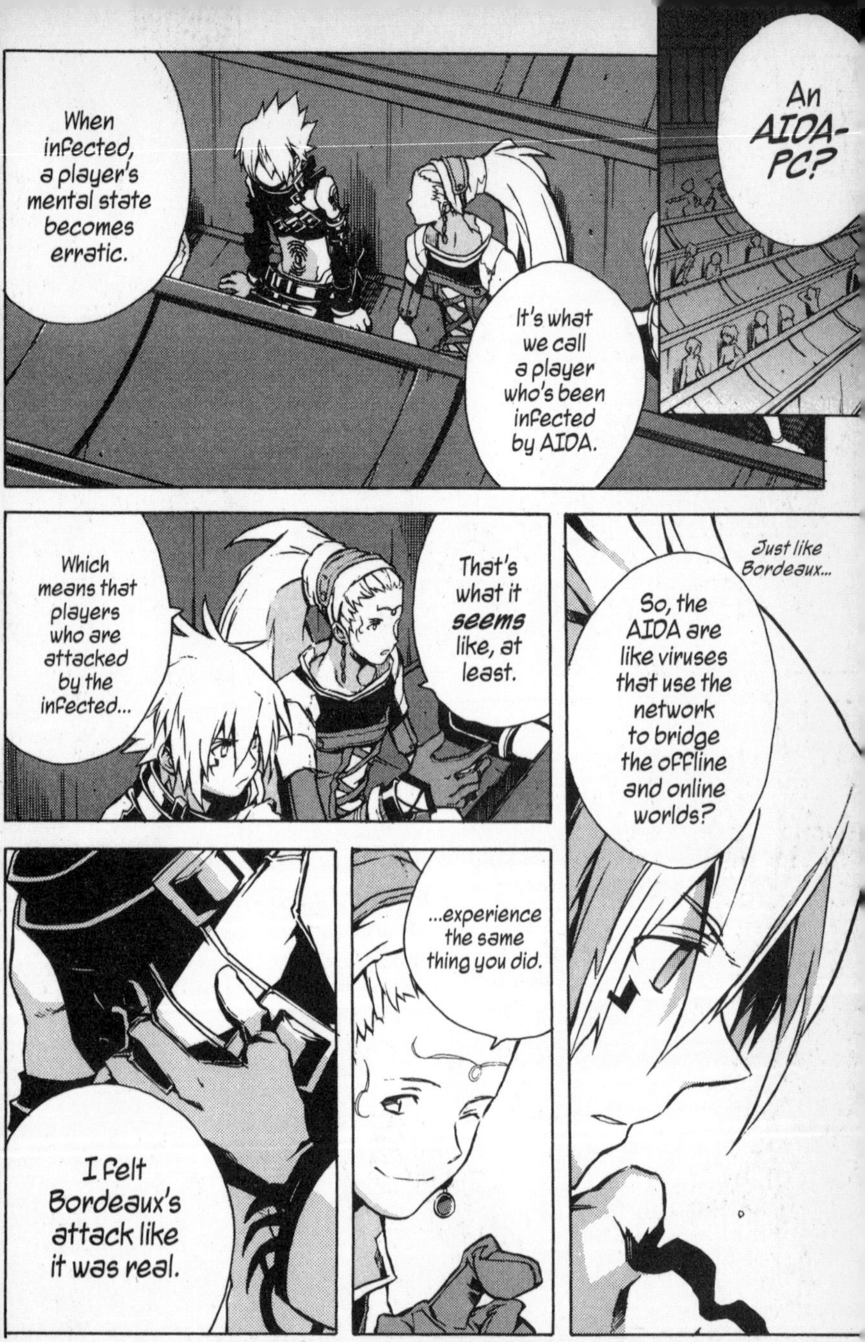
An AIDA-PC?
It's what we call a player who's been infected by AIDA.
When infected, a player's mental state becomes erratic.
Just like Bordeaux...
So, the AIDA are like viruses that use the network to bridge the offline and online worlds?
That's what it *seems* like, at least.
Which means that players who are attacked by the infected...
...experience the same thing you did.
I felt Bordeaux's attack like it was real.

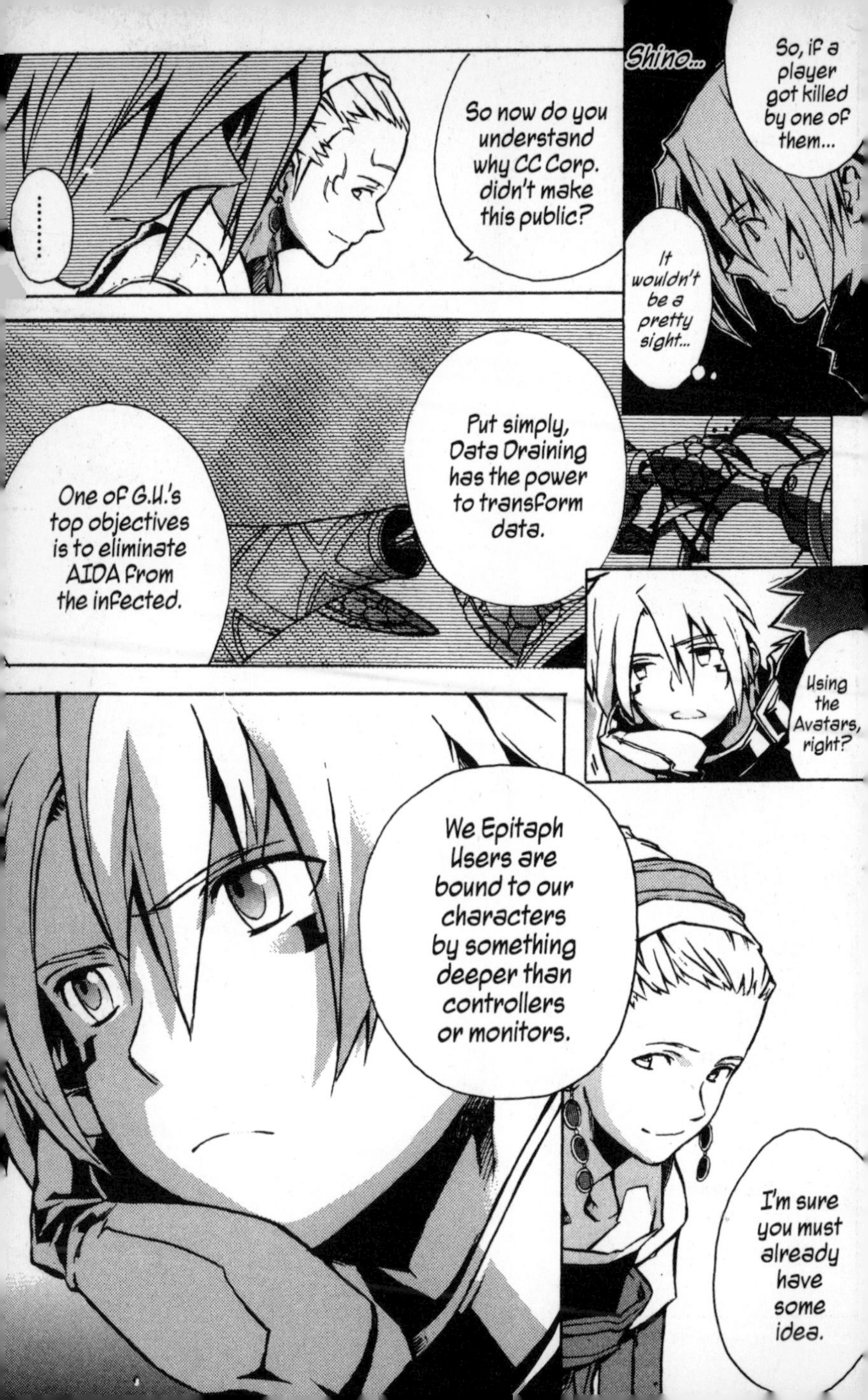
So, if a player got killed by one of them...
Shino...
It wouldn't be a pretty sight...
So now do you understand why CC Corp. didn't make this public?
......
Put simply, Data Draining has the power to transform data.
One of G.U.'s top objectives is to eliminate AIDA from the infected.
Using the Avatars, right?
We Epitaph Users are bound to our characters by something deeper than controllers or monitors.
I'm sure you must already have some idea.

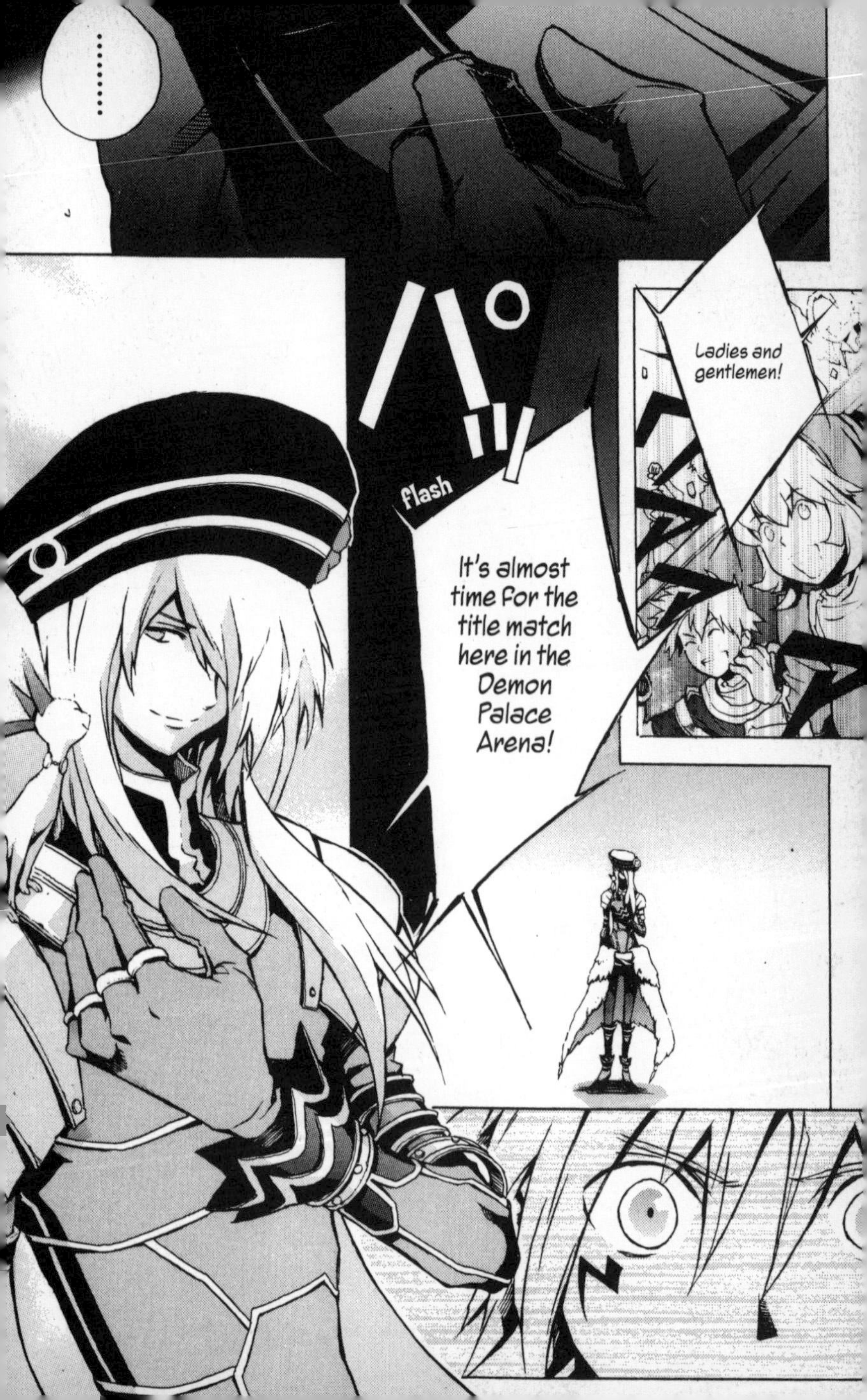
......
flash
Ladies and gentlemen!
It's almost time for the title match here in the Demon Palace Arena!

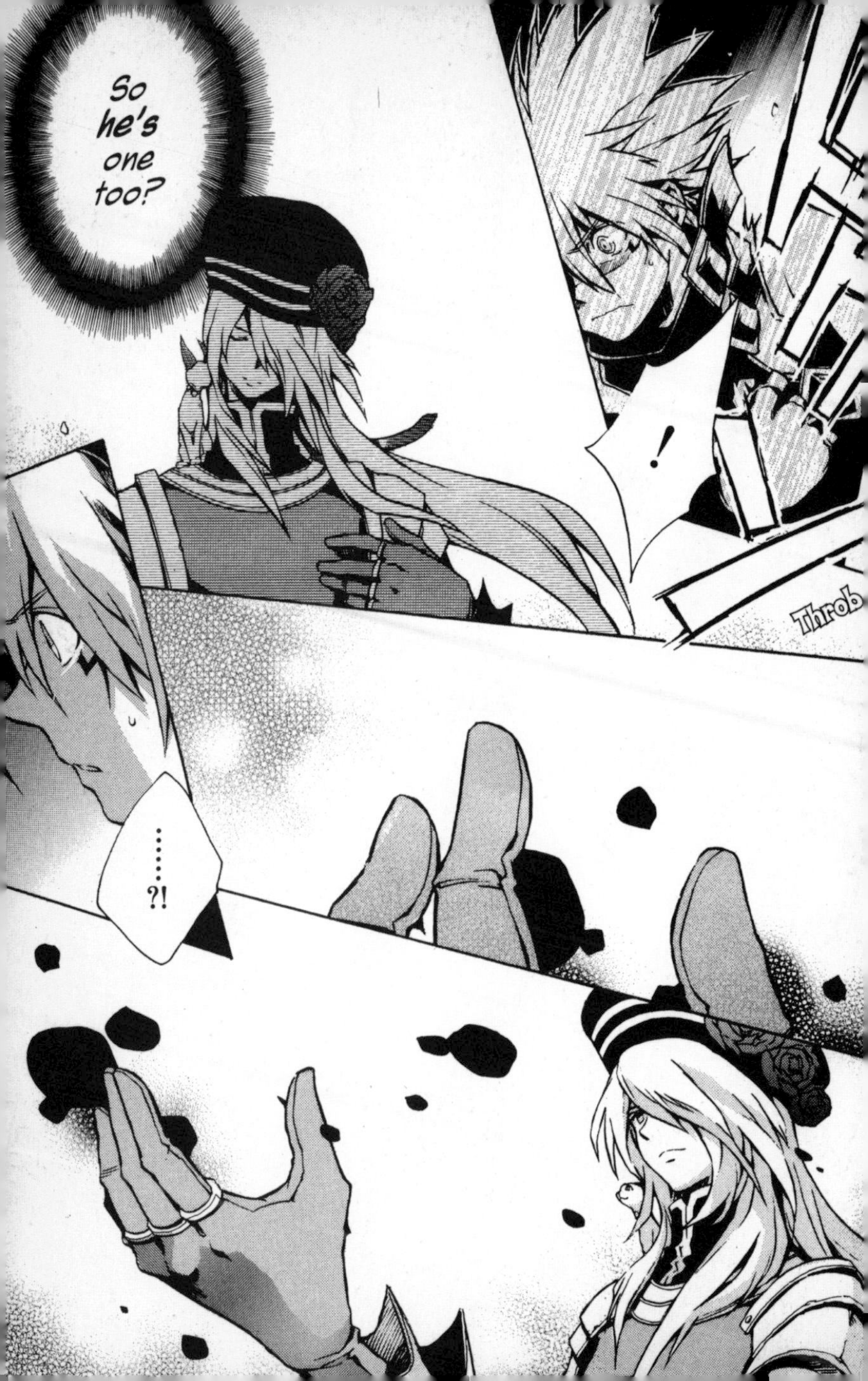
!
Throb
So he's one too?
......?!

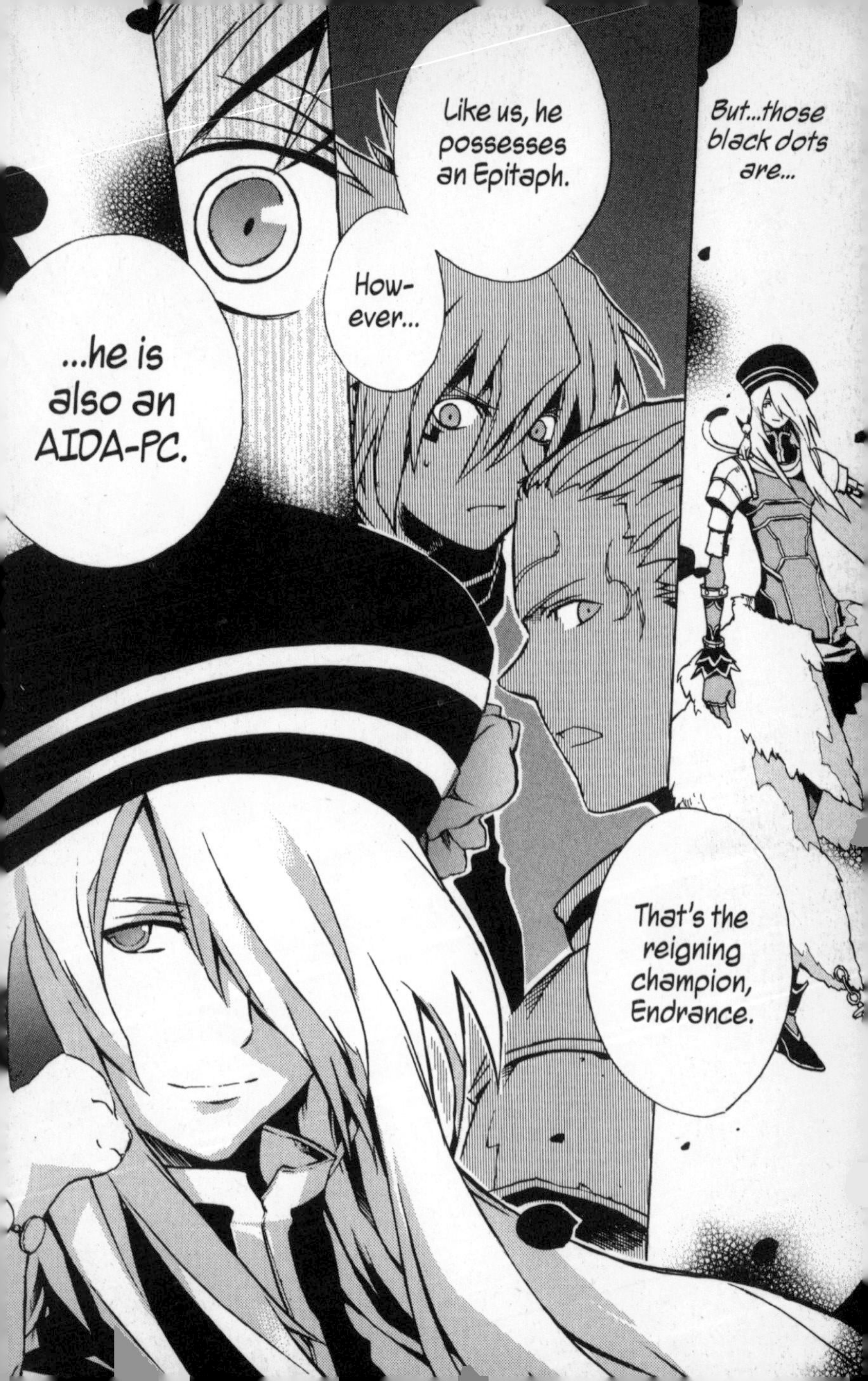
But...those black dots are...
That's the reigning champion, Endrance.
Like us, he possesses an Epitaph.
How-ever...
...he is also an AIDA-PC.

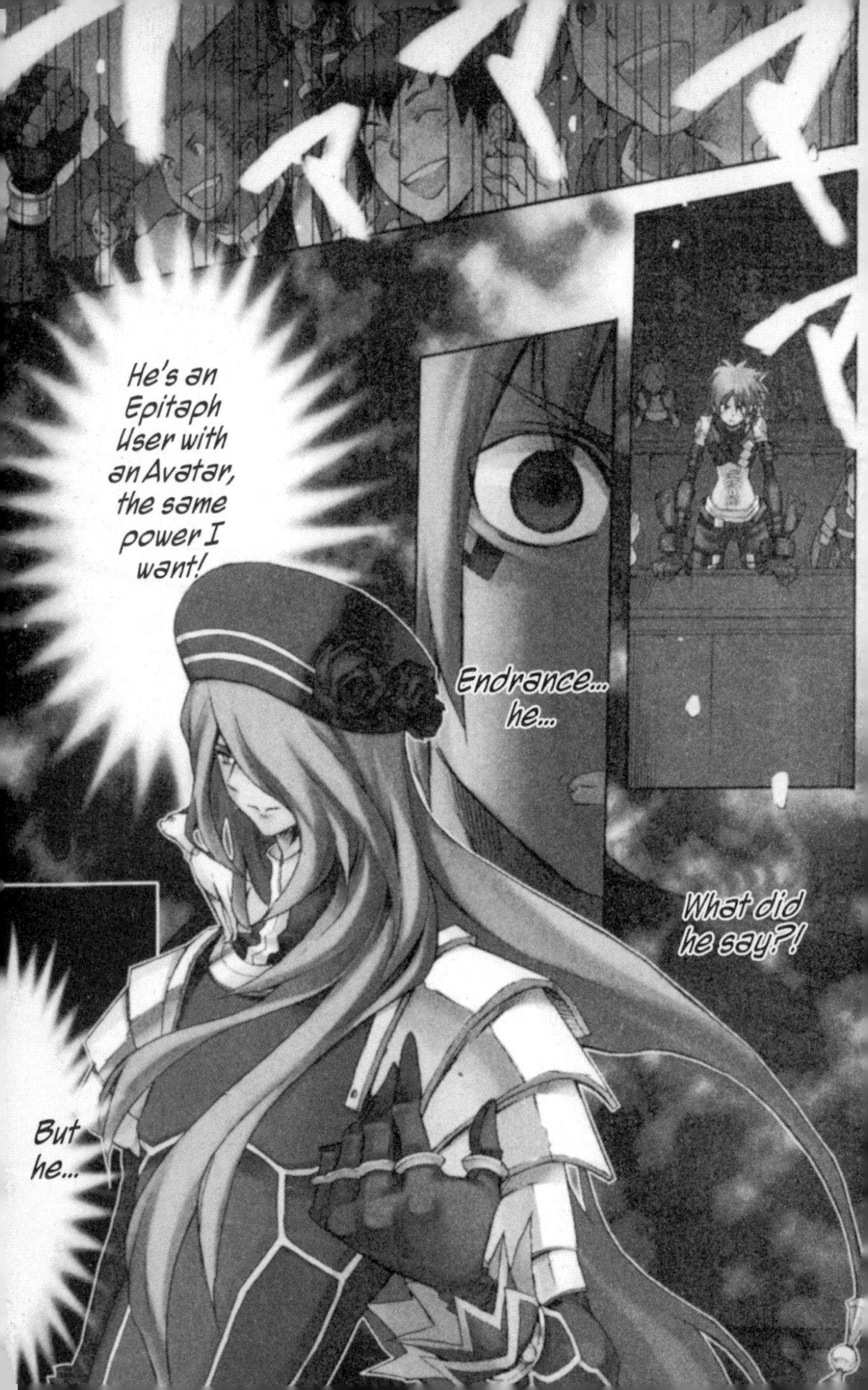
Endrance... he...
What did he say?!
He's an Epitaph User with an Avatar, the same power I want!
But he...

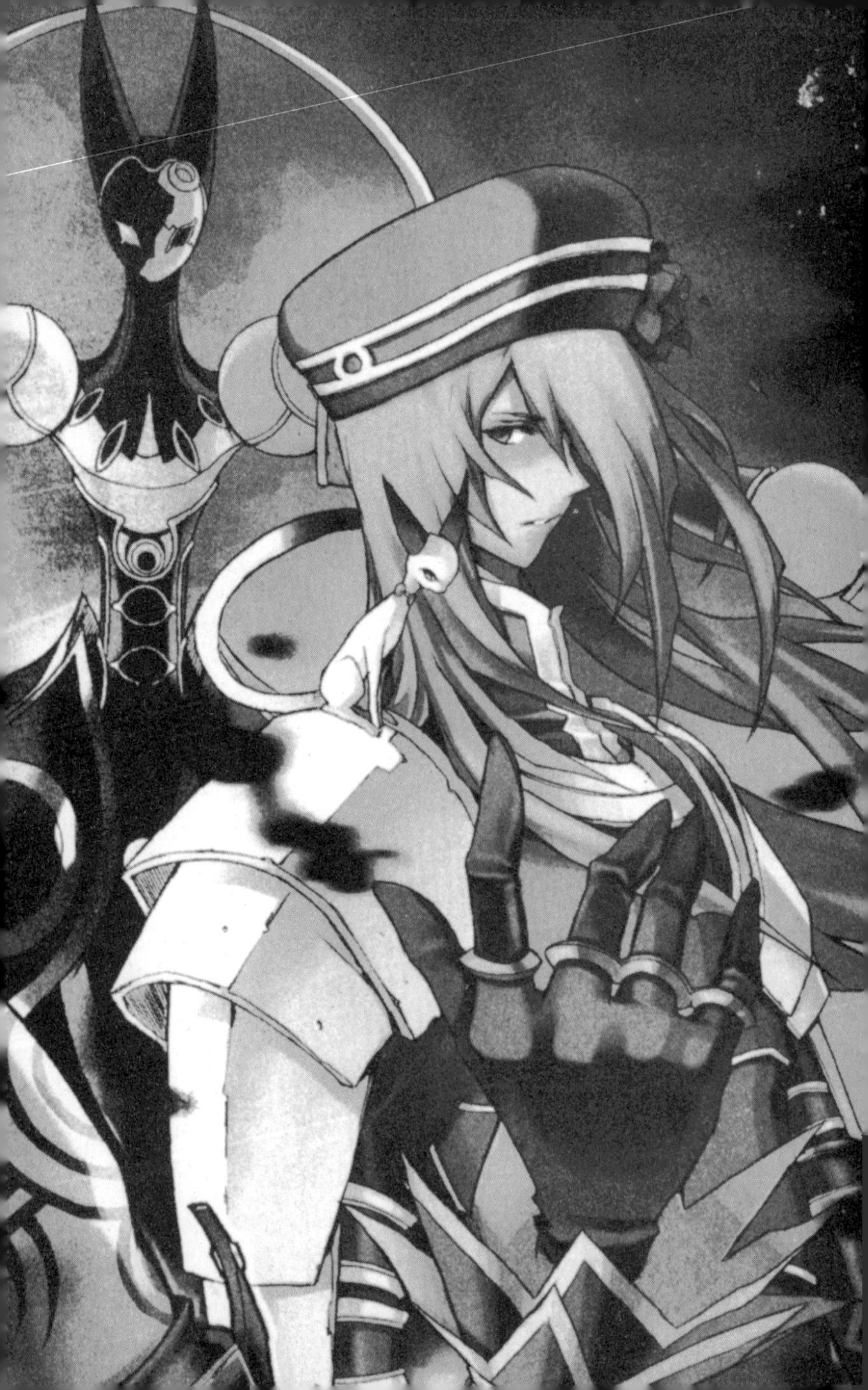

Chapter 4: Endrance's Cat

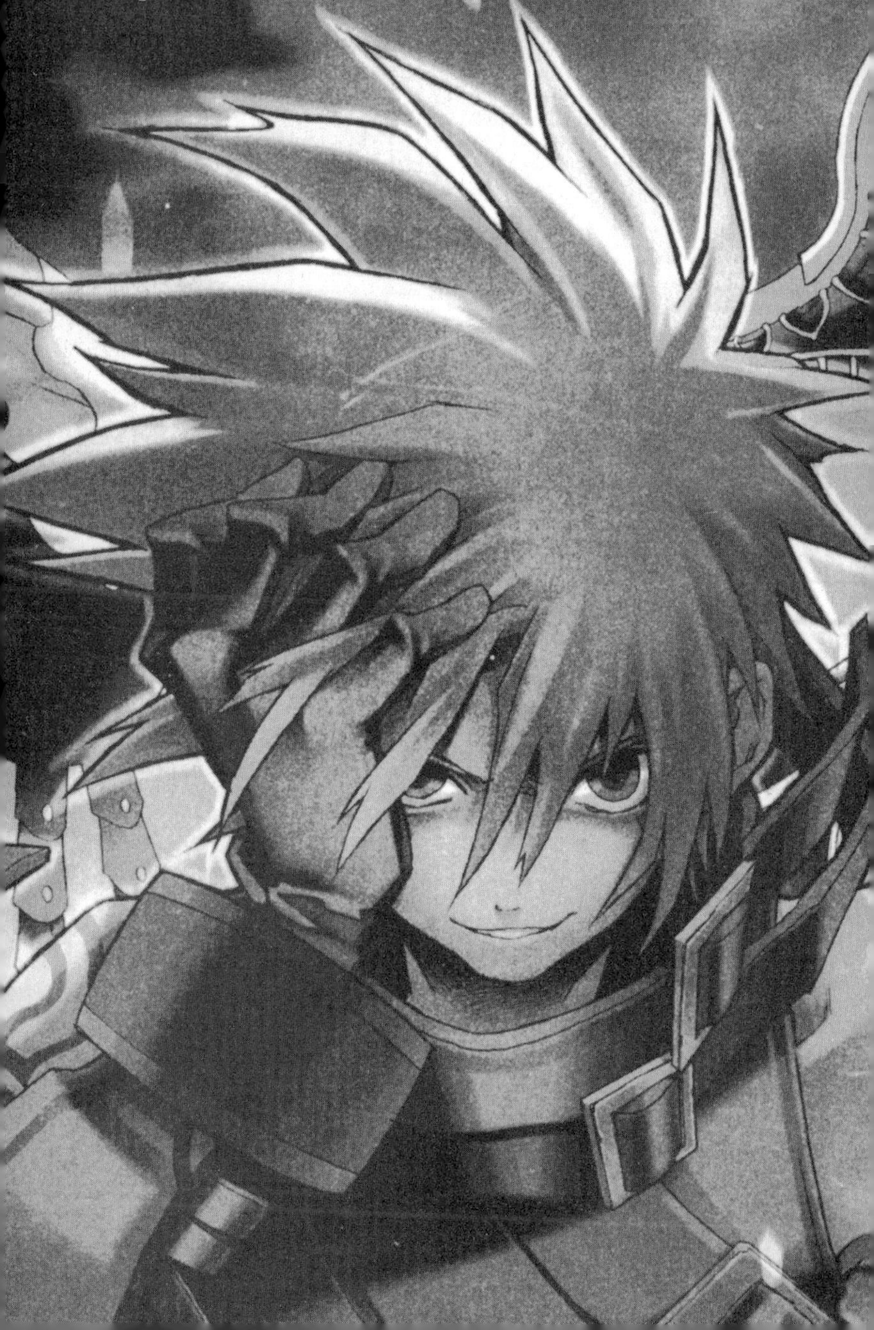

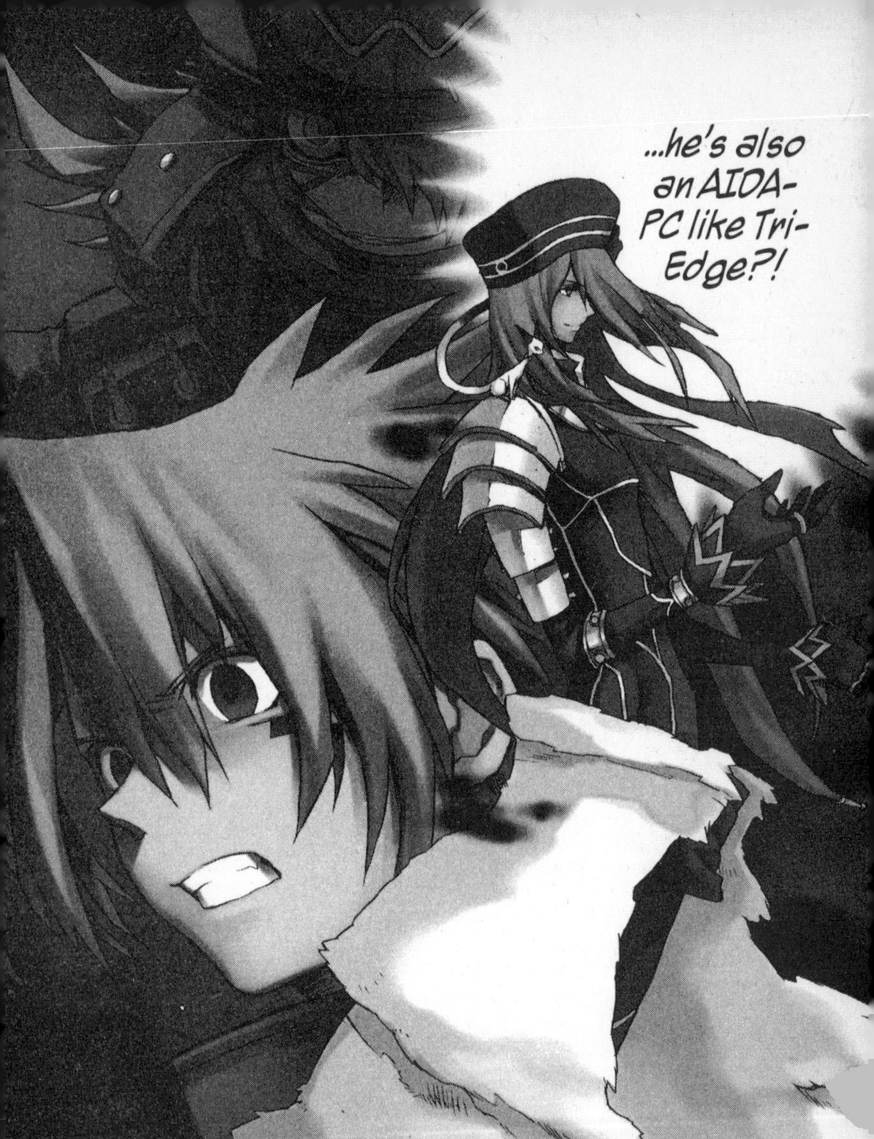
...he's also an AIDA-PC like Tri-Edge?!

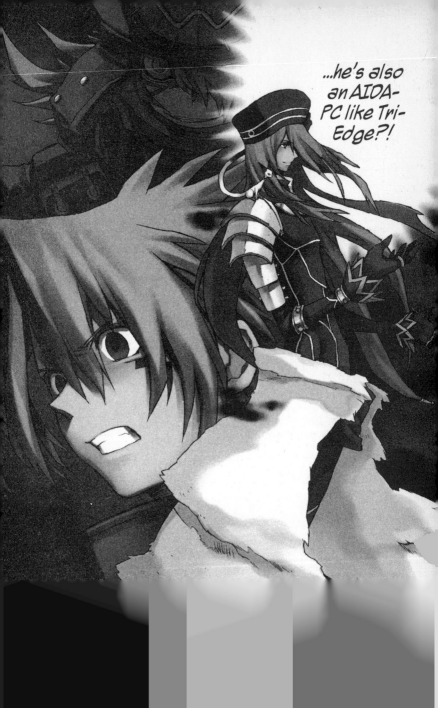

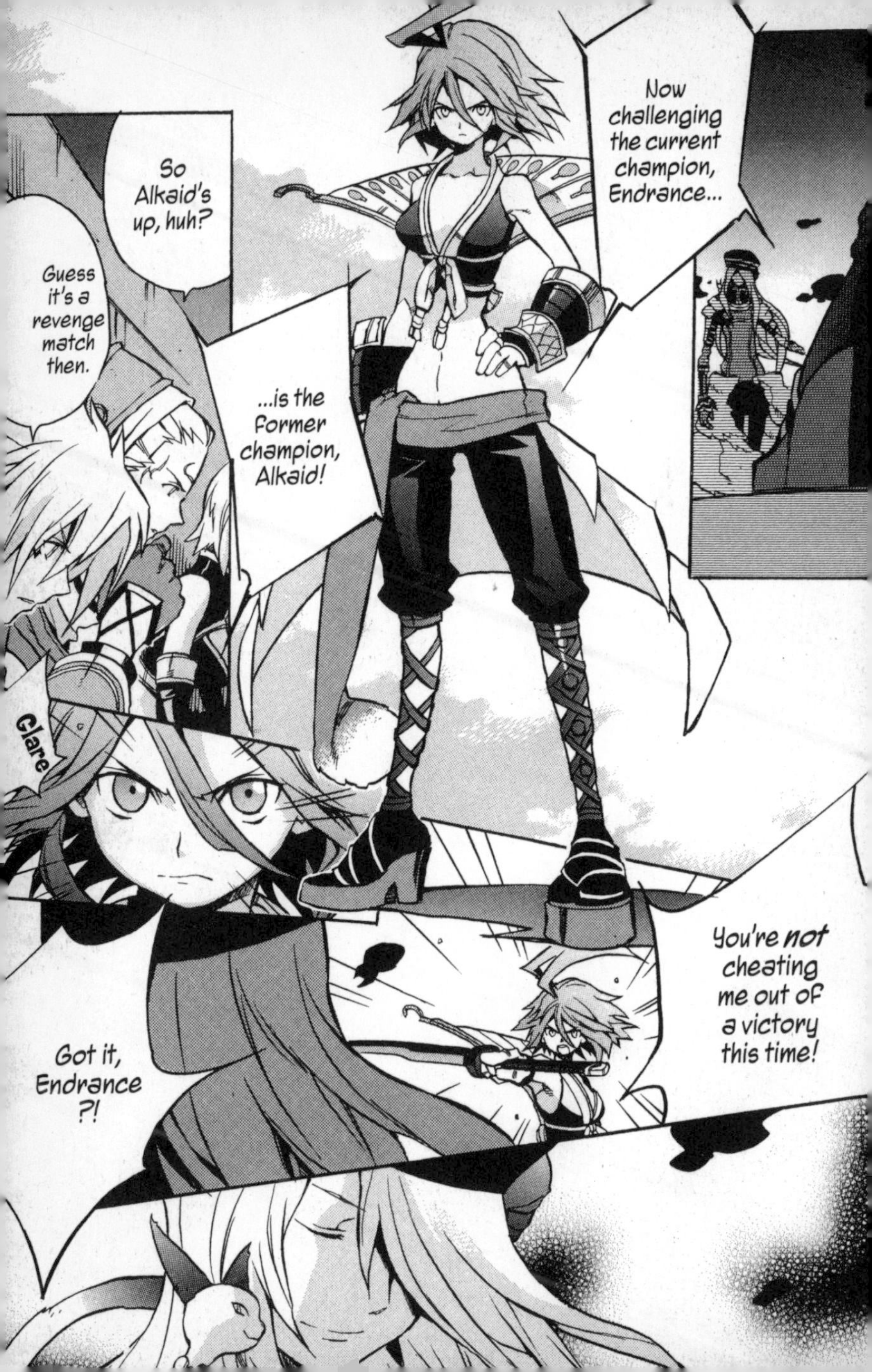

Now challenging the current champion, Endrance...
...is the former champion, Alkaid!
So Alkaid's up, huh?
Guess it's a revenge match then.
Glare
You're *not* cheating me out of a victory this time!
Got it, Endrance ?!

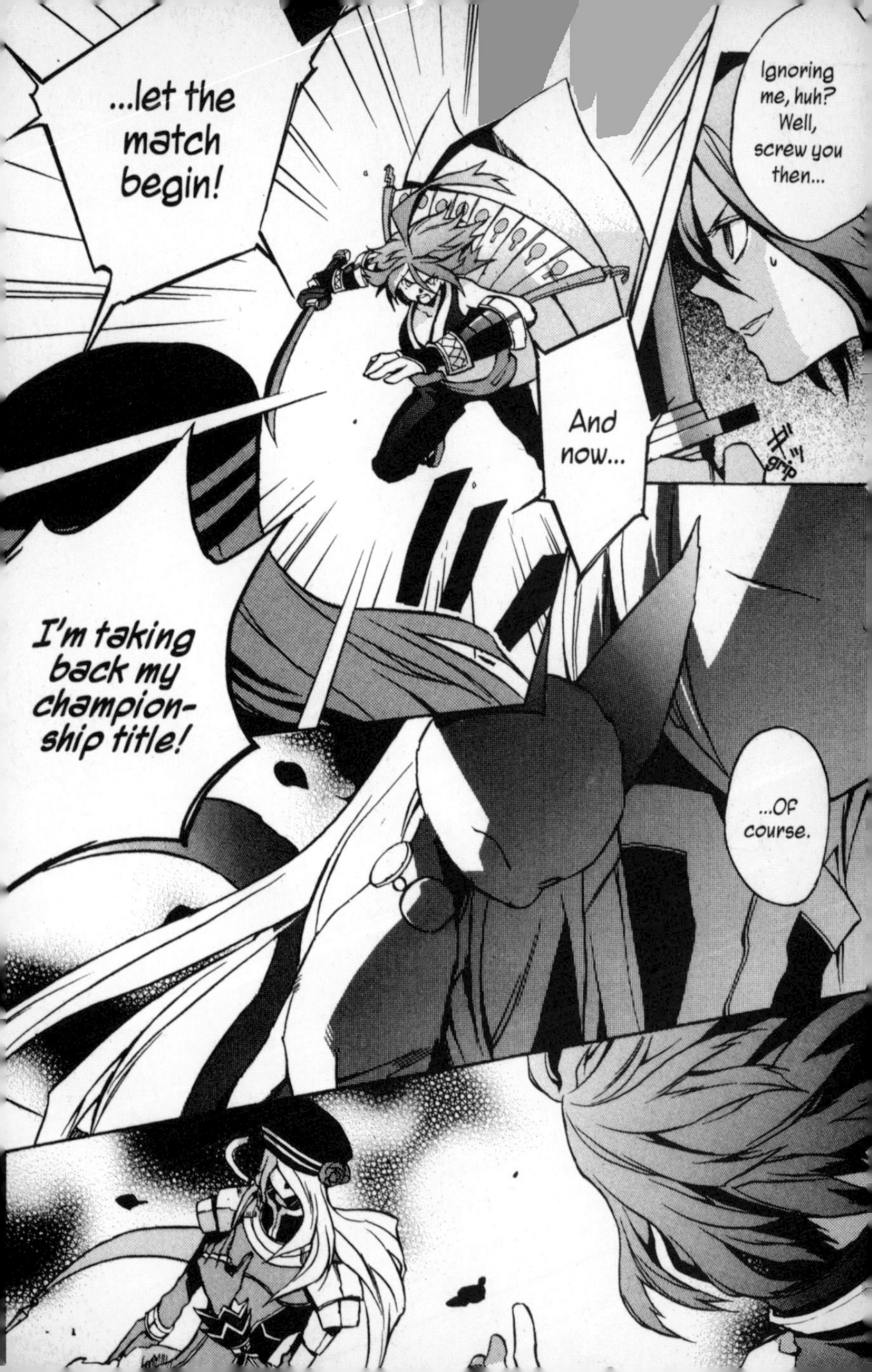
Ignoring me, huh? Well, screw you then...
grip
And now...
...let the match begin!
I'm taking back my championship title!
...Of course.

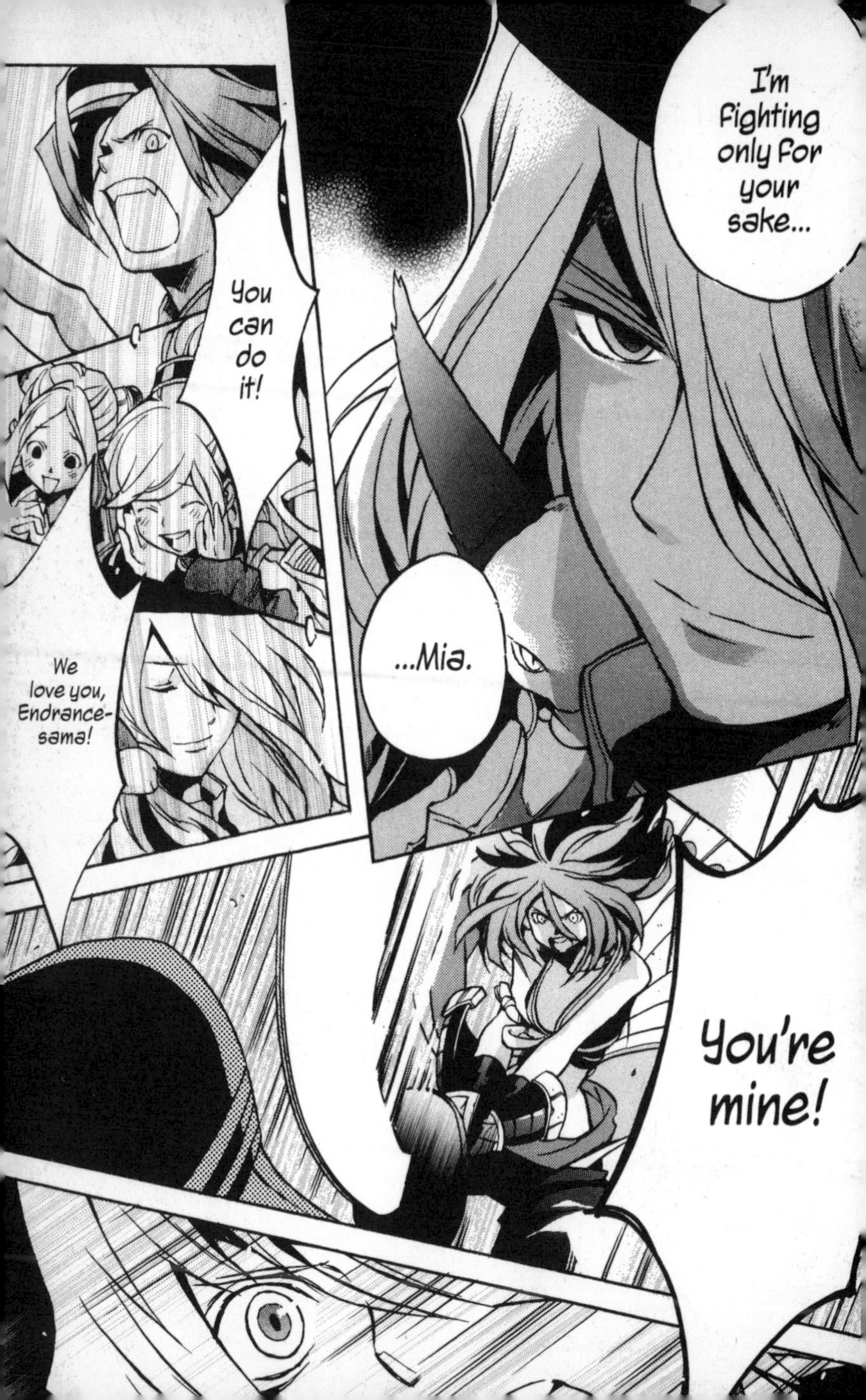
I'm fighting only for your sake...
...Mia.
You can do it!
We love you, Endrance-sama!
You're mine!

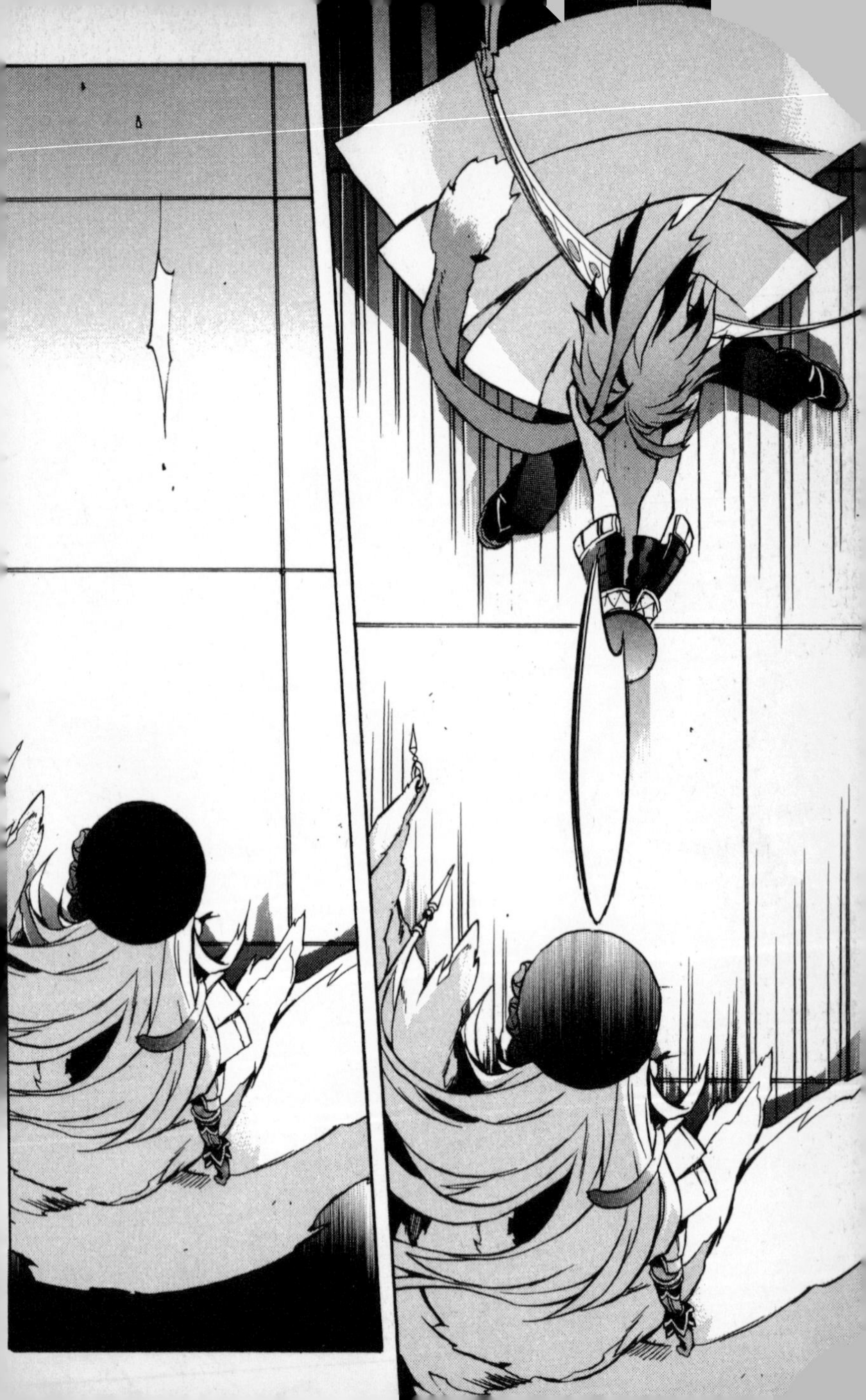

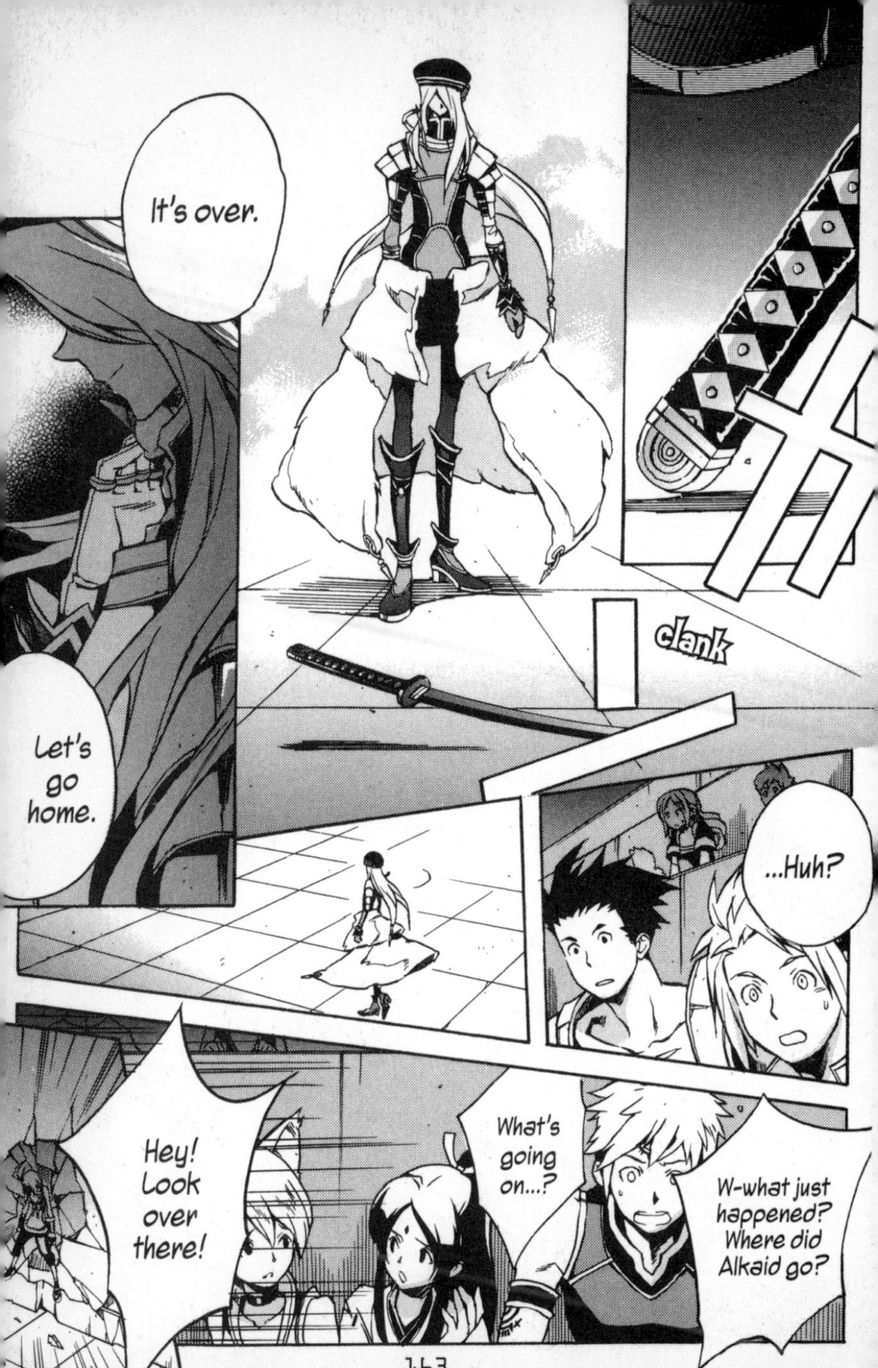
clank
It's over.
Let's go home.
...Huh?
W-what just happened? Where did Alkaid go?
What's going on...?
Hey! Look over there!

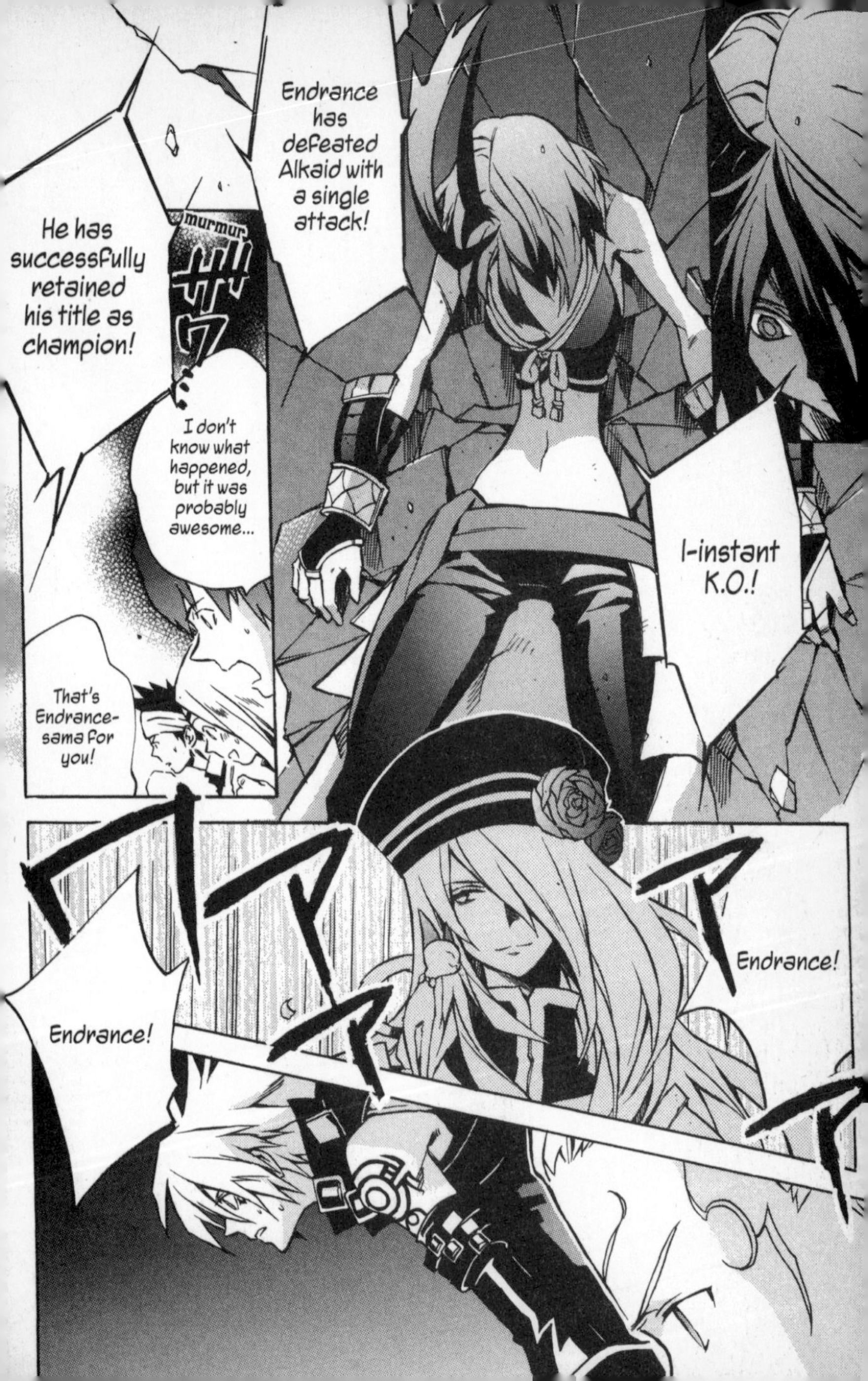
Endrance has defeated Alkaid with a single attack!
I-instant K.O.!
He has successfully retained his title as champion!
murmur
I don't know what happened, but it was probably awesome...
That's Endrance-sama for you!
Endrance!
Endrance!

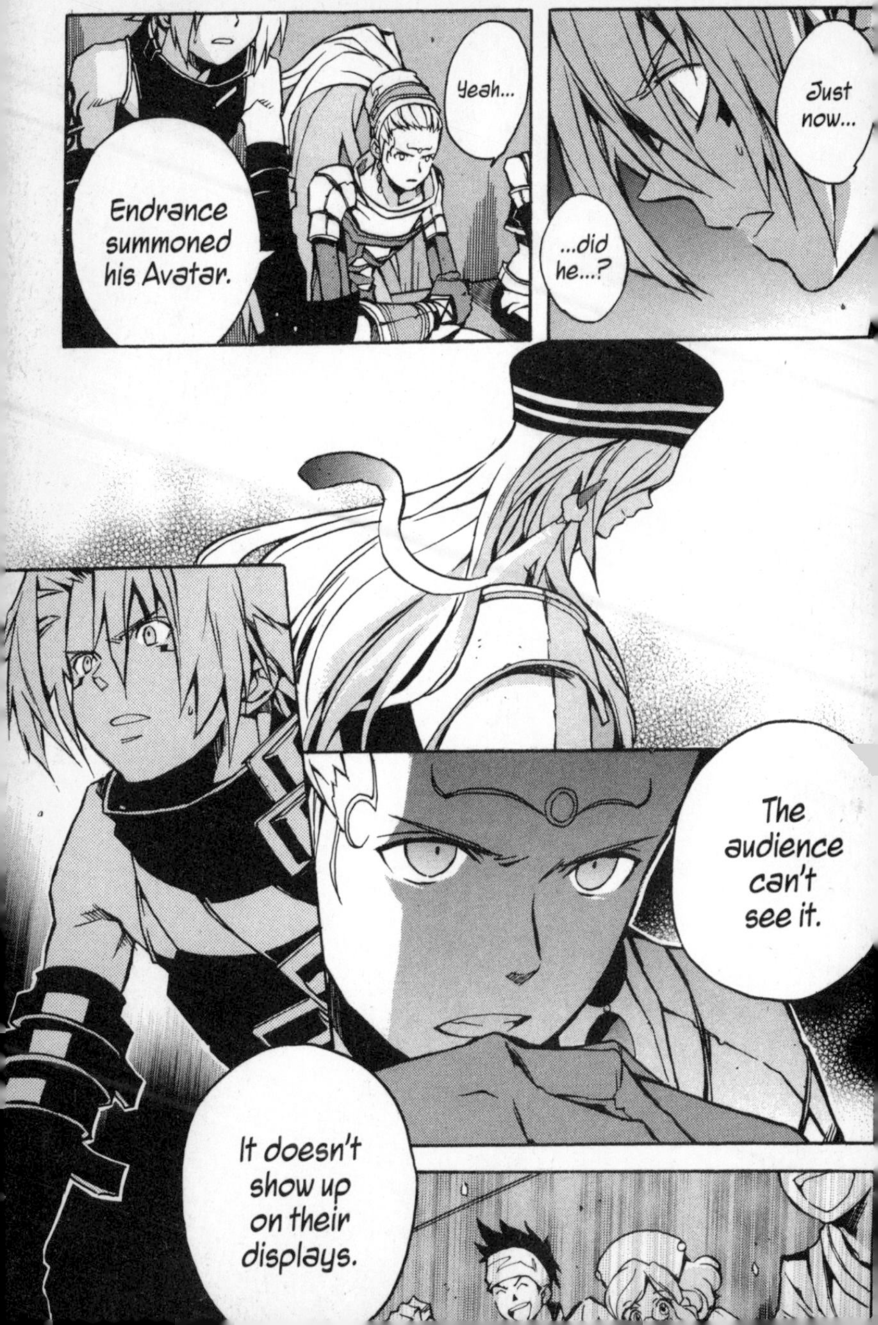
Just now...
...did he...?
Yeah...
Endrance summoned his Avatar.
The audience can't see it.
It doesn't show up on their displays.

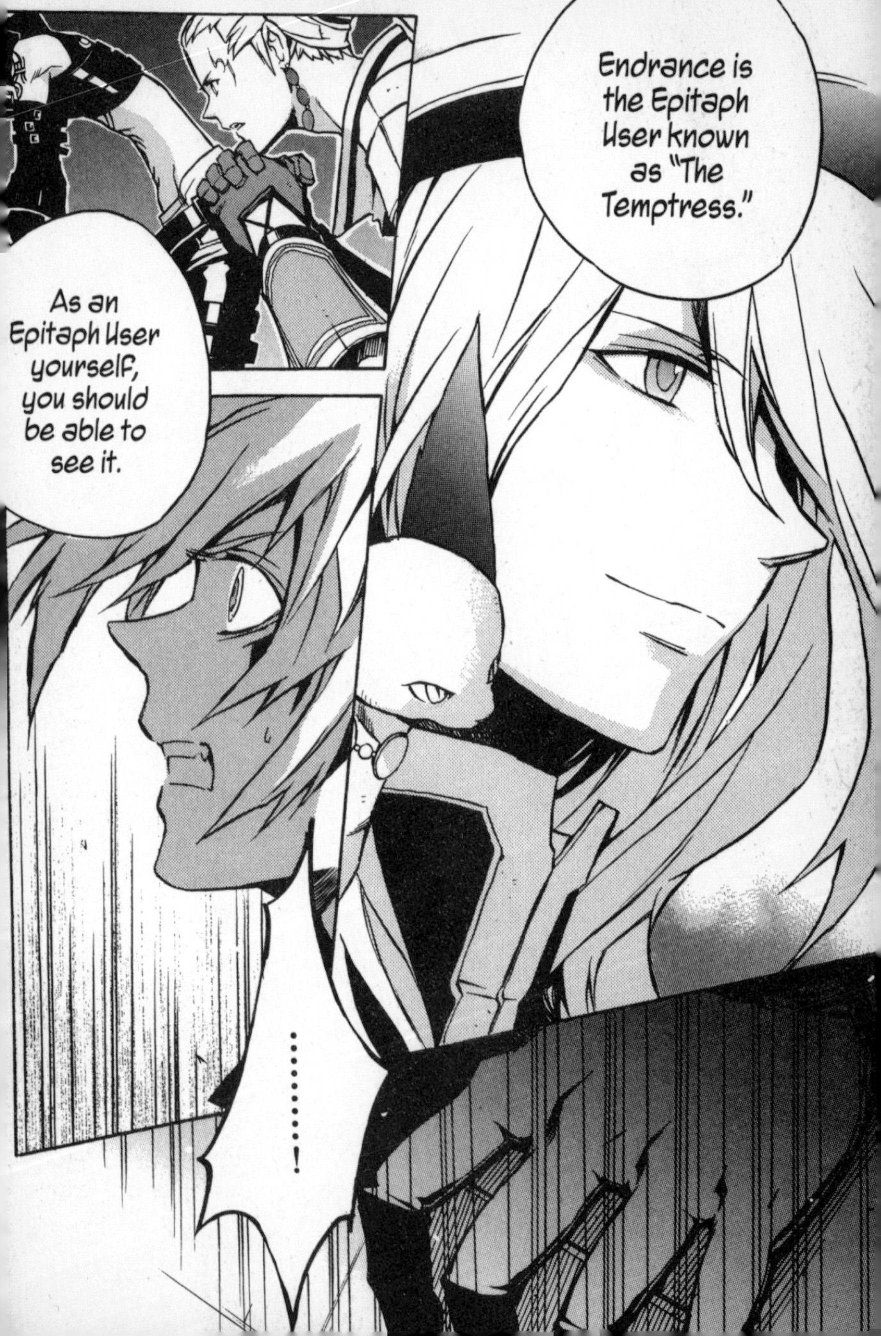
Endrance is the Epitaph User known as "The Temptress."
As an Epitaph User yourself, you should be able to see it.
.........!

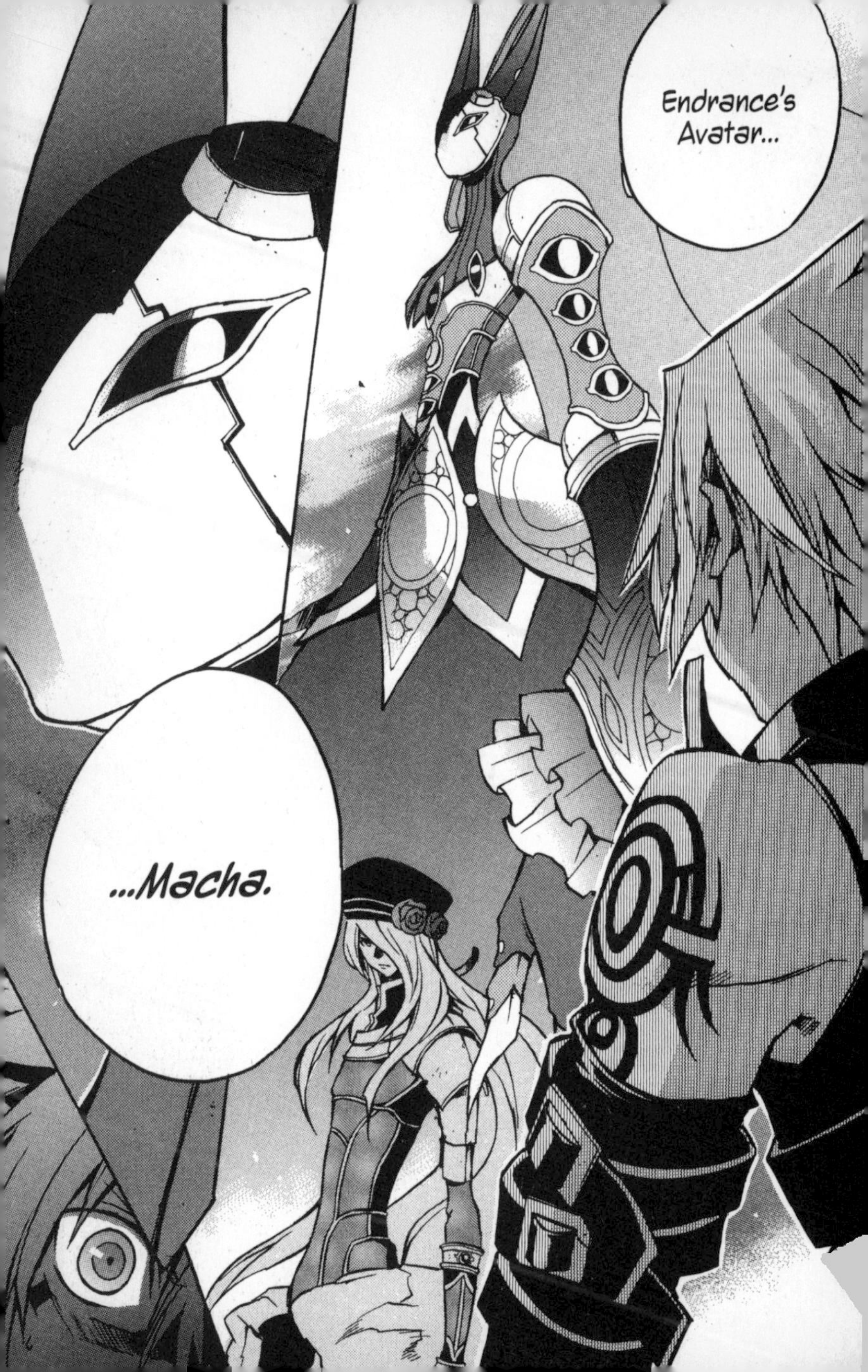
Endrance's Avatar...
...Macha.

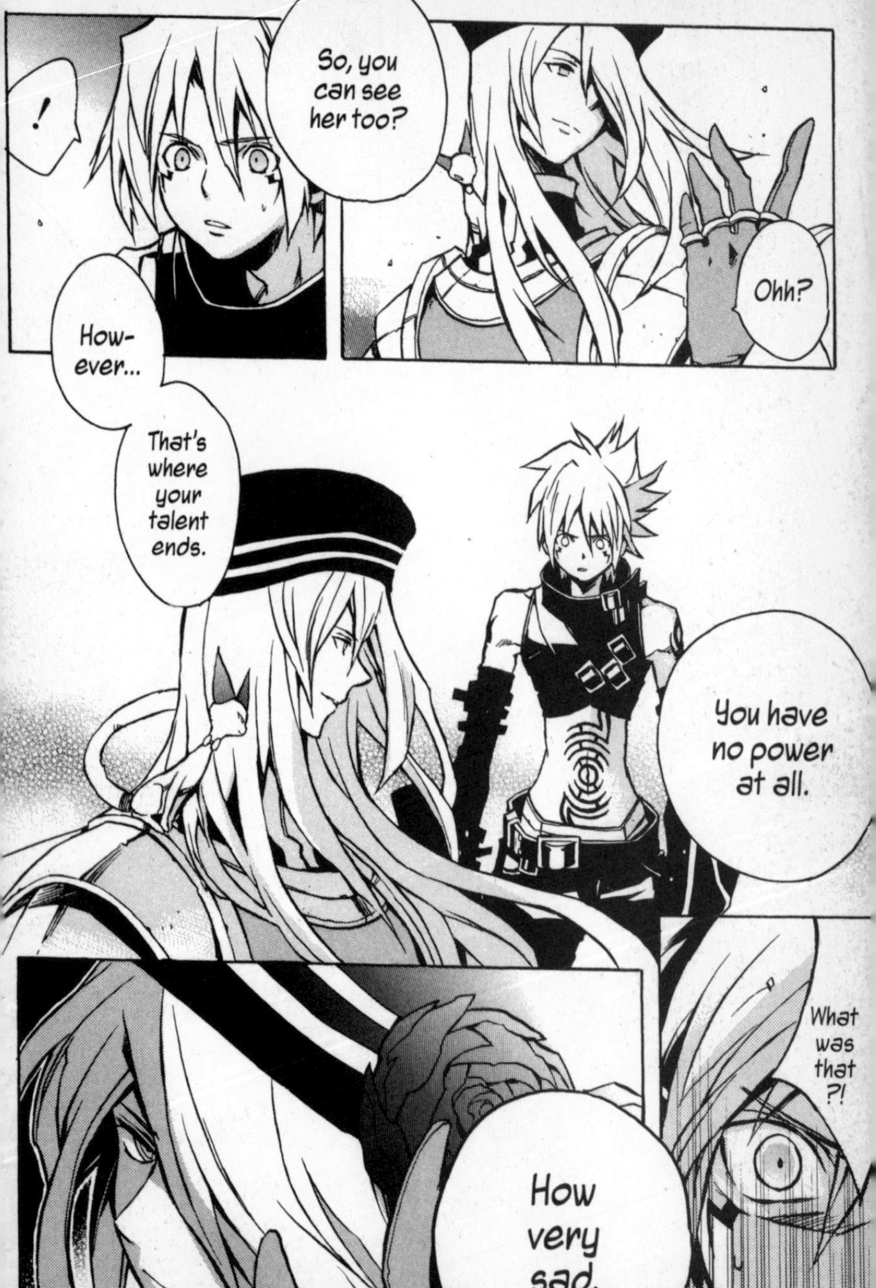
So, you can see her too?
Ohh?
!
How-ever...
That's where your talent ends.
You have no power at all.
What was that?!
How very sad.

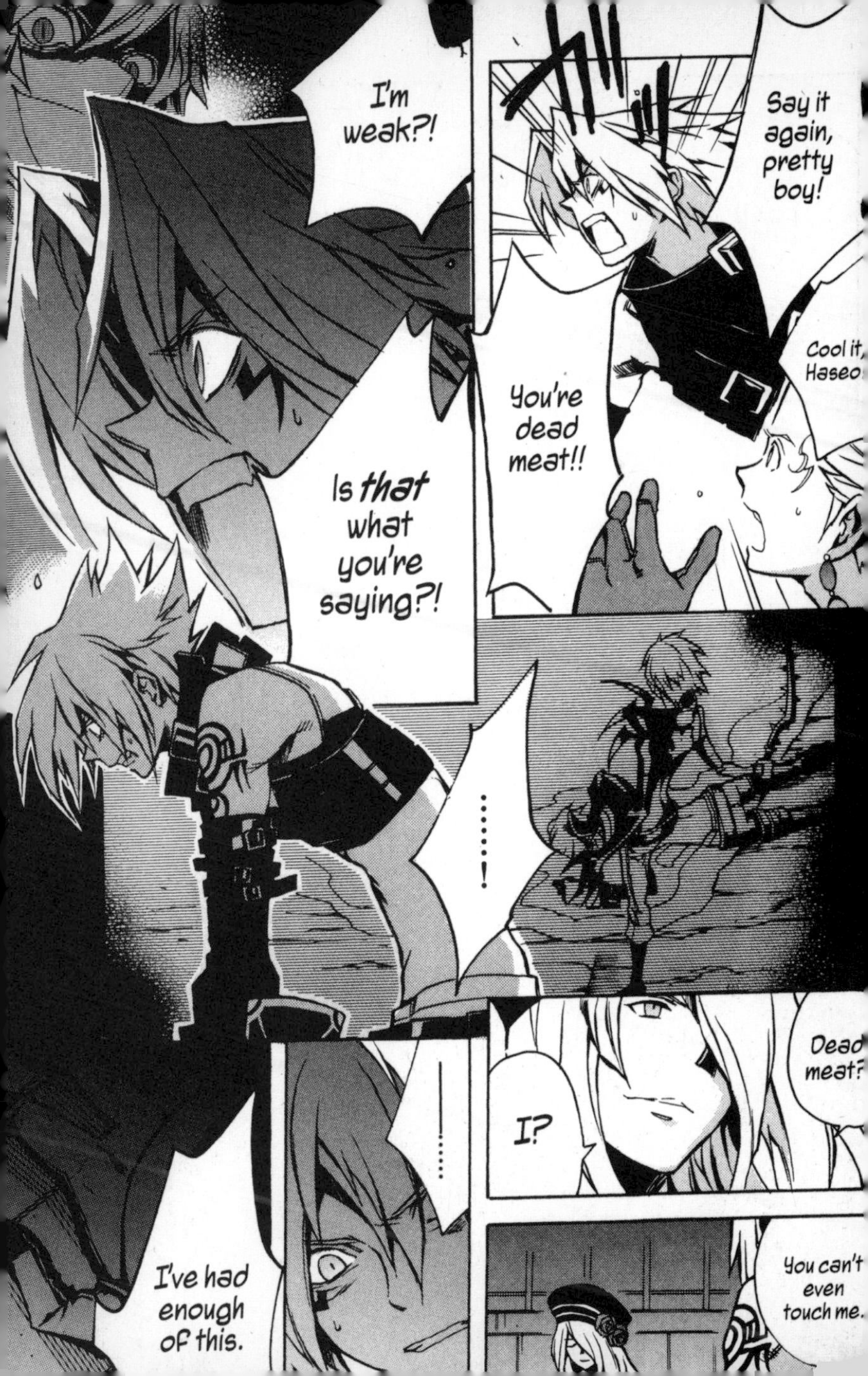
Say it again, pretty boy!
Cool it, Haseo!
You're dead meat!!
I'm weak?!
Is *that* what you're saying?!
......!
Dead meat?
I?
You can't even touch me.
......
I've had enough of this.

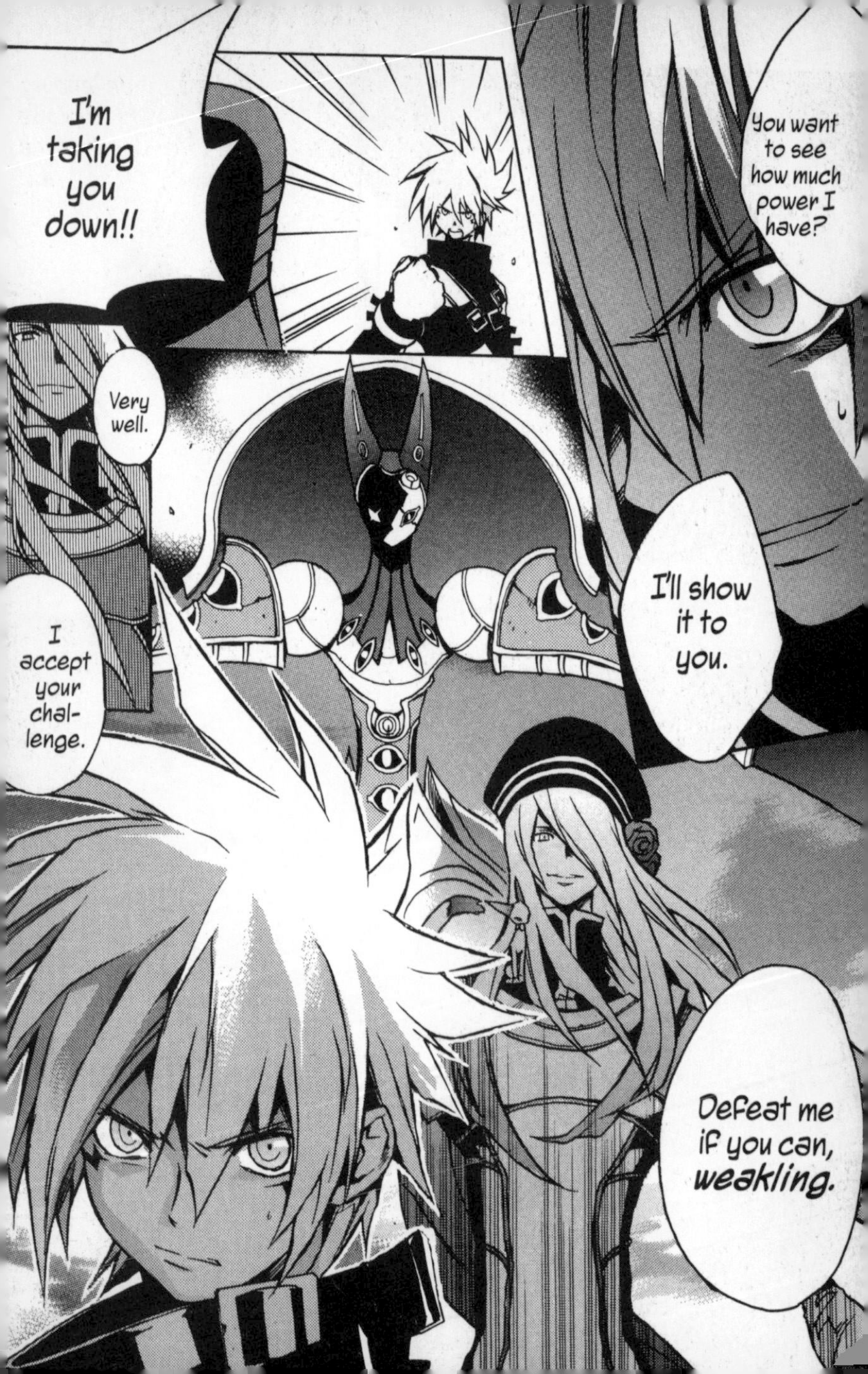
You want to see how much power I have?
I'll show it to you.
I'm taking you down!!
Very well.
I accept your chal-lenge.
Defeat me if you can, ***weakling.***

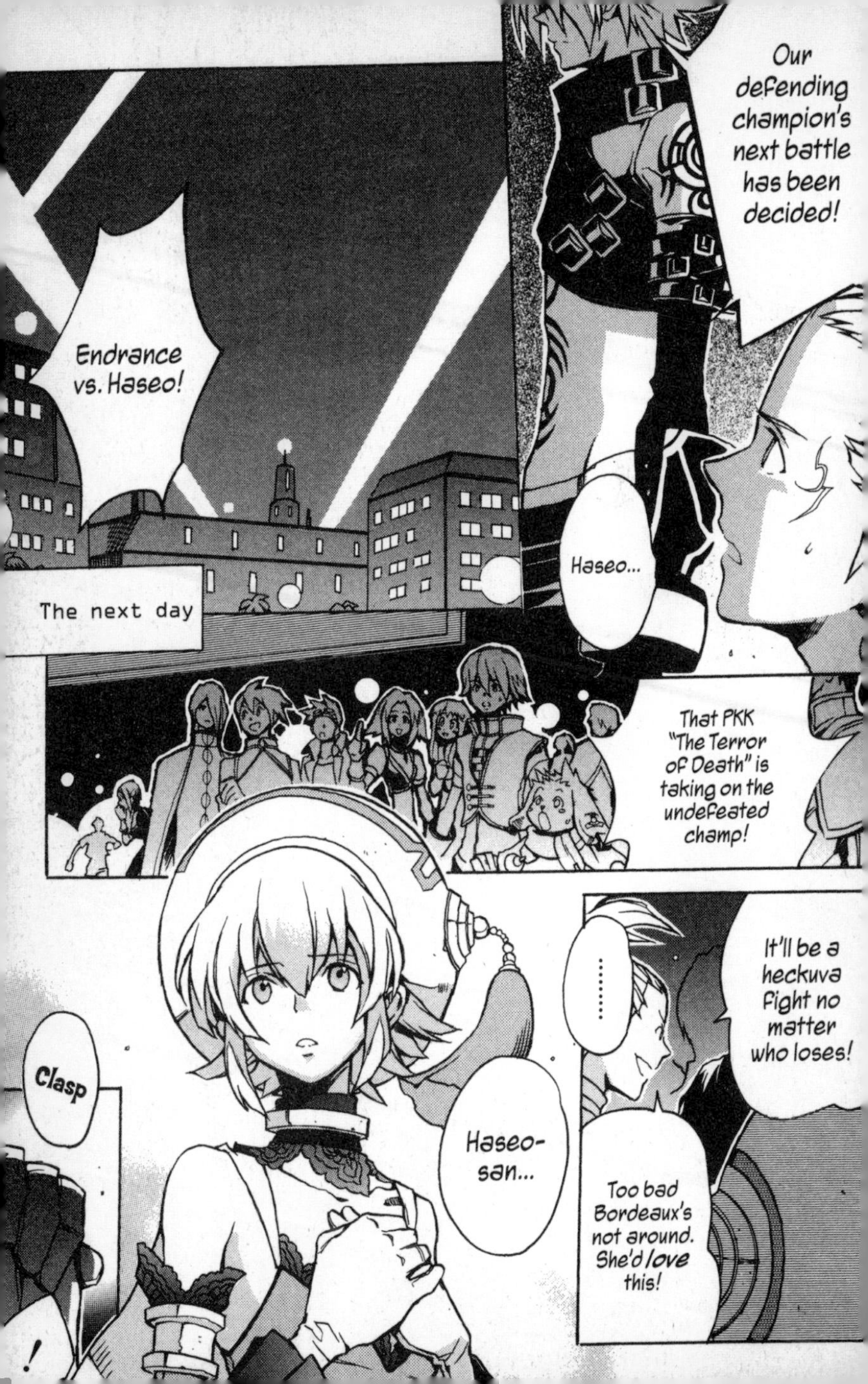
Our defending champion's next battle has been decided!
Haseo...
Endrance vs. Haseo!
The next day
That PKK "The Terror of Death" is taking on the undefeated champ!
It'll be a heckuva fight no matter who loses!
......
Too bad Bordeaux's not around. She'd *love* this!
Haseo-san...
Clasp
!

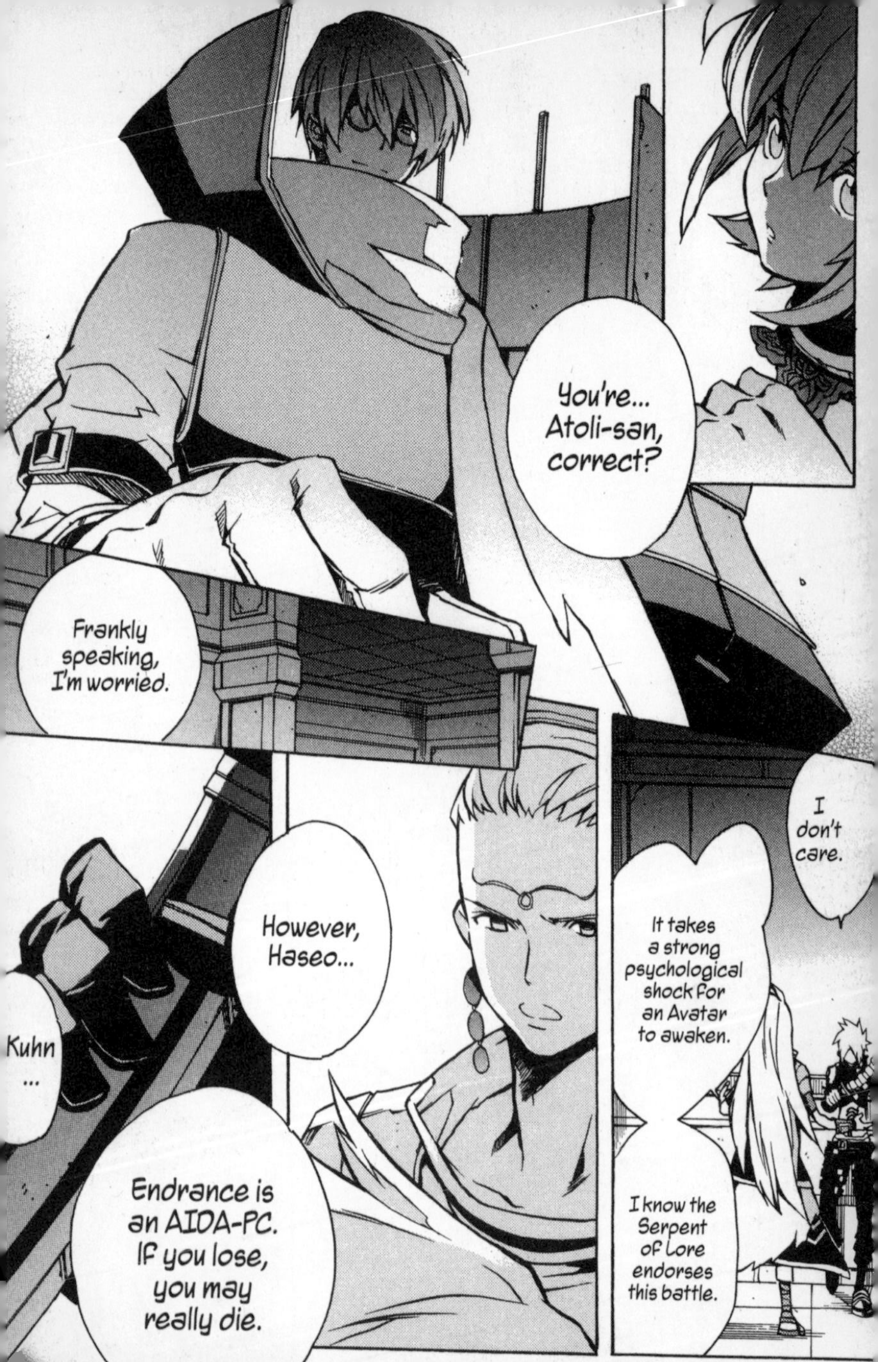
You're... Atoli-san, correct?
Frankly speaking, I'm worried.
I don't care.
It takes a strong psychological shock for an Avatar to awaken.
I know the Serpent of Lore endorses this battle.
However, Haseo...
Kuhn ...
Endrance is an AIDA-PC. If you lose, you may really die.

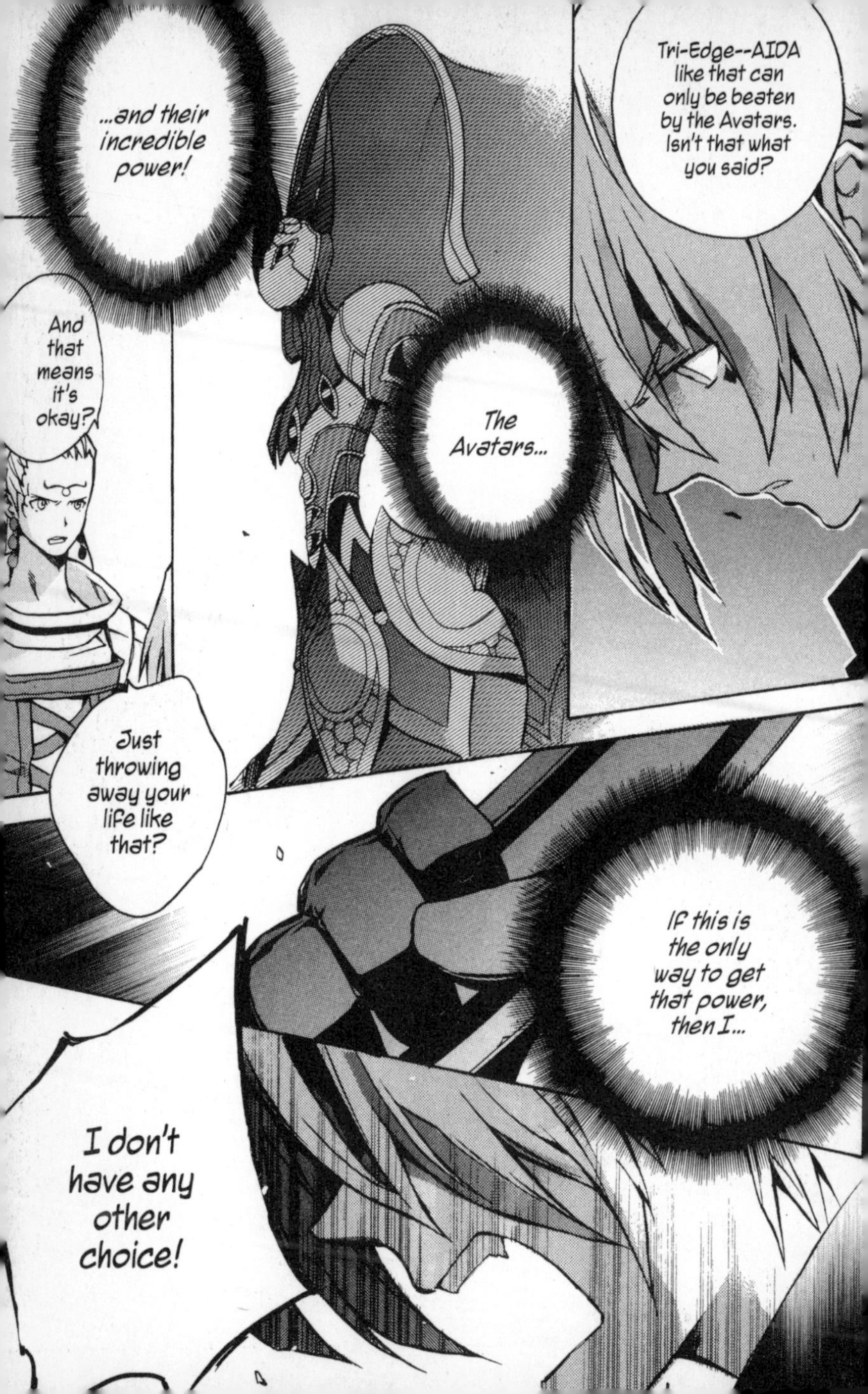
Tri-Edge--AIDA like that can only be beaten by the Avatars. Isn't that what you said?
The Avatars...
...and their incredible power!
And that means it's okay?
Just throwing away your life like that?
If this is the only way to get that power, then I...
I don't have any other choice!

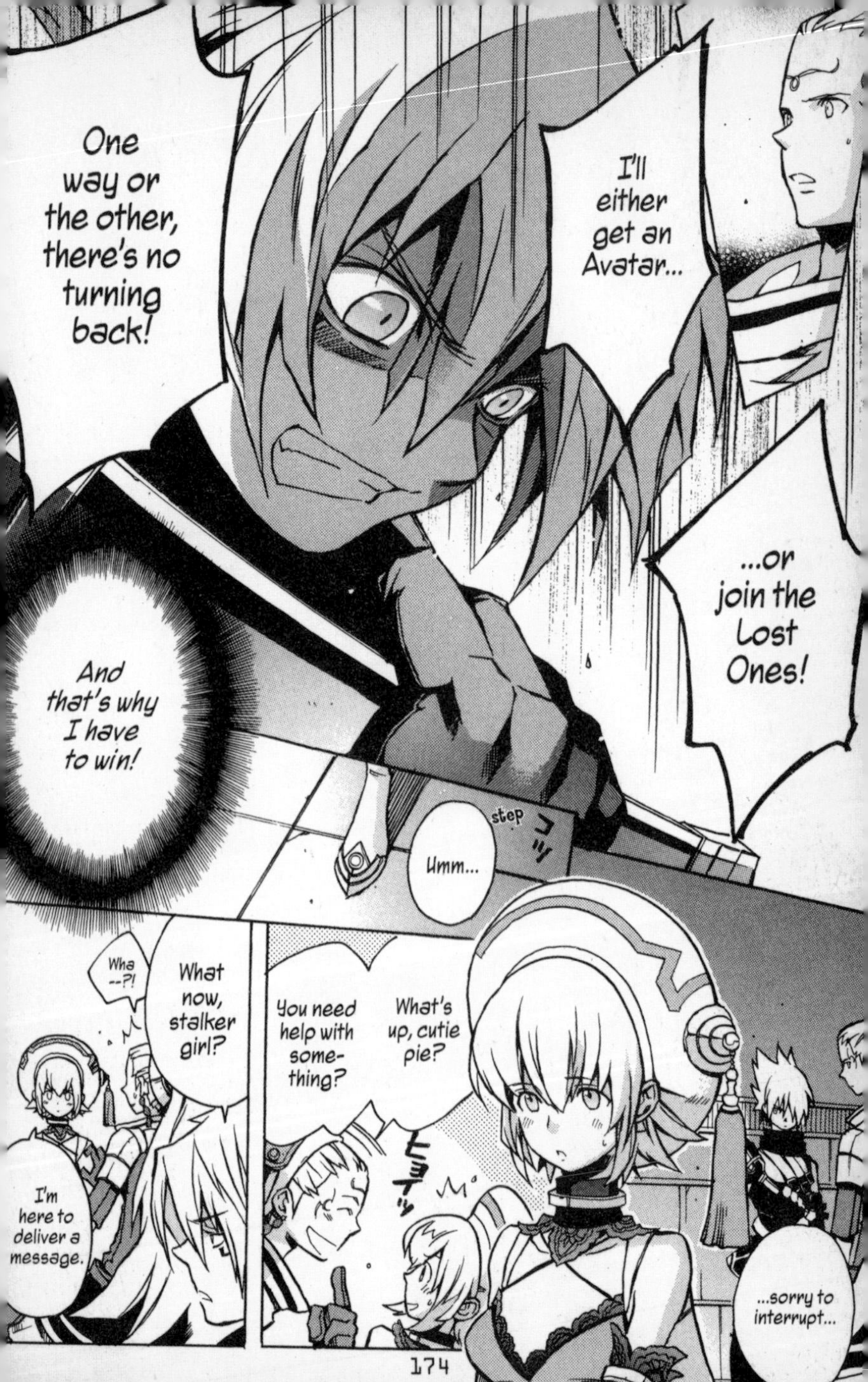
I'll either get an Avatar...
One way or the other, there's no turning back!
...or join the Lost Ones!
And that's why I have to win!
step コツ
Umm...
What's up, cutie pie?
You need help with some-thing?
ヒョイッ
...sorry to interrupt...
What now, stalker girl?
Wha --?!
I'm here to deliver a message.

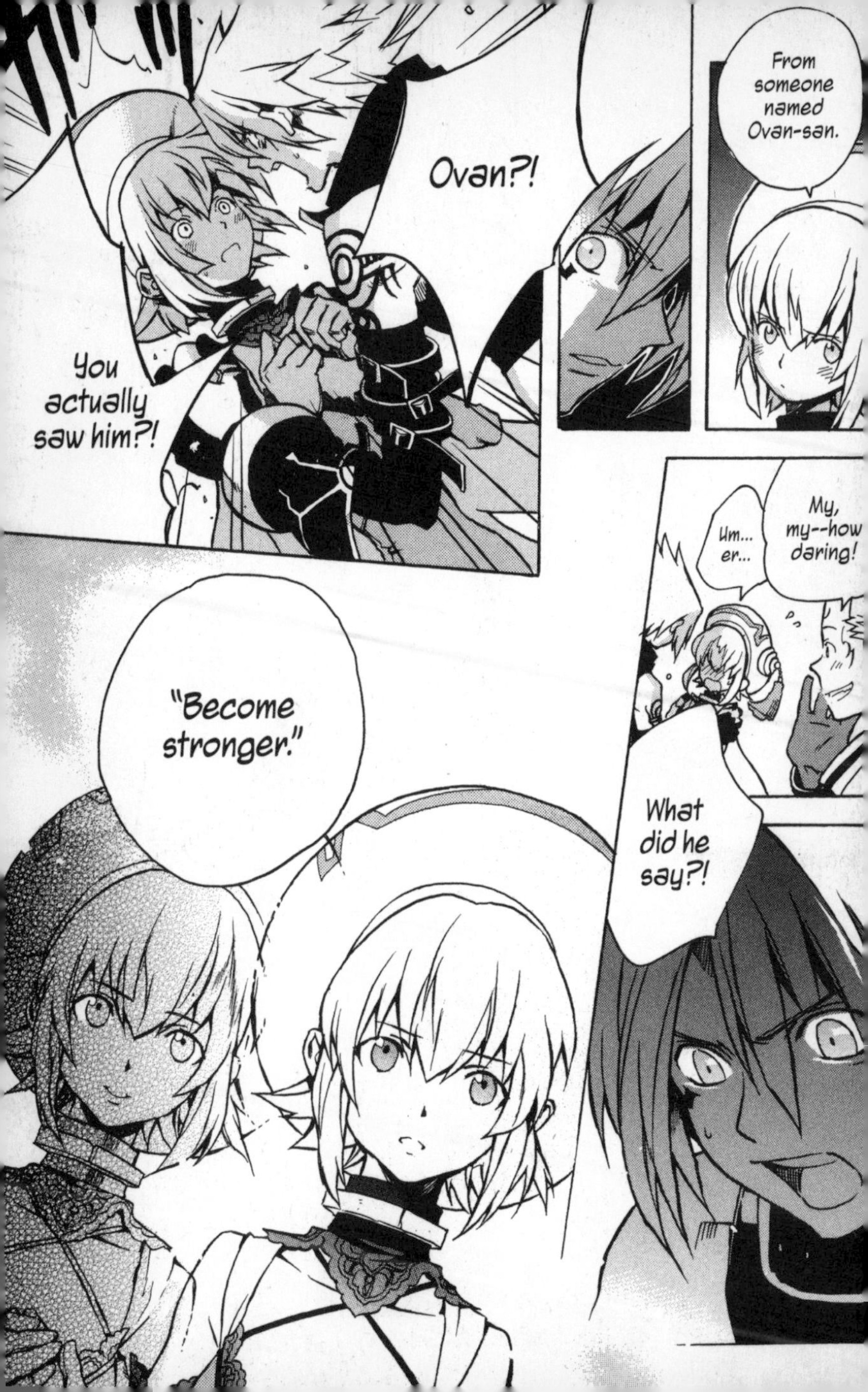
From someone named Ovan-san.
Ovan?!
You actually saw him?!
My, my--how daring!
Um... er...
What did he say?!
"Become stronger."

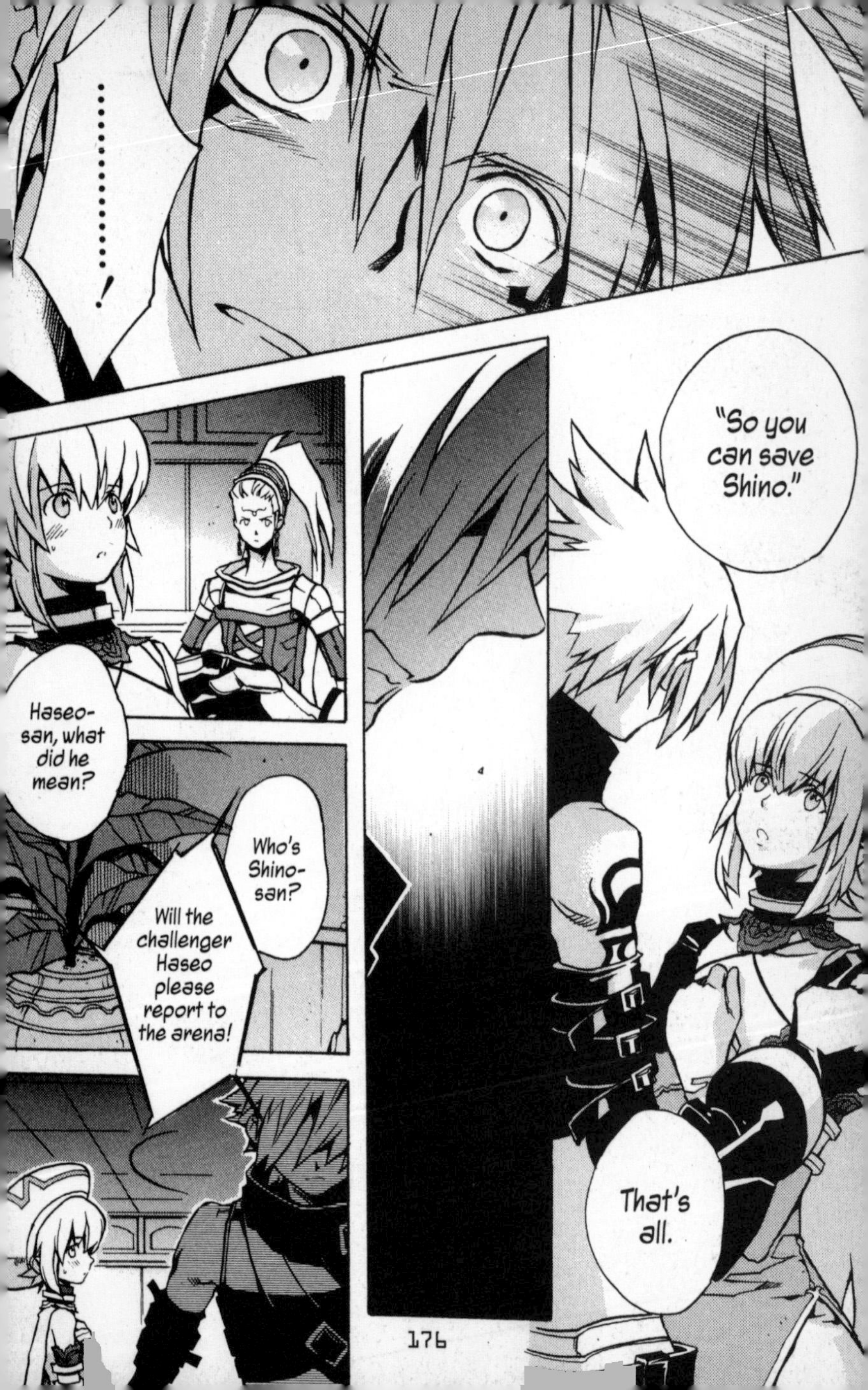
......!
"So you can save Shino."
That's all.
Haseo-san, what did he mean?
Who's Shino-san?
Will the challenger Haseo please report to the arena!

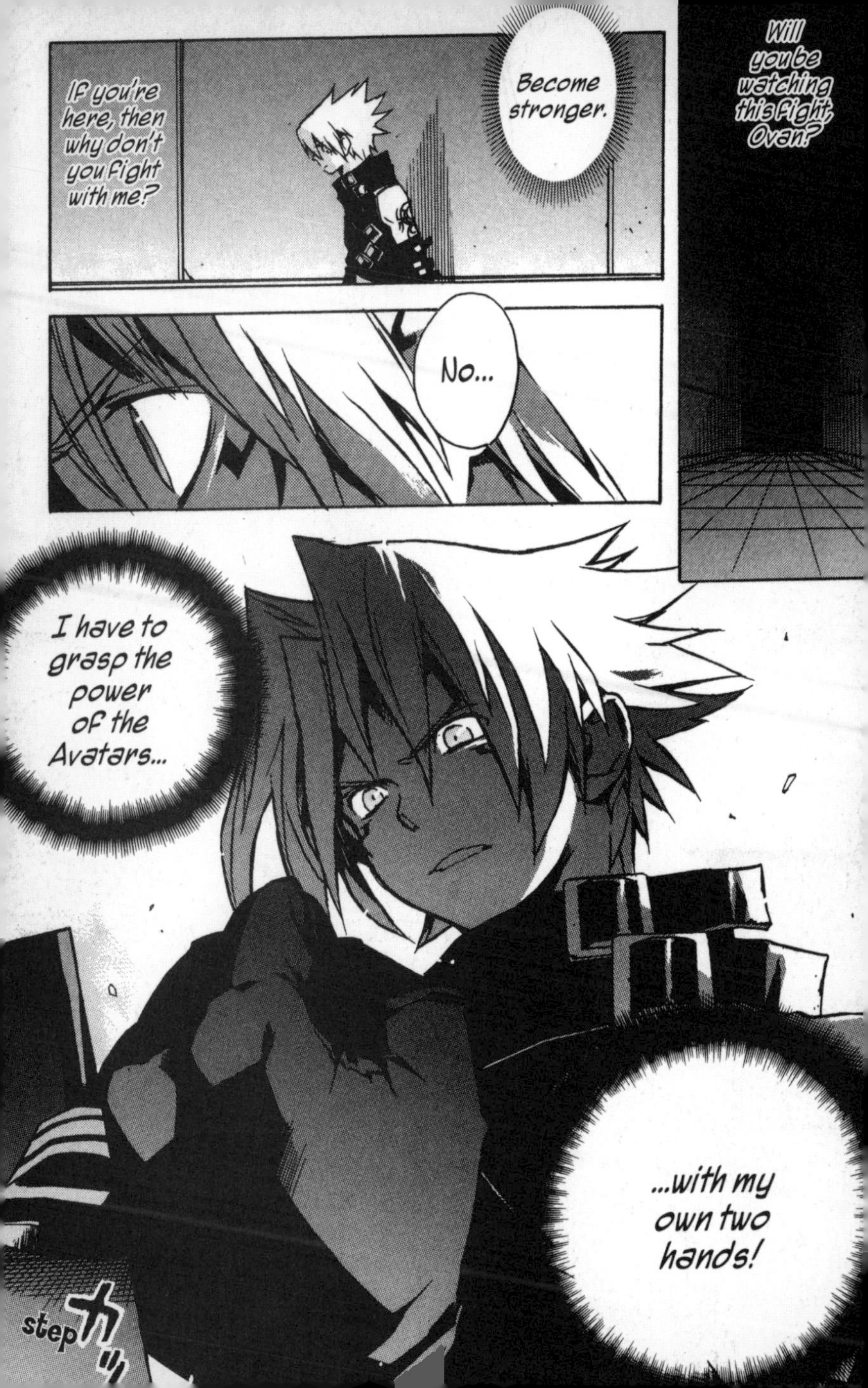

Will you be watching this fight, Ovan?
Become stronger.
If you're here, then why don't you fight with me?
No...
I have to grasp the power of the Avatars...
...with my own two hands!
step

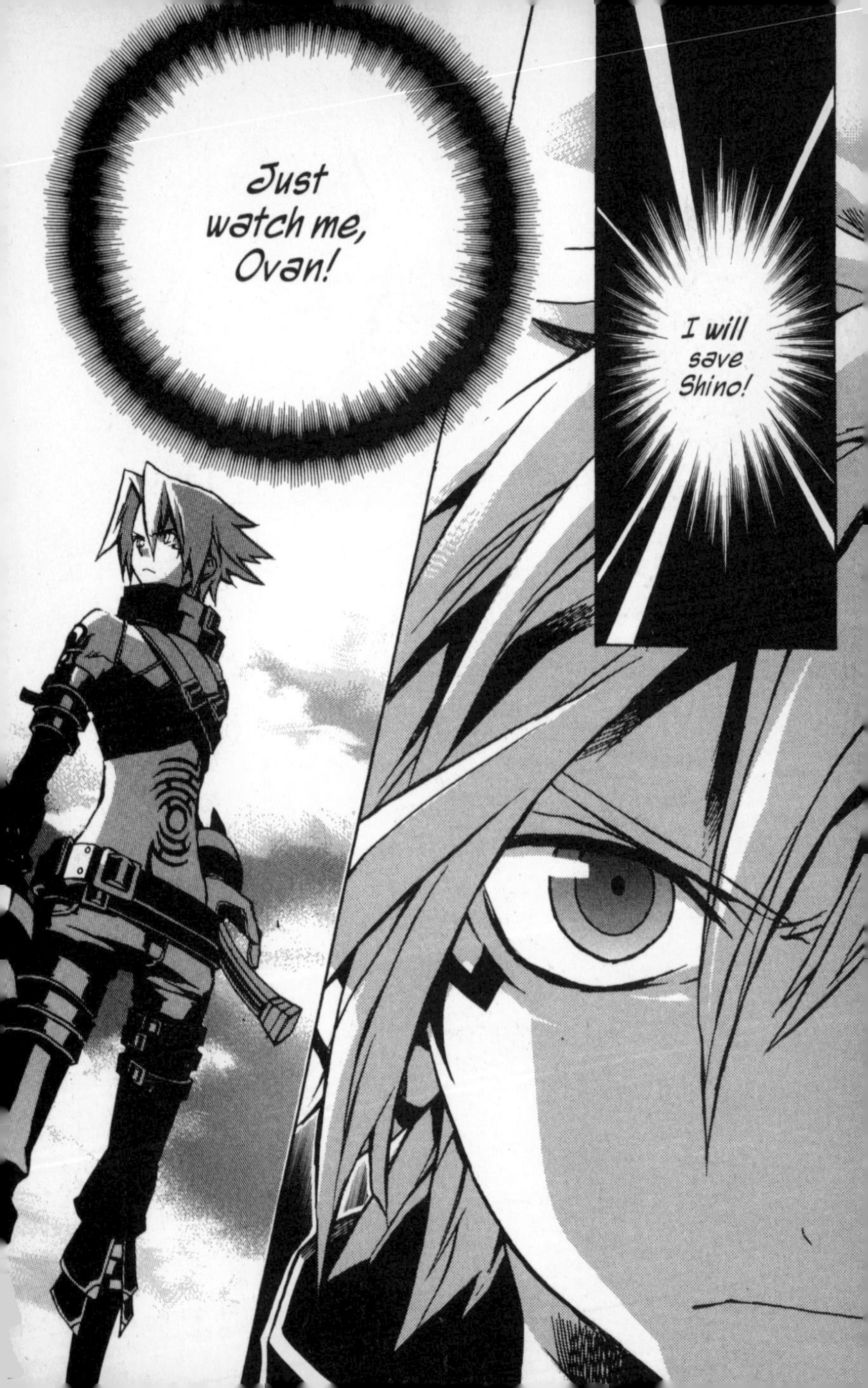
I will save Shino!
Just watch me, Ovan!

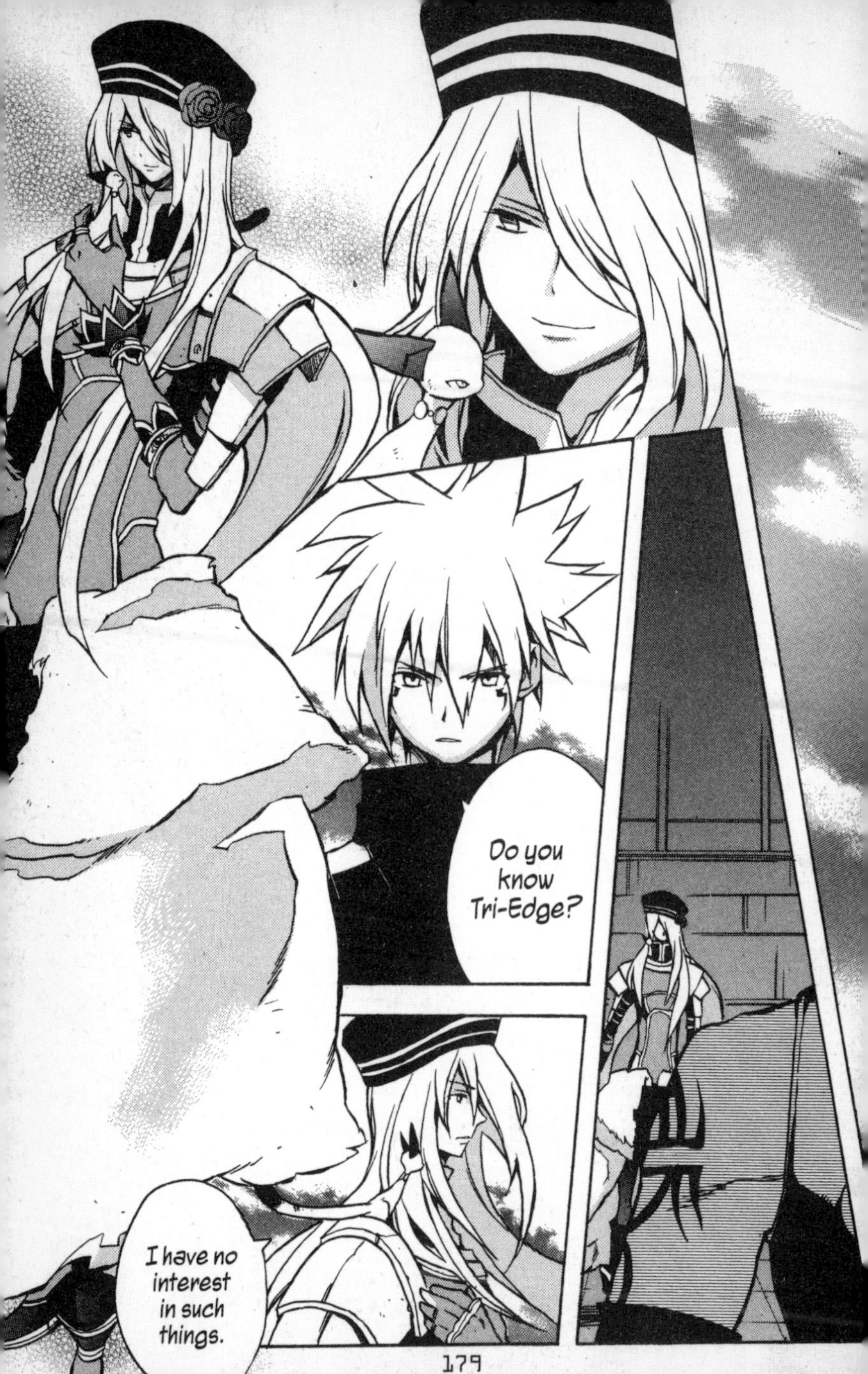
Do you know Tri-Edge?
I have no interest in such things.

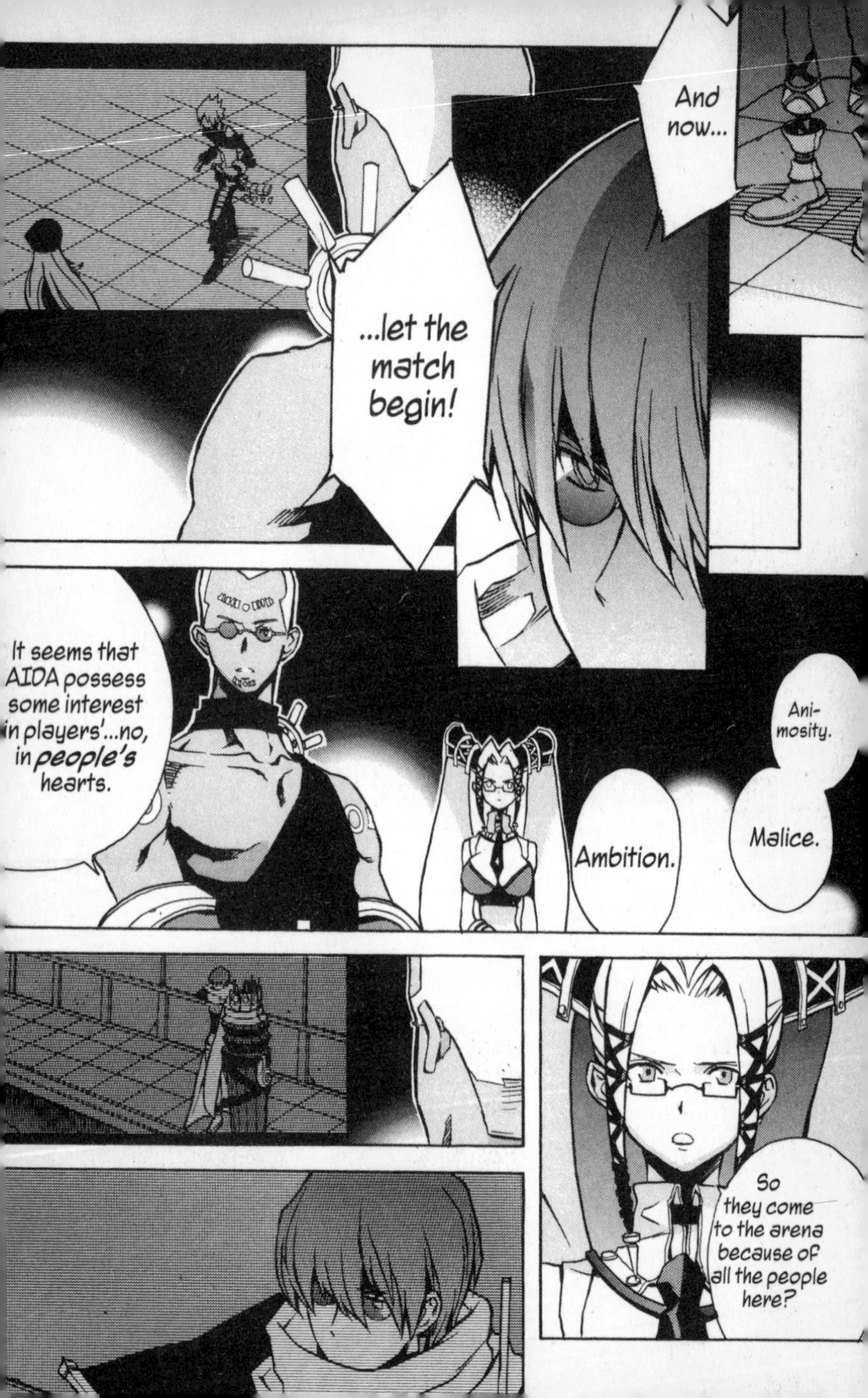
And now...
...let the match begin!
Ani-mosity.
Malice.
Ambition.
It seems that AIDA possess some interest in players'...no, in *people's* hearts.
So they come to the arena because of all the people here?

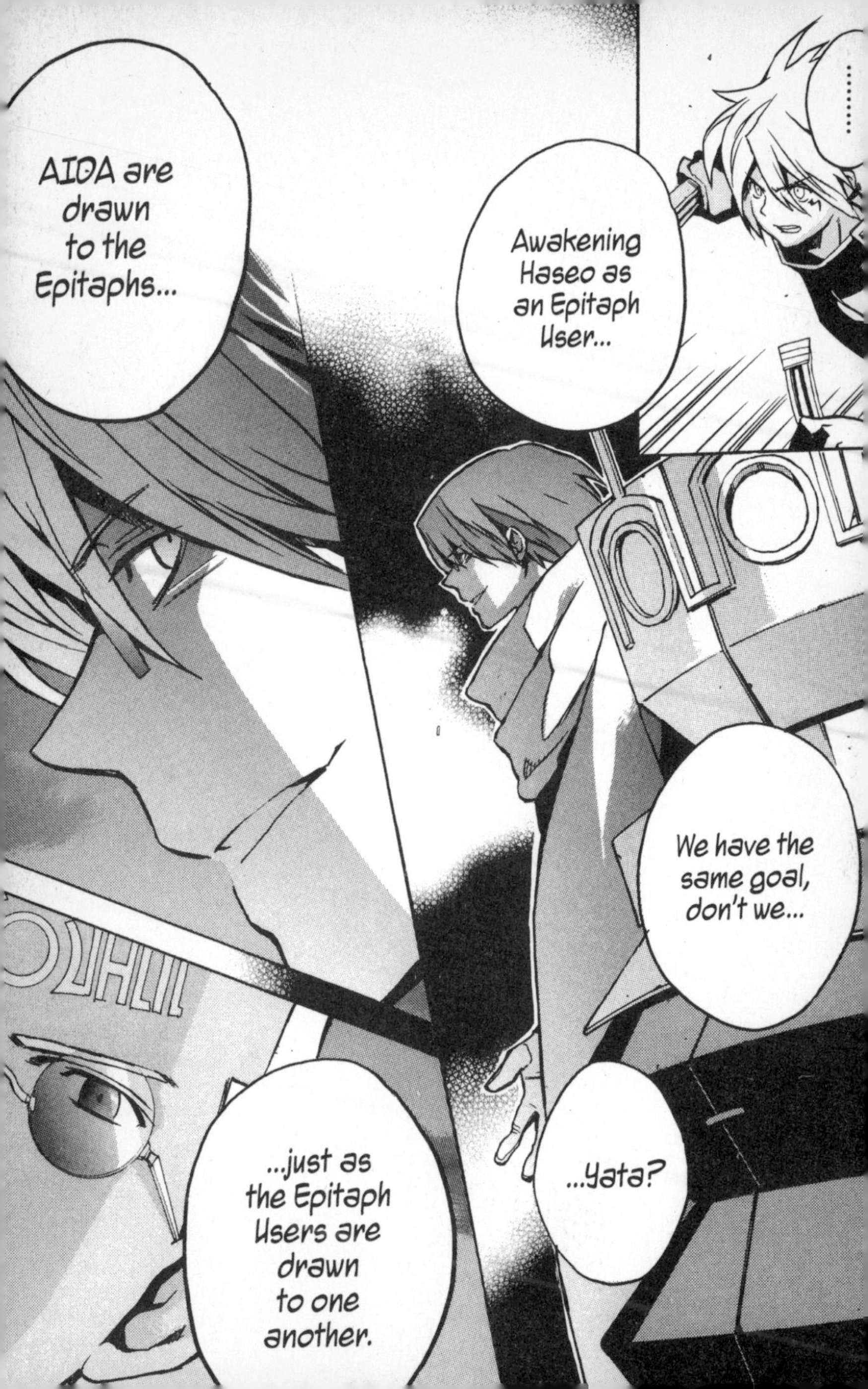
......
Awakening Haseo as an Epitaph User...
AIDA are drawn to the Epitaphs...
We have the same goal, don't we...
...Yata?
...just as the Epitaph Users are drawn to one another.

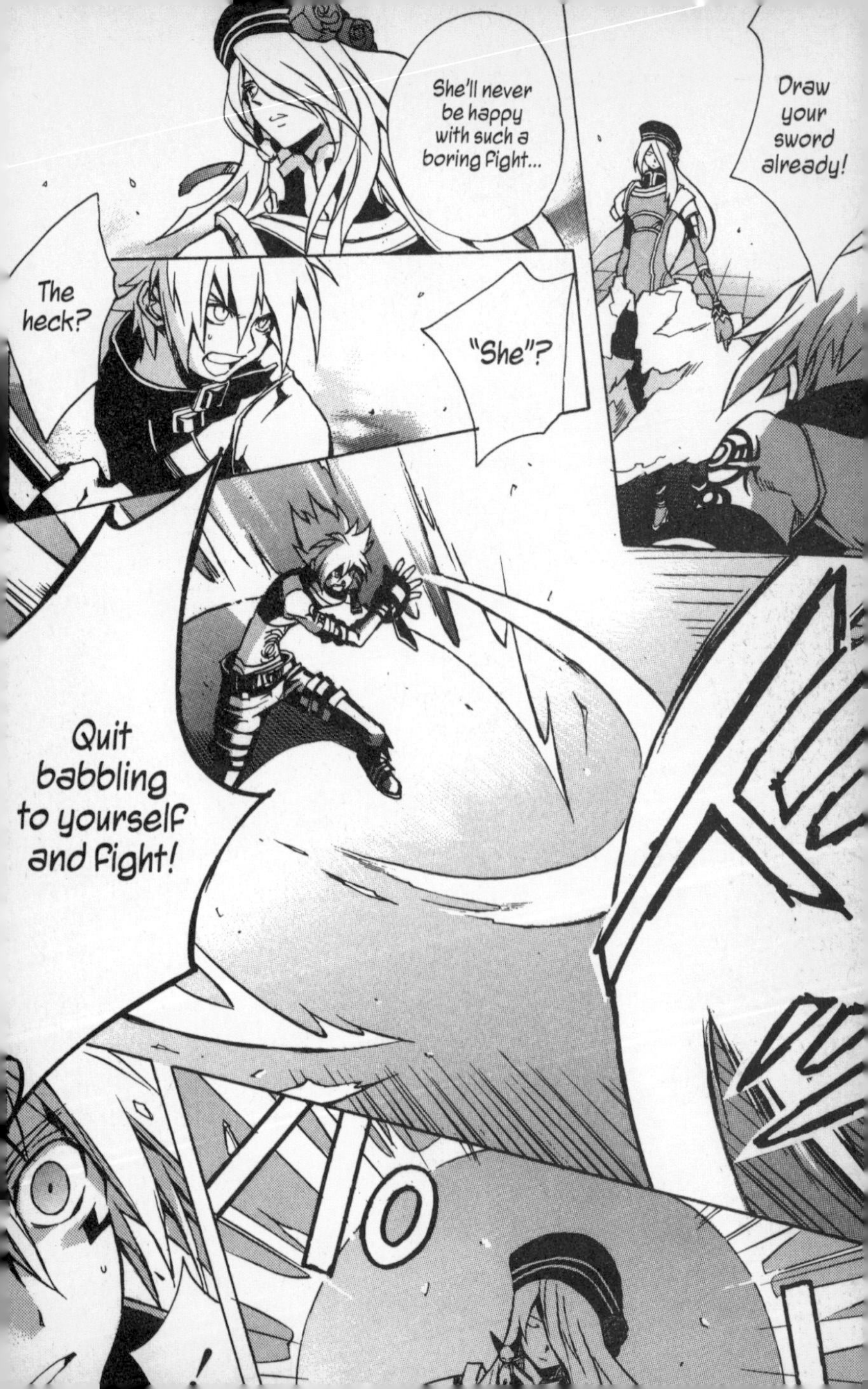
Draw your sword already!
She'll never be happy with such a boring fight...
The heck?
"She"?
Quit babbling to yourself and fight!

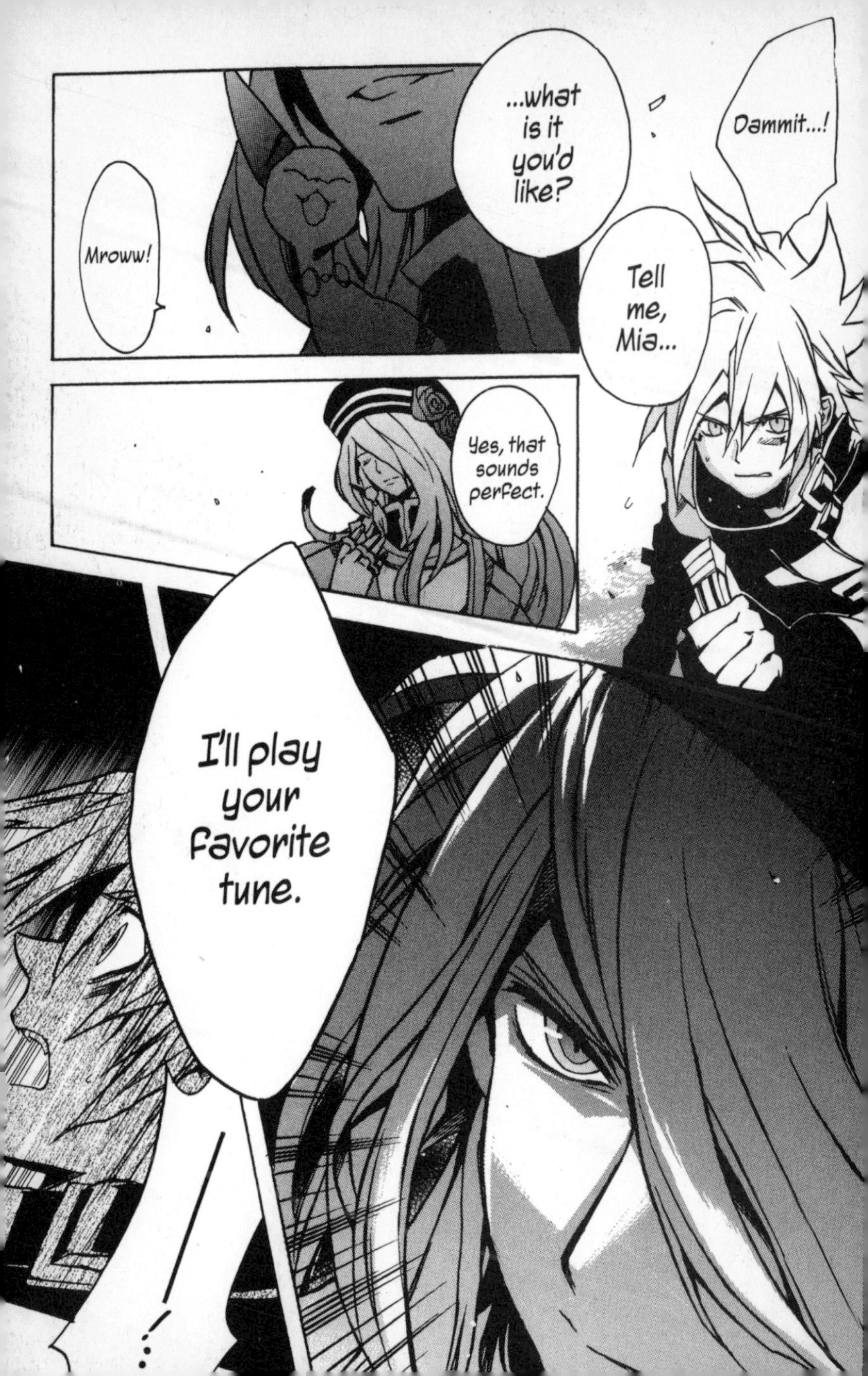
Dammit...!
Tell me, Mia...
...what is it you'd like?
Mroww!
Yes, that sounds perfect.
I'll play your favorite tune.
...!

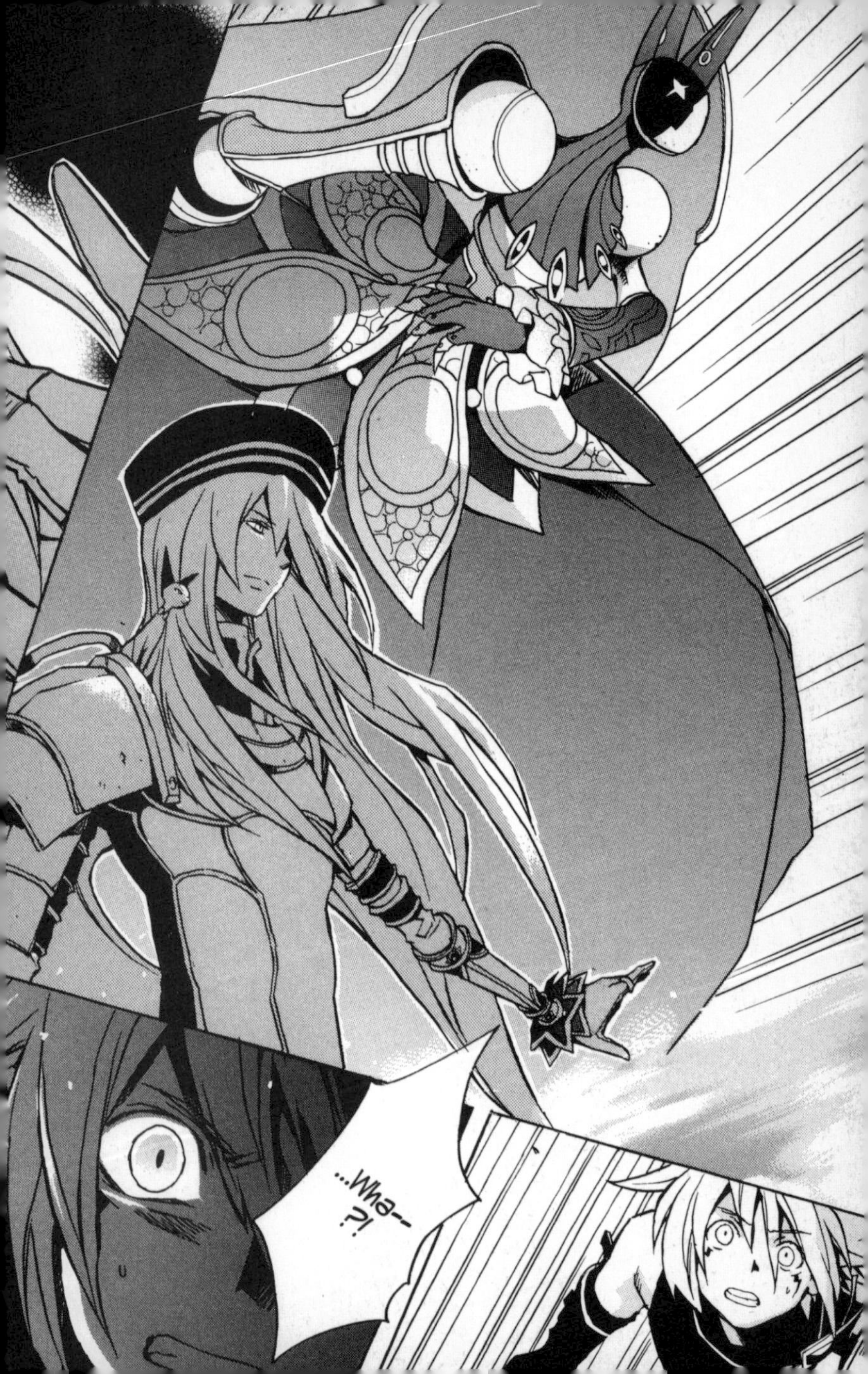
...Wha--?!

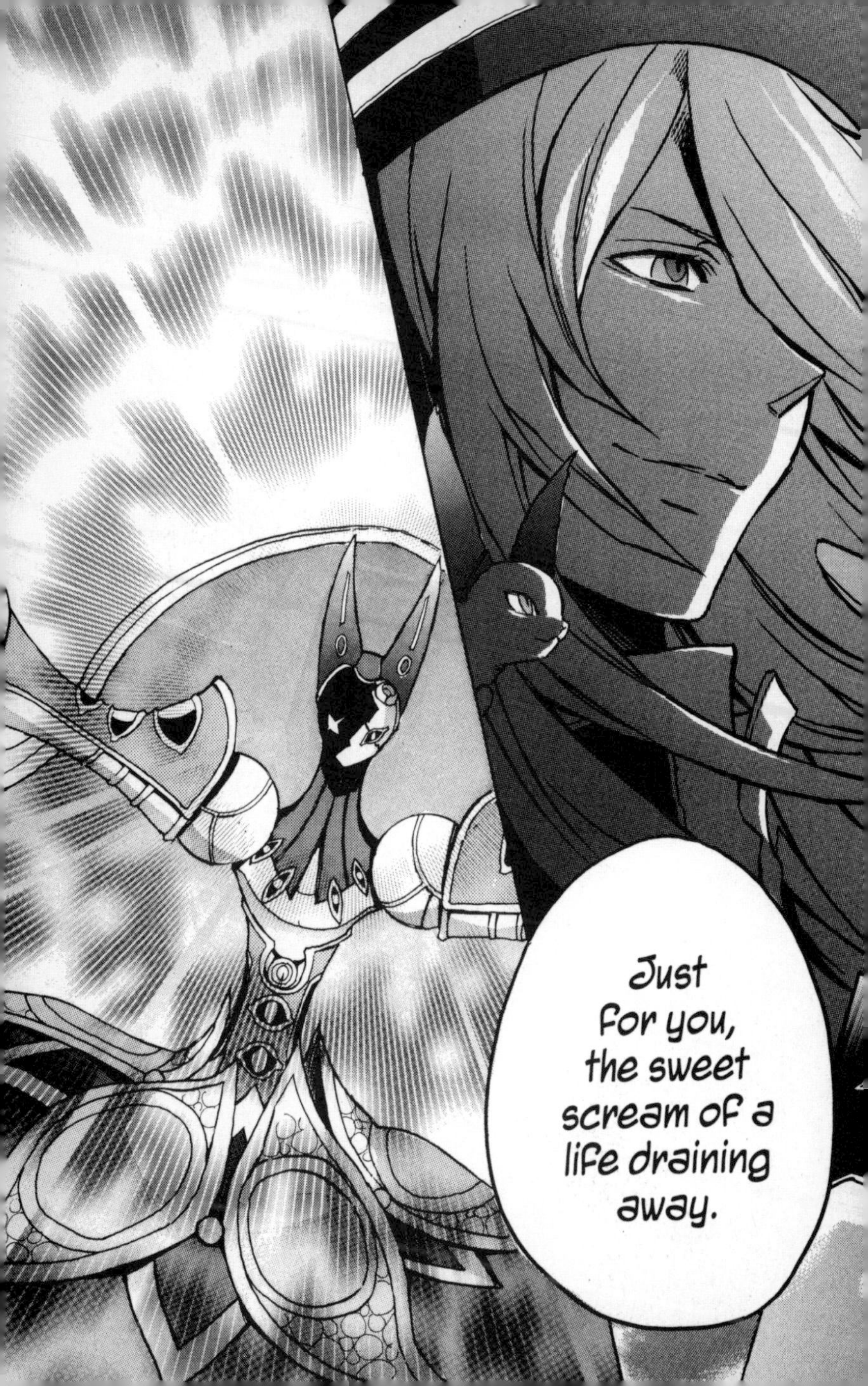
Just for you, the sweet scream of a life draining away.

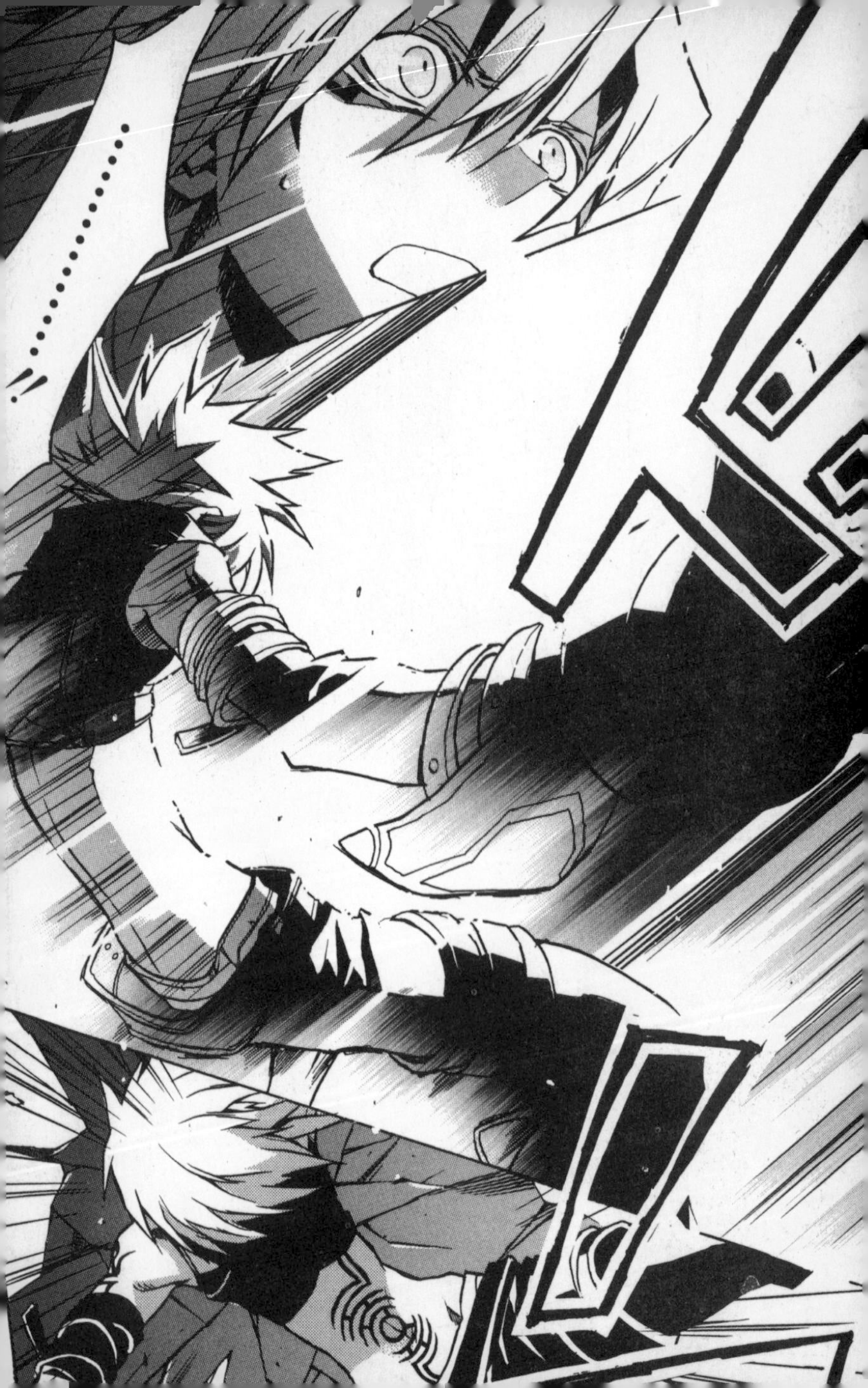
......!!

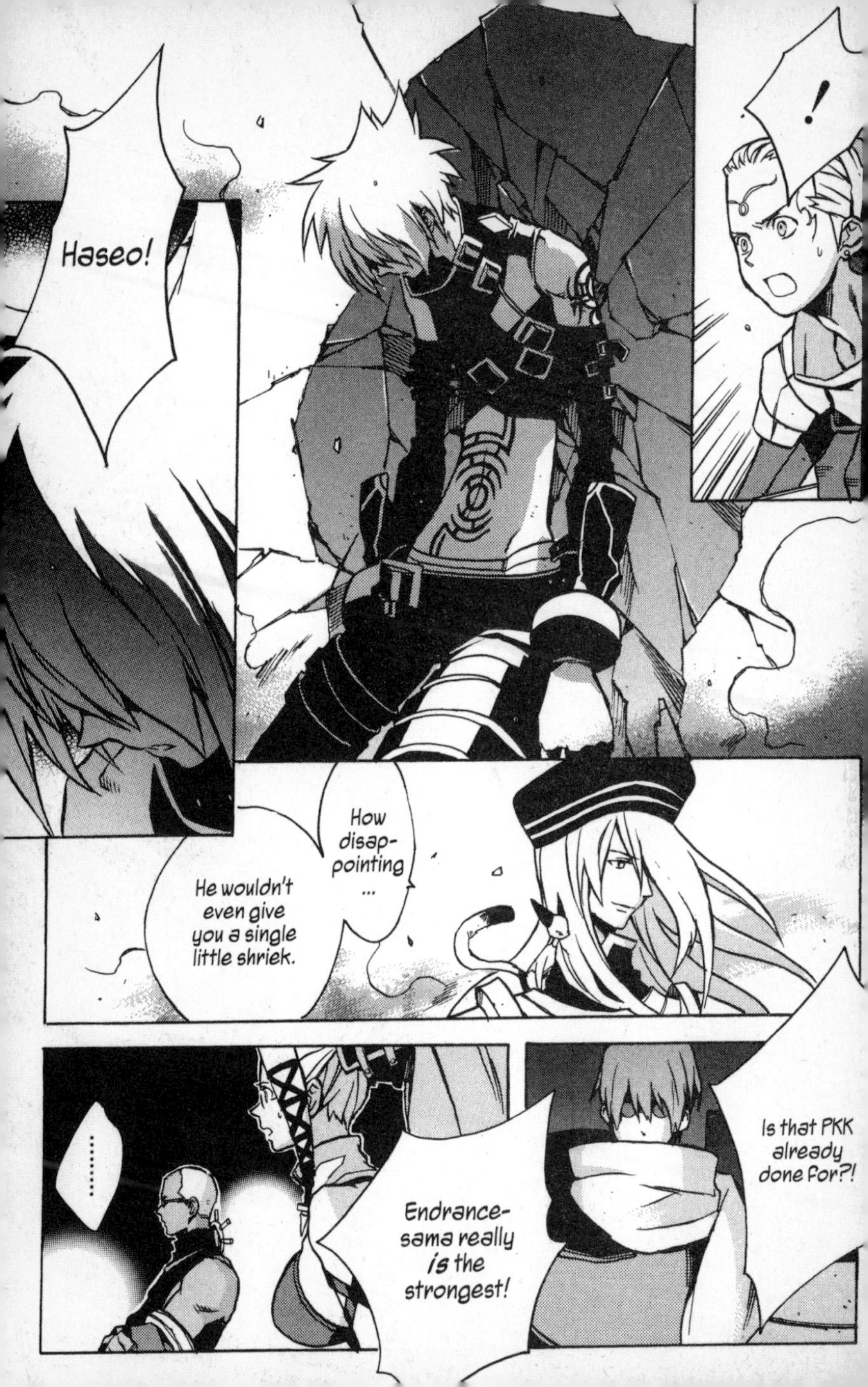
!
Haseo!
How disap-pointing ...
He wouldn't even give you a single little shriek.
Is that PKK already done for?!
Endrance-sama really *is* the strongest!
......

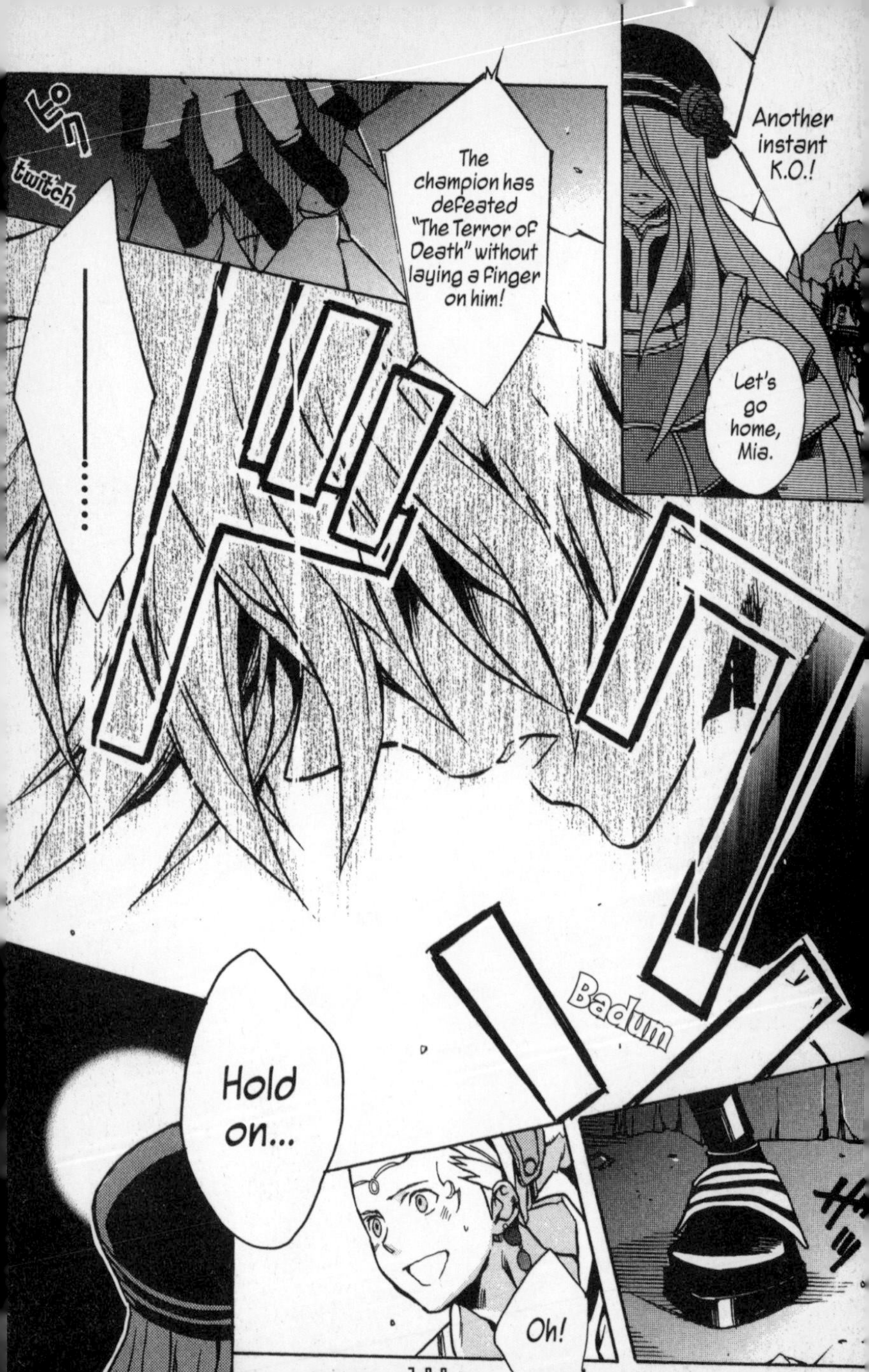

Another instant K.O.!
Let's go home, Mia.
The champion has defeated "The Terror of Death" without laying a finger on him!
twitch
......
Badum
Oh!
Hold on...

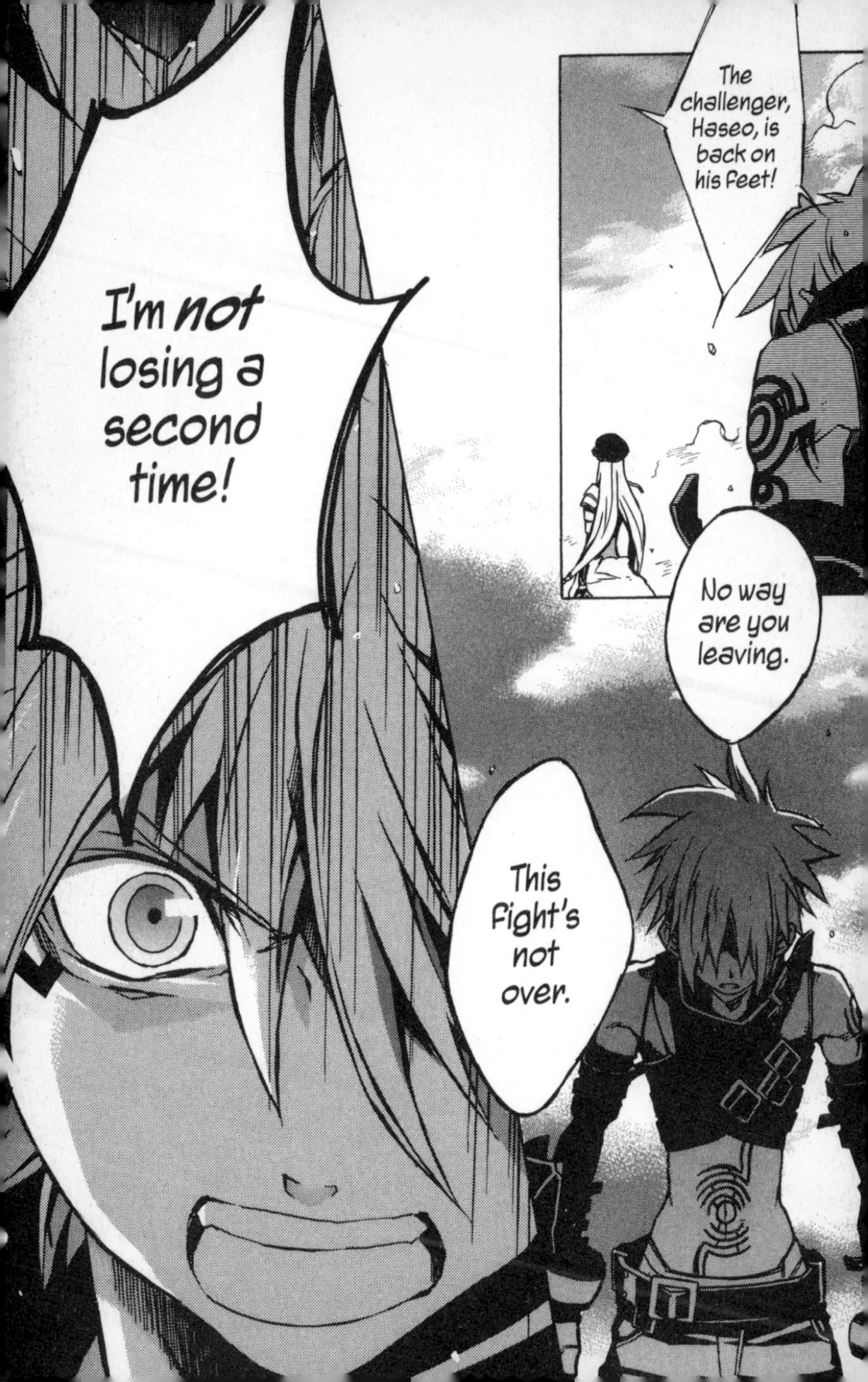
The challenger, Haseo, is back on his feet!
No way are you leaving.
This fight's not over.
I'm not losing a second time!

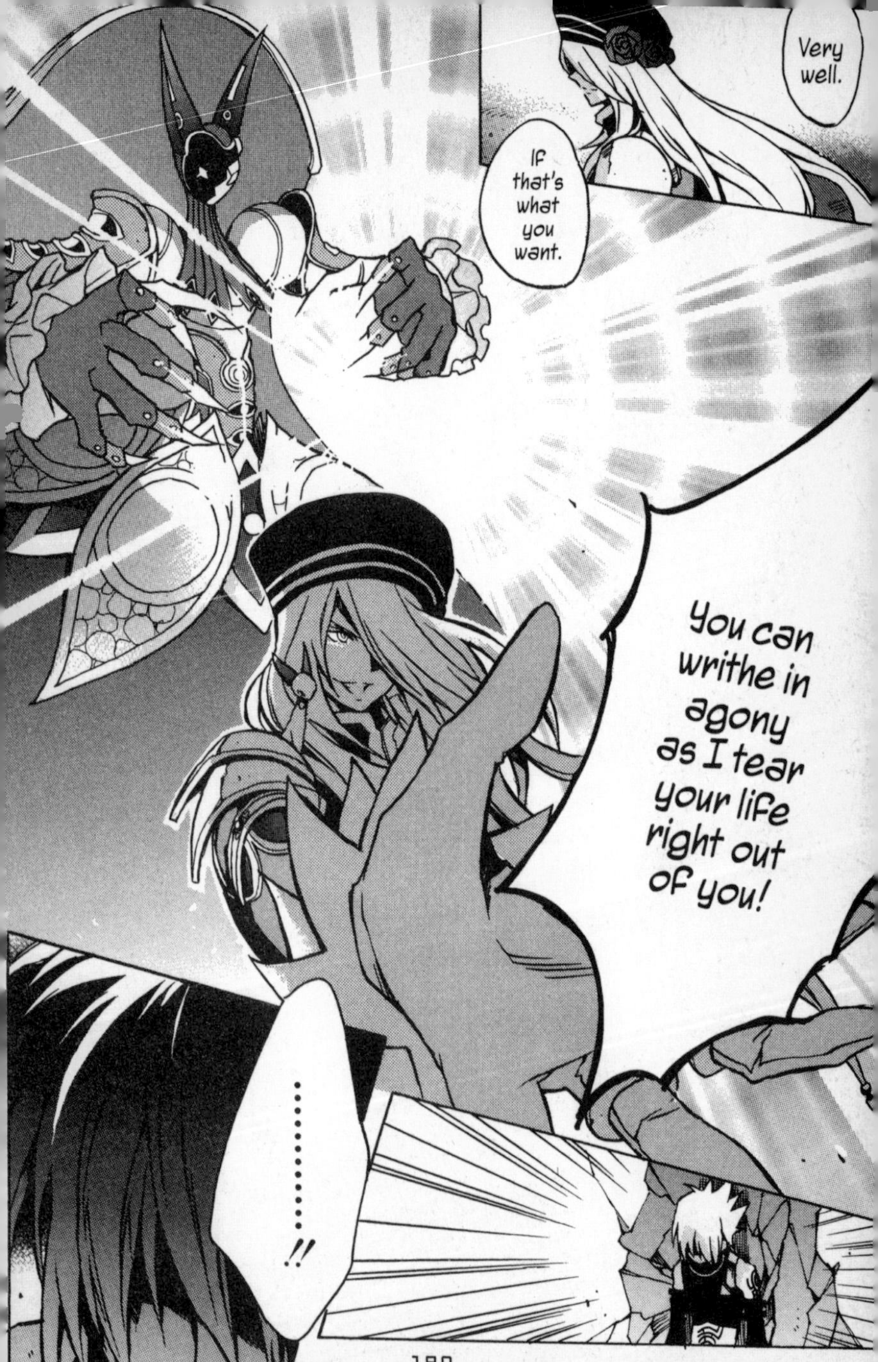
Very well.
If that's what you want.
You can writhe in agony as I tear your life right out of you!
.........!!

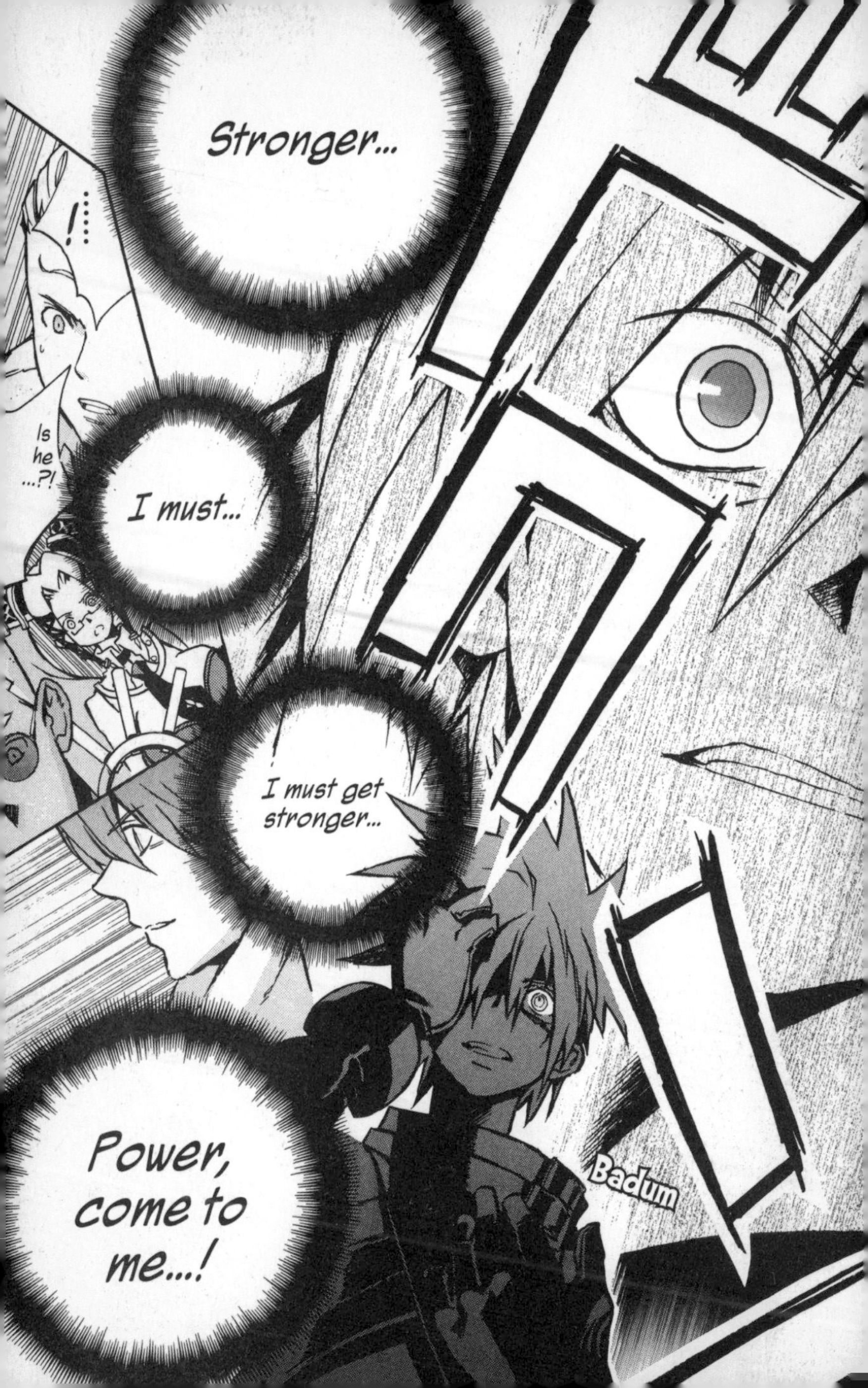
Stronger...
!......
Is he ...?!
I must...
I must get stronger...
Badum
Power, come to me...!

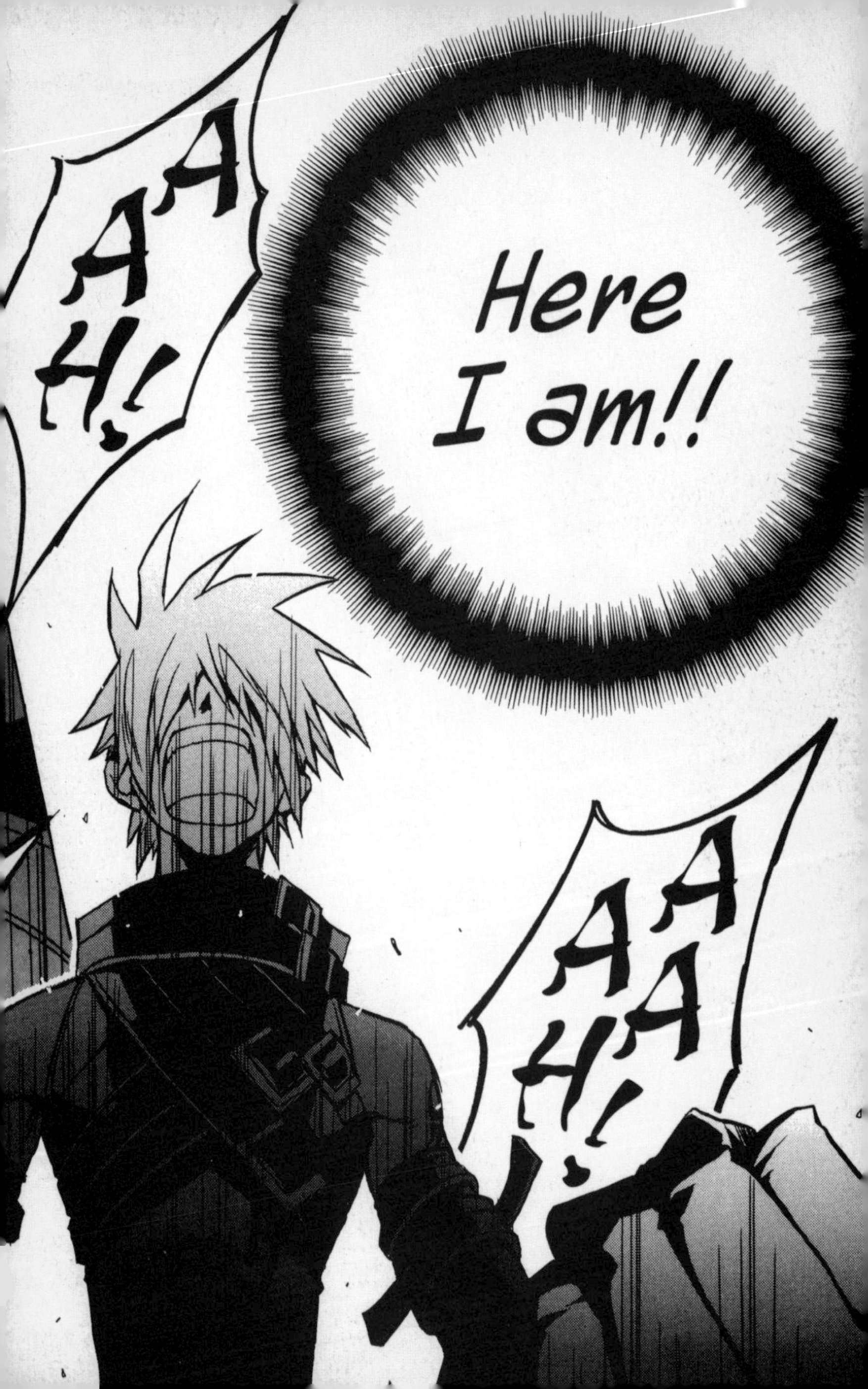
Here I am!!
AAAH!
AAAAH!

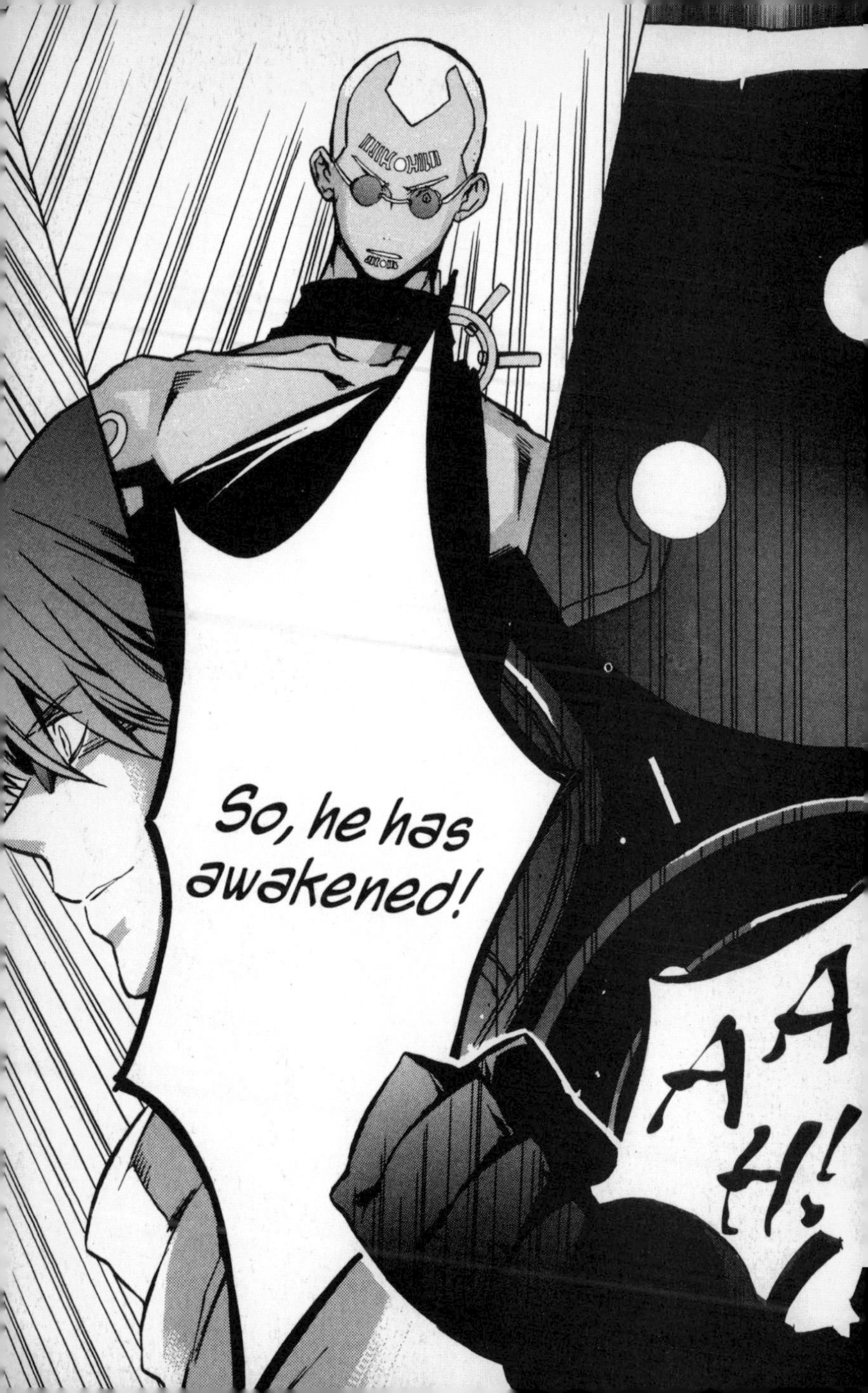
So, he has awakened!
AAAH!

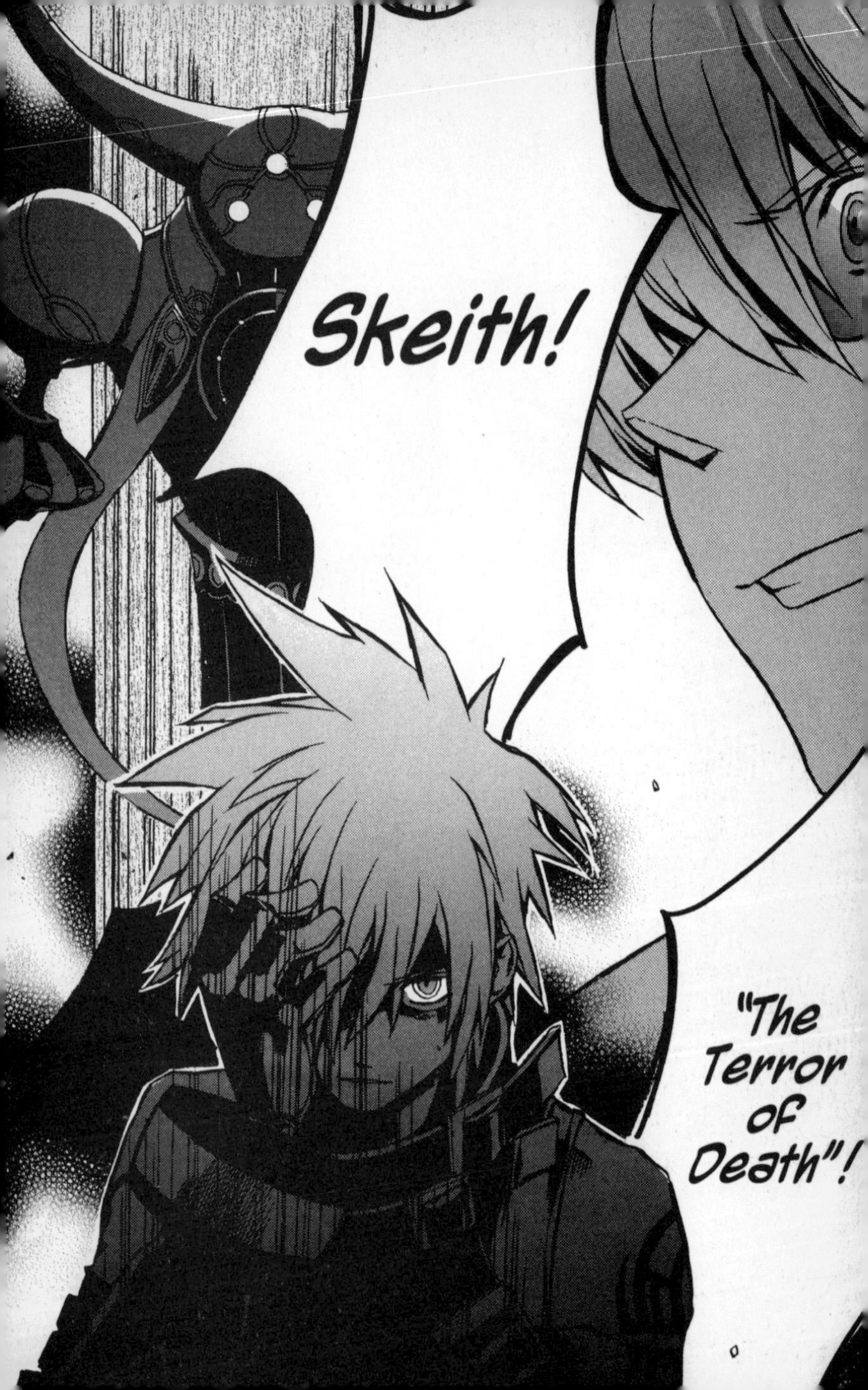
Skeith!
"The Terror of Death"!

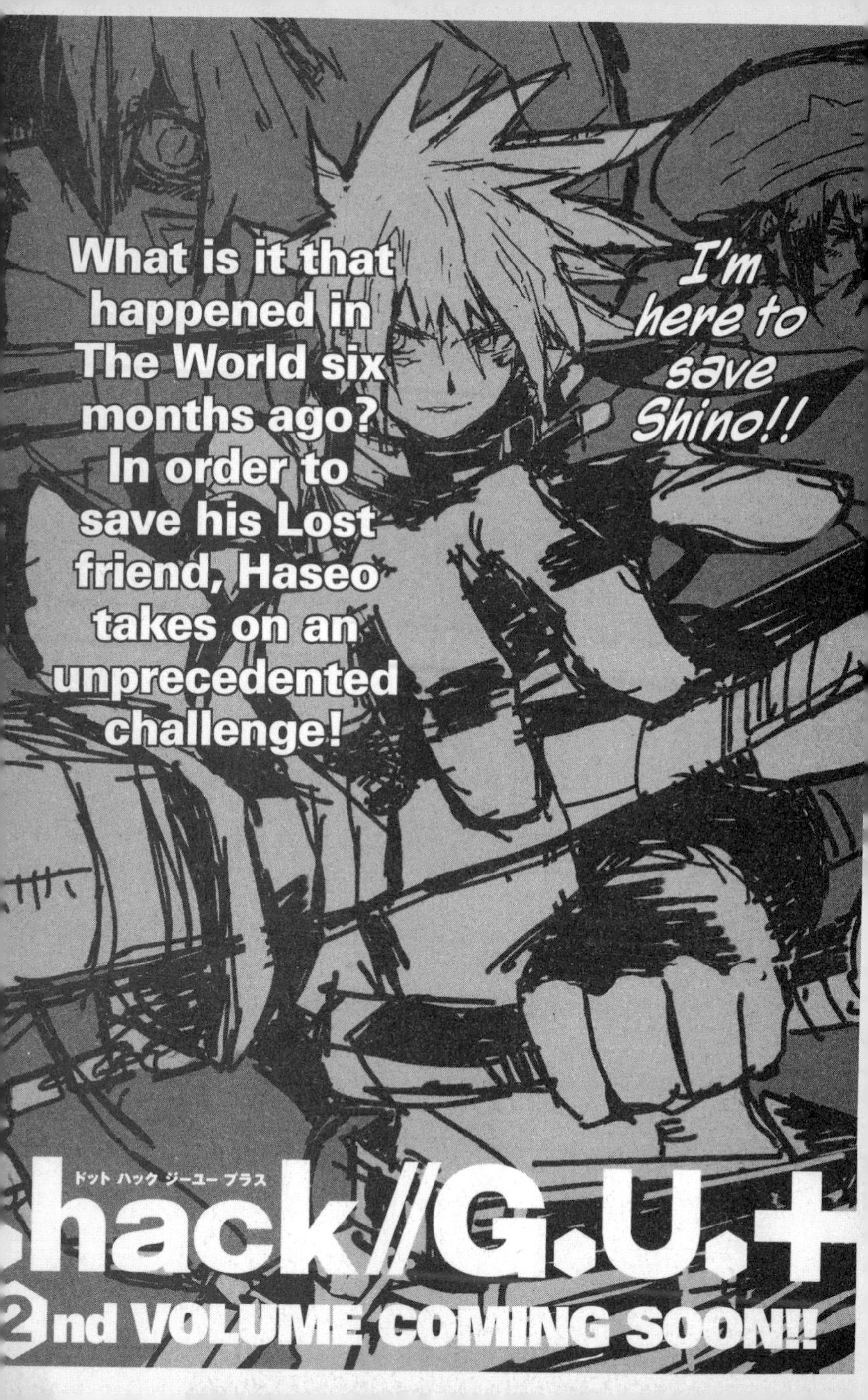
What is it that happened in The World six months ago? In order to save his Lost friend, Haseo takes on an unprecedented challenge!
I'm here to save Shino!!
ドット ハック ジーユー プラス
.hack//G.U.+
2nd VOLUME COMING SOON!!

CHARACTER GUIDE

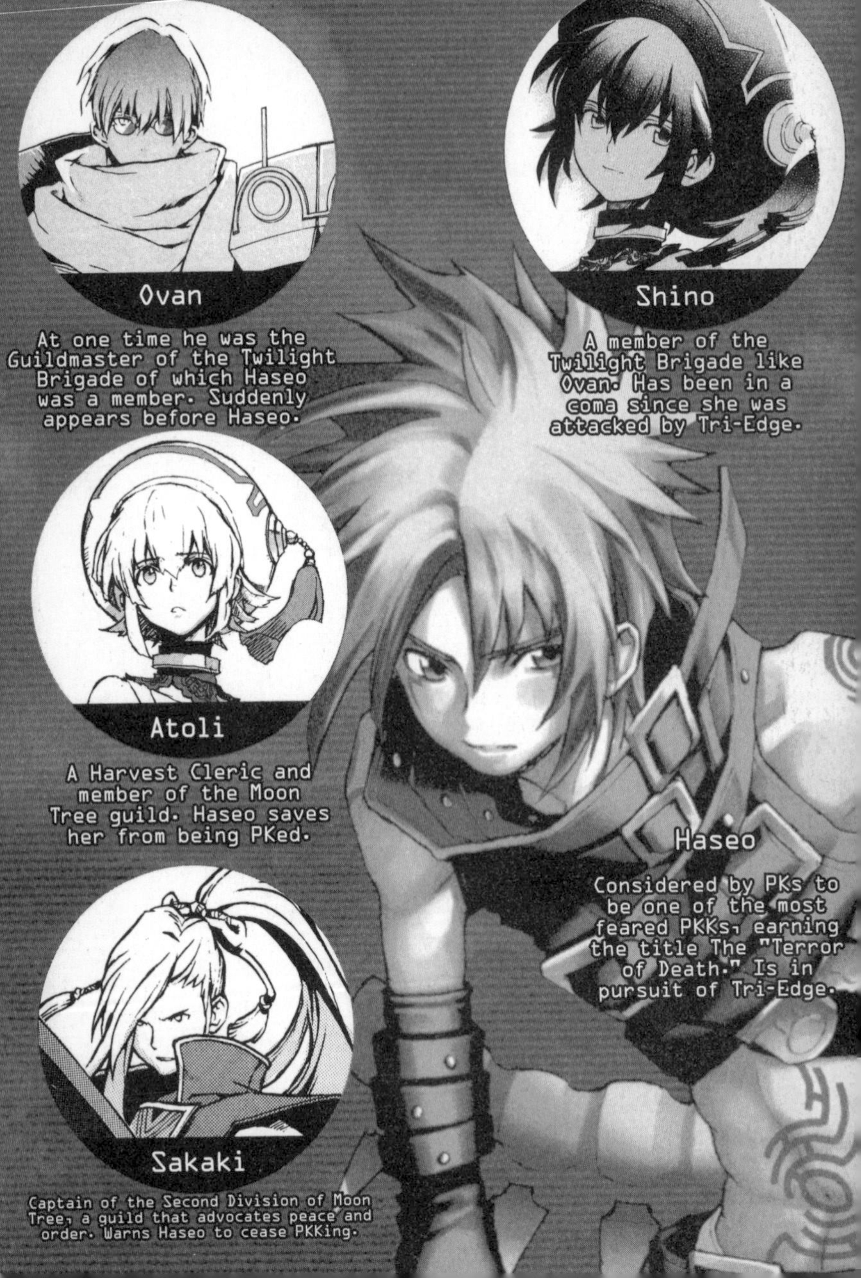

Ovan

At one time he was the Guildmaster of the Twilight Brigade of which Haseo was a member. Suddenly appears before Haseo.

Shino

A member of the Twilight Brigade like Ovan. Has been in a coma since she was attacked by Tri-Edge.

Atoli

A Harvest Cleric and member of the Moon Tree guild. Haseo saves her from being PKed.

Haseo

Considered by PKs to be one of the most feared PKKs, earning the title The "Terror of Death." Is in pursuit of Tri-Edge.

Sakaki

Captain of the Second Division of Moon Tree, a guild that advocates peace and order. Warns Haseo to cease PKKing.

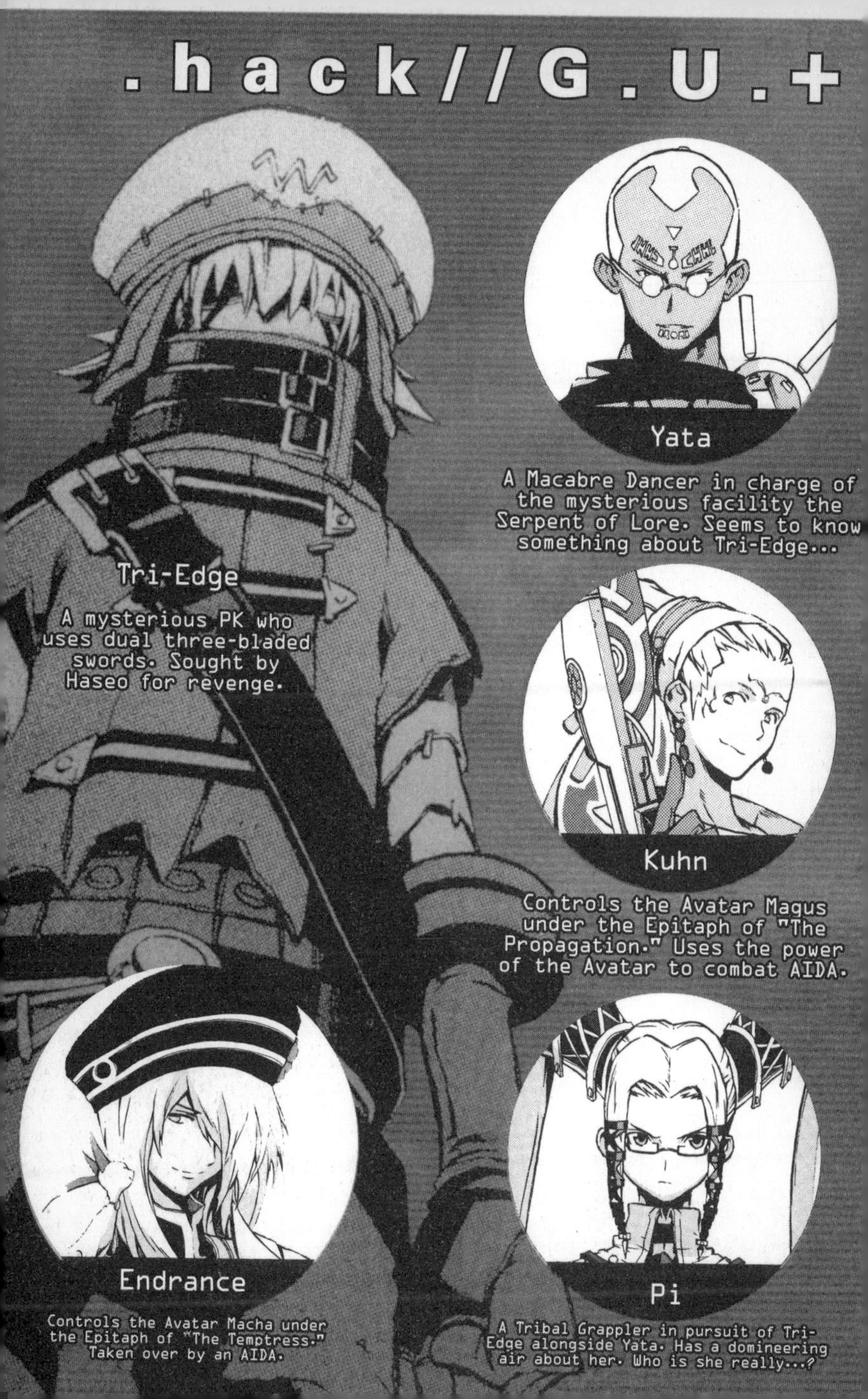
.hack//G.U.+
Yata
A Macabre Dancer in charge of the mysterious facility the Serpent of Lore. Seems to know something about Tri-Edge...
Tri-Edge
A mysterious PK who uses dual three-bladed swords. Sought by Haseo for revenge.
Kuhn
Controls the Avatar Magus under the Epitaph of "The Propagation." Uses the power of the Avatar to combat AIDA.
Endrance
Controls the Avatar Macha under the Epitaph of "The Temptress." Taken over by an AIDA.
Pi
A Tribal Grappler in pursuit of Tri-Edge alongside Yata. Has a domineering air about her. Who is she really...?

Hardcore! Game .hack//G.U.!!

Cyber Connect 2
Piroshi Matsuyama

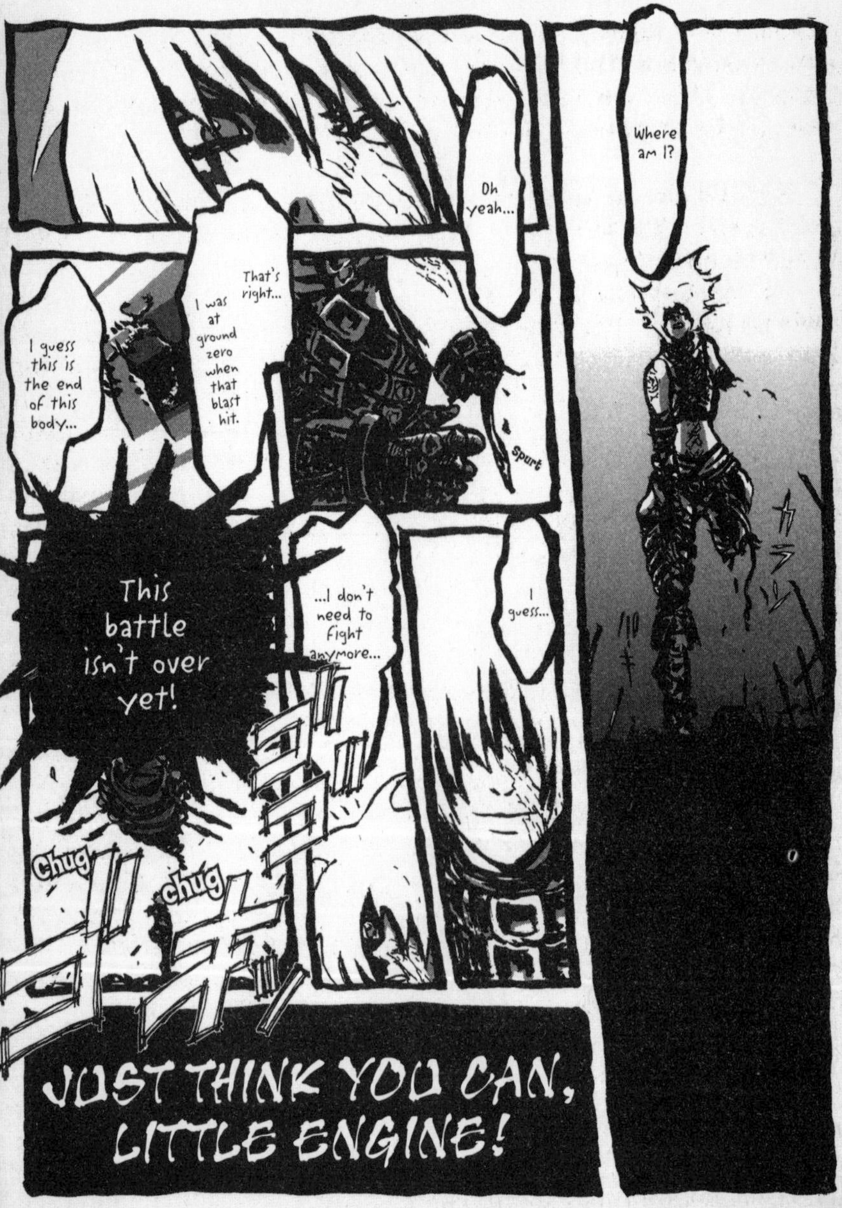
Where am I?
Oh yeah...
Spurt
That's right...
I was at ground zero when that blast hit.
I guess this is the end of this body...
I guess...
...I don't need to fight anymore...
This battle isn't over yet!
Chug
chug
JUST THINK YOU CAN, LITTLE ENGINE!

G.U. and G.U.+

Tatsuya Hamazaki

.hack//G.U. takes place seven years after the first *.hack* tetralogy and three years after the events of *.hack//Legend of the Twilight*. Here in G.U.+, we take the essence of the game version and change the story around a bit.

First, I'd like to bring to your attention the fact that *G.U.+* is published in the *.hack//G.U. The World* magazine and is scheduled to run twelve chapters.

It's quite unusual for a manga based on a game to start serialization six months before the game is released. Usually that would be impossible, not only because of concerns about spoilers, but because at that point a game wouldn't be completely finalized. In this case, the primary factor that made it possible for us to release the manga in this fashion is that it's been serialized in a magazine focused exclusively on *G.U.* Another reason is that I, the scriptwriter for the game, am also the writer for the manga. Now, you may be interested in the changes made to the dramatization of this manga. I won't make a point-by-point analysis of the individual differences, but they are mainly based off the difficulty of compressing three games into three volumes of manga, the difficulty of avoiding spoilers and the priority of which scenes were needed from the RPG.

Regardless, creating and working on the *.hack* franchise, in both the past and the present, has made me feel alive.

Many creators have put together the games, anime, manga and novels of this series. The story of *G.U.* was crafted upon the feedback received from the original game. It first came alive when users' eyes lit up. If this manga invokes a similar reaction in its readers, please feel free to check out the rest of the series, as I'm sure you'll discover something quite new. *.hack* is built on the curiosity of its readers, players and general audience.

It's quite fortunate that we were able to invite the artist Ms. Yuzuka Morita to this project. I'm sure we've been able to gain new audience members due to the strength, delicacy and gentleness depicted in each of her images. I believe that she can help to make the *G.U.+* story into a masterpiece.

ARTIST'S NOTE

Hello there! I'm Yuzuka Morita, and I draw the.hack//G.U.+ manga. I'm still learning a lot about being an artist, and I wouldn't be anywhere if it weren't for the great people who surround me. I'm sorry for everything I've put you through! Thank you so much!!

I'm extremely grateful for the experience of being able to work with these amazing people. I've done nothing to repay their kindness yet, but I'm trying my best to change that!

Yuzuka Morita

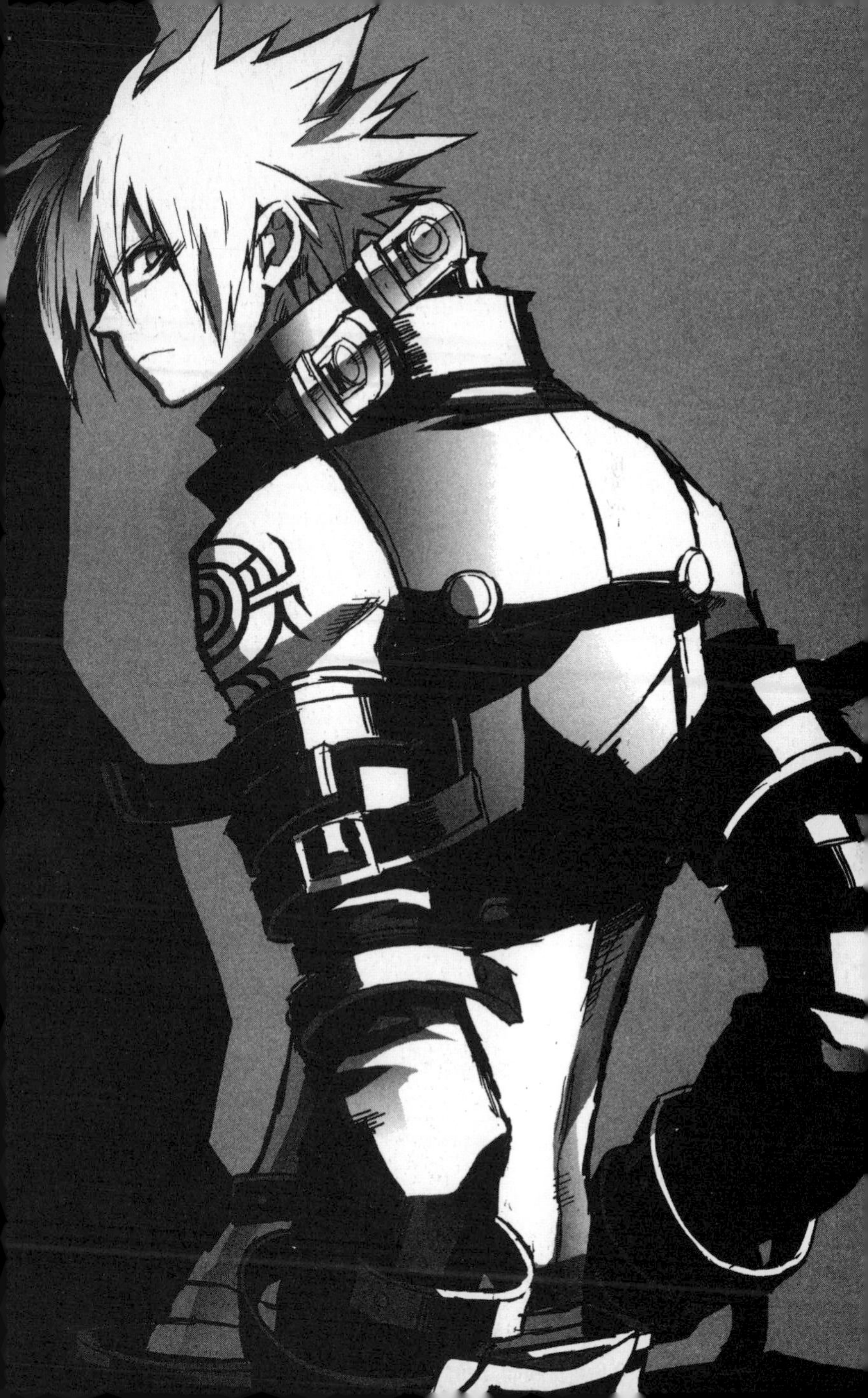

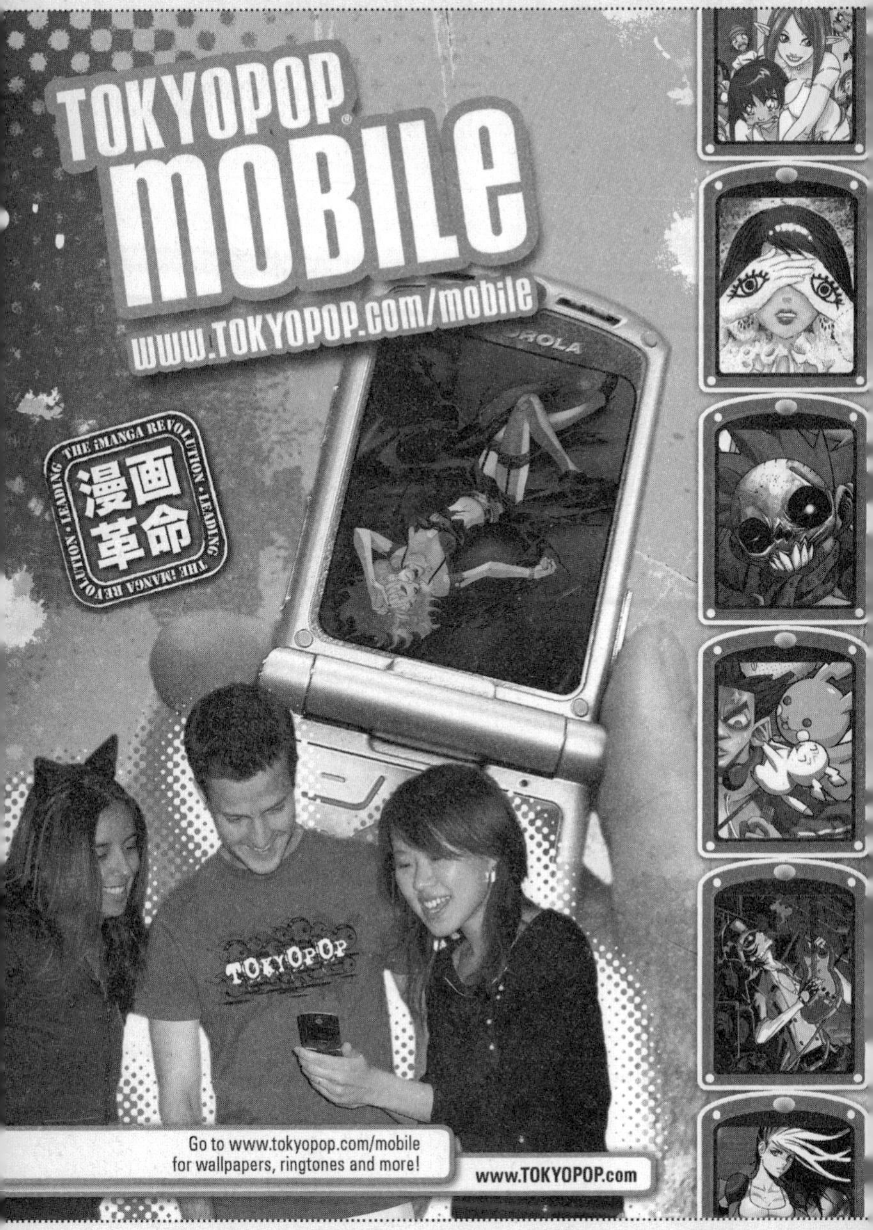
TOKYOPOP®
MOBILE
www.TOKYOPOP.com/mobile
THE iMANGA REVOLUTION · LEADING
漫画
革命
Go to www.tokyopop.com/mobile
for wallpapers, ringtones and more!
www.TOKYOPOP.com

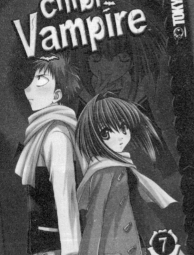

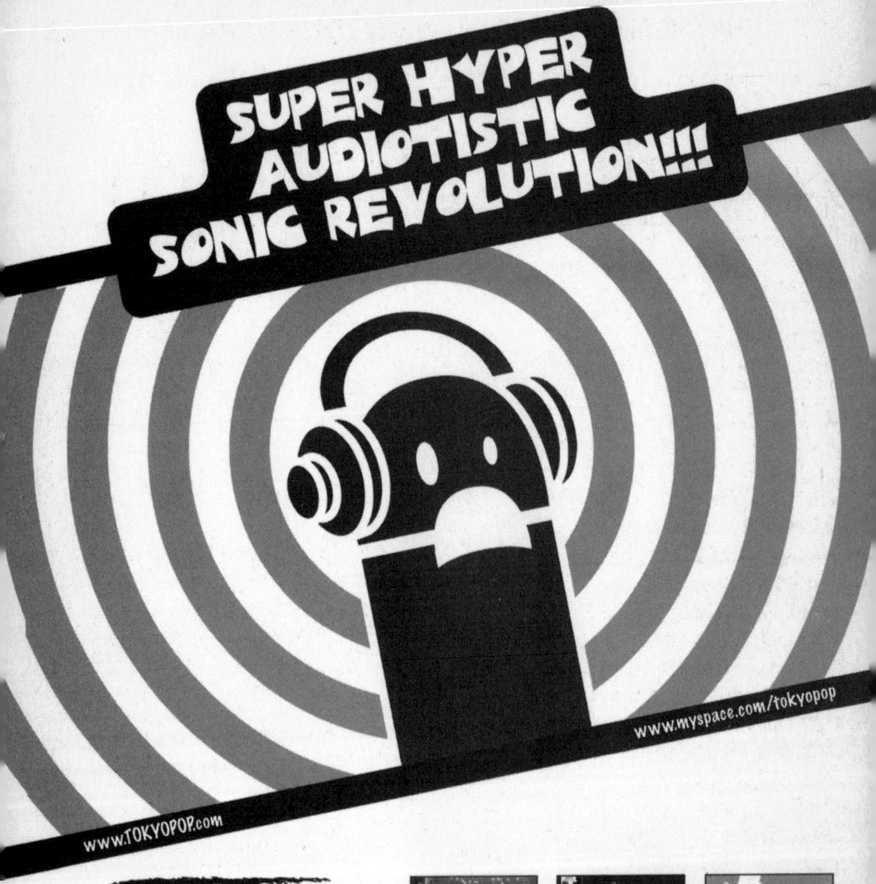
SUPER HYPER
AUDIOTISTIC
SONIC REVOLUTION!!!
www.myspace.com/tokyopop
www.TOKYOPOP.com

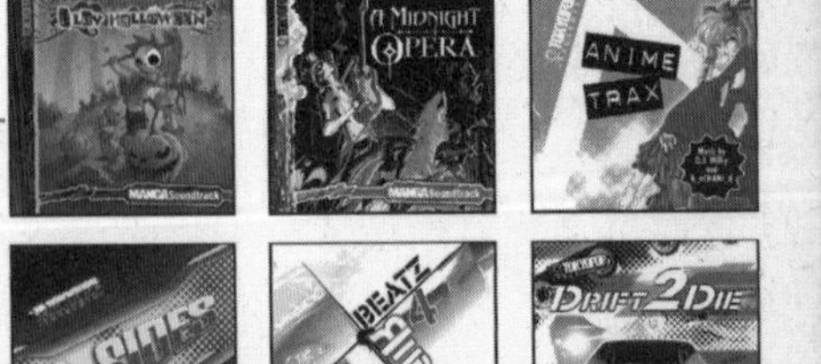
A MIDNIGHT OPERA
ANIME TRAX
DRIFT 2 DIE

"Laugh out-loud funny" –IGN.com

pearl pink™

By Meca Tanaka

4

The bumpy and funny romance between bubbly Tamako and her stardom-obsessed crush Kanji continues!

When Tamako moves in with her mother, will absence finally make Kanji's heart grow fonder? The mysteries of Tamako's past—as well as their consequences for her future—are revealed in this exhilarating finale to *Pearl Pink*!

ROMANCE

T
TEEN
AGE 13+

FOR MORE INFORMATION VISIT: WWW.TOKYOPOP.COM

STOP!

This is the back of the book. You wouldn't want to spoil a great ending!

This book is printed "manga-style," in the authentic Japanese right-to-left format. Since none of the artwork has been flipped or altered, readers get to experience the story just as the creator intended. You've been asking for it, so TOKYOPOP® delivered: authentic, hot-off-the-press, and far more fun!

DIRECTIONS

1
2
3
4
5
6
7
8
9
10

If this is your first time reading manga-style, here's a quick guide to help you understand how it works.

It's easy... just start in the top right panel and follow the numbers. Have fun, and look for more 100% authentic manga from TOKYOPOP®!

漫画革命 · LEADING THE MANGA REVOLUTION